Political Theology
Reimagined

Political Theology Reimagined

Alex Dubilet and Vincent W. Lloyd,
Editors

Duke University Press
Durham and London
2025

© 2025 Duke University Press
All rights reserved
Project Editor: Livia Tenzer
Designed by A. Mattson Gallagher
Typeset in Arno Pro by Westchester Publishing Services

Library of Congress Cataloging-in-Publication Data
Names: Dubilet, Alex editor | Lloyd, Vincent W., [date] editor
Title: Political theology reimagined / Alex Dubilet and
Vincent W. Lloyd, editors.
Description: Durham : Duke University Press, 2025. |
Includes bibliographical references and index.
Identifiers: LCCN 2024054589 (print)
LCCN 2024054590 (ebook)
ISBN 9781478032205 paperback
ISBN 9781478028932 hardcover
ISBN 9781478061144 ebook
Subjects: LCSH: Political theology | Critical theory
Classification: LCC BT83.59 .P657 2025 (print) |
LCC BT83.59 (ebook) | DDC 261.7—dc23/eng/20250605
LC record available at https://lccn.loc.gov/2024054589
LC ebook record available at https://lccn.loc.gov/2024054590

Cover art: Rafat Asad, *Mediterranean Sea #2* (detail), 2020. Acrylic on canvas,
130 × 130 cm. Courtesy of the artist.

Contents

Part 3. Race, Blackness, and Modernity

Part 4. Itineraries in Feminism and Gender

Introduction

POLITICAL THEOLOGY IN RIOTOUS TIMES

Alex Dubilet and Vincent W. Lloyd

"Love always means non-sovereignty," asserts Lauren Berlant. "I think sovereignty badly conceptualizes almost anything to which it is attached. It's an aspirational concept and, as often happens, aspirational concepts get treated as normative concepts, and then get traded and circulated as realism."[1] These lines condense a knot of challenges for political theology. There is the challenge of genealogy: critically undoing what appears as natural and necessary by tracing the hidden normative investments that make it function. There is the challenge of sovereignty and its others: theorizing politics that acknowledge the materialized dreams and realities of statist modernity no less than the ways they are never as exhaustive as they claim. There is the challenge of conceptual distinction and scale: The problem of sovereignty is not circumscribed to the arena of the state but can arise on the level of an individual or a citizen, a comportment or a disposition. And there is the challenge of the persistent lives and afterlives of the sacred: to eschew sovereignty, a turn to love, but this turn takes place in the ineradicable shadow of theology, since what is God if not love, at least in the Christian tradition that shapes the Western imagination (and its detractors)?

Tracing subterranean interactions and conceptual links between sovereignty and its others, reflecting on the impact of theological and other violent legacies on the psyches and bodies of the living and the dead, and doing so via surprising sites (whether they are textual, historical, or material): This is some of what political theology has to offer.

The Cree poet Billy-Ray Belcourt concludes his collection *This Wound Is a World* (2017) with Berlant's definition of love and adds, "Love is a process of becoming unbodied; at its wildest, it works up a poetics of the unbodied."[2] There are no clean divides: On the obverse side of political sovereignty and the body politic, one does not find love purified of politics. To be bodied or unbodied does not just happen. Settler colonialism, white supremacy, heteropatriarchy, capitalism: These are the interlocking forces that body and unbody. The rigor of poetry does not merely name these abstractions; nor does it allow them to remain abstract. Instead, it renders them visceral, somatic. A poetics of the unbodied explores what happens when the distinctions between corporeal and incorporeal, the living and the dead, cease being obvious conditions of intelligibility. The claim to *have* a body remains within an analytic of possession and sovereignty, but intimacy with unbodying renders bodies inseparable from historical violence and from text: "sometimes bodies don't always feel like bodies but like wounds" (23). At other times, the body remains in the conditional, "if i have a body, let it be a book of sad poems" (18).

In addition to Berlant's, Belcourt takes up another motto, this one from the Nishnaabeg writer Leanne Betasamosake Simpson: "i think we fucked, and maybe i should say make love, but maybe not because we didn't actually make love. it was sadder than that. we were sadder than that. but it wasn't bad and it wasn't wrong. it wasn't desperate. i think it was salvation" (55). Hesitation is layered, and ambiguity disturbs conceptual certainty. One might see here a love sadder than love. But it matters what we call things, and there is precision even amid ambiguity. To call experience love carries a normative force that would cover over the raw encounter. We fucked; we didn't make love. Avoiding the language of love does not condemn: "it wasn't bad and it wasn't wrong." What is being described is a libidinal encounter without disavowal, and to it is ascribed the power of salvation. Yet not unambiguously. The culminating transfiguration falls short of asserting objectivity ("*i think* it was salvation"), and this is confirmed in Belcourt's subsequent redoubling through personal meditation of being "sadder than that" and yet making "love anyway and it felt like salvation." Thinking and feeling are real, but their addition here invites doubts about salvation's standing. It is as though these invocations of salvation carry with them the political-theological insight that salvation has not been an innocent concept, entangled as it is with dreams and aspirations, sometimes positioned in opposition to sovereignty but frequently as sovereignty's very promise.[3]

Salvation, like sovereignty, is an aspirational concept treated as normative, circulated as realism, mediated politically. As is love. Yet this does not permit one to simply abandon them. That would be not only to ignore their tremendous historical effectivity but also, for example, to discount the powers of encounters that feel like salvation. Such diagnoses—without a concomitant all-too-easy dismissal of concepts such as salvation, sovereignty, and love—is at the heart of the political-theological enterprise. This

Dubilet and Lloyd

entails determining hermeneutic frames and fields of intelligibility no less than tracing out conceptual narratives and discursive histories that have given meaning to such terms.

It may also entail finding sovereignty's alterity not in love or salvation but, for example, in dwelling with and giving language to the ghosts on which sovereignty's kingdom has been built. *This Wound Is a World* conjures ghosts out of the archives, inhabits states of ghostly apparition, meditates on the two-way porosity of the living and the dead. As Belcourt announces, "the poem: an ontology of ghosts" (52). Yet as his poetics suggest, there are no easy demarcations. The living are spectral, and ghosts can have bodies and fuck. Libidinal encounters without disavowal that may feel like salvation have effects that greatly exceed the subjective realm. There is a repeated, unsettling imbrication of libidinal economies and settler colonial ones, which sometimes meld into one and at other times break each other apart: "i wanted to taste / a history of violence / caught in the roof of his mouth" (22). Remaining suspended between love and fucking, violence and ecstasy, corporeality and the incorporeal, the living and the dead is perhaps too subtle a maneuver for theological and political grand narratives. The task remains how, amid the ongoing inheritances and disinheritances of history and its abstractions, to form a conceptuality and a language that do not simply reproduce or disavow that ongoing history of violence—an urgent task for political-theological reflection understood from the perspective of the colonized and racialized, the violated and the poor.

This is a task that Belcourt undertakes in verse. Woundedness is world making, so the title seemingly announces. But Belcourt resists converting unbearable and inescapable loss into possibility and salvation by inviting the reader into the ambivalent attachments and desires that make *this* wound not a lack but a source for a poetics where attention is trained to structure ecstasy and where ecstasy shatters structure. The world remains in the wound, and the wound attests to the world's violent undoings and to the violating promises—whether of sovereignty, love, or salvation—it carries. There is a persistent liminality at the heart of the psycho-geography of Belcourt's poems that undoes the kind of heroic centering that words such as *possibility* and *world* might suggest. The lyrical voice unapologetically locates itself—"i am from the back alley of the world" (21)—or declares, "we need not to pretend that love was to be found in wastelands like these" (23). In back alleys and wastelands, the dead are not left to bury the dead; there, a communion takes place between the dead who have afterlives and the living who live in intimate proximity to death. The past is not past but persists in violent fragmentation, never easily sublated or superseded, despite the claims of theologico-political narratives of salvation and progress.

The vision of the poet constructs a conceptuality that binds and unbinds, that diagnoses the violence of the past but does not stop there. Rather, it intensely weaves the past with the present, the ghosts of the dead with the living. It links the holy and the material, the mythical and the natural, violence and ecstasy. Untethered from sovereignty, from a vertical chain between God and the sky and the king on the throne and the soul as individuated and self-possessed, the political and theological link and unlink, igniting thought and the imagination. Less assured than either sovereignty or salvation, the poet confronts "history's barb-wire door" (49) by starting to look for other "doors, not enclosures. Doors without locks. Doors that swing open" (43). This is hardly a vision of personal escape since, to follow Belcourt's elliptical formulation, "a theoretics of the doorway is a revolutionary undertaking" (52), an undertaking of the unbodied that includes the ghosts of (settler colonial, heteropatriarchal, capitalist) modernity.

The essays that follow denaturalize the vertical chain of sovereignty and experiment with the resulting political-theological productivity. They diagnose narratives of secularization, their displacements and disavowals, their violent promises and realities. They attend to the ways narration and genealogy can confront modern colonial visions of universal history and disturb its ontological presumptions about who and what is dead and living, past and present. They explore the complex affiliations of the material, the bodily, the economic, and the mythical, and they listen to the theoretics and poetics fostered in the struggles of liberation.

No longer is political theology a branch of Christian thought. No longer does it name the contested legacy of fascist legal theory. Today, political theology is a field engaged across a variety of disciplines, from cultural studies to anthropology, from comparative literature to Black studies. As we become increasingly aware of the dangerous and liberatory entanglements of religion, secularity, and power, political theology names a crucial site for research and teaching, discussion and collaboration. Yet misconceptions (*it's Christian, it's Nazi*) about this burgeoning field remain prevalent. This book brings together a constellation of essays that, collectively, offer an account of what political theology means today, and where it is headed tomorrow.

Each of the essays models what it means to do critical scholarship in political theology. The essays stake out the field's emerging new identity by engaging critical theory from diverse and global perspectives. No longer are Carl Schmitt, Jacques Derrida, and Giorgio Agamben the only cornerstones of political theology. Now Black, decolonial, queer, and feminist theory, and new movements in continental thought, are front and center. This volume opens new itineraries in political theology by expanding its conceptual references, theoretical topoi, and conversation partners. The essays experiment with what political theology might become while at the same time offering a guide to the field's ongoing scholarly dynamism. This experimental mode means that the voices that follow do not offer a unified program, and sometimes their inclinations diverge and even conflict. We welcome such moments of discord, as they invite readers to take a position, to participate in the dialogical development of the field.

What holds together the field of political theology and the essays collected? Scholarly fascination by and critical suspicion of the secular and its ontology. Creative exploration of the imbrications and intertwinements of the theological and the political. Rigorous investigations of legitimation and delegitimation and how religious operations haunt these processes. Commitment to insurgent struggles for liberation, to impossible justice, to assertions of freedom antagonistic to the reign of law and order. Nuanced attention to the effects of conceptual narratives on our understanding of what constitutes religion and the secular, the theological and the political. The imperative to attend to religious ideas, practices, and imaginaries and the way they are inflected by anti-Blackness, patriarchy, caste prejudice, and colonial legacies. The power of genealogy to constellate history anew and make visible ambivalent attachments in our critical practice. In short, political theology grapples with religion in all its complexity and with critical thought in all its complexity, combining them in ways that trouble regnant sureties and commonplaces.

Within this common horizon, the volume's essays pursue a variety of paths to probe the nature, shape, and orientation of political theology. Reflecting the rich diversity and interdisciplinarity of the field, contributors range from early-career scholars to senior faculty members and include scholars of literature and philosophy, political theory and anthropology, religious studies and theology. The essays, however, are not intended as a survey of the ways various disciplines approach political theology; nor do they seek to discipline the field of political theology. Instead, the essays put discipline and method to use in ways that are intended to inform and transform what political theology might mean. In doing so, they share certain scholarly virtues: They pursue novel theoretical lines of investigation; they read texts (literary, philosophical, and cultural) carefully; they construct creative conceptual constellations; and they marshal often unexpected resources to address aporias in the scholarship and in the world. Each essay resists, in some way, the two most common starting places of political theology: the classics of Christian theology and the classics of modern political theory.

To what standards ought we hold scholarship in political theology? Standards follow from disciplinary contexts—not just the syllabi of theories and methods courses but the soft norms inculcated in conferences, workshops, and peer reviews. One of the awkward features of conversations happening under the label "political theology" is that their disciplinary context remains ambiguous. Or because scholars formed in multiple disciplines are participating in these conversations, in these multiple clusters of conversations, it is not clear whether political theology itself has standards or a characteristic methodology. There are Christian theologians (of various stripes), Continental philosophers (often situated in an uncertain disciplinary positions), political theorists, and, in recent years, anthropologists, literary scholars, and scholars of cultural studies. The result has been that the label "political theology" is attached more to those who claim it for themselves than to those who approach their work in a certain way, and those who claim it often do so in reference to someone who claimed it before them: Schmitt, Agamben, Jürgen Moltmann, or Jacob Taubes, to take a few popular examples.

Indeed, colleagues relate to the phrase "political theology" in quite different ways. Christian theologians are often comfortable saying, "I am a political theologian"—by which they mean, "I am situated in the discipline of theology, and my particular interests are in politics." Christian theologians will also say, "I work in political theology," signaling that political theology is a field (of Christian theology) that can serve as a primary research interest, if not an identity. In contrast, scholars formed in any other discipline would shrink from saying, "I am a political theologian," though they may say, "I work in political theology." The latter locution, sometimes resulting in "political theology" listed among other research interests—next to, say, African American literature, phenomenology, or affect theory—suggests not only a set of questions but also a set of theoretical resources with which to engage those questions. But rarely is there any overlap between the theoretical resources that secular scholars associate with political theology and those Christian theologians have in mind when they say, "I work in political theology." Staging conversations to overcome this divide, as much dispositional as disciplinary, is difficult. Even if, somehow, colleagues who sit in these two corners of the academy find themselves in the same room, it is not only different points of reference that inhibit dialogue. If some colleagues identify so strongly with the field that they claim it as an identity and others take it as one tool among many, there is necessarily some awkwardness, even incommensurability.

As a scholarly approach, political theology is not essentially bound to any particular religious, intellectual, or discursive tradition.[4] In recent years, scholars have debated the significance of political theology for Judaism and Islam (with both cases necessitating further reflection on the relationship among law, ethics, and politics) as well as in Hinduism, Buddhism, and Indigenous religious traditions—in addition to explorations of various forms of Christianity, from the Eastern Orthodox to Mennonite and Mormon. Scholarly gatherings and forums have sought to "provincialize" European political theology and to probe the shapes that decolonial political theology might take, with contributions from scholars of religion and politics in Chile, China, Colombia, Korea, Nigeria, Poland, South Africa, and beyond.[5] In dealing with the histories of colonialism, capitalism, and the modern state that constitute global modernity, such investigations confront head on the reality that there is no easy abandonment of the analytics deemed "European," even for those struggling against its legacies.

In addition to expanding outward, the theoretical apparatus of political theology has become increasingly sophisticated. Not only are critical tools from decolonial, feminist, and Marxist theory part of the conversation, but the theoretical practices of genealogy and speculation have also become creatively imbricated. This has entailed reconceptualizing classic moments of European thought through novel theoretical lenses, resulting in conceptual experimentation—with the world and the Earth, theodicy and legitimation, and much else. For example, when examined with the conceptual tools elaborated by Denise Ferreira da Silva, Fred Moten, or François Laruelle, German Idealism becomes an expansive and unfamiliar terrain for reassessing the complex interconnections of theology and the political and philosophical aspects of secular modernity.[6] Approaching fundamental categories of modernity with an entwined genealogical and speculative attunement to theological materials presents a particular task for political theology: to refuse the triumphalist visions of secular modernity and to do so without recourse to the authority, order, and continuity of tradition.[7]

One of the goals of this volume is to showcase the rapidly expanding breadth of conversations in political theology while, at the same time, offering resources to orient them. The tools employed by scholars working in political theology in different traditions, in different discursive sites, need not be the same, but it is important to self-consciously reflect on those tools: why they are chosen, when they are effective, and when new tools are needed. Colleagues and students whose intellectual homes are at a distance from core discussions of political theology often encounter political theology for the first time through a small set of canonical theorists, which can lead to the paradoxical result that those whose scholarly interests are most outside of modern Europe lean most heavily on modern European theoretical resources. It is, of course, hardly an accident that the home of capitalist and colonial modernity would be the home of theoretical abstraction and universality, while other sites are relegated to the realm of particularity and become objects of ethnography or the mere application of theory.[8] Yet this does not need to be accepted as fate, as anticolonial, postcolonial, and decolonial theoretical developments demonstrate. Whether out of specific traditions or their catastrophe and ruination, such contemporary theoretical dislocations have forced us to rethink the presuppositions of Eurocentric theory, and this volume aims to continue this innovative line of research.[9]

It is important to acknowledge that the sites of insurgent thought and activity to which contemporary political theology turns were already, in a sense, practicing political theology. If we attend to the words, images, and actions of movements struggling against domination the world over—say, Zapatistas in Mexico, Dalit organizers in India, Aboriginal organizers in Australia, land reformers in South Africa—we will surely find religion and politics mixing in ways that are complex and generative and that shift what we think counts as religion and what we think counts as politics. And the organic intellectuals formed by these movements, whether Houria Bouteldja in France or Essex Hemphill in Black America, must certainly be *doing* political theology. What does a volume such as *Political Theology Reimagined*, which pushes outward from a Eurocentric, poststructuralist frame in feminist, queer, Black, and decolonial directions, add when political theology is already happening, in sophisticated ways, outside of that narrow frame? And would additional scholarship—more attuned to the lives and afterlives of religion and theology—in cultural studies, anthropology, literature, and other fields, where the turn beyond poststructuralism happened a generation ago, not suffice?

Our contention is that political theology, whatever its limitations, has become an important site of inquiry that has generated novel theoretical tools and perspectives on the complex interrelations of religion and politics that remain frequently unavailable in established disciplinary spaces. It has developed critical approaches to rigorously conceptualize the historical junctures and disjunctures of the theological and the political, which have continued to structure the colonial, racialized, capitalist modernity we inhabit. This interdisciplinary conversation has produced inventive ways to interrogate the status of religion: its historical formation as a concept out of Protestantism and liberal modernity, its continuities and discontinuities with Christianity and its visions of particularism and universalism, its status as the default object of critique for secular philosophy or of management for the secular state. Political theology has provided a critical vantage on the ways that religion is shaped by power but also on the ways that forms of power are shaped by disavowed religious genealogies, and it has taught us to attend to assemblages—material and ideal, historical and contemporary—that weave together the theological and political across the long histories of modern religion and the state. Our hope is that critical perspectives developed within political theology can help attend to texts and archives of those struggling against domination by rendering theoretically visible how forms of insurgency *and* counterinsurgency can enact political and religious dimensions in intricate ways. And its inventive modes of reading can unsettle common assumptions about the discourse of religion, which limit our approach to those texts and archives and their power to insurgently challenge regnant terms of order. Showcasing these expanding conversations can attune scholars across the humanities and critical social sciences to political theology in ways that deepen and problematize their own scholarly and political itineraries.

Whether in Christian theology or political theory, Continental philosophy or the anthropology, political theology often brings with it a radical edge. Those who think that the powers that be get things right most of the time, or need only the occasional gentle nudge, rarely gravitate toward political theology. The field grows out of crises, times when fundamental assumptions come into play, times when the order of the world loses its solidity. You will find a crisis at the center of whichever origin story for political theology you choose. There was a crisis for Augustine in the late Roman empire. There was a crisis for Schmitt in Weimar Germany. There was the post-1989 crisis of the left that generated novel political-theological theorizing by the likes of Agamben and Slavoj Žižek; after September 11, this line of investigation only intensified, now becoming dominant in the

US academic context, as well. In each case, the unsettling of the order of the world necessitated a rethinking of the foundations, and this could not avoid a reengagement with the theological dimension.[10] In each case, the wealthy and powerful sought to exploit crises for their own ends, at times using the lexicon of political theology. Fending off these attempts, whether Hindutva or Christian nationalist or Zionist, requires developing the tools to cleave insurgent political theology from the political theology of order, purity, and domination—a key task of this volume.

This narrative of crisis is worth interrogating: Crisis for whom? Is an intellectual crisis equivalent to a political crisis? It does, however, suggest an important truth: that struggles born of vulnerability engender creativity. The experimental itineraries in political theology that occupy the pages that follow could also be said to grow out of the 2008 financial crisis and the decade of social movements that followed: Occupy Wall Street, the Arab Spring, Black Lives Matter, Idle No More, Standing Rock, #MeToo, the fights for public education and prison abolition. These movements captured the imagination of young scholars who, with increasing frequency, have one foot in the academy and another in activism. Social movements challenged scholarly fields to ask new questions, to create new tools, and to orient themselves in a clearer way to calls for justice that exceed the order of the world. They have also opened new theoretical vistas, ranging from riotous insurgency to the commune form. Scholars of color, first-generation scholars, and queer and trans scholars entered conversations in political theology motivated not only by theoretical concerns but also, frequently, by existential concerns—concerns about life and death, faith and hope, violence and oppression. A shift of perspective occurred: From an exclusive focus on the state, political theology came to investigate insurgent theories, affects, and vernaculars that oppose domination.

With their intellectual and political formations entangled, scholars attracted to political theology have often brought an organizing spirit to their intellectual labor. The result has been an explosion, over the past decade, of collaborative projects and infrastructure, from the growth and transformation of the journal *Political Theology* to the proliferation of online forums, reading groups, seminars, and workshops. It has also led to regular conferences, some hosted by a new professional organization, the Political Theology Network, and the development of streams focused on political theology within established professional organizations, including the American Philosophical Association, the American Studies Association, and the American Academy of Religion.[11] This is the context that gave birth to the chapters that follow, and many of the contributors have participated in or led organizing projects in the field.

Like many academic projects, this volume grows out of a mix of excitement and frustration. We see political theology moving in multiple promising directions, enlivened by adjacent fields in the humanities and critical social sciences and by a cohort of colleagues coming to their work with deep political commitments. But we also see risks. Political theology is easily misunderstood and dismissed. A focus on first-order political commitments can shrink interest in the sort of theoretical reflection that requires intellectual patience and rigor—tracing networks of concepts, making distinctions, considering counterarguments, and reading and writing with care. There is the risk of insularity for discussions of political theology within particular contexts—for example, Jewish political theology, political theory and political theology, ethnography and political theology—and we hope readers can find inspiration in the essays that follow to bring new energy and creativity to their work. We are concerned, as well, that work in political theology can remain unserious when it comes to understanding the complexity of religion, reducing dense networks of practice, thought, and imagination to a few key concepts that are easily legible to secular (or Protestant) interlocutors. Or it can remain narrowly Christian, without working through the paradigms of critical theory that have transformed understandings of power and the political, the material and the economic, in ways that implicate Christianity itself.[12] In compiling this volume, the two of us—one located in an English Department, the other in a Theology and Religious Studies Department—showcase promising developments that might serve as antidotes to these concerns.

The four groups of essays that follow map out distinct trajectories within the field of political theology. The first group expands the canon of European critical theory relevant for political theology. These contributions retrieve novel conceptual perspectives, topoi, and problematics from leftist political theory, speculative philosophy, and contemporary critical theory for use in political theology. They investigate what purchase these approaches have for political theology and what becomes visible when they are interrogated from a political-theological perspective. The second section collects essays that ask what happens to political theology when it is examined through novel sets of coordinates, from the colonial to the cosmic. Moving across diverse sites and events, from the decolonial to Islam and from India to the scale of the planetary and beyond, they explore how the thought and structure of political theology is transformed, deformed, refused, and expanded by such encounters. The third set of essays traces what attunements to racialization and Blackness do to political-theological contours and how such perspectives transform the concepts and narratives that ground political theology. They make the case that political theology necessarily goes wrong when it does not grapple with anti-Blackness. The interventions of the final section are framed by questions of feminism and gender. They ask what happens to political theology when gender difference and subversion of identity, no less than sentimentality and gendered violence, are situated at the heart of political-theological investigations.

These frames are hardly the exclusive way to organize the contributions. The essays that take up Sylvia Wynter's thought as a theoretical node (David Kline, James Ford, Beatrice Marovich) are as much about Blackness as they are about colonial modernity, with questions of gender never far from view. Feminist thinkers such as Silvia Federici (explored by Adam Kotsko) must also be understood as part of an expanded canon of European leftist critical theory. Other contributions make productive use of European concepts and genealogies within an expanded frame—for example, in Aseel Najib's exploration of Claude Lefort's conceptualization of the political in relation to Islam or Alex Dubilet's reconsideration of the status of Christianity and secularism through the prism of general antagonism and the undercommons.

The essays in this volume respond to a number of open questions in the field. By making these questions explicit, we hope to encourage readers to enter the conversation and articulate new answers themselves. We also hope to make visible some of the conceptual sites with the greatest intellectual energy in political theology today, which have shifted from where they were even a decade ago. For example, the edited volume *Race and Political Theology* (2012) shared with this volume a desire to move beyond both sectarian and dogmatically secular approaches to the field, but that volume focused on Jewish and Black American inflections on paradigms set by Schmitt, with only gestures toward coloniality, patriarchy, and capitalism as essential questions.[13] Indeed, even the reflections in that volume largely approached Jewish and Black thought from a multicultural paradigm that has now been challenged by new currents in Black feminism, Afropessimism, and critical explorations of "Judeopessimism."[14]

One open question in political theology today, in a sense a prerequisite for all others, concerns the significance of storytelling and narration. In 2008, the literary theorist Regina Schwartz suggested that poetics ought to be read as a modality of secularization, and in 2014, the early modern literary scholar Victoria Kahn centered the Greek concept of *poiesis* in a critique of political theology.[15] In subsequent years, not only literature scholars but political theorists and philosophers have increasingly attended to these questions in ways distinct from, but not unrelated to, the call in 1991 by the Christian theologian John Milbank for political theology to be the project of "out-narrating" secular modernity.[16] What does it mean for political theology to attend to genre, to tarry with the tragic or comic, to understand the tropological power of discourse, or to explore how narrative structures determine the distribution of the possible and impossible?

George Shulman's essay in this volume argues for the centrality of the creative imagination and mythopoetic techniques for political theology understood as a study of what he terms "organizing faiths." Drawing on an archive of voices that includes the Hebrew prophets, William Blake, Friedrich Nietzsche, and James Baldwin, Shulman argues for a political theology grounded not in logos but in poesis, in collective imaginative inventions that "engender creative capacities for enlarged affiliations, self-organizing nomos, and resonant meaning making." Situating political theology less in relation to secularization than to the global color line, Shulman proposes Fred Moten's explorations of fugitive sociality and a sociopoetic insurgency of dispossession in common as a countertheological voice to the grammar of an anti-Black world. Marovich reevaluates the significance of narrative differently through her exploration of the biomythological mode of storytelling. Taking political theology as a discourse that deals with the persistence under erasure of the theological—as a discourse that takes seriously, that is, the shadow cast when the divine is absented—Marovich turns to Wynter's theorization of humans as beings that are at once biological and mythological, living beings with capacity to tell stories about themselves, to unpack the theoretical and political-theological underpinnings of breath in Luce Irigaray's oeuvre, in both its emancipatory and constricting modalities. Kline, meanwhile, explores the necessity, already latent in Wynter's work, of political-theological storytelling for the "new science of the word," which Wynter elaborates in opposition to colonial modernity's dominant paradigms.

One particular mode of storytelling, secularization, has long been closely associated with political theology. Twentieth-century debates among figures such as Schmitt, Taubes, Karl Löwith, and Hans Blumenberg probed which concepts count as secularized, what mechanisms were involved in secularization, and whether secularization might give rise to critique itself. The debate around secularization remains a critical touchstone in the present, its parameters expanding to include the critical study of the formation of secularism and the ontology of the secular.[17] An important conceptual frame for analyzing the reordering of relations between the religious-theological and secular-political realms, secularization has been complemented by the insight that religion and the political are themselves not ahistorical constants but emerge through complex processes of differentiation in modernity. What does it look like to revisit debates about secularization, but with Europe now understood through the lens of colonialism and empire or altogether displaced by forms of theorizing and politics of the Global South? Our contributor Rafael Vizcaíno offers one answer to this question by turning to the works of Enrique Dussel to argue that traditional secularization narratives are "a colonialist and imperialist myth of modernity" that have obscured the violence of colonialism. As a result, Vizcaíno argues that epistemic decolonization in political theology is necessary, and decolonial struggle is essentially political-theological in nature.

What might it mean to do political theology by juxtaposition? Unlike comparison—a mode of inquiry long suspect in the study of religion—this would entail a joint exploration of the conceptuality and practice of political theology in two quite different sites. Rather than enumerate similarities and differences, such a project would inquire into what we can understand more clearly about political theology through decentering, destabilizing encounters. In a certain way, Agamben introduced this question to the field with the provocative juxtapositions that form the core of his *Homo Sacer*, yet his work leaves lingering questions about the determining role of the European tradition for all political theology.[18]

In this volume, Ford shows that Agamben's theoretical framework is essentially, and not accidentally, incompatible with the forms of exception developed in colonialism and chattel slavery. Agamben's approach, Ford's analysis shows, suffers from "a phobic avoidance of the racialized sites, discourses, movements, and events"—even more so, paradoxically, than Schmitt's own. Resisting the equation of Black life and bare life, Ford turns to W. E. B. Du Bois's account of the general strike to trace the generativity that irrupts and interrupts the discourse of sovereign political theology. Meanwhile, Dana Lloyd stages an encounter between Adriana Cavarero and voices of Indigenous feminism to approach one of the concepts most associated with political theology—sovereignty—with "bad intentions" or irony. Taking her lead from Cavarero's feminist challenge to regnant philosophical concepts, Lloyd constellates Indigenous voices not only to think a decolonial philosophy of nonviolence but also to rethink a sovereignty that may be about sharing and nurturing. She offers a path for political theology "liberated from its commitment to settler colonialism and to violence."

Recent years have seen other methodological innovations expand what it means to do political theology. Anthropologists, in particular, have explored the power of ethnography to put pressure on familiar concepts of political theology—all the while being guided by similiar concerns.[19] European intellectual historians interested in political theology have moved beyond their initial focus on early modernity to track connections between the political and the theological from late antiquity all the way to the twentieth century.[20] Comparativists have asked, for example, what connections exist between theological visions and political accounts of monarchy across traditions.[21] Given this explosion of approaches, what methodological tools are best equipped for political-theological inquiry?

Kotsko finds methodological inspiration in the work of Federici, whose genealogies reject the religious-secular dyad and remain intersectional all the way through. Guided by a strategic presentism, Kotsko proposes that political theology's genealogical perspective could seek "to transform our vision of the past to make it usable for the transformation of the present." The volume also features indirect methodological interventions arising out of encounters staged between political theology and its disciplinary outsides. Drawing on Judith Butler's work, Siobhan Kelly, for example, refuses the reduction of gender to identity to explore "how an analysis of gender subject formation can instead serve as a crucial backbone of political theology moving forward." Ada Jaarsma's contribution explores the role of affects and institutions in political theology. Challenging the presuppositions of secularity and the secular-religious binary, Jaarsma elaborates Isabelle Stengers's conceptualization of passionate thinking as a way to probe what Deleuzian and process-based approaches might do for political theology. Lucia Hulsether, meanwhile, centers affect and feeling in examining Christian nationalism as a category of public discourse in the aftermath of the January 6, 2021, attack on the US Capitol. What structures of feeling, she asks, are involved not only in Christian nationalism but also in packaging "Christian nationalism" as a discursive object?

The conjuncture of Marxism and political theology is a charged but highly productive site of exchange. In his early writings, Karl Marx was poignantly attuned to the essential analogies and transmutations occurring between the theological and the political, formulating a proleptic rebuttal to Schmitt's vision of political theology.[22] While Marx-influenced thinkers have worked on issues proximate to political theology (think of not only Dussel and Federici but also Alain Badiou, Walter Benjamin, and Ernst Bloch), recent discourse on political theology tends to range from anarchist to liberal (as well as, of course, to conservative).[23] What would it look like to construct generative engagements between Marxist thought and ongoing conversations in political theology?

Inese Radzins responds to this question by excavating the critical force of Michel Henry's phenomenology of life. Influenced by Marxism and Catholicism, Henry diagnoses the violence of objectification at the heart of modernity, driven by scientific reason and capital accumulation. The antidote Radzins proposes is opening up political theology to poesis—in a move that can be put in conversation with Shulman and Marovich—to affirm the irreducible activity and creativity of life. Martin Shuster, meanwhile, turns to the contemporary Japanese Marxist Kōjin Karatani to rethink the status and underpinnings of secularism. He shows the political-theological importance of Karatani's displacement of modes of production in classical historical materialism with modes of exchange. Shuster proposes that it is essential for political theology to appreciate what Karatani calls the "Borromean knot" of nation, state, and capital.

As it enters the commerce of theory, political theology seems to harbor ambitions to the universal. It may appear to tell us what politics, as such, and theology, as such, are really about—but it has usually done this with reference to Western Christianity and the modern state. How constitutive are claims of universality to political theology? Are there ways to think rigorously and abstractly from a political-theological perspective that would not reproduce colonial pretensions of European thought?

Basit Iqbal and Milad Odabaei's provocation puts into question the all-too-easy translatability and convertibility enacted by "theory," of which political theology serves as one instantiation. Problematizing the operations of abstraction necessary for political theology to function as a concept, Iqbal and Odabaei turn to Talal Asad's anthropology of the secular and explore its attunement to the grammars of concepts as they emerge from and remain embedded in collective forms of life. Using examples of Asad's analysis of laïcité and political fear, they show the necessity of remaining aware of how knowledge and critique are embedded and transmitted through concrete forms of life. Convergently, Prathama Banerjee explores how B. R. Ambedkar's avowal of the irreducible copresence of different religious traditions—and thus also of dissensus as to the very definition of religion—helps him develop a "religious criticism as a legitimate form of public ethics, constitutive of the condition of living with multiple religions." Wandering and itineracy—both spiritual and epistemological—across multiple religions becomes the basis for this religious criticism as an essentially anti-statist perspective. For Banerjee, "While operating in the neighborhood of political theology," such religious criticism "cannot quite be reduced to it." But if political theology is understood broadly as a space that itself may unsettle statist visions, as other contributions in this volume suggest, then Banerjee's contribution may be read as showing an example of the way non-European sites of critical encounter can productively unsettle key aspects of the political-theological terrain.

A related question to that of universality is: What can political theology offer the study of religious traditions other than Christianity, and how do such encounters transform political theology? For Najib, postcolonial political theology must attend as much to geographical difference as to historical difference, its "attention to colony and metropole [must be] mirrored by its consideration of the past and the present." Her essay rethinks Lefort's theorization of the political as a tool and a method for studying precolonial Islamic tradition, which she enacts by turning to the Abbasid Caliph al-Ma'mun. For Agata Bielik-Robson, meanwhile, political theology must begin with the theological origin of critique, which she locates in the Jewish messianic tradition's account of transcendence: "In Jewish messianism the divine transcendence is most of all a standpoint from which the metaphysical totality can be seen and judged." In opposition to what she diagnosis as the Jewish Gnostic perspective on negation embodied by Taubes and Benjamin, Bielik-Robson turns to Theodor Adorno's *Negative Dialectics*, which successfully elaborates "a critique executed from within the world and out of *compassion* for its imperfect beings." Meanwhile, Vincent Lloyd explores the spiritual (and usually not religious) Black feminist discourse on healing. He queries whether it fulfills its critical promise and suggests that Hortense Spillers's writings on Black Christianity offer an immanent critique of the secularized Christianity found in Black feminist theory.

Sovereignty has been one touchstone of traditional accounts of political theology, and where there is sovereignty, there is also legitimacy. What happens to legitimacy with the demystification of the sacred aura on which it relies? Are there theological forms, in the realm of concepts, practices, or ways of life that offer alternatives modes of legitimation? Or, by contrast, is demystification an insufficient substitute for more radical drives to delegitimation? What concepts, what terms of order, are troubled when legitimacy is unsettled: authority, tradition, or, perhaps, modernity itself?

In his chapter, Kirill Chepurin theorizes what he terms "cosmic delegitimation." Chepurin decenters secularization debates by returning to a foundational event of modernity: the Galilean-Copernican revolution that inaugurates the transition from the hierarchized cosmos to the decentered infinite universe (an event also at the heart of essays that engage Wynter). His contribution asks, with the contemporary French speculative philosopher Quentin Meillassoux: What does a political-theological thinking proceeding from the Copernican revolution look like? Meanwhile, if state legitimacy is grounded in overcoming civil war does Christianity, as its theological precursor, perform a more originary form of pacification? To answer this question, Dubilet's essay revisits Augustine's retort to Gnostic dualism and theorizes the Gnostic "a-cosmic revolt" as a rebellion against interpellation and the political. Igniting a cosmic general antagonism and refusing individuation, gnosis delegitimates political theology by showing it to be fundamentally a counterinsurgent project. Rather than reject political theology for a secular politics, Dubilet argues for the necessity of critiquing their essential co-imbrication, but this, paradoxically, requires inhabiting a political-theological attunement.

Behind the variety of questions explored in these essays, one detects a more basic one: What is to be done with political theology? Careful readers of this volume will detect different answers, both explicit and implicit, to this question. For some authors, it is simply to be used, a tool to struggle against oppressive alternative visions of political theology or against self-assured secularisms. For others, it is an accepted intellectual terrain within which certain kinds of conceptual or genealogical work can be pursued. And for still others, it is an ambivalent structure or object to be critiqued—to be clarified, transformed, or entirely abandoned. Even as the meaning and direction of political theology across the essays varies, they demonstrate distinct ways of working with political-theological materials.

The questions that we have separated analytically are deeply overlapping, and each essay responds to multiple pressing questions in the field. Yet the essays do more than this: They create new concepts and open new trajectories of investigation. Taken together, these essays do not produce political theology as a homogeneous terrain but trace multiple throughlines within its contemporary formation. Which direction seems most productive to creatively or critically pick up will depend on the reader's theoretical tastes. It may be the articulation of a fundamental critique of modernity's theory and practice with recourse to countertheology (Shulman), to cosmic immanence or upscaling (Chepurin), or to auto-religion (Kline). It may be theorizing against the primacy not only of the state but even of the political, whether through Ambedkar's religious criticism and epistemological and spiritual itinerancy (in Banerjee) or through cosmic general antagonism and undercommon gnosis (in Dubilet). Or linking the precolonial and the postcolonial (in the Islamic context, as in Najib) or the colonial and decolonial (in Latin America, as in Vizcaíno) in novel ways that trouble both modernity and tradition. Or intervening into contemporary political debates and their presuppositions and imaginaries, whether on the national level (Hulsether) or on the grassroots one (V. Lloyd). We hope readers will diagnose other conceptual clusters across the volume, which they will take as invitations for their own creative reimagining of political theology.

These essays grow out of a set of ongoing, iterative projects that take political theology as an occasion for conversation, for gathering—simply gathering, with the belief that those who gather will fruitfully push one another and inspire one another, yielding not a shared program but an increasingly sophisticated web of inquiry. While critics worry that political theology names a very specific theoretical move or is necessarily rooted in a given religious tradition, and so yields distorted results, the essays that follow demonstrate that the rich diversity of intellectual work in political theology today is better understood in terms of resonance than origin, in terms of disposition and orientation than dogma.

This collection came together at a time when conversation, gathering, was made difficult by the COVID-19 pandemic. The pandemic's uneven effects across populations, and across the academy, shaped which colleagues could participate in this volume and partially determined the burden of participation on each. The pandemic is among the many factors that give this project its contingent shape and its silences. This is nothing new: Pandemics and plagues have often been intimately interwoven with political theology in modernity. Below the famous figure of the sovereign as a composite body on the frontispiece of Thomas Hobbes's *Leviathan*, two tiny figures observe the well-ordered city landscape devoid of living beings. Identifiable by their clothing and beaked masks, the two are plague doctors, and they look down at a city that appears to be in lockdown.[24] Modern sovereignty and its dreams of perfect order, it turns out, were never far from the plague, a site where obedience is exchanged for security.[25]

The effects of pandemic on political theology may seem distinct from, or even at odds with, the effects of radical social movements. The former isolates and stills; the latter collectivizes and impassions. Yet both contexts, both sets of crises, put similar sorts of pressure on the way that political theology has previously been understood. As Butler points out, *pandemic* etymologically calls forth a vision of collectivity, all the people, and while the powers that be naturalize a world of division and domination, social insurgency of recent years has rethought social reproduction and reactivated radicalism as collective force from below.[26]

While Butler takes the pandemic as an opportunity for reexamining the relationship between world and worlds, the contemporary English poet Sean Bonney explores pandemic's more unsettling associations. Meditating on the Moscow plague of 1771, in which the masses rose up against quarantine restrictions, Bonney recounts that the populace attacked a monastery and murdered the archbishop. Today, according to Bonney, instead of the theological authorities as symbols of uncontrolled disease, we have the police: "every cop, living or dead, is a walking plague-pit."[27] Bonney is not taking sides in partisan debates about pandemic response (he died in 2019); rather, he attempts to map out the paradoxical proximities of plague and riot for a contemporary moment that is marked equally by both.

We conclude as we started, with poetry, to explore another way that a political-theological attunement—which is something less programmatic but no less efficacious than a method—might help delineate and intervene in the contemporary. Bonney's experimental poetics explore "riot, plague, any number of un-used potentialities" to create "a chart of the spatio-temporal rhythm of the riot-form . . . A map that could show the paths *not* taken. And where to find them, those paths, those antidotes, those counter-plagues" (117). As a result, even the plague itself does not remain the same: "Plague. The opposite of solidarity. Or rather, solidarity itself: the solidarity of isolation and quarantine, of the bomb-zone or the ghetto. The great silence is full of noises" (117). Time is also transformed, by riot no less than pandemic. "Antagonistic time, revolutionary time, the time of the dead . . . packed with unfinished events: the Paris Commune, Orgreave, the Mau Mau rebellion" disrupts, tears asunder "normative time, a chain of completed triumphs, a net of monuments, dead labour, capital. The TV schedules, basically" (116). Antagonistic, revolutionary time irrupts into the unfolding catastrophe of history, "the unmarked grave [of] ALL history," to name the specters of those who struggled against or succumbed to the violent imposition of order at the hands of theological and political authorities.[28] Like Belcourt, Bonney invents a language to commune with the dead, freeing the dead to haunt the present, disjointing and dislocating its time, to join the ongoing riot: "A riot is a haunt."[29] It calls forth an antagonistic poetics for an antagonistic reality, one that sides with "all the beggars of history" against "the inheritors of the law" (17).[30]

The riot "is formative by virtue of what it makes visible."[31] Its insurrectionary force against the world discloses multiple experiences of time and illuminates other political imaginaries that reweave the histories of victory and defeat. Disrupting providence and justification, antagonistic time calls forth, in material and poetic ways, counter-Earths, counter-plagues, and counter-rhythmic interruptions.[32] Riotous times break apart the policing counterinsurgent epoch and connect with past insurgents and victims in a general antagonism as "a riotous production of difference."[33] They elaborate an abolitionist chorus with anarchic and communist dreams that exceed what is commonly contained by those proper names, a chorus Saidiya Hartman speculatively reimagines: "All of them might well have shouted, No slave time now. Abolition now. In the surreal, utopian nonsense of it all, and at the heart of riot, was the anarchy of colored girls: treason en masse, tumult, gathering together, the mutual collaboration required to confront the prison authorities and the police, the willingness to lose one-self and become something greater—a chorus, a swarm, an ensemble, a mutual aid society."[34]

We turn to Bonney to show that one can find elements of political theology in unlikely places if one only knows how to look. In the poem "What Teargas Is For," Bonney describes the omniscience, omnipresence, and omnipotence of the police: "Cops, being neither human nor animal, do not dream. . . . [They] got access to the content of all of our dreams." Bonney reflects that police need not dream because "they've got teargas"—supplied globally by a company connected to the British crown. In a way, this is a reminder to scholars of political theology that the abstractions of sovereignty are never more than a few mediations away from its material manifestation in police violence. Bonney sardonically speculates that the monarch's relative "probably thinks of teargas as being somehow related to the Cloud of Unknowing, and, in a sense, he's kind of right."[35] The poet is dismissive, though not wholly. But how exactly do we understand the relation between teargas and the anonymous fourteenth-century work of Christian mysticism and to the contemplative apex that gives it its name?

We are certainly far from the legitimating comforts of the king's mystical two bodies or the mystical foundations of authority. This political mysticism is of a different, radically material sort, which we might name a mysticism of teargas. "You come to have a very real understanding of the nature of things, both visible and invisible, by having your sensory system hijacked and turned against you by a meaningful dose of teargas." The poem covertly restages aspects dear to mystical theology: the path of contemplation, the visible and the invisible, the sensual and supersensual, and knowledge and unknowing, as well as the undoing of spatiotemporal organization ("loss of geographical certainty"). There is even a perverse permutation of the imperative mode of spiritual direction so dear to medieval manuals: "Next time things are starting to kick off a little bit just go out on the street and run straight into the middle of the biggest cloud of teargas you can find."[36]

The dialectical dance of the poem shifts from an abrasive dismissal of the theological as a mystifying discourse of sovereign power to tracing its unexpected material transformations in relation to teargas and the police. But you can detect this shift only with a political-theological attunement. The "small and silent point of absolute Unknowing," the spiritual peak of apophasis, occurs not in unity with God but in a cloud of teargas. The spiritual power of teargas displaces the theater of the soul into the theater of police power—or, rather, it is still very much the theater of the soul, now caught in a cloud of teargas, which forcefully corporealizes it by imposing an "absolute regulation and administration of all the senses." The Cloud of Unknowing is a Cloud of Teargas. Thinking this statement in its speculative and material complexity requires a political theology that has severed its ties with sovereign power and its modes of legitimation to side with its victims. It requires a political theology proximate to "an anti-police mystical theology," a disordering insurgency harboring visions and weapons that remain unrecognizable to those political theologies that are, wittingly or not, actually police theologies of order.[37]

This is not the only reference to the Cloud of Unknowing in *Our Death*. Ruminating in "Letter Against the Language" on the status of the inexpressible located in the culminating scream of the father character in Pier Paolo Pasolini's film *Teorema* (a scream containing "all that is meaningful in the word 'communism'") and on "hearing inexpressible things" in the Letter to the Corinthians (which Pasolini cites in his unfinished screenplay on Paul), Bonney catches himself. He declares, "Don't get me wrong. I'm not about to disappear into some kind of cutrate Cloud of Unknowing."

He goes on to explain that Pasolini, whose rage and heterodox commitment to communism Bonney inherits, made clear, in a 1974 article, that by "inexpressible things" he meant "the names of power," names responsible for massacres that are "impossible to pronounce . . . and continue simply to live."[38] Bonney's oblique reference is to Pasolini's "What is this coup d'état? I know," which is structured by an almost incantatory repetition of "I know the names," declaimed as parrhesiastic accusations to political and theological authorities responsible for coups, massacres, and repression in Italy. Pasolini published the essay a year before his murder in Ostia, which, in a political-theologically significant contingency of history, was the site of the foundational mystical vision of Christianity: Augustine's so-called vision at Ostia.[39]

The names of power, however, have a complex relation to unknowing. Are not the first and ultimate names of power, the names of God, those divine names that legitimate theological-political hierarchies? Apophatic unsaying has always been the other side of the kataphatic saying of the divine names, for the entire Christian mystical tradition from Dionysius the Areopagite to *The Cloud of Unknowing* and beyond. Perhaps, then, the cut-rate Cloud of Unknowing remains in the delimited domain of the theological, but at full price, it forces us to traverse the inexpressible names of power up to the massacres and murders carried out in its name.[40] Here, what we see are theological imaginaries traversing the material world of violence and the police, insurgency and counterinsurgency. Political theology allows us to abandon the purely theological domain and transversally defamiliarize interrelated elements such as apophasis, power, knowledge, and the senses. Fragments of a theological imaginary are mutated within the political reality of the present in ways that, as theologians no less than historicists would undoubtedly remind us, betray the original orientation of *The Cloud of Unknowing*. But neither is the secular left undisturbed by political-theological ways of reading that suspend self-legitimating secular presuppositions about history and liberation and that free past insurgencies, relying on millenarianism, the Gods, and other theological weapons, from the condemnation of being premodern: Peasant revolts from sixteenth-century Germany to nineteenth-century India become contemporary in their struggle against hierarchy, established authority, and modern property relations.[41] A political theology that sides with riotous social insurgency against the police will not itself remain unchanged when it confronts the linguistic chain of implication that binds the political to policy and the police.[42] It may become something more and less than political and more and less than theological, seeing both terrains as imbricated in insurgency and counterinsurgency, in riot and order, in denouncing and legitimating the names of power.

Mapping normative rhythms and their interruptions, recovering voices and lines of antagonism, conjuring counter-plagues: These are the decisive imperatives for the riotous times of the present, and they animate the essays that follow. The goal is less to subsume all this under the proper name of political theology than to explore the lives and afterlives of theological shards in the present and thereby undermine all facile claims to secularity and all easy demarcations of religion. This entails creating new constellations of concepts and texts, reconsidering our basic narratives and genealogies, remaining attentive to the ruses of justification and rationalization, and experimenting with the many folds of transcendence and immanence. Critically engaging with the archives of insurgency across the catastrophes of counterinsurgent modernity means discerning when riotous and insurrectionary direct action opens onto forms of leveling and communizing assembly, insurgent universalities, and destituent freedoms, and when, by contrast, they enact xenophobic reimpositions of identity, counterrevolutions of property, or racist scapegoating in response to neoliberal precarity and, through this discernment, refuse the neutral perspective of the state for which all riotous insurgencies are equal, merely a temporary disorder to be overcome by declaring a state of emergency.[43] As Bonney concludes an epistolary poem, commending the joy of the critical task in political-theological terms, "The deep truth is imageless. When you know that, you know there's everything to play for. All else is madness and suffering at the hands of the pigs" (44). And if the entanglements of sovereignty and sense, of the normative and the imaginary, prevent the formulation of a unified vision of justice, this does not prevent the poets from voicing different senses of this impossibility. Let us end with their words. Belcourt: "i mouthed the word justice / and then forgot how to speak" (12). Bonney: "say no justice no peace and then say fuck the police" (29).

Notes

We express our appreciation to Shayla Jordan for her editorial help, to Sandra Korn for her initial excitement about the project, to Courtney Berger for her continual support for the project at Duke University Press, to all of the contributors to this volume, and to our families.

1   Davis and Sarlin, "On the Risk of a New Relationality."

2   Belcourt, *This Wound Is a World*, 55. Hereafter, page numbers are cited in parentheses in the text.

3   Assmann, *Herrschaft und Heil*.

4   The status of tradition has been a key theoretical site of inquiry influential for political theology: see Asad, "The Idea of an Anthropology of Islam"; Asad, "Thinking about Tradition, Religion, and Politics in Egypt Today"; MacIntyre, *After Virtue*; Mahmood, *Politics of Piety*, 113–17; Stout, *Democracy and Tradition*.

5   See, e.g., the Routledge Transforming Political Theologies book series; "Deprovincializing Political Theology," the 2022 special issue of *Political Theology* (23, nos. 1–2); and An, *The Coloniality of the Secular*.

6   For an instantiation of this approach, see Chepurin and Dubilet, *Nothing Absolute*.

7   See Dubilet, "An Immanence Without the World." For a perceptive critique of the scholarly opposition between colonial modernity as source of abstraction and tradition as source of embodiment and concretion, see Ahmed, *Archaeology of Babel*. There is also an important dissenting tradition of critical scholarship that follows Edward Said in embracing the aspiration to the secular and the worldly. For a collection exemplifying this line of scholarship that articulates a critique of postsecularism, see the "Why I Am Not a Postsecularist" special issue of *boundary 2* (40, no. 1). See also Said, *The World. the Text, and the Critic*. For one critical assessment of secularism and the secular and its essential relation to Christianity, see Anidjar, "Secularism."

8   For one example of the persistence of European universalism, see Masuzawa, *The Invention of World Religions*.

9   For two quite different examples of rethinking of European abstraction, see Chakrabarty, *Provincializing Europe*; Pandolfo, *Knot of the Soul*. For catastrophe, see also *Critical Times*'s special issue "The Destruction of Loss" (6, no. 2).

10   In one classic political-theologically inflected account, modernity itself arises out of crisis; see Koselleck, *Critique and Crisis*.

11   Four book series now address political theology: Transforming Political Theologies (Routledge), Political Theologies (Bloomsbury), Political and Public Theologies (Brill), and Transdisciplinary Theological Colloquia (Fordham), the last of these growing out of regular conferences convened at Drew Theological School.

12   For theoretical accounts of Christianity's multifaceted relation to the secular, see Anidjar, *Blood*; Anidjar, *The Jew, The Arab*; Barber, *On Diaspora*; Stimilli, *The Debt of the Living*; Sullivan, *Church, State, Corporation*.

13 Lloyd, *Race and Political Theology.*

14 See Armstrong, "Losing Salvation"; Kaplan, "Notes Toward (Inhabiting) the Black Messianic in Afro-Pessimism's Apocalyptic Thought"; Magid, *Meir Kahane,* 75–106.

15 Kahn, *The Future of Illusion*; Schwartz, *Sacramental Poetics at the Dawn of Secularism.*

16 Milbank, *Theology and Social Theory,* 331.

17 For a contemporary critique of the earlier debates, see Davis, *Periodization and Sovereignty.* For critical study of the secular, see, e.g., Asad et al., *Is Critique Secular?*; Fernando, *The Republic Unsettled.*

18 Agamben, *Homo Sacer.* For his reflections on method, see Agamben, *The Signature of All Things.*

19 See, e.g., Agrama, *Questioning Secularism*; McAllister and Napolitano, "Political Theology/Theopolitics."

20 See, e.g., Shortall and Jenkins, *Christianity and Human Rights Reconsidered*; Stroumsa, "God's Rule in Late Antiquity."

21 Moin and Strathern, *Sacred Kingship in World History.*

22 Dubilet, "On the General Secular Contradiction."

23 For a recent anarchist articulation of political theology, see Martel, *Anarchist Prophets.*

24 See Agamben, *Stasis*; Falk, "Hobbes' Leviathan und die aus dem Blick gefallenen Schnabelmasken."

25 On plague and dreams of order, see Foucault, *Discipline and Punish,* 195–209. See also Agamben's controversial meditations on the COVID-19 pandemic in *Where Are We Now?*

26 Butler, *What World Is This?*

27 Bonney, *Letters Against the Firmament,* 115. Hereafter, page numbers are cited in parentheses in the text.

28 Bonney, *Our Death,* 46.

29 Bonney, *Our Death,* 11.

30 Bonney, *Our Death,* 29.

31 Invisible Committee, *Now,* 15. For a Marxist reading of riot as a contemporary form, see Clover, *Riot, Strike, Riot.*

32 For an innovative theorization of insurgency, multiple temporalities, and paths violently repressed, see Tomba, *Insurgent Universality.*

33 Harney and Moten, *The Undercommons,* 109.

34 Hartman, "The Anarchy of Colored Girls Assembled in a Riotous Manner," 485.

35 Bonney, *Our Death*, 73.

36 Bonney, *Our Death*, 73.

37 Dubilet, "The Just without Justification," 18.

38 Bonney, *Our Death*, 18.

39 See Hollywood, "Introduction."

40 For a recent theorization of negative theology in relation to political theology in an insurrectionary key, see Dubilet, "The Just without Justification." For alternative readings, see Newheiser, *Hope in a Secular Age*, and the "Negative Political Theology" special issue of *Modern Theology* (36, no. 1).

41 See Banerjee, "In Memoriam Ranajit Guha"; Guha, "Prose of Counter-Insurgency."

42 On politics, policy, and the police, see Harney and Moten, *The Undercommons*.

43 We completed this introduction as the far-right "anti-immigrant" (i.e., racist) riots began to spread across the United Kingdom. One of the first to receive a criminal sentence was a counter-protestor, Ashkan Kareem, who was jailed for twelve months for "violent disorder" while protecting a mosque from attack in Darlington. This offers another illustration of what the neutrality of the state amounts to in practice.

Expanded Horizons
in Critical Theory

1

From Negation to Critique

ADORNO ON TRANSCENDENCE

Agata Bielik-Robson

Does critical theory have theological roots? In this essay, I attempt to show that it does indeed: Its very concept of critique was made possible by the Jewish messianic tradition, which involves a highly specific notion of transcendence.[1] Unlike in the Platonic metaphysics, where *epekeina tes ousias* (beyond being) designates the superessential highest point of the great chain of beings, in Jewish messianism the divine transcendence is most of all a standpoint from which the metaphysical totality can be seen and judged. The Jewish messianic transcendence, therefore, signifies not the highest possible ontological perfection but, rather, a place from which it is possible to criticize the whole of creation as lacking thereof: It constitutes the transcendental possibility of the critique as such.

In *Twilight of the Idols*, Friedrich Nietzsche famously refutes the idea of such vantage point as illogical. It is simply unfathomable from the perspective of a single creature, which is always thrown into being and thus cannot pretend to be able to judge it: "There is nothing that can judge, measure, compare, or condemn our being, because that would mean judging, measuring, comparing, and condemning the whole. . . . *But there is nothing outside the whole!*"[2] The Jewish tradition begs to differ precisely on that point: If there is any need to acknowledge the concept of the transcendent God, it is precisely because it allows one to formulate by proxy "the biggest objection to existence."[3] For, if God can judge—we, his *tselemim* (likenesses), can, too. According to Nietzsche, however, this judgment always amounts to an outright No—a "negative attitude towards life," which always tends to evaluate the whole of being in a deleterious manner.[4] "Judging, measuring, comparing" the enterprise of being inevitably leads to "condemning the whole." Critique merely disguises negation—hence, Nietzsche's conviction that it is the "spirit of revenge" that operates behind the critical attitude toward the world. Its true aim is not an improvement of what appears imperfect in the order of being but its total, uncompromised rejection.

Is Nietzsche's critique of critique relevant in reference to critical theory? Yes and no. After all, as Nietzsche himself remarks, "This is why the Jews were dialecticians."[5] In late works of Theodor Adorno—*Minima Moralia* and *Negative Dialectics*—the possibility of critique is discussed in regard to two different standpoints (*Standorte*): one strictly transcendent, lending an external view on things, and the other, more immanent and implying a transfer of the sacred into the sphere of the profane. While the former can indeed be accused in the Nietzschean manner of reducing critique of the world to a simple negation, the latter is dialectical, maintaining and reconciling two moments—negation and affirmation—simultaneously.

"Critical Energy": Adorno's Secular Use of Jewish Messianism

In his recent book, *Migrants in the Profane*, Peter Eli Gordon presents Adorno as the thinker who, unlike Walter Benjamin and Max Horkheimer, "did not seek in religion a substantive remedy for [the deficient condition of the world]. Instead, *he found in religion the critical energy that could make the deficit visible*. He thereby honored religion even while he sustained a principled commitment to the dialectical redemption of secular society from within."[6] According to Gordon, the particularly abundant religious source of such "critical energy" was, for Adorno, the Lurianic Kabbalah, which for the first time depicted the migration of the sacred into the profane as the dialectical intertwinement of both realms in the metaphor of the shell and the kernel: "In Adorno's view it is the task of criticism to expose the negativity of the world. One must break open the shells, or conceptual categories, that lend the world its illusory perfection. The imagery of the Lurianic Kabbalah here becomes an allegory for the critique of ideology. Adorno pays homage to the metaphysical concept of the messianic, *but* uses this concept for the sake of this-worldly critique."[7] The most famous of Adorno's epigrams on revelation confirms his Lurianic choice: "No theological content will last untransformed; every single one will have to face the test and enter the sphere of the profane."[8] Yet in the light of this aphorism, there is no need to oppose—as Gordon does in his seemingly innocuous use of *but*—"the metaphysical concept of the messianic" and "this-worldly critique." The latter is precisely the test of the Real for the former. In Adorno's view, the transcendent is meaningless unless it wanders into the world and gets "crucified" on the cross of the immanent present.[9] Does the *but* in Gordon's formulation indicate that, despite the right diagnosis, he misreads the kabbalistic influence on Adorno's late work by insisting on the traditional "untransformed" theological content of the metaphysical transcendence as the vantage point that resists any migration into the profane?

In what follows, I try to show that such, indeed, is the case. When interpreted truly radically, Adorno's Lurianic commitment will prove capable of elucidating what, from the more traditional theological point of view still embraced by Gordon, must seem to be an outright contradiction: "the dialectical moment [of critique] that permitted [Adorno] to see in modernity the *realization rather than the betrayal of a religious truth he could not affirm.*"[10] Gordon's conclusion is both intriguing and aporetic, for how could Adorno affirm secular modernity as a critical realization of the religious truth of the transcendence that he simultaneously refused to affirm? How could he endorse the modern development of critical theory, impossible in any other epoch and, at the same time, the essentially premodern notion of the transcendent vantage point to "this-worldly critique"? Or, putting things bluntly, how could he decide to use the "messianic optics" without believing in the Messianic Light?

The answer to this aporia lies in Adorno's ingenious appropriation of the Lurianic theologoumenon: the *total* migration of the sacred into the profane, conceived and maintained precisely as a *theological* maneuver or a *new* "religious truth," replacing the old one, focused on the traditionally conceived otherworldly transcendence. In contrast to the latter, what is now metaphysically and theologically *true* is the becoming-worldly of God, the *divine self-secularization* as a procosmic choice of stepping out of godself, inherent in the very process of creation. Just like Hannah Arendt and Hans Jonas, Adorno reacts with enthusiasm to Gershom Scholem's *Major Trends of Jewish Mysticism,* which presented the kabbalistic mystical thought not as an a-cosmic negation of the inner-worldly dimension (as Nietzsche would like to see all metaphysics involving the notion of transcendence) but as a dialectical pro-cosmic affirmation of the world (*saeculum*), playing a major role in the theological process called a "holy history" (*Heilsgeschichte*).[11] Here transcendence does not disappear completely. Rather, it undergoes a "diminution" that dethrones the sacred from the position of the eternal Absolute and makes it complicit with things transient and finite. "This is the *transmutation of metaphysics into history,*" Adorno writes. "It secularizes metaphysics in the secular category pure and simple, the category of decay. Philosophy interprets that pictography, the ever new Mene Tekel, in microcosm—in the fragments which decay has chipped, and which bear the objective meanings. No recollection of transcendence is possible any more, save by way of perdition; eternity appears, not as such, but diffracted through the most perishable."[12]

Gordon equates the Lurianic position of *Negative Dialectics*—the dialectical moment of critique made possible by the "religious truth"—with negative theology, but this equation is highly misleading. In fact, there is palpable tension between Adorno's use of negative theology, to which he resorts at the end of *Minima Moralia*, and his use of Luria's dialectical messianism, to which he alludes in the concluding sections of *Negative Dialectics*. The former approach is called by Adorno an "inverse theology," which brings him closer to the anti-cosmic standpoint of Benjamin and Franz Kafka; the latter, associated with the Lurianic Kabbalah, Adorno calls "Hegelianism without closure," which openly declares "kabbalistic" pro-cosmism.[13] This tension once again brings to mind the Nietzschean warning against the notion of critique as making a secular use of the "messianic optics." For what does it mean to be critical—and not just negative? What should be the standpoint of the critique *proper*, not inherently hostile to the idea of reconciliation with transient reality? And finally, if the concept of transcendence is supposed to offer such a vantage, then to what extent can it truly migrate into the profane—that is, the inner-worldly?

In *Minima Moralia*, Adorno famously states that critique must be undertaken from the point of view of redemption:

> The only philosophy which can be responsibly practised in face of despair is the attempt to contemplate all things as they would present themselves from the standpoint of redemption. *Knowledge has no light but that shed on the world by redemption: all else is reconstruction, mere technique.* Perspectives must be fashioned that displace and estrange the world, reveal it to be, with its rifts and crevices, as indigent and distorted *as it will appear one day in the messianic light.* To gain such perspectives *without velleity or violence*, entirely *from felt contact with its objects*—this alone is the task of thought. It is the simplest of all things, because the situation calls imperatively for such knowledge, indeed because *consummate negativity*, once squarely faced, delineates the mirror-image of its opposite.[14]

In Jewish messianic theology, the concept of redemption is tinged with ambivalence that never escaped Scholem and of which Adorno is also aware: On the one hand, it suggests something good and welcome—

Agata Bielik-Robson

an ultimate liberation from all the "imperfections" of the present state of being: sin, decay, and death. On the other, however, it implies that the road to freedom must lead through the gates of the apocalyptic Last Judgment over the world as a whole. To appeal to the instance of the Last Judgment means to evoke the most radical transcendence as the strongest possible vantage point: an absolute unalloyed "exteriority" (to use Emmanuel Levinas's term), which, by its very essence, *cannot* migrate into the profane and assume a contaminated form of the infinite in the finite. Not only does it not wander into the world. By staying totally *outside* as the Levinasian "otherwise than being," it reserves the right to destroy what it created—the right to form "the strongest objection to existence" and thus to the apocalyptic negation of the world. Thus, when Adorno states that he wants to use the Messianic Light "without velleity or violence" (*ohne Willkür und Gewalt*), he immediately demonstrates his knowledge of the danger that he wishes to avert: the threat of the violent No as the Nietzschean dark reverse of the critical desire leading to "critical negation."[15] But unlike Benjamin, who openly sided with the divine violence and its "destructive character," passing a lethal verdict on existence, Adorno thinks that he can make a controlled and restricted use of the Messianic Light by bracketing the metaphysical reality of transcendence so the "velleity and violence" can be safely avoided. Aware of its "impossible" standpoint, critique would not be so assured in its destructive attitude toward the "consummate negativity" of the world as it is the case with the overt apocalyptic discourse, strongly relying on the reality of the "unconditional." Adorno thus hopes that the weakening of the "religious truth" of transcendence to the philosophical truth of the transcendental condition will do the trick by creating a *pure* vantage point, free from any theological content usually attached to it, including the apocalyptic *Willkür und Gewalt*:

> But it [critical knowledge] is also the utterly impossible thing, *because it presupposes a standpoint removed, even though by a hair's breadth, from the scope of existence* [Aber es ist auch das ganz Unmögliche, weil es einen Standort voraussetzt, der dem Bannkreis des Daseins, wäre es auch nur um ein Winziges, entrückt ist], whereas we well know that any possible knowledge must not only be first wrested from what is, if it shall hold good, but is also marked, for this very reason, by the same distortion and indigence which it seeks to escape. The more passionately thought denies its conditionality for the sake of the unconditional, the more unconsciously, and so calamitously, it is delivered up

to the world. Even its own impossibility it must at last comprehend for the sake of the possible. *But beside the demand thus placed on thought, the question of the reality or unreality of redemption itself hardly matters.*[16]

Seemingly "the simplest of all things," the critique turns out to be an unachievable task: It must be articulated from "a standpoint removed, even though by a hair's breadth, from the scope of existence," even if it does not believe in the "reality of redemption." The critique is uneasily poised between the Scylla of full immanentism, where it is affected "by the same distortion and indigence which it seeks to escape," and the Charybdis of too much naïve trust put in the idea of "the unconditional" as the traditional religious transcendence, full of the all-too-human spirit of revenge toward the world. In theoretical terms, therefore, critique is *impossible* (Nietzsche was right), and it is only the practical "demand placed on thought" that makes it simultaneously *necessary*. The clash between pure reason and practical reason thus leads straight to the aporia in Gordon's striking formulation: Critical knowledge is a realization of a religious truth that the modern secularized mind cannot affirm. It needs a negative, but it does not need theology: "We must conclude that what Adorno wishes to retain from theology amounts to little more than a *conceptual* gesture, like a vanishing point on the distant horizon that remains infinitely behind us as we move forward in time."[17]

Jacob Taubes, who was very critical of Adorno, called this position of a vanishing point an *aestheticized "as if" messianism*—and perhaps rightly so.[18] The attempts to keep transcendence as the transcendental vantage of critical attitude, *which only wanders into the profane as something that cannot ever wander into the profane*, inescapably leads to the paradox that cannot be resolved even by an "as if" proviso. Such migration of the non-migratable, says Taubes, can never *work*, because it will either remain an ineffective *als ob* (as if), never to be taken fully seriously—or, when taken seriously and no longer "as if," it will immediately regress to the old "religious truth" and issue in the apocalyptic wholesale negation of the world (which Taubes endorses). Adorno is indeed stuck here in an unproductive antinomy. On the one hand, he admits that any knowledge or judgment of the world must stem from this world, from the "felt contact with objects," and thus partake in its disfigurations and imperfections. On the other, however, he insists on the transcendent vantage as the ideal point of critique, regardless of its metaphysical status (true or not), as the only *Standort* that can save us from the immanentist distortion. Its sterilizing "as-if-ness" does not solve anything. If criticism is rooted in the "exteriority" of the transcendence, it inevitably turns into a severe negation of this world as a "consummate negativity." But when it is left hanging in the air, it sinks back into "the same distortion and indigence which [the critique] seeks to escape." This way or another, the "critical energy" goes to waste.

Of course, Adorno knows that critique should be a *dialectical* position: It cannot be a simple negation, but neither can it allow for a simple affirmation of the status quo. Yet, this is precisely why his first attempt to formulate the standpoint of critical theory constitutes a failure. The lack of dialectics in the finale of *Minima Moralia* makes him particularly exposed to the Nietzschean skepticism: Is Adorno critical here—or is he merely negative? Is his critical theory truly what it promises: "a gain of such perspective without velleity or violence, entirely from felt contact with its objects," that is, a critique executed from within the world and out of *compassion* for its imperfect beings—or is it yet another version of the apocalyptic-punitive sentence passed over the world in the ruthless vein of *pereat mundus, sed fiat iustitia*?

From Vantage to Leverage, or, The "Revelation from Below"

In the decade separating *Minima Moralia* and *Negative Dialectics*, a radical change occurs in Adorno's theory of critique, which corresponds to the shift in his understanding of the very idea of the "messianic optics." The "inverse theology," with which Adorno begins to toy already in his dissertation on Søren Kierkegaard and that eventually leads him to the *as if* position in *Minima Moralia*, is surpassed by a more dialectical standpoint that no longer involves pure "exteriority" of transcendence. "Exteriority" is replaced by a different, more immanentist *Standort* that nonetheless preserves the metaphysical dignity of the "unconditional." In *Negative Dialectics*, Adorno calls this position a new Archimedean point that would correct "the [old] delusion that the transcendental subject is the Archimedean fixed point from which the world can be lifted out of its hinges" (181). Already the change of nomenclature suggests a contrast with the former view: Unlike the cold, critical gaze executed from the judgmental beyond (and then secularized in the transcendental view from nowhere), this alternative *Standort* is rooted in material immanence as the point of leverage, capable of moving the whole reality from within. This seemingly contradictory infinite in the finite is the experience of pain as "physical suffering," which G. W. F. Hegel, here preceding Adorno, called "the prerogative of all living natures."[19] That is, he called it a *privilege* to hold a separate and nonnegotiable point of view that cannot be explained away or relativized by any theodicy:

> The physical moment tells our knowledge that suffering ought not to be, that things should be different. *Woe speaks: "Go."* Hence the convergence of specific materialism with criticism, with social change in practice. . . . This dignity is the mind's negative reminder of its physical aspect; its capability of that aspect is the only source of whatever hope the mind can have. The smallest trace of senseless suffering in the empirical world belies all the identitarian philosophy that would talk us out of that suffering. (203)

For Adorno, pain is noumenal: It touches the very core of the Real; it is the spark of the "unconditional" that has now fully migrated into the profane and phenomenal. The pain, therefore, does not belong to the realm of appearances. It is a kernel of the transcendence in the immanence, which cannot (yet) recognize itself in the distorted worldly kingdom of necessities and, because of that, manifests primarily in pain. But its true destiny is happiness—a future possible state of being, no longer marked with distortion that now causes nothing but suffering. In that sense, the new Adornian "unconditional" resembles the impersonal spark in Simone Weil, which, located in the noumenal sphere of "human personality," constantly asks the painful question: *Why am I being hurt?* In Weil's account, the noumenal spark is a soft spot of the soul where only joy was expected, and this is precisely why it is so mercilessly exposed to pain. The only difference between Weil and Adorno is that, in Adorno's Lurianic variations, the spark is no longer purely pneumatic. Here the spark fuses fully with matter, giving rise to the new "theological materialism."

The crucial gain of this change is that one can also see, criticize, and move the world from the new Archimedean point of leverage without assuming the vantage of transcendence as the instance of severe judgment. Moreover, this specific form of *theological materialism* can be perceived as a secularized variant of what Scholem, in his early studies on the lament of Job, called the "revelation from below": the Joban experience of the creature limited by the conditions of actuality and subject to afflictions of which the transcendent God has no knowledge and therefore cannot be a judge.[20] Thus, while for the Christian Hegel it is the divine incarnation that attenuates the instance of the Last Judgment with a touch of mercy, for Scholem—but also for Adorno of *Negative Dialectics*—it is the figure of Job, the suffering creature who can judge the world through the ultimate perspective of its pain and oppose it to the divine judgment that does not know or care for attenuating circumstances. This certainly is a better standpoint of the critique—truly "without velleity or violence," entirely from felt contact with its suffering objects, instead of the "revelation from above" and the thundering verdict of the absolute justice that is about to doom the world because it never lived in it. In that sense, *Negative Dialectics*, as well as Adorno's late essays on literature, constitute a critical enterprise that fortunately does *not* follow the finale of *Minima Moralia* and, precisely for that reason, can be properly critical—that is, free from the imminent threat of *absolute* negation. According to Gordon, who insists on the validity of the strictly transcendent *Standort* for the whole of Adorno's late works, "Religious norms [had] to be evacuated of all metaphysical authority: They would be permitted to retain only as much of their redemptive meaning as was necessary for them to serve the task of *critical negation*. This was the necessary price of religion's trial of secularization. Negative theology became negative dialectics."[21] In my view, however, something else occurred: a more radical change of *theological* perspective, in which the "religious truth" of divine transcendence transformed into a different, but equally religious, truth of the sacred inadvertently fused with the profane. Just as in Hegel, for whom suffering is the place of the first uneasy awakening of the infinite Spirit in finite nature, in Adorno, the Joban "physical moment" of each and every single creature is the topos of the "unconditional," revealing itself in the midst of the material world "from the felt contact with its objects."

This is precisely where Adorno departs from Benjamin, to whom he was hitherto deeply indebted as his main theological authority (certainly more than to Scholem). Benjamin, from his earliest *Theological-Political Fragment* to his latest *Concept of History*, remained a Jewish Gnostic (or, as Taubes called him, a "Jewish Marcionite"), taking the apocalyptic standpoint of "critical negation" without mercy.[22] Contrary to this, Adorno's *Negative Dialectics* gives up on the *vantage of transcendence* to make room for the *leverage of immanence*, perceived no longer as "consummate negativity" but, rather, as a realm in which the sacred and the profane, the kernels and the shells, hope and pain mix beyond the possibility of separation. From this perspective, the "negative theology" of *Minima Moralia* can be regarded as Adorno's Gnostic failure of the nerve: completely understandable from the point of view of a Jew who witnessed the atrocities of the Shoah, but in philosophical and theological terms not crucial to—in fact, not even compatible with—his merciful appreciation of the creaturely condition that he develops in his later works. Just like Scholem, therefore, Adorno could have said that his secularism is not secular and that his atheism is of a pious type.[23] But he would go even further than Scholem, whom he reproached for a certain theological timidity in dealing with the "explosive" potential of the Lurianic Kabbalah. While Scholem still harbors hopes for a new "revelation from above"—the awakening of the divine transcendence to the status of active *das Erscheinende*—Adorno stakes his critique only on the grassroots "revelations from below," in the immanence alloyed with transcendence that irrevocably wandered into the material realm, never to leave it again. For Adorno, the Lurianic Kabbalah thus becomes a source of a truly modern "theological materialism" and forms a new "metaphysical authority" that affirms the migration of the sacred into the profane "ruthlessly" (*rücksichtlos*) and turns it into a *new* "religious truth."[24] Adorno's negative dialectics as the modern execution of *peregrina in saeculo*, migration in the profane, does not occur, as Gordon claims, because of the secularized (as well as sterilized) remnants of the "negative theology" in his critical theory, but because of a quite successful *realization* of the new "religious truth" of the Lurianic Kabbalah, which made God commit a *tsimtsum* (diminution, contraction) and exteriorize himself into the profane in a truly *rücksichtlos* manner—that is, without any transcendent remainder and without any nostalgia for the recovery of the original form of Godhead. This new truth, in fact, is the very opposite of negative theology in which God retains his transcendent counter-position to the world as *die Gegenprinzip*, exposing the world as the "consummate negativity." Adorno does not reduce theology to the pragmatic means of secular "critical negation." Rather, he seeks *another* theology that would affirm secularization as the new "religious truth."[25]

Theology of Miniaturization: The Kabbalistic Paradigm of *Tsimtsum*

In *Negative Dialectics*, the kabbalistic paradigm of *tsimtsum* (contraction, reduction, withdrawal) emerges as the modern rule of "miniaturization" of the theological content to "almost nothing." This, however, does not refer to the "vanishing point" of transcendence as pure exteriority. The apparent fall of the traditional metaphysics—being also the fall of transcendence into the immanence—is simultaneously a rise of a new metaphysical truth, that of the Absolute taking the form of "the smallest intramundane traits":

> Enlightenment leaves practically nothing of the metaphysical content of truth—*presque rien,* to use a modern musical term. *That which recedes keeps getting smaller and smaller,* as Goethe describes it in the parable of New Melusine's box, designating an extremity. It grows more and more insignificant; this is why, in the critique of cognition as well as in the philosophy of history, *metaphysics immigrates into micrology.* Micrology is the place where metaphysics finds a haven from totality. *No absolute can be expressed otherwise than in topics and categories of immanence,* although neither in its conditionality nor as its totality is immanence to be deified. . . . *The smallest intramundane traits would be of relevance to the absolute,* for the micrological view cracks the shells of what, measured by the subsuming cover concept, is helplessly isolated and explodes its identity, the delusion that it is but a specimen. There is solidarity between such thinking and metaphysics at the time of its fall. (407–8, emphasis added)

In *Notes on Literature,* the collection of essays composed mostly in the 1960s, Adorno devotes one essay to "the most enigmatic work Goethe produced"—*Neue Melusina*—whose magical heroine is diminished to the size of a doll and lives in a little treasure chest that protects her from the violence of the outside world and thus also from the reifying "disgrace of adaptation."[26] In *Negative Dialectics,* the reference to New Melusina alludes to the two topoi at once: to the kabbalistic metaphor of the shell and the kernel, where the little queen symbolizes the "smallest intramundane trait" of the "messianic light," deposited in the box, and to the Benjaminian image of "ugly and wizened theology," distorted and reduced to the size of a dwarf, hidden in the chest under the table and invisibly pulling the strings of the chess-playing puppet.[27] The "little chest in the Melusina story," therefore, is a modern semi-secular avatar of the Arc of the Covenant as the shell that preserves and protects *Shekhinah,* the trace of the divine presence in the world. Thus, it is precisely the sacred that wandered into the profane, whose "religious truth" opposes the purely immanentist world of myth: "The little chest in the Melusina story, one of the most enigmatic works Goethe produced, is the *counterauthority to myth;* it does not attack myth but rather undercuts it through nonviolence."[28]

In Adorno's portrait of the Goethean Melusina, the motif of *Shekhinah* appears in its later kabbalistic figuration: the contracted divine dwelling on Earth, a miniaturized gentle glory (*kavod*) that agreed to withdraw and reduce to live *among* the creatures of the world, by sharing their limitations and imperfections *with* them and not *against* them. The Goethean motif of *Ermattung* as fading and diminution alike, which Adorno associates with the Lurianic *tsimtsum*, thus leads to a source of metaphysical *counterauthority* that is different from the former, purely transcendent *counter-principle* (*Gegenprinzip*).[29] It opposes the mythic violence with nonviolence of the spark that refuses to adapt to the violent world and still hopes for happiness. For Adorno, myth as the principle of pure immanence (*der Bannkreis des Daseins*) is inescapably associated with violence that maintains and perpetuates the dominion of the ideological shells (*Schallen*) over the singular sparks of life, desperately trying to free themselves from the "subsumption by the cover concepts." But if the treasure chest protects from violence and thus creates a *Standort* for a possible critique of the violent world, itself *ohne Willkühr und Gewalt*, then the model of "critical negation" from the finale of *Minima Moralia*, using the scorching light of the Last Judgment, would be still very mythic. It is thus only in his late works, where Adorno experiments freely with the concept of *Ermattung* (the *tsimstum*-like diminution), that he finally achieves what he always wanted from his critical theory: an Exodus out of Egypt of mythic violence. The "Messianic Light," with which he previously wanted to scorch the world of decay, dims and produces a softer version of the critique that steers away from the pitfalls of wholesale negation. Adorno is now fully a theological migrant into the material profane: "At its most materialistic, materialism comes to agree with theology" (207).

For many Jewish thinkers of late modernity, the instance of the Last Judgment represents the last stronghold of religious transcendence; for Karl Kraus, Benjamin, Taubes, and, finally, Levinas, to defend transcendence is to call on the ultimate severity of *die Weltgericht*.[30] But late Adorno begs to differ in redefining his idea of transcendence according to the paradigm of *tsimtsum* as the wandering of the divine into the irreducible otherness of the world that will never again become one with God, will never dissolve its "imperfections" and return to the perfect One. For late Adorno, the true transcendence lies in the "one-way-street" self-limitation of the divine power that irrevocably migrates into the world to share its finite fate as the miniaturized *Shekhinah*-Melusina: the flickering spark of life simultaneously exposed to pain and hoping for happiness.

In the end, therefore, Adorno's political theology gives up on the negative concept of critique as "critical negation," executed in the name of absolute justice, and acquires a more affirmative compassionate tone that unknowingly brings him closer to the worldly tolerant tune of ancient rabbis. In *Genesis Rabbah*, the collection of rabbinical commentaries to the first book of the Torah, Abraham challenges the transcendent God, who threatens to end the experiment of creation, by teaching him a "religious truth" about creaturely being that God simply cannot know: "You desire the world and you desire absolute justice. Take one or the other. You cannot hold the cord at both ends at once."[31] In *Negative Dialectics*, this pro-cosmic wisdom appears as "the object's preponderance" (183) or the love of things (191) that stubbornly sides with the otherness of the material world as non-judgeable from the immaterial vantage point of *otherwise than being*: Nietzsche's lesson learned. *Pace* Nietzsche, however, Adorno's pro-cosmic affirmation does not mean that the world cannot be criticized at all. As long as there is pain and suffering, there must be a critique—but, as Adorno finally realizes, that critique must truly emerge "without velleity or violence, from the felt contact with objects" themselves. His "messianic optics," therefore, undergoes a "miniaturization" according to the merciful paradigm of *tsimtsum*: It no longer operates from outside of the world to effect a violent "a-cosmic revolt"; instead, it operates within the world to change its violent status quo.

Notes

1   My essay can be regarded as a corollary to the debate that took place in 2007 at the University of California, Berkeley, under the title "Is Critique Secular?" with Judith Butler, Talal Asad, and Saba Mahmood. In her introduction to the volume, Wendy Brown formulates the rationale behind the topic in the manner that closely resonates with mine: "The question, *is critique secular?* would seem to imitate critique's direct interrogative modality and secularism's putative transparency": Asad et al., *Is Critique Secular?*, 8. It is precisely this putative secular transparency of the critical mode of thinking that I want to put to the test.

2   Nietzsche, *Twilight of the Idols*, 182.

3   Nietzsche, *Twilight of the Idols*, 182.

4   Nietzsche, *Twilight of the Idols*, 163.

5   Nietzsche, *Twilight of the Idols*, 163.

6   Gordon, *Migrants in the Profane*, 142, emphasis added.

7 Gordon, *Migrants in the Profane*, 129, emphasis added.

8 Adorno, "Vernunft und Offenbarung," 608.

9 Adorno was well aware of the Hegelian formula *die Rose im Kreuze der Gegen-wart* (The rose in the cross of the present), the antecedents of which he saw in the sixteenth-century kabbalistic teaching of Isaac Luria. Hegel resorts to the Rosicrucian symbol few times but most extensively in his *Philosophy of Right*: "To recognize reason as the rose in the cross of the present, and to find delight in it, is a rational insight which implies reconciliation with reality" (19).

10 Gordon, *Migrants in the Profane*, 141, emphasis added.

11 In his letter to Walter Benjamin from March 4, 1938, Adorno reports on his meeting with Scholem and his understanding of the Lurianic Kabbalah as an atypical form of procosmic mysticism: "But when one takes a closer look at the things which [Scholem] himself presents . . . , then their most essential characteristic seems to be the fact that they 'explode.' He himself insists upon a sort of radioactive decay which drives us on *from mysticism . . . towards enlightenment*. It strikes me as an expression of the most profound irony that the very conception of mysticism which he urges presents itself from the perspective of a philosophy of history precisely as that same migration into the profane with which he reproaches both of us": cited in Gordon, *Migrants in the Profane*, 126.

12 Adorno, *Negative Dialectics*, 360, emphasis added. Hereafter, page numbers are cited in parentheses in the text.

13 The mysterious term—*inverse theology*—appears for the first time in Adorno's letter to Walter Benjamin from December 17, 1934, devoted to Benjamin's essay on Franz Kafka. "Let me only mention my own earliest attempt to interpret Kafka, nine years ago—I claimed he represents a photograph of our earthly life from the perspective of a redeemed life, one which merely reveals the latter as an edge of a black cloth, whereas the terrifyingly displaced optics of the photographic image is none other than that of the obliquely angled camera itself . . . it could indeed be called an 'inverse' theology": Adorno and Benjamin, *The Complete Correspondence, 1928–1940*, 66–67.

14 Adorno, *Minima Moralia* (2005), 153, emphasis added.

15 Adorno, *Minima Moralia* (1951), 480. This danger was well spotted by Margarete Kohlenbach, who writes, "While the straight theologian sees redemption in both God and God's hidden dominion on earth, the inverse theologian sees nothing but damnation, absolute alienation, universal blindness, and the hell of history": Kohlenbach, "Kafka, Critical Theory, Dialectical Theology," 153. Hent de Vries, commenting on Kohlenbach's diagnosis in his essay devoted to the comparison between Adorno and Karl Barth, confirms that "the divine promise—the 'hope of redemption,' as Adorno

says—would then be stripped of any foothold in being": De Vries, "Inverse Versus Dialectical Theology," 498.

16 Adorno, *Minima Moralia* (2005), 247, emphasis added.

17 Gordon, *Migrants in the Profane*, 129.

18 "Compared to [Benjamin] Bloch is just wishy-washy, and especially Adorno. Think of *Minima Moralia*, the last part. There you can tell the difference between substantial and as-if, and you can see how the whole messianic thing becomes a *comme si* affair": Taubes, *The Political Theology of Paul*, 74.

19 "Pain is the *prerogative* of living natures. . . . It is said that contradiction is unthinkable; but in fact, in the pain of a living being it is even an actual existence": Hegel, *Science of Logic*, 770. In both Hegel and Adorno, the contradiction consists in the contrast between life's expectation of happiness and its current painful state—and it is precisely this contrast, showing in the "inverse" state of suffering how things could have been *otherwise*, that lends the new critical standpoint. As Ansgar Martins nicely puts it in his magnificent study, *Adorno und Kabbalah*, "For Adorno, who sometimes expresses this with the Lurianic phraseology of messianic 'sparks,' the experience of happiness includes the silent contradiction as to the 'damned' human life under capital" (184).

20 For Scholem, the Book of Job is the paradigmatic case of *kinah*: a lamentation of a single creature over the order of creation, addressed to—but also against—the Creator. See Scholem, *Tagebücher nebst Aufsätzen und Entwürfen bis 1923*, 550.

21 Gordon, *Migrants in the Profane*, 146, emphasis added.

22 Taubes, "Walter Benjamin," 56.

23 See Scholem, *On Jews and Judaism in Crisis*, 283.

24 See Adorno to Scholem, February 17, 1964, in Adorno and Scholem, *Der liebe Gott wohnt im Detail*, 308.

25 In his essay in this volume, Alex Dubilet also addresses the problem of Gnosticism, but, contrary to my argument, sides with the Gnostic view, even if deeply modified in the post-metaphysical formula deprived of the strong reference to transcendence. He thus defends the Gnostic dualistic "combat myth," which underlies the whole apocalyptic genre, as the "revolt against the monotheistic doctrine of the power and creation" versus Augustine's and generally Christian neutralization of its subversive appeal. While I agree with him that Gnosis should not be simply neutralized by any theodicy, I also want to show that there is another way by which Gnosticism can—and should—be overcome.

26 Adorno, *Minima Moralia* (2005), 111.

27 See Benjamin, "On the Concept of History," 389.

28 Adorno, *Notes to Literature*, 169.

29 Adorno, *Notes to Literature*, 169.

30 The portrayal of Karl Kraus as the apocalyptic prophet of the doom and the paradigmatic thinker of *pereat mundus, sed fiat iustitia* stems from Walter Benjamin for whom "he stands on the threshold of the Last Judgment. . . . If he ever turns his back on creation, if he breaks off in lamentation, it is only to file a complaint at the Last Judgment. Nothing is understood about this man until it has been perceived that, of necessity and without exception, everything—language and fact—falls for him within the sphere of justice": Benjamin, "Karl Kraus," 254.

31 Genesis Rabbah, "Lekh Lekha," 39:6.

2

Political Theology's Antagonisms

BETWEEN STASIS AND GNOSIS

Alex Dubilet

On Civil War

A hostile intimacy links sovereignty and civil war. They remain bound to each other through a complex interplay of presence and absence. The claim to have successfully overcome civil war grounds sovereignty's legitimacy and acts as a crux in narratives of political modernity. Take, for example, Carl Schmitt on the aftermath of the Peace of Westphalia: "Every state sovereign became a representative of the new spatial order within the confines of his own territory, and thus was in a position to overcome civil war with a sovereign decision."[1] Where one was, the other shall be. Or, more precisely, where the two (civil war) was, the one (sovereignty) shall be. Even where this transition occurs successfully, specters of civil war do not stop haunting the space of sovereignty. Civil war is the very worst that can befall a polity: This is the perennial lesson of political thought.

Against this sanctimonious consensus, which conjures up the horrors of disintegration to uphold political unity, Michel Foucault conceptualized civil war as a "permanent state."[2] More recently, affirmative theorizations of civil war have extended this thesis, arguing that civil war "continues even when it is said to be absent or provisionally brought under control . . . [and] the modern state, which purports to put an end to civil war, is instead its continuation by other means."[3] From this perspective, state sovereignty is a secondary operation of disavowal, a result of pacification and neutralization that are never final or complete: Before—but also during and after—the sovereignty of the state is the rebellion of civil war. Civil war disturbs sovereignty from the beginning, or even from before the beginning, because civil war is primary and unsurpassable, never overcome except by a temporary imposition of unity. This position recalls nineteenth-century understandings of civil war as permanent rather than exceptional, exemplified in Karl Marx's formulation of class struggle as a "more or less veiled civil war, raging within existing society."[4] Such injections of disunity into dominant political metaphysics of unity reject the Hobbesian view that sovereignty's breakdown yields atomized conflict, seeing the individual instead as the correlate and even the product of the state itself. Rebelling against the state, its individuations, and its individuating possessions, "the real movement that elaborates, everywhere and at every moment, civil war" is, according to one contemporary perspective, another name for communism.[5]

Recent attempts to articulate an affirmative paradigm of civil war have returned genealogically to the ancient Greek concept of stasis. Etymologically a contronym, stasis names both mobility and immobility. Against the traditional line of political and philosophical thought, Dimitris Vardoulakis argues that mobility comes first; in turn, democracy precedes sovereignty, and resistance precedes unity: "Mobility is that which causes immobility. Resistance is the cause of unity and stability."[6] His reappraisal draws on the classicist Nicole Loraux's groundbreaking *The Divided City*, which showed how the forgetting of stasis is foundational to the polis. Naming an originary fracturing, stasis carries a temporal and ontological primacy but must be consigned to the past, its violence no longer a threat to the polis constituted in peaceful equality. For Loraux no less than for Vardoulakis, affirming the priority of stasis remains in a dialectical dance with unity: "Although it is always put in the category of the two because it divides, [stasis] would make one out of two, with provisions that there is a rift in the middle of this one."[7] Stasis operates within and reaffirms the delimited interiority of the polis in contrast to its antonym, *polemos*, which indicates a relation of war toward the outside.[8]

Affirming a two but always within a one, stasis opposes sovereignty's affirmation of a one without division. Under the rubric of agonistic monism, as Vardoulakis makes explicit, stasis names the democratic political practice of dissensus that precedes and unsettles the neutralizing effects of political theology understood in the Schmittian way as essentially imbricated with state sovereignty. Solon's law, the classic legal articulation of stasis, certainly demonstrates it to be a process of extreme politicization: "If when the city was torn by strife anyone should refuse to place his arms at the disposal of either side he should be outlawed and have no share in the city."[9] Participation in political life becomes mandatory. The consequence of not taking a stand during stasis is political exclusion. In stasis, "neutrality does not exist," and this demands a "remainderless engagement."[10] Exhaustive imposition of the political, elimination of neutrality, imperative inclusion, and threats of exclusion—all of these characteristics, however,

Alex Dubilet

make stasis resemble its purported opposite: the sovereign approach to the political, which Schmitt defines formally through the distinction of friend and enemy, "the utmost degree of intensity of . . . association or dissociation."[11] Recapitulating the self-conception of the Greek polis, Schmitt understands the proper enemy to be the external object of *polemos*, whereas those who affirm stasis as the originary site of politicization strive to invert the "ideal distinction between what is a vocation for the city [i.e., war] and what is an absolute threat [i.e., civil war]."[12] However significant, this opposition downplays a shared investment: It masks that stasis works—no less than sovereignty does—to (re)assert the primacy of the political. Civil war and sovereignty function within and performatively reproduce the interiority of the political field, whether divided or not, in contrast to what is relegated to the outside.

The Greek unity delimited by the division of stasis will subsequently be transmuted, as Domenico Losurdo has argued, into the civilizational unity of Christianity (of the *res publica christiana*) and ultimately that of Europe.[13] This will be the proper space of politics, in contrast to the barbarian and uncivilized outside, which will be dealt with differently, with unlimited violence.[14] This demarcation of the political is a chapter in the broader history of the political-theological inheritance structuring the identity of Europe.[15] As a result, breaking with political theology cannot merely entail freeing the political from its grasp but, rather, must include unsettling the primacy and inexorability of the political as such. Escaping the perpetual oscillation between sovereignty and civil war, those "two faces . . . of a single political paradigm," requires understanding political theology in its ambivalence, not only as the apparatus that binds the Christian to the secular or as the locus of sovereign fantasies but also as a critical attunement to the power of theological materials to dislodge—if also, of course, to legitimate—the imposition of the political as ineluctable destiny.[16]

It requires appreciating political theology as a singularly productive contemporary site for interdisciplinary genealogical investigations of the complex entwinements of the theological and the political. Tracing systematic analogies and historical transfers between the two realms, political theology develops the insight that the fundamental concepts of political modernity remain imbued with theological traces and inheritances. Undermining modernity's self-legitimating narratives, political theology names a mode of reading that diagnoses elements that the theological passes to the political, that Christianity bequeaths to the secular modern: formations of universalism and difference, structures of law, exception, and decision, and patterns of temporality.[17] The question I pursue can be initially formulated within this capacious perspective: If concepts of the modern state are secularized theological concepts, according to Schmitt's famous dictum, and arise through the pacification of civil war, how did Christianity, as its theological precursor, perform a more originary form of pacification—of a more originary form of rebellion?

Gnostic Cosmic General Antagonism

To begin elucidating this question, I want to turn to two perhaps surprising figures: Cedric Robinson and Hans Blumenberg. In *The Terms of Order*, Robinson critiques the political as the basic grammar of the West, as at once the transcendental principle of order and the instrument for its production. To speak of order is to speak of authority, "the ontological boundary, the cosmic end-point," the foundation and endpoint of legitimacy and assurance.[18] Significantly, for Robinson, political authority in the West originates as a "monstrous issue of the Christian church and the Christian state."[19] It emerges as a fundamentally theologico-political problem with the formation of the church as a legal structure: The church arrogates to itself the authority of truth and the power of its enforcement through the struggle with what it deems heresy or, more specifically, what becomes the Ur-heresy, Gnosticism, in opposition to the truth of its own orthodoxy. Christianity becomes worldly, legal, and political—that is, it becomes fully itself—only through the repression of Gnostic revolt: "The historical seal of the Church's authority was its successful resistance to 'rebellion.'"[20]

Blumenberg offers a complementary argument about Christianity's formation out of its struggle with Gnosticism. His fuller thesis is that Gnosticism must be overcome twice: first, partially and unsuccessfully, by Christianity, and second, by modernity, the epoch of reason's self-assertion.[21] Naming the tendency to withdraw all legitimacy from the world, Gnosticism is equally intolerable for the Christian church and for modernity, across their shared but differential investments in the world and its future. In diagnosing Christianity and modernity's common enemy, *The Legitimacy of the Modern Age* offers an important political-theological insight even as it explicitly critiques political theology and secularization in its attempt to reestablish modernity's legitimacy and autonomy.

Contested as a vague historical category lacking a determinate scope, Gnosticism nevertheless maintains an irreducible and constitutive relation to dualism.[22] "However divergent," writes a leading historian, "the different

Gnostic cosmogonies were invariably underlain by a marked anti-cosmic dualism and repeatedly identified the Gnostic Demiurge of the material universe with God the Creator of the Old Testament."[23] Gnostic dualism divided salvation from creation to side with the former in what Jacob Taubes aptly characterized as a "revolt against the monotheistic doctrine of the power and creation."[24] An unstable historical name for a set of heresies of the late Antique period, Gnosticism has remained an object of recurrent fascination up to the present centrally due to its refusal to grant any legitimacy to creation and its creator. It has come to function, across various theoretical reactivations, as a name for the generic and general tendency of world refusal or "a-cosmic revolt," and it is this aspect that preoccupies me in the chapter.[25]

For Blumenberg, Augustine is the apotheosis of early Christianity's attempt to overcome Gnostic dualism, which condemned the created world as a site of failure and its creator as a malicious deity. Against Gnostic delegitimation of the cosmos as the prison of the demiurge, Augustine sought to reestablish the fundamental goodness of creation and thereby to justify its creator. The justification of God and his providential order occurs "at the expense of man, to whom a new concept of freedom is ascribed expressly in order to let the whole of an enormous responsibility and guilt be imputed to it."[26] For creation to be absolved of essential corruption, Augustine elaborates human freedom in the form of the will, strong enough to be accused and bear responsibility but not to escape sin and merit salvation. Bestowing freedom was the mechanism for ensnaring in guilt. As Blumenberg argues, "The dogma of original sin was the 'reoccupation' of the position of the demiurge, of the counterprinciple to the foreign or good god."[27] With Man responsible for what has gone wrong in God's providential dispensation, the whole theological-political realm connecting the Earth and the sky is acquitted of all charges of evil and corruption. Overcoming the Gnostic threat requires not only the doctrine of original sin but also that of the Trinity, since in elaborating the difference in unity of the Father and the Son, the Trinity reconciles the God of creation and the God of salvation. Jared Hickman synthesizes the logic well:

> Augustine effectively redeemed Gnosticism's bad Creator-God by sliding him into the position of the good Savior-God—through the doctrine of the Trinity—and then sliding Man up to the position vacated by the bad Creator-God—through his signature doctrine of original sin—thereby leaving Man rather than God to bear the onus

of the blighted immanent sphere of creation. The price of exonerating Creator-God from the world's evil was demonizing but also aggrandizing Man as, in effect, the "creator" of the fallen world through Adam and Eve's paradigmatic abuse of freedom in Eden.[28]

Gnosticism and Blumenberg's thesis on its double overcoming are thematized in the concluding pages of Schmitt's final remarks on political theology. Published late in Schmitt's life, *Political Theology II* is known for its defense of political theology against Erik Peterson's much earlier attempts to theologically negate it. Less often remarked on is the turn, in the postscript, to defend political theology against its scientific negation undertaken in Blumenberg's legitimation of modernity.[29] Political theology, in Schmitt's definition, is "a transposition [or reoccupation (*Umbesetzung*)] of concepts" between the "systematic thought of the two . . . historically most developed constellations of 'Western rationalism,' the Catholic church with its entire juridical rationality and *the state of ius publicum Europeaum.*"[30] Any attempt, such as Blumenberg's, to conceptualize the transition to modernity as a scientific de-theologization remains blind to political theology's second element and thus to the irreducibly political dimension of modernity. That Schmitt might critique Blumenberg for ignoring the political dimension is hardly surprising. What *is* surprising is his elliptical appreciation of Blumenberg's thesis on Augustine's overcoming of Gnosticism.

On one side, Schmitt formulates political theology as a narrative continuity of the West across the discontinuity of secularization, and its first element, the Catholic Church, arises out of "the overcoming of its Gnostic opposite [*Gegenposition*]" (124/119). On the other, Schmitt avows the "tenacity and near irrefutability [*Schwer-Widerlegbarkeit*]" of Gnostic dualism (124/120). The irreducible structure of antagonism between the God of creation and the God of love and salvation forms its "core structural problem" and applies to "every religion of salvation and redemption" (125/120). Restricted neither to Gnosticism nor even to the theological domain, this problem is "immanently given, inescapably and ineradicably, in every world in need of change and renewal" (125/120). An all-too-direct secularizing translation renders Gnostic dualism into political idiom: "The lord . . . of a failed world" (the God of Creation) and "the liberator" (the God of salvation) "are essentially enemies" locked in "a hostile struggle [*eine feindliche Auseinandersetzung*]" without any possible mediation (125/121). The two Gods maintain a "relationship of unbridgeable alienation" characterized by the most intense enmity, which Schmitt compares, in a startling political-theological analogy, to "a kind of dangerous Cold War" (124/119–20). For Schmitt, it seems, the decisive significance of Gnostic dualism is its theological articulation of the inexorable persistence of enmity and political antagonism.

Such a political vantage point, however, necessarily distorts the Gnostic a-cosmic rebellion, making it appear as merely one side of a political antagonism or a struggle for domination. It erases the intolerable impropriety it harbors for the political and the theological, in their (dis)continuity, in their division and imbrication. It is not a political rebellion but a rebellion against the political and the world as such, a "rebellion as a total spiritual war against the world."[31] It instantiates Christian Jambet's insight that rebellions, in their generalizing radicality, express not political positions but "a slipping outside the lines of political servitude, outside of the world devoted to the masters who subjugate."[32] The appellation *abasileutos*, which appears in certain Gnostic texts, confirms this insight.[33] The kingless, the undominated, or even those without sovereignty or the unsovereign, these translations could be alternative ways to refer to the Gnostics.[34] Moreover, I would read the alpha privative in *abasileutos* as suggesting less a positive identity or a coherent tradition, guaranteed and reproduced by authorities across history, than an insistence prior to all origination that expresses a "refusal of authority and tradition as transcendent."[35] Against the endless parade of victors, with their thought and speech acts of legitimation, the undominated and the unsovereign are names within a discontinuous and improper nontradition, a dispersive and deviating counterhistory of rebellion against the unitary orders that proclaim God, the world, and authority as necessary and good.

Gnostic fabulation of insurgency and rebellion on a cosmic scale fought against the providential machine that became Christianity's inheritance to modernity. Proliferating convoluted dramas of creation and salvation, these flamboyant cosmic struggles refused to justify the things as they are or should be, the Good God, and the providential order of creation. For Augustine and the entire Christian tradition, this endless multiplication of divine agents and events amounted to nothing but "ridiculous and unholy fables."[36] Yet, their cosmological visions, expressed in a wild and unruly mythological poetics, conjured an excessive cosmic insurgency that overwhelmed all attempts to make the individual bear responsibility for evil. Their speculations on the origins of evil never ceased to appall defenders of orthodoxy because their internal reasoning inevitably led to the condemnation of God, the world, and the theologico-political hierarchies that legitimate them.[37]

Recovering Gnostic rebellion for genealogies of civil war can productively add to them a missing political-theological dimension. If "the point of view of civil war is the point of view of the political," then Gnostic dualism would reveal it to be, more fundamentally, the point of view of the political-theological: Civil war cuts across the theological and the political—in antagonism to God, the state, and the world they uphold. Gnostic rebellion, however, exceeds the framework of stasis and the political, which stasis reinforces through division: Extending to the cosmos and the gods, its antagonism is not delimited but absolute.[38] Indeed, more than simply rendering political antagonism political-theological, their rebellion expresses a general antagonism on a cosmic scale, a cosmic general antagonism that bursts open the delimitations of the political.

As Stefano Harney and Fred Moten formulated in their ongoing study within the Black radical tradition, general antagonism is "a constant and ongoing rebellion and insurgency against identity."[39] Operating on multiple levels—importantly, below and in excess of the political—general antagonism indicates a "riotous production of difference" that precedes and breaks apart all identity and oneness.[40] It indicates an interminable disruption of the imperative regulations of totality and identity, on whatever level they occur. Prior to sovereign pacification and confounding the demarcation of the political field, general antagonism occurs at once at the inner essence of things—or even preceding the very constitution of essence and thing—and comes from the outside or the surround. Moving immanently to its own rhythm, rebellious insurgency comes first, prior to the field of the individuated and the imposition of discreteness and coherence. Or, anterior to totality, whose determination it disruptively repels, general antagonism retains priority to what counts as first, an ante- and an-originary displacement (never fully) covered over by the imposition of the individuated subject as necessary and unsurpassable.

Undercommon Gnosis Against Individuation

The Gnostic revolt unsettles the primacy and inexorability of the political: Occurring beyond the proper site of politics, it also makes available an a-cosmic subtraction that is below it. General antagonism extended to the cosmos and the gods appears hyperpolitical but also allows a movement of withdrawal from proper identity and individuation, which appears as apolitical. One of the fundamental Gnostic mythologemes, the divine spark, suggests precisely such a refusal of worldly interpellations. The divine spark rejects guilt and moral responsibility for a corrupted world and, if theoretically elaborated beyond its theological context, repudiates politics, since "in the trick of politics we are insufficient . . . [and] politics proposes to make us better."[41] While, for Augustine, there is nothing wrong with God and the world, but only with us, then for the Gnostics, there is an unfolding cosmic catastrophe but, ultimately, nothing wrong with us, despite what the world and its authorities declare.[42] Divine sparks are foreign to the world, or, to use a different figure from the Gnostic lexicon, they persist as alien life.[43] They are strangers to the world, to the appalling cosmos of oppression and domination upheld by worldly power and the political theologies binding the heaven and the Earth. Alien life and divine spark are both Gnostic conceptual gestures that indicate an ante-originary incommensurability to the world, but they carry distinct valences. The former emphasizes the outsider's exposure to the world's violence, while the latter emphasizes an ante-cosmic and ante-nomian blessedness.[44]

It is common to interpret Gnostic formulations such as the divine spark, and Gnosticism more generally, as promising self-deification or concerning individual salvation alone. This is as true for Orthodox heresiologists and the modern historians who inherit their modes of thought as for sympathetic readers of the Gnostics. Take Taubes, for example, who admires the singularity of the Gnostic revolt but still sees it as a moment in the world-historical genesis of the individual, which arises out of the alienation and desacralization of the cosmos.[45] Or Peter Sloterdijk, who considers the Gnostic articulation of the world as an object of universal deixis "a revolution in the power of negation" and understands their revolt as "general strike against the astral factory," yet nevertheless locates the proper and authentic site for this revolution and general strike within the individual.[46]

As alien, life displays an essential foreignness to the world and its mediational thought. It is not synonymous with individual life but acts as a prism that shows individuation to be a worldly mechanism for interpellating life into the theologico-political paths of justification. It refuses what it is refused by: the coercive frames of appearance and intelligibility that produce subjects who are properly individuated, operative in the world, and theologico-politically accountable. For the individual is a reactive formation, a worldly effect of individuation produced to quell insurgency and neutralize antagonism: The individuated subject encloses and forecloses what is too improper, too improperly in common, too proximate to "the general antagonism of earthly anarrhythmia and displacement."[47]

Moreover, the individual invested with free will, strong enough to be held responsible for the corruption of the world, emerged as a node within the Christian apparatus of theodicy that justified the world and God as good against the Gnostic threat. And it operates as a counterinsurgent site of guilt and responsibility well beyond Christianity's pacification of Gnostic dualism. As Schmitt noted, the presupposition of man's sinfulness is an essential mechanism for legitimating all theological and political authority.[48] The Gnostic articulation of divine sparks refuses this destiny of original sin by rendering souls anterior and exterior to the cosmos and its theologico-political hierarchies. In this refusal, the Gnostics add one more historical name to the lineage of those that Schmitt positions as his political-theological enemies—or, rather, as the enemies of political theology as such: anarchists and communists, who elaborated a positive anthropology. Yet more than just a positive or affirmative anthropology, alien life and divine sparks reveal the individual to be a coercive effect of individuation in the world imposed by orthodoxies, whether secular or religious. They index an ante-originary subtraction from worldly interpellations, individuations, and subjections, an a-cosmic freedom incommensurable to the enclosure of the world, which asserts that there is nothing but individuals in dialectical bondage to the law.[49]

Whereas individuation occurs in relation to (sovereign, interpellating, and legitimating) transcendence, alien life inhabits "an eternally alien immanence" in perpetual dispersal against the world and its legitimating powers.[50] This eternal immanence of alien life registers, to follow François Laruelle, a mystical core of lived experience unilaterally subtracted from the world, revealing the world itself to be a transcendent apparatus and a hallucinated imposition of hierarchical division and relation, which forecloses the radical immanence of the real.[51] Remaining in debt to Moten and Harney's gift of general antagonism as an ongoing insurgent experiment occurring in intimate proximity to and within the intimacy of the undercommons, I want to propose the formulation *undercommon gnosis*.[52] Understanding gnosis as undercommon gnosis registers at once the forsaking of the imperatives of transcendence (under) and of the imperatives of individuation (common). It situates alien life in radical immanence, irreducible and antagonistic to all operations of individuation and transcendence—of the world, its God, or their paths of mediation and justification.[53]

The expansive undercommon experiment of eternally alien life and divine sparks inhabits a freedom from interpellation and individuation that are imposed exhaustingly, if not exhaustively, as the materialized reality

Alex Dubilet

of the world. Insurgently tearing the cosmic canvas, Gnostic a-cosmic underground remains in subtraction from the realm of proper speech and action, from the tiring imperatives of the political community, from the enclosures—and thus also the exclusions—constitutive of the political and of political theology. The a-cosmic refusals arising out of the visions of cosmic insurgency combine the insufficiently political with the excessively political, leading not to a different politics but to something entirely different from politics and its distributions of sites and positions. Refusing individuating interpellations into theaters of speech and action, undercommon gnosis conjures a field more open, more unruly and expansive, than politics could ever allow.

Gnosticism and the Gnostics are but historical names generated in the policing orbit of Christian orthodoxy, which sought to uphold the world, its continued persistence, its order and authority. Names demarcate and divide, unify and separate, determine one identity in contrast to others; they interpellate agents into the world and into history, whose identity can subsequently be contested or denied. They thereby capture and regulate a force that is impersonal, nameless, and (under)common. As Daniel Colucciello Barber has suggested, Christianity inscribed Gnosticism as a heretical identity into the world to foreclose gnosis as a radical insistence on unpossessable knowledge.[54] I would also say that the positive identity coercively interpellated into the world covered over a generic drive of worldly delegitimation, a destituent gesture abdicating justification and forestalling individuation. To move from a name inscribed into the world and its history back to a generic field below that world and that history, we might return to the alternative appellation *abasileutos*, the undominated or the unsovereign, to see a generic tendency of insurgency and rebellion discontinuously emerging in the face of counterinsurgent repression by theologico-political authorities enforcing individuation. We might add another deviant translation and render it the masterless, seeing in them the scattering of those anonymous and common, those too idle and workshy, too vagrant and wayward, too riotous and without property or place in the order of things—those who were repeatedly disciplined and terrorized into the capitalist and racist order of modernity.[55] I am tempted to add another deviant and devious translation to the mix, the ungovernable, to allow this discontinuous nontradition to clandestinely resonate with the contemporary anarcho-communist desire "to become ungovernable and to remain that way."[56] The undominated, the kingless, the unsovereign, the masterless, the ungovernable: These may be dispersed further into proletarian gnosis or gnosis in blackness, into underground heretical forces or itinerant antinomians, into those in riotous marronage or abolitionist insurrection.[57] Naming imposes identities and inscribes them into the order of the world order and the narrative of history, but before and across this naming, an uncontained swarm without identity, improper all the way down—a dispersive collection of cosmic misfits and cosmic hobos, which is also to say, a-cosmic hobos and a-cosmic misfits—endlessly disrupts the world and its history by withdrawing the primacy of their operations.[58]

Political Theology as Counterinsurgency and as a Mode of Reading

Although Gnostic rebellion may be read within an expanded political-theological genealogy of civil war, its cosmic general antagonism occurs excessively beyond (and below) the proper threshold of the political. How, then, should we understand the relation between gnosis and stasis? Although this question is never explicitly posed in *Political Theology II*, its discussion of Gnostic dualism does suggestively begin and end with references to stasis. It appears first when, elucidating the Trinitarian reconciliation of Gnostic dualism in his defense of political theology, Schmitt returns to Gregory of Nazianzus's articulation of the Trinity used by Peterson in his critique of the possibility of Christian political theology. "The One—*to Hen*—is always in upheaval—*stasiazon*—against itself—*pros heauton*" (122/116). For Schmitt, the presence of stasis within the supposedly nonpolitical Trinity demonstrates, contra Peterson, the irreducibility of the political problem of enmity: "At the heart of the doctrine of Trinity we encounter a genuine politico-theological stasiology" (123/118).

Still, what is the relation between stasiology and Gnosticism or simply between stasis and gnosis? Miguel Vatter proposes one interpretation: "Schmitt was skeptical that the Trinitarian doctrine could counter Gnosticism because he thought this doctrine harbored the Gnostic teaching of a 'civil war' (stasis) between a God of Love, the savior-God who is not of this world, and the Creator God who lords it over an evil world."[59] While Schmitt certainly points out the presence of stasis within the Trinity, to say the Trinity harbors Gnostic dualism underestimates the difference, even for Schmitt, that finally obtains between Christian Trinity and Gnostic dualism. Significantly, Schmitt uses stasis to describe only Christianity Trinity and *not* Gnostic dualism. In the Trinity, the division of stasis is an internal division, present but sublated: Creation and salvation are unified in the Trinity, whereas in Gnostic dualism, the lord of this world and the liberator are essential, irreconcilable enemies. Displaced from the polis to the Trinity, stasis remains a division in dialectical dance with unity. The term's second evocation, which follows Schmitt's elaboration of the core structural problem of Gnostic dualism, confirms the essential interiority of stasis: "If every unity is immanently a duality and therefore contains a possibility of upheaval, a stasis, then theology seems to become a stasiology" (126/123).

A different interpretation is necessary. Christianity indicates the transformation of Gnostic cosmic antagonism, a sort of irreducible hyperpolitical *polemos*, into the unity of Trinity, which is riven but never broken apart by stasis. This explains Schmitt's use of stasis as proof of the irreducible presence of unrest, division, rebellion—and thus of the political—a use at odds with the one found in *The Concept of the Political*, where stasis registers only the weakening of political unity ("civil war is only a self-laceration").[60] In *Political Theology II*, I want to suggest, Schmitt must be understood as fighting a hidden two-sided war, affirming the irreducibility of political antagonism against those who would deny it—Peterson in Christianity and Blumenberg in modernity—but also combating the absolute enemy (i.e., Gnosticism), which he interprets as provoking revolutionary wars of liberation. Schmitt admits local civil wars within the proper field of the political and of political theology when faced with the threat of cosmic general antagonism against the world and its theologico-political authorities.[61] In affirming stasis, Schmitt staves off the claims of apolitical theology, but more profoundly, he combats the Gnostic generalizing vector of insurrection, which comes from the outside and delegitimates all demarcations of the political and of the theological.

I would thus revise my earlier assessment to say that, rather than interpret Gnostic dualism as theologically articulating the irreducibility of the political, Schmitt reads it as the threatening specter of the hyperpolitical. This, however, still occludes the more complex Gnostic oscillation between cosmic general antagonism and undercommon gnosis; between the excessively political cosmological visions of insurgency and the insufficiently political a-cosmic subtraction of alien life and divine sparks, which refused theologico-political authority to proclaim that there is nothing wrong with us. Rather than one side of a political struggle, this Gnostic oscillation indicates an anarchic refusal of proper individuation and delimitation of position, enforced in extremis by political antagonism.

It indicates not one of two, but a totality (of the world) and the alien immanence of a dispersive undercommons that interrupts every enclosure and position. The Gnostic ante- and antinomian, ante- and anticosmic, tendency remains illegible to the imperative gaze of the political, which detects and sanctions only what is enclosed and delimited, individuated and claiming sovereignty.

Gnosticism is the historical, worldly name ascribed to a tendency that must be neutralized for the constitution of Europe in its political-theological continuity across Christianity and statist modernity. The formation of political theology as a unitary apparatus requires the naming and delimitation of Gnosticism and, ultimately, its expulsion outside of the frame. The structural problem of gnosis, understood as both cosmic general antagonism and anarchic refusal of proper individuation and political interpellation, does not, however, stop haunting the field of political theology. Cosmic insurgency and alien life decenter and delegitimate the political and political theology by showing them to operate as regulative enclosures that produce the space of interiority. The political in its structural analogy to the theological legitimates authority and order, proper forms of interpellation and coercion, while sanctioning the illimitation of violence toward the outside. Here we again face the ambivalence at the heart of political theology, since this Gnostic retrieval requires a political-theological attunement or mode of reading: Without it, one remains trapped within the illusory secular desire of purifying the political of political theology, never confronting the structural inseparability of its two elements.

Christianity and the modern state suppress scission and division in favor of the legitimacy of unitary order, sovereignty, and authority. Theologically and politically, they pacify rebellion and render it a specter to be warded off, imposing a neutralized domain of individuated subjects relying on transcendence for their salvation and security. Cosmic general antagonism and undercommon gnosis expose this theologico-political matrix of individuation and sovereignty as an apparatus of pacification and political theology as a counterinsurgent project. They show that the individual—that exalted, treasured, and legitimating inheritance of the West—is in reality a counterinsurgent mechanism and a sign of successful counterinsurgency. For these delegitimating disclosures, they inescapably provoke the venomous reaction of Christian and secular-modern theodicean machines striving to achieve the essential goal of counterinsurgency, which up to the present day remains: the maintenance of "legitimacy" and "the acceptance of an authority."[62]

Notes

I thank Joe Albernaz, Andrea Gadberry, Jessie Hock, and Ross Lerner as well as the participants of the Political Theology Reimagined Workshop and the University of California, Irvine, Critical Theory mini-seminar on my current project, *Interminable Disorder*.

1   Schmitt, *The Nomos of the Earth in the International Law of the Jus Publicum Europaeum*, 157.

2   Foucault, *The Punitive Society*, 13.

3   Tiqqun, *Introduction to Civil War*, 60, 79.

4   Marx and Engels, "Manifesto of the Communist Party," 495.

5   Tiqqun, *Introduction to Civil War*, 63.

6   Vardoulakis, *Stasis Before the State*, 95–109.

7   Loraux, *The Divided City*, 103.

8   See Plato, *The Republic*, 470b.

9   Aristotle, cited in Loraux, *The Divided City*, 102.

10   Loraux, *The Divided City*, 102–4.

11   Schmitt, *The Concept of the Political*, 26.

12   Schmitt, *The Concept of the Political*, 28–29; Loraux, *The Divided City*, 32.

13   Losurdo, *War and Revolution*, 151–54. In this transition, *stasis/polemos* becomes *seditio/bellum*.

14   These concerns remain operative in genealogies of civil war centered on Rome as well; see Owens, "Decolonizing Civil War."

15   See Anidjar, *The Jew, The Arab*; Guénoun, *About Europe*.

16   Agamben, *Stasis*, 4.

17   See Anidjar, *Semites*, 39–63; Arendt, *On Revolution*, 178–86; Dubilet, "On the General Secular Contradiction"; Meister, *After Evil*.

18   Robinson, *The Terms of Order*, 33.

19   Robinson, *The Terms of Order*, 33.

20   Robinson, *The Terms of Order*, 80.

21   Blumenberg, *The Legitimacy of the Modern Age*, 126. For a transformative new reading of Blumenberg's thesis of the double overcoming, see Albernaz and Chepurin, "The Sovereignty of the World."

22   For one skeptical take on Gnosticism as a category, see King, *What Is Gnosticism?*

23   Stoyanov, *The Other God*, 90.

24   Taubes, *From Cult to Culture*, 72.

25   Taubes, *From Cult to Culture*, 104.

26 Blumenberg, *The Legitimacy of the Modern Age*, 133.

27 Blumenberg, *Work on Myth*, 199.

28 Hickman, *Black Prometheus*, 56. In addition, in justifying God and the world, Christianity neutralizes Gnostic dualism but does not wholly eliminate it, displacing and transmuting it into the difference between the elect and the rejected, the *massa damnata* or the condemned mass: Blumenberg, *The Legitimacy of the Modern Age*, 135. In its exclusion from the history of salvation, the *massa damnata* may be read as a moment in the theological-political genealogy of what Frantz Fanon will describe as *les damnés de la terre*.

29 Discussing *Political Theology II*, Agamben focuses exclusively on its exchange with Peterson: see Agamben, *The Kingdom and the Glory*, 6–16.

30 Schmitt, *Political Theology II*, 117; Schmitt, *Politische Theologie II*, 110. Hereafter, page numbers from the English edition, followed by German pagination, are cited in parentheses in the text. I have silently changed translations where necessary, since the English edition contains numerous mistakes and infelicities.

31 Laruelle, *Future Christ*, 11.

32 Cited in Grelet, "Proletarian Gnosis," 96.

33 See Fallon, "The Gnostics."

34 Thiellement, *La victoire des Sans Roi*, follows this path. The provocative translation of *abasileutos* as unsovereign comes from Albernaz, "Impossible Freedom."

35 Smith, "Against Tradition to Liberate Tradition," 154.

36 Augustine, *The De Haeresibus of Saint Augustine*, 87.

37 See Peters, "What Was God Doing?"

38 Tiqqun, *Introduction to Civil War*, 36.

39 Harney and Moten, "Wildcat the Totality."

40 Harney and Moten, *The Undercommons*, 109.

41 Harney and Moten, *The Undercommons*, 19–20.

42 On the claim "there is nothing wrong with us," see Harney and Moten, *The Undercommons*, 20, 50–52, 65–66.

43 For alien life as a central Gnostic motif, see Jonas, *Gnostic Religion*, 48–51.

44 Aland, "Was ist Gnosis?" suggests that the Gnostic message is one essentially of joy and not alienation.

45 Taubes, *From Cult to Culture*, 90.

46 Sloterdijk, *After God*, 50–60.

47 Harney and Moten, *All Incomplete*, 3.

48 Schmitt, *The Concept of the Political*, 64–65.

49 On individuation, interpellation, and political theology, see Dubilet, "A Political Theology of Interpellation."

50 Moten, *Black and Blur*, 67.

51 Laruelle, *A Biography of Ordinary Man*; Laruelle, *Future Christ*. For Laruelle, however, radical immanence describes the ordinary man, the One, the human-in-person, as though individuation has always already occurred in the real rather than being imposed by the world.

52 Harney and Moten write, "Wherever and whenever that experiment is going on within the general antagonism the undercommons is found": Harney and Moten, *The Undercommons*, 109–10.

53 Whatever hyper-transcendence of the alien God that Gnostic dualism may invoke, it never legitimates the cosmos and its theologico-political hierarchies, but offers an evanescent lever, an almost a-theological void, which allows for an alien life in ante-originary subtraction from all cosmic interpellations and dominations.

54 For this distinction, see Barber, "Unpossessed Knowledge," 227–28.

55 On the masterless, the wayward, and the work-shy, see Gordon, *The Hawthorn Archive*, 339–44; Hartman, "The Anarchy of Colored Girls Assembled in a Riotous Manner"; Hill, *The World Turned Upside Down*, 39–56.

56 The Accused of Tarnac, "Spread Anarchy, Live Communism."

57 On proletarian gnosis, see Grelet, "Proletarian Gnosis," 93; on gnosis in blackness, see Armstrong, "Losing Salvation."

58 On the cosmic hobo, Harney and Moten, *The Undercommons*, 140. On namelessness, see Dubilet, "The Just Without Justification."

59 Vatter, *Divine Democracy*, 243.

60 Schmitt, *The Concept of the Political*, 29.

61 Useful as it may be for Christian and liberal commentators to equate Schmitt and Gnosticism, this equation is untenable: Schmitt sides with established authority legitimated by the creator God, while the Gnostics side with the God of salvation against all worldly power. They are absolute enemies.

62 US Army, *Field Manual 3-24* MCWP 3-33.5, section 1.27.

3

Exchange Beyond Exchange

KŌJIN KARATANI AND THE PERSISTENCE
OF THE RELIGIOUS

Martin Shuster

In a remarkable passage in "Science as Vocation," Max
Weber writes:

> It is the destiny of our age: given the rationalization and intellectual-
> ization of the times, and especially given the disenchantment of the
> world—its loss of magic—the ultimate and most sublime values have
> retreated from public life, into either the otherworldly realm of mys-
> ticism or the direct brotherly communities of individuals with one
> another. It is no accident that our highest art is an intimate one, not
> monumental; nor that today it is only in the smallest circle, between
> individuals, *pianissimo*, that something pulses corresponding to what
> once blazed through large communities as the breath of prophecy,
> fusing them together.[1]

The sorts of so-called secularization theories that have followed this invocation are legion (essentially by now too numerous to name here in any
sort of economical fashion).[2] Think about how Weber's claims are bound
up with the rest of his account—notably, for example, how the (alleged)
waning of religion also prompts certain kinds of social organization to retreat (say, institutions organized around the sanctity of religion), making
room for the possibility of a bureaucratization of politics (we might say,
the divine right of kings gives way to the management of experts).

At a very high altitude, we may tie this story about secularism to a
story about Marx(ism). As one commentator notes, "It is a commonplace
in the history of ideas that Marxism is little more than a messianic faith in
secular disguise."[3] Such claims about Karl Marx revolve chiefly around his
philosophy of history, which maintains—at least on a certain reading—a
progressive view of history.[4] On such a view, the way "fully" to secularize
Marx is simply to present a Marx that jettisons any such progressive view
of history. But what if the parameters of the very discussion itself must be

fundamentally shifted? What if Marx (or, at least, a certain reading of him) presents an opportunity to think about the entire problematic of secularism in a different light? The thought of the contemporary Japanese Marxist Kōjin Karatani exactly offers an opportunity to think differently about the entire schema of secularism as it has emerged in many contemporary discussions, and it does so exactly because it develops an allegedly overlooked element of Marx's thought.

To see how this is the case, at least in preliminary form, let me cite two quite common pictures of secularization. On one hand, take Carl Schmitt's claim that "all significant concepts of the modern theory of the state are secularized theological concepts."[5] Schmitt presents this idea in what might be termed an "analogical" register, where concepts are "transferred" (*übertragen*) from one realm to another (what makes this possible are exactly alleged structural similarities between jurisprudence and theology).[6] As he puts it, "The omnipotent God *became* the omnipotent lawgiver."[7] Just as I may transfer an object from one space to another (say, this desk from my office to the living room), so I may transfer one concept from one faculty to another. On the other hand, take an account such as Charles Taylor's in *A Secular Age*, where his explicit target is "subtraction stories"—stories alleging that humans have "lost, or sloughed off, or liberated themselves from earlier, confining horizons, or illusions, or limitations of knowledge."[8] On such a view, secularism reveals something that had somehow been occluded by religion. Taylor rejects such views, opting instead to see secularism as itself a distinct worldview, one that is an alternative to religion and that ultimately puts an end to "the naïve acknowledgment of the transcendent or of goals or claims which go beyond human flourishing."[9] Even in the wake of such secularism, though, Taylor maintains that belief or unbelief is an *option*, albeit one in which religion can be pursued only "in full awareness" of what it in fact is.[10]

Even as they envision the religious and the secular in two quite different ways—Schmitt seeing the secular as a sort of transfer of something from one domain to another; Taylor seeing it as the emergence of a new "exclusive humanism"—what they share is a vision of the secular and the religious as two realms or worldviews. There are countless variations on these themes in the mammoth bodies of literature surrounding these topics (with these two ends envisioned in various ways and in all kinds of relation). But what if the religious and the secular are better understood as not entirely distinct phenomena (of whatever kind) but, rather, as something like two dimensions of the same phenomenon? The analogy may be to a quantum entity, where differing properties are exhibited under different conditions, or, more vividly, perhaps to the way in which two cities occupy the same space in China Miéville's remarkable novel *The City and the City*. If this is the case, then they are neither as analogizable as Schmitt suggests nor as open to optionality as Taylor does.

Karatani's work offers us an opportunity to present an understanding of the secular and the religious along the lines of this metaphor of a quantum entity (say, light as both wave and particle), but it does so by means of a serious development of Marx's thought. It thereby both advances our understanding of the contemporary social, economic, and political situation (as Karatani's recent prestigious Beggruen Prize also affirms) *and* invites us to rethink the ways in which we conceive of the relationship between the secular and religious. These two features go hand in hand, and the aim of this chapter is to sketch exactly how. (Put another way, Karatani's thought pushes strongly against Weber's claims as cited in the beginning of this chapter, but it does so in a way quite different from most accounts.)

Modes of Exchange

A proper understanding of Karatani's significance for understanding the secular and the religious requires unpacking the Marxist theory core at the heart of his work. Central to that account is Karatani's suggestion that what must be prioritized is an analysis of "modes of exchange." Such a focus makes him a controversial figure as a commentator on Marx, since it is taken as a commonplace assumption that Marx's chief focus is on modes of production, not modes of exchange. Nonetheless, Karatani's focus on modes of exchange is central to any understanding of his thought and, thereby, his thought in relation to anything else.

Of course, Karatani acknowledges, with most accounts of Marx(ism), that a central locus of analysis in Marx revolves around modes of production, focusing chiefly on the means and ownership of production. It is thereby commonplace to stress, on Marx's behalf, that "relations of production constitute . . . the economic structure of society, *the real foundation*, on which rises a legal and political superstructure and to which correspond definite forms of social consciousness."[11] While Karatani does not disagree with such approaches, he does believe they should be tempered in a particular way: Karatani's unorthodox claim is that, if we want to address questions of "capitalism, state, and nation in a fundamental way," we should consider—and, indeed, prioritize—modes of exchange as our locus of analysis.[12]

What might this mean exactly? Note that, like a range of nontraditional Marxists, from members of the Frankfurt School to someone like Cedric Robinson, Karatani believes that "traditional" Marxism is confronted with certain problems.[13] One way to bring this into focus is to note that if, for example, modes of production are prioritized—and thereby reified—as the "economic base," then culture, politics, art, and so on are potentially viewed "merely" as an ideological superstructure. It becomes difficult, if not impossible, to situate these features of our lives in any but the most reductive ways. Equally crucial, however, is that such approaches fail properly to account for the ways in which such reductionist accounts force us into naïve or mistaken views of history, whether past or present. For example, it (1) becomes difficult to understand in significant Marxist terms earlier phases of history where there was no neat split between economics and politics (as there is in capitalist society); and (2) fails to account for the ways in which "ideological" structures—for example, state, nation, and religion—continue to exert a strong influence separate from or, at times, even counter to the interests and movements of capital.

Karatani is, of course, aware that there are Marxist traditions that take a more nuanced view of things and that are thereby capable of addressing our ideological superstructure in autonomous terms. What is unique to Karatani, at least on his own estimation, is that such approaches begin allegedly to lose Marx's own synoptic view, leading to increasingly fragmented approaches that are not faithful to the sort of systematic impulses that animate Marx's account. For our purposes, such approaches would also not offer the opportunity to rethink the relationship between the secular and the religious in the way that I am suggesting Karatani's thought makes possible.

A focus on modes of exchange, then, is a way—Karatani believes—to present Marx's central aspirations as a thinker while equally offering important insights about the contemporary world that might otherwise be unavailable or hidden, thereby improving our possibilities for significant worldly change. Or, in Karatani's words, alternative approaches "resulted in the loss of any totalizing, systematic perspective for comprehending the structures in which politics, religion, philosophy, and other dimensions are interrelated, as well as the abandonment of any attempt to find a way to supersede existing conditions."[14]

According to Karatani, Marx evinces an interest in exchange (conceived in broad terms) from his earliest work. Karatani's story stresses here Marx's focus on various relations of exchange, whether between humans and nature or within human societies; thus, there is an elaborate and multifaceted account of material exchange—covered by the German term *Verkehr* (traffic)—wherein there are several species of exchange, understood in metabolic terms as traffic between natural materials and human bodies, between these and human constructions such as money or particular societies, and between these and other human constructions.[15] Karatani's claim is that after the late 1840s, Marx turns his attention exclusively to commodity exchange, limiting "his observation of exchange to a specific modality."[16] *Capital* is thereby meant to understand in detail the various features of commodity exchange, but those features, according to Karatani, should not be understood apart from a broader consideration of exchange more generally, whereby observations of "the state, community, and nation" can also be brought to the fore, especially to the extent that they suggest or involve other forms of exchange.

Commodity Exchange

Before elaborating the broad notion of mode of exchange operative for Karatani—a notion that is, in fact, central for understanding Karatani's understanding of religion and secularism—note the tenor in which his analysis of commodity exchange proceeds. Following Marx, Karatani is very clear that the salient phenomenon of analysis here is the sort of commodity exchange that arises between communities, not between individuals.[17] Karatani highlights this feature to stress that, even with a broader shift to commodity exchange as a social, political, and economic mode of organization, pockets of society remain where other forms of exchange are dominant or chiefly operative (think, for example, of the sort of exchange operative amid families, various kinds of cooperatives, gift exchanges, and other experiments in organization that continue to exist *within* capitalist society, even now).

The normative principles that animate commodity exchange originate from (at least an implicit) mutual consent and mutual recognition between two communities. Such exchange specifically hinges on the recognition of a "universal equivalent form (money)."[18] Importantly, though, any such recognition does not lead to equality under or by means of the operations of commodity exchange; in fact, quite the opposite is true. Because money is what allows for commodity exchange, its valorization allows for possibili-

Martin Shuster

ties of association that exhibit and prioritize vastly differing power relations. Put simply, money allows for the purchase of commodities; in this context, the most notable commodity is the commodity of labor. The purchase of labor can, in turn, create surplus value—that is, profit. The possibility of profit in such a context, however, creates the possibility for inequality.

It is worth pausing here to understand exactly how Karatani's story, while iconoclastic, is nonetheless incredibly consonant with a core element of Marx's account, engaging it in an exceedingly serious fashion. To bring this into focus, let me rehearse one way in which mainstream (non-Marxist) accounts understand commodity exchange. Commonly, it is understood that capitalism's basis is in the *finding* of value. On such a view, at some point in the evolution of commodity exchange some smart people allegedly realized that one could buy something at one price and then sell it at some higher price, whether as it currently is or by doing something to it (e.g., making it into something else). I can, say, buy this lumber, turn it into a desk, and then sell it to you for twice the price I paid for the lumber. What such a traditional account prioritizes is the market. It is seemingly just the market that generates value; what it tends to minimize, if not outright overlook, is the human element involved here: Something must be *done to* the lumber by *someone* for there to emerge the possibility of value. (Otherwise what we have is mere mercantilism: trade.) What such a view makes mysterious, then, is the actual creation of wealth. A central feature of Marx's project in *Capital* is exactly to show how we constantly ignore such (human) features of the entire capitalist framework. Only human labor can generate surplus value. Surplus value and the exploitation of labor go hand in hand on such a view. This is one way to understand why Marx saw the sort of philosophy that he practiced as "the self-clarification of the struggles and wishes of the age."[19] He was no mere scholar of capitalism; he was rather a scholar of capitalism exactly because it was brutal (and exploitative).

Modes of Exchange in Context

Another way to put this last thought is to stress that central to such a mode of exchange are relations of class. Because some own the means of production while others do not, relations between those who labor and those who control the means of production emerge by means of which labor is possible. We should not underestimate here, though it is not a central locus of interest for Karatani directly, the extent to which questions around class and race intersect with each other.[20] In a similar way, as a variety of feminist and Marxist thinkers have stressed, the costs required to reproduce labor for the very functioning of these modes of exchange are hidden, unacknowledged, and certainly not paid for by those who own the means of production. Included here most prominently are the functions involved with domestic care. I highlight this point about relations of class here because, again, at a certain level of abstraction, they can also be viewed as relations of class; when such functions are traditionally performed by women—as they traditionally have been in capitalist societies—then it is possible to conceive such divisions around sex as divisions of class.[21]

Note for a moment these claims about class relations. Keep them in mind as I present another crucial aspect of Karatani's story—namely that commodity exchange is just *one* kind of exchange. In fact, Karatani believes it is essential to situate Marx's account of commodity exchange amid three other possibilities of exchange, for only then will the true significance of the entire analysis come into view.

Karatani cites a mode of exchange, theorized by Marcel Mauss and others, that involves reciprocal exchange.[22] A society oriented around such a principle may use gift giving or the pooling of resources to create relations of reciprocity, where individuals might be bound to one another by honor or duty or some conception of the gift as a mediated practice that establishes relations across society. Such a form of exchange is prominent, for example, in tribal societies.[23] As with all of the other modes of exchange Karatani discusses, note that "actual social formations consist of complex combinations of these modes of exchange."[24] Taking this point seriously allows us to recognize elements, perhaps implicit, of such a mode of exchange in other social forms. Thus, for example, while Karatani stresses that the notion of a nation arises at a historical moment due to the synthesis of two other modes of exchange.[25] It is possible to note that certain forms of nationalism conceive of relations within the nation on the model of a large family, thereby implicitly referencing such a reciprocal form of exchange.[26] (Karatani himself puts this idea as the suggestion that "the nation is something that appears within the social formation as an attempt to recover, through imagination" such reciprocal exchange as it disintegrates in modernity.[27])

Another mode of exchange that hearkens back to much earlier times is plunder. Such a mode of exchange depends on one community plundering the possessions of another. Why call this a mode of *exchange*? Karatani highlights that any such plunder requires distribution: The community that does the plundering has some means of assimilating the plunder among itself (it need not be equal, but whatever is plundered is distributed *somehow*). Karatani highlights how it is here that we might find the origins of the state. As he puts it, "The origin of the state lies in conquest."[28] It is exactly when a state pursues a monopoly on violence, in Max Weber's words, that it also transforms "plunder and violent compulsion into a mode of exchange."[29]

In addition to commodity exchange, then, we have before us three distinct modes of exchange, each involving elements of human social organization throughout history. In this way, for example, looking to the past, Karatani is able to highlight possibilities of exchange around plunder by repurposing the theory of "oriental despotism" elaborated by Karl Wittfogel (an early associate of the Institute for Social Research) to account for the functioning of precapitalist states.[30] Looking to the present and beyond, Karatani stresses that the pull and continuing role of reciprocal exchange offers possibilities for understanding the continuing relevance of nations and nationalism. Equally, a proper understanding of these modes of exchange in relation to one another offers a possibility for understanding the continuing significance of religion. (More on this shortly.)

The Borromean Ring

To see all of this, note that there is no form of exchange that is basic or primary, either logically or historically. Instead, various forms of exchange can, and often do, coexist within historical milieus and social configurations. For this reason, Karatani notes that "when the capitalist economy leads to class disparity and struggle, which is inevitable, the nation demands equality and the state alleviates class opposition by means of taxation and redistribution."[31] Even in the time of the dominance of commodity exchange, the existence of the state and the nation (not to mention a range of experiments in social organization with each one) guarantees that other modes of exchange remain operative. In this way, Karatani highlights that there is a Borromean knot where there is a deep—and unbreakable—relationship between these modes of exchange and the sociopolitical institutions that are most closely linked to them (the state to plunder; the nation to reciprocal exchange; and capital to commodity exchange). If this is true, then "it is impossible to overthrow one of them alone. If we try to overcome capitalism by means of either the state or nation, we will end up reinforcing the state or nation; Stalinism is the former case while Nazism is the latter."[32]

The image of a Borromean ring, or knot, highlights that, allegedly, the capitalist formation is a *synthesis* of all three modes of exchange. As the earlier quotes suggest (and as Karatani pursues in more detail), the qualitative nature of commodity exchange within capitalism is such that it gives rise—materially and conceptually—to other forms of exchange and organization. Karatani's account doesn't rely merely on ahistorical abstractions about the intersections and interactions of these modes of exchange; rather, he also highlights that the *historical* formation of capitalism gives rise to the Borromean knot of Capital-Nation-State. Note how this picture of the Borromean knot determines how Karatani reads the present moment:

> One often hears the prediction that, thanks to the globalization of capital, the nation-state will disappear. It is certain that economic policies within nation-states do not work as effectively as before, because of the growing network of international economic reliance on foreign trade. But, no matter how international relations are reorganized and intensified, the state and nation won't disappear. When individual national economies are threatened by the global market (neoliberalism), they demand the protection (redistribution) of the state and/or bloc economy, at the same time as appealing to national cultural identity. So it is that any counteraction to capital must also be one targeted against the state and nation (community). The capitalist nation-state is fearless because of its trinity. The denial of one ends up being reabsorbed in the ring of the trinity by the power of the other two. This is because each of them, though appearing to be illusory, is based upon different principles of exchange. Therefore, when we take capitalism into consideration, we always have to include nation and state. And the counteraction against capitalism also has to be against nation-state. In this light, social democracy does nothing to overcome the capitalist economy but is the last resort for the capitalist nation-state's survival.[33]

Seeing this assessment and understanding the Borromean ring that Karatani suggests exists allows us to bring into focus the political-theological importance of Karatani's work.

Karatani and Political Theology

Because of the connections between nationalism and religion, on one hand, and the state and religion, on the other—not to mention the connections between capitalism and religion—the Borromean knot that Karatani diagnoses guarantees that religion will continue to be a central category, and political theology a central site of inquiry, for any consideration of our contemporary form of life.[34] Furthermore, such a Borromean ring highlights that the vast archive that is the archive of the political that orients these modes of exchange (in their various logical and historical contexts) in fact overlaps in many moments with—if not potentiates or orients—the archive of religion. Speaking the language of a contemporary commentator, we can note that the archive of religion will not be exhausted any more than these various modes of exchange can or will be exhausted.[35]

This is not the only way, however, in which Karatani's account offers opportunities to prioritize religion in this context. Note that there is a fourth mode of exchange that we have not yet considered but that is central to Karatani's account. Related to the mode of exchange involving reciprocity, there is also another logical possibility of exchange, one that pursues reciprocal exchange *outside* the confines of either the state or the nation. Karatani stresses that such societies "have been given various names: socialist, communist, anarchist, associationist, and so on."[36] Imagine potentially an entire system (in Karatani's Immanuel Wallerstein–inspired language, a world system) grounded by the principle of reciprocity but divorced from the workings of the aforementioned Borromean knot of Nation-State-Capital. Karatani prefers to refer to such a mode of exchange simply as X, highlighting that it exists currently only as an (on his understanding, Kantian) idea—that is, solely as something that regulatively guides our reasoning. To name or sketch this mode of exchange in any significant detail would thereby be already to betray it, to the extent that such sketches would involve drawing on present conditions and categories for such an elaboration. (In this way, the historical formations that Karatani names are not realizations of X, but hints about its contours.[37]) One way to think about this mode of exchange is exactly as something that is foreclosed by present society and relations (including, I ought to note, within academia itself).[38]

To begin to conclude, note that Karatani himself stresses the connection between this notion of exchange and religion in a remarkable section in *The Structure of World History* titled "Universal Religions." There, Karatani sketches the evolution of religions across the globe, highlighting that, strikingly, "religion . . . is indivisible from politics and economics."[39] Karatani traces out the ways in which magicians, priests, and others were intimately involved with the various forms of exchange listed earlier. The details are rich, but what interest me are some crucial features of the account. Karatani points out, for example, that the emergence of the state structure coincided with the transformation of magic into religion. Here he closely links the emergence of agriculture in the context of the state with a contemporaneous move away from shaman and animists and their influence on the weather. Irrigation and the good governance of the ruler become intimately linked to the religious rather than to the magician who consorts with the weather. In turn, every particular state began to organize itself also with a particular divinity in mind, and this is one way to account for the henotheism that was common in the ancient world. Over time, the structure of the state became stronger, leading eventually to the possibility of empire and, Karatani argues, thereby to the possibility of monotheism. Once again, religion is "indivisible from politics and economics." Karatani further specifies this thought, noting that "the development of religion is also the development of the state."[40]

He further clarifies this close link between religion and politics through a discussion of universal religion (i.e., a religion that is not exclusionary, that is open to all). Karatani stresses that with the rise of empires there emerged the possibility of a world empire. World empires arise where and when modes of exchange B and C expand "spatially."[41] Karatani explains that, in part, the emergence of world empire arises through a strengthening of the state and, thereby, a prioritization of plunder; at the same time, however, the emergence of world empire occurs in part through the "development of trade and markets" and thereby a prioritization of commodity exchange.[42] Once political and economic development reaches a point at which a world market and world money make their appearance, then universal religion emerges as a possibility, since it is fundamentally a "criticism of modes of exchange B [plunder] and C [commodity exchange], which were the dominant modes in world empires."[43] This is why "universal religions appeared independently from one another at roughly the same time in all of the regions that produced ancient civilizations" (a point Karatani pursues in some detail).[44]

Conclusion

Karatani presents universal religion as carrying the possibility of the aforementioned mode of exchange X, a possibility, as already noted, augured by the very evolution of economics and politics to the present moment. Relying on Sigmund Freud, Karatani, terms this a sort of "return of the repressed."[45] It is not some mere "nostalgic restoration." It cannot be such because it has not yet existed. While it has structural analogies to the mode of exchange known as reciprocity, it is also wholly different from that because it is understood as a *world* phenomenon. It is for this reason that it has never yet existed.

It is worth pausing here to reflect explicitly on the significance of Karatani's account for what might be termed contemporary political theology. Note that Karatani shows how proper consideration of the history of modes of exchange across global human history reveals a deep connection between the evolution of religion and politics. It is not that concepts are merely transferred from one realm to the other; nor is it the case that the two develop in opposition to or by means of starkly distinguishable kinds of content. The two, rather, are already always interpenetrated exactly because they are underwritten by modes of exchange that cut across the gamut of human activity. Every political program, every political project, every political option already always carries with it a religious aspect to the extent that each is irrevocably altered by the modes of exchange that facilitate it.[46] Returning to an image I invoked at the beginning of this chapter, we have here a sort of quantum entity, where different properties can be discerned and exhibited under different conditions. But now we might add the equally physics-inflected caveat that the appearance of certain properties is intimately linked to the observer.

With that point in mind, let me turn for a moment to Karatani's own imperatives in the face of this picture. He stresses that the Borromean knot of Capital-Nation-State demands that we continue to pursue an actualization of the mode of exchange X and the sort of world system it demands. Karatani frequently invokes Immanuel Kant's political theology, especially around the sort of picture of federated nations introduced in *Perpetual Peace*.[47] To his credit, Karatani is sober enough to realize that "nation, state, and capital will persist. No matter how highly developed the forces of production become, it will be impossible to completely eliminate forms of existence produced by these modes of exchange. . . . [Y]et so long as they exist, so too will mode of exchange [X]."[48] In this way, Karatani clearly shows that religion, and its concomitant archives, will remain central for what we may term, with the musician Katie Stelmanis, any "future politics."[49]

Given this modal orientation to the future, one significance of Karatani's thought to the field of political theology is the suggestion, not so much pursued by Karatani or generally by Marxists, that religion—we may even say here *theology*—itself may play a part in significant political change. It is important to specify exactly what I mean here: Oftentimes in political theology, but also in our common understanding of theology in politics, it is, of course, understood that theological positions have political consequences. What if, however, the very working out of theological problems *as* theological problems, without necessarily an explicit eye toward politics, will turn out during this particular moment to have political power—not because it will or can be "transferred" to the political realm, but because its political significance is already intimately bound up with its theological significance? Put another way: Karatani's close linkage between religion and politics cuts both ways—from politics to religion but also the other way around. The analogy here may be to a thought of Theodor W. Adorno's, on display in a work such as *Minima Moralia* (and influenced by Walter Benjamin), that critical explorations of particular aesthetic works could produce political insights, since the political inheres in a sort of micrological form in the aesthetic. (And let us not ignore here the close proximity and deep connections between religion and art.) The pursuit of a truly universal religion—mode of exchange X—may itself then be of the utmost political significance, even as it is a project not yet properly pursued in the modality of either religion or politics, exactly because to pursue it requires rethinking our prosaic distinctions between the secular and the religious.[50]

Notes

1   Weber, *Charisma and Disenchantment*, 40.

2   For a powerful introduction to many of these themes and issues see, alternatively, Smith, *A Short History of Secularism*.

3   Gordon, "Secularization, Genealogy," 151.

4   On this point, see Shuster, "The Philosophy of History." For an argument that pushes back against such readings of Marx, see Anderson, *Marx at the Margins*.

5   Schmitt, *Political Theology*, 36.

6   On this point, see Vatter, "The Political Theology of Carl Schmitt."

7   Schmitt, *Political Theology*, 36, emphasis added.

8   Taylor, *A Secular Age*, 22.

9   Taylor, *A Secular Age*, 21.

10   Taylor, *A Secular Age*, 389.

11   Singer, *Marx*, 46.

12   Karatani, "Beyond Capital-Nation-State," 569.

13   On the point of the Frankfurt School, see, e.g., Jay, *The Dialectical Imagination*, 48. On the point of Robinson, see especially Robinson, *An Anthropology of Marxism*; Robinson, *Black Marxism*.

14   Karatani, *The Structure of World History*, ix–x.

15   On this point, see especially Karatani, "Beyond Capital-Nation-State," 571; Karatani, *The Structure of World History*, 2–6.

16   Karatani, "Beyond Capital-Nation-State," 572.

17   Karatani, *The Structure of World History*, 13.

18   Karatani, *The Structure of World History*, 13.

19   Marx, "Letter to A. Ruge," 209.

20   This has become a renewed topic of discussion in recent debates, especially as the notion of "racial capitalism" has come to the fore in, e.g., the uptake of Cedric Robinson's work but also the work of Ruth Wilson Gilmore and others: see Gilmore, "Race and Globalization," 261; Robinson, *Black Marxism*.

21   For such a point, see, e.g., Firestone, *The Dialectic of Sex*.

22   Mauss, *The Gift*.

23   Karatani, *The Structure of World History*, 8.

24   Karatani, *The Structure of World History*, 9.

25   See Karatani, *The Structure of World History*, 210.

26   Balibar, "The Nation Form."

27   Karatani, *The Structure of World History*, 209.

28   Karatani, *The Structure of World History*, 69.

29   Karatani, *The Structure of World History*, 68.

30   Wittfogel, *Oriental Despotism*.

31   Karatani, "Beyond Capital-Nation-State," 585.

32   Karatani, "Beyond Capital-Nation-State," 585.

33   Karatani, *Transcritique*, 281.

34   Gellner, *Nations and Nationalism*; Kantorowicz, *The King's Two Bodies*; Weber, *The Protestant Ethic and the Spirit of Capitalism*.

35   See especially the way in which our lives may be "colored" or "burdened" by this archive. See De Vries and Sullivan, *Political Theologies*.

36   Karatani, "Beyond Capital-Nation-State," 576.

37   There are potential avenues of dialogue here to the way in which the Marxist-inspired analyses of the Frankfurt School invoke the Jewish ban on images (*Bilderverbot*). On the latter, see especially Cook, "Through a Glass Darkly";

Gordon, *Migrants in the Profane*; Pritchard, "Bilderverbot Meets Body in Theodor W. Adorno's Inverse Theology"; Shuster, "Adorno and Negative Theology." Equally, see the first chapter in this collection, by Agata Bielik-Robson, and especially the way in which she explores the potential alternative theological understanding (of things) it raises.

38 On this point, see especially Inese Radzin's discussion in this volume and her development of Michel Henry's Marx inspired/inflected notion of life.

39 Karatani, *The Structure of World History*, 131.

40 Karatani, *The Structure of World History*, 132.

41 Karatani, *The Structure of World History*, 134.

42 Karatani, *The Structure of World History*, 134.

43 Karatani, *The Structure of World History*, 134.

44 Karatani, *The Structure of World History*, 135.

45 Karatani, *The Structure of World History*, 141.

46 Once again, as suggested earlier, such claims might be seen as the "objective" formal counterparts to the sort of "subjective" claims Inese Radzins develops around Henry's notion of lived subjectivity in the last chapter.

47 Kant's political theology is much more complex and requires more normative commitments than Karatani acknowledges. For more on these, see Shuster, *Autonomy after Auschwitz*, chap. 2.

48 Karatani, *The Structure of World History*, 307.

49 This is the title of her 2017 album, created under the moniker "Austra." I listened to this album while writing portions of this chapter.

50 There emerge here possible points of comparison to the sort of "future politics" that you have in Jacques Derrida (democracy to come) and Ernst Bloch (not-yet-conscious), but this is something I cannot pursue in any detail here. Karatani himself mentions the connection to Bloch in Karatani, *The Structure of World History*; Karatani and Wainwright, "'Critique Is Impossible Without Moves.'"

4

Keeping Life Living

THINKING WITH MICHEL HENRY

Inese Radzins

> In this inaugural act of science and modern thought, it is
> what we are that gets set aside. . . . Physics, chemistry, bi-
> ology, social, or human sciences, political economy—you
> know so little about the human! And that is not because
> you still have a lot of progress to make but because life is
> not situated where you are looking or within your field
> of vision.
>
> Michel Henry, *From Communism to Capitalism*

Michel Henry offers a sweeping dismissal of many aca-
demic endeavors, claiming they know little about their purported subject
matter: the human. His work suggests that knowledge as produced in our
day (and perhaps also that created by many of us in this volume) ignores,
displaces, and even deadens *life*. In other words, much of what we take to be
knowledge is inadequate because it misunderstands its subject. The misun-
derstanding is due to a much broader and very modern phenomenon: the
objectifying tendencies of the scientific method and its economic counterpart, Capital. Henry argues that these two forces determine knowledge
production in our day to the detriment of the *human* and what he designates
Life. This chapter considers how Henry's analysis can be used to interrogate
political theology. My concern is to show how the discipline may actually
ignore what it takes as its subject matter, the human, and thereby distort
what it attempts to analyze, understand, and improve: social and political
life. What distinguishes Henry's oeuvre and what I suggest is of relevance
for political theology is his emphasis on the *knowledge of life*: the creative
"unfolding of a singular life" in all its various needs and abilities. This *life*, as
we will see, is characterized by Karl Marx's living labor and the need for
creative and cultural production. My contention is that Henry's attention to

life and to individual subjectivity encourages political theology to consider very mundane activities and *human* labor itself as the locus of social life. Another modality for reconsidering the *human* can be found in Prathama Banerjee's chapter in this volume on B. R. Ambedkar. There, Banerjee suggests that Ambedkar focuses on "the pre-social, archaic question of human creaturely, species condition on Earth," a designation that could resonate with Henry's thought.

It may sound obvious that *life* be placed at the center of political theology. However, Henry contends that *life* itself has been displaced by the modern world, and especially by the emphasis on the scientific method and the forces of Capital. Much like Marx's analysis of Capital, which erases living labor by deadening it, Henry's oeuvre suggests that academia, too, neutralizes the most spiritual of activities, *living*. I am concerned with how political theology might participate in this neutralization. Henry maintains that in the West, life has been erased by various systems that claim to foster it, whether economic, philosophical, theological, political, or scientific. What these systems all have in common is a tendency toward reification. In other words, the system itself is considered a living entity that determines and shapes individuals. When these systems are reified, a problematic reduction of individual life occurs as the subject comes to be regarded only as an object that can alternatively be thought, perceived, theorized, used, measured, or valued. Life is thereby objectified by philosophers who think it, capitalists who use or purchase it, theologians who sacralize it, and politicians who organize it. Henry calls this a *principal inadequation* that characterizes modern life, substituting unreal entities, such as ideas, theories, money, or even data, for what is most real—life, with all of its needs and abilities. In the process, he observes, our singular knowledge of life is reduced to thoughts about "it." Politics and theology thus come to operate just like the economic and scientific worlds: turning subjects into objects, whether believers into numbers or citizens into data points. I suggest that Henry's contribution to political theology lies in identifying and avoiding this kind of objectification by providing a robust account of life that includes a fascinating appropriation of Marx.[1] Another novel interpretation of Marx for political theology can be found in Martin Shuster's contribution to this volume, which argues that Kōjin Karatani (much like Henry, I think) moves beyond "traditional" Marxism by focusing on "modes of exchange" to rethink secularism.

     Inese Radzins

Political Theology and Culture

As a discipline, political theology traditionally has been concerned with a twofold dynamic: historically, it was the relationship of theology and politics, and more recently, it is that of religion and politics.[2] Many of its discourses are determined by dualistic terminology, such as *secular-sacred*, *public-private*, or *friend-enemy*. Roberto Esposito has observed the permanence of these dichotomies, characterizing the discipline as a "machine" defined by opposition: "Both historically and conceptually, the two poles of the political and the theological enter into relationship with each other in the continuous attempt to overcome the other."[3] Recently, a number of works have questioned the oppositional nature of the dualism, allowing for different trajectories in the field. One such work is Victoria Kahn's *The Future of Illusion*, which sheds light on the way a third element—*poiesis*—has been neglected in these conversations. Although her focus is on late modern appropriations of early modern texts, especially as they concern the Jewish question, she points to the way the traditional discourses of political theology exclude other, often more creative, realms of life.[4]

Kahn suggests that the category of *poiesis* provides creative resources for thinking political theology more imaginatively: "I use the term to refer both to the new anthropology elaborated by Hobbes and Vico, with its emphasis on making, and to the attendant emphasis on works of art as exemplary of this human capacity."[5] Key to her analysis is the observation that poesis, often considered a personal endeavor, cannot be confined to the "private" realm or to the theological side of the dualism. Instead, she argues that culture permeates public life, thereby undermining some of the dualisms so often used in political theology. In other words, Kahn wants to understand how aesthetics shape the social and the political. Her concern is to highlight the critical role of art, thereby "rescuing a positive idea of culture from the charge of complicity with the status quo."[6] To regard culture is to consider its potential to challenge normative conversations and discourses and thus to provide a space to think differently and more creatively about social life. In this way, her work pushes us to rethink the role culture might play in discussions of political theology in our own day.[7] I argue that Henry's work does something similar.

Like Kahn, Henry emphasizes a creative modality—culture—to consider life together. He also highlights the capacity of human beings to create and make their worlds. Whereas Kahn notes the possibility of creating fictions of—and for—the political order, Henry focuses on more mundane creations.[8] Also like Kahn, he suggests that culture is both constructive and critical. However, Henry's culture differs from Kahn's because it is more materially inflected and, perhaps, more all-encompassing. For him, there are "cultures of food, shelter, work, erotic relations or relations to the dead—such relations provide an initial definition of the human."[9] Culture includes very mundane activities, such as cooking or building or child-rearing. In other words, Henry emphasizes quotidian activities as providing the roots for culture. His concern is to allow the human space for creating oneself and one's life. The whole notion of culture is thus displaced toward subjectivity. In this way, his thinking may have similarities to Ambedkar, who, Banerjee notes, "was more invested in the idea of a critical *self* than in the anthropological idea of a community or culture." Henry's focus is on whether or not the individual can be such a critical self.[10]

Emphasizing the more mundane elements of cultural life calls for another kind of consideration of political theology. Whereas Kahn's work offers a third modality, *poiesis*, with which to think political theology, thus enriching the traditional twofold dialogues, Henry's work questions how the discipline itself is structured. Ultimately, his work points to the limitation of the discipline to account adequately for its subject, the human. But before turning to these limitations and his criticism, it is important to define what he means by life, living subjectivity, and the cultures produced thereby.

Henry's Life and Lived Subjectivity

Henry's philosophy is characterized by *Life* and, in particular, life as lived by any single individual: "The a priori of all a prioris—is the absolute Life in which we are alive."[11] This Life is a transcendental affectivity that each individual senses uniquely. He also refers to it as lived—or at times *living*—subjectivity, ipseity, and auto-affection. It is, he asserts, "what is most intimate" and the "actualization of the force of life in a living body."[12] Considering *life* in this way prompts him to reconfigure the philosophical category of subjectivity and to consider the human more robustly. The rethinking is apparent in his use of tangible examples—studying for an exam, running, holding a child, tasting an apple, hammering a nail, feeling a kiss, or baking bread. That these mundane practices are significant and not trivial will be made clear in his critique of politics explained in the section that follows. Crucial to this lived subjectivity is the "effort of labor." Living *is* the ability of any one human to be active, creative, and productive.

What is surprising in Henry is how life and living subjectivity are connected to a particular reading of Marx that focuses on living labor. Regarding the connection between the two, he asserts:

> Life, in turn, cannot be disconnected from what constantly holds it in its grasp: from the air that it breathes, from the ground that it treads, from the tool that it uses, or from the object that it sees. The original co-belonging of the living individual and the Earth is essentially practical. It is located in life and based on it. The force of life is the force through which the Individual and the Earth cohere in this ageless origin (*primitivitè sans âge*). Living labor is the implementation of this force.[13]

Henry appropriates Marx's concept of living labor to explain how life *is* activity. This implies that living—at its best—is laboring. But one must be careful here because *Henry's labor is not to be equated with work or any form of Capitalist production.* Rather, it is a creative capacity of attending to life. It is, as Marx observed, praxis, or life production: an engagement with the world to produce life's necessities. Labor is the activation of the force of life *and is thus not to be confused with wage labor.* As such it is also practical, a co-belonging with and in the Earth. What characterizes Henry's living subjectivity is the capacity to freely sense and engage reality practically—creatively, attentively, and productively. Laboring freely is a key component of life and "what we are." Raphaël Gély describes this very human capacity as an "originary inventiveness."[14]

Although all people share this capacity for inventiveness, the knowing of it is unique to each individual. Henry designates this immediate experiencing as "knowledge of life."[15] He contrasts this with a more traditional philosophical epistemology characterized by "knowledge of consciousness and of science." This contrast between life and consciousness is critical: Living life differs from thinking life. Thought depends on reflection and cognition; representing objects to myself to think and also taking myself as an object of thought. Sensing oneself is fundamentally different from thinking oneself, or thinking anything. Henry's "knowledge of life" is thus a unique and singular capacity that no two persons will ever share; as such, it is irreducible to thought. And it is this uniqueness, the singularity of lived subjectivity and its active ability to labor, that distinguishes his oeuvre and offers a reimagining of political theology.

To understand the difference between *knowledge of life* and *knowledge of consciousness*, Henry offers the example of a biology student sitting in a library, reading about the genetic code. The contrast he draws is between the student's subjective and objective modes of knowing. The genetic code is an object the student is reading about. It is presented to her in the book as a theory to understand. However, Henry is clear that "it is not scientific knowledge that allows her to acquire the scientific knowledge contained in the book. It is not in virtue of this knowledge that she moves her hands or eyes or focuses her thought. Scientific knowledge is abstract."[16] The word *abstract* is critical because it points to a distance between the knower and what is known. The genetic code is a theory, or idea—an object—that one studies. This kind of knowing pervades the world in the form of theories, hypotheses, or concepts, such as *political theology*. Lived subjectivity, however, cannot be abstracted. It cannot be made into a theory—even a theory of the subject, for example. Instead, knowledge of life is *immanent*, *felt*, or *sensed*: "The knowledge that made possible the movement of the hands and the eyes, the act of getting up, climbing the stairs, drinking and eating, and resting is the knowledge of life."[17]

What distinguishes lived subjectivity and its knowledge of life—and what makes it absolutely different from Capitalist modes of production—is its aesthetic quality. This is what links it to Kahn's *poiesis*. Henry's life, understood as living labor, involves creative production and never production for profit. The effort of labor is fundamentally creative and productive of culture. It is, as Marx noted, a very human ability and a primary *need* of the self. Not surprisingly, what Henry means by culture is very specific: "Because culture is the self-fulfillment of life, it is essentially practical."[18] That culture is practical appears an odd sentiment and points to a difference with Kahn. Henry asks us to consider culture in very basic terms: taking care of life's necessities, whether providing food, shelter, or clothing. In living and addressing our needs, human beings create: cuisine, architecture, design. It is in these types of cultural creations that *life* is found. As noted earlier, the relations that define humans are found in "cultures of food, shelter, work, erotic relations or relations to the dead."[19] What is surprising in Henry is that culture arises in attending to need. His *culture* is thus unique because its focus is on the individual's ability to produce, to live laboring.

Life is determined by the ability of lived subjectivities to engage in cultural productions, not just individually but as part of communities. If lived subjectivity is a transcendental affectivity, it is always situated amid a culture, milieu, place, space, and community. Social life is thus characterized by individuals working and producing culture together. Notably, lived subjectivity does not imply an isolated, or autonomous, individual. The *Life* in which we are alive is both unique to each individual and always shared. "In a society understood as a community of the living within life," Henry writes, "culture is thus everywhere. Everything has a value because everything is done by and for life."[20] The key to Henry's *human* is this suggestion of doing everything "by and for life." The living that each person does brings them together with others in sharing various communal/cultural productions—of food, shelter, work, erotic relations, and relations to the dead. In other words, where living labor and life flourish, culture lives. Consequently, culture cannot be limited to its "high" forms or to "individual" genius, whether the paintings in museums or music in opera houses (although it is also there). Culture *is* cooking, building, loving, writing; it is inherently practical, mundane even. We will see later in this chapter that it is this "inherent practicality" that economics, politics, and theology all too often ignore.

Henry's culture is also, I suggest, the location of spirituality. As such, it offers a key insight for political theology by proposing a radically immanent theology. This spirituality lacks any form of transcendence, or separation into sacred and secular or private and public spheres. It cannot be relegated to a separate domain—whether church, temple, doctrine, liturgy, or prayer. Neither does it involve any kind of higher Being or beings. Living itself takes precedence over any logos, theory, or divinity. It is thus much more mundane: "It designates the inner connection of the living to the life from which it derives its condition as alive, in which it experiences (*eprouve*) all that it experiences."[21] For Henry, individuals flourish when this connection to life is cultivated. In other words, when producing and participating in culture, one is most human, most alive, and thereby spiritual. Consider the way the student senses their studying; the chef, their baking; the painter, their painting; or the carpenter, their building. Spirituality is alive in these spaces—the places where culture thrives. In other words, life is grounded in the very worldly activities that an individual undertakes and undergoes in daily living. The meeting of our very quotidian needs is thus in and of itself spiritual. The question Henry's work raises for political theology is how to attend to these kinds of mundane and yet very spiritual sensibilities.

When everything is done "by and for life," the needs and abilities of individuals take center stage. The critical piece for Henry is the consideration of individual life and its "originary inventiveness." His philosophy begins by asking how this inventiveness, understood in terms of living labor, is fostered. Life, living, and the joy and effort involved are in and of themselves spiritual—a spirituality evidenced by the various cultures produced, such as those of food, shelter, and work. The problem for Henry is that these kinds of cultures and the focus on individual human *living* are diminished and deadened by global capital and its various political figurations, where the economy and buying, selling, and financial valuing come to determine society. In other words, various social forces limit one's spiritual capacities. Here, Henry's spirituality may again have resonances to Ambedkar, who, Banerjee observes in this volume, emphasizes the notion of "*dhamma*, an alternative form of religious being that helped individuate those who were denied their individuality in the name of social being." Ambedkar's context differs radically from Henry's, but the dynamic they point to is similar: Social being often denies and minimizes the human and, thus, also an individual's spirituality. The critical piece in Henry's work, to which I now turn, provides a description of how a simulacrum of life—*objectification*—comes to displace culture and lived subjectivities.

Objectification and Reification

This brings us to the second insight Henry's work provides to political theology. If the first was identifying lived subjectivity in mundane practices as the locus of life and spirituality, the second is identifying a key dynamic that displaces life: our various conceptions of social life, or politics. Although politics is typically understood as a force to promote the public good, Henry's work suggests the opposite. In the West, he asserts, politics "deals with public affairs that are supposed to be the affairs of those who it claims to serve, but in reality they are only the affairs of the capitalists."[22] Just as Marx observed that the factory should have made life better for individual workers, Henry notes that politics should enhance life for individuals. Instead, workers remain enslaved by Capital, and individuals are ignored by politics.

His most complete description of the deadening that occurs with politics is found in *From Communism to Capitalism: A Theory of Catastrophe*. The "catastrophe" he identifies is the "elimination of subjective life."[23] It manifests differently in communism than in capitalism, but Henry is clear that *all* political systems, including democracy and socialism, fall prey to it. His analyses of the limitations of both communism, which subverts living labor, and capitalism, which manipulates it, are prescient and worth engaging. The fundamental problem he identifies is that life and living labor—the most singular of capacities—are displaced by social totalities

Inese Radzins

that generalize and homogenize life. This problem, for him, is a result of a very modern dynamic (already identified by Marx) that privileges the scientific method and valorizes Capital.

Rejecting the narrative of Western cultures as "civilizing" the world, Henry argues that they have, instead, barbarized life.[24] He situates this barbarism in the rise of the scientific method: "With Galileo, . . . the encounter with the world is stripped of its essential subjectivity. The task of understanding the world in its true being is no longer assigned to *bodily sensible knowledge* nor to the *subjective force* that inhabits the body."[25] Instead, knowledge increasingly depends on three characteristics: the demand for a neutral observer, a reliance on experts, and, most notably, an emphasis on objective knowledge. What is problematic for Henry is the process whereby the scientific method and its call for objectivity has come to determine all forms of knowledge, including, I suggest, political theology. "The new 'human sciences' themselves seek to be objective, whether it concerns their methodology or their 'object': The human is reduced to homogenous phenomena."[26]

This homogenizing of the human is the problem Henry identified in his criticism of academia. Recall the example of the student studying and the difference between objective forms of knowing and subjective knowledge. Her knowledge of life is her sensing of herself studying; fidgeting; getting up to take a break; feeling tired, exhilarated, or confused, and so on. This is how she knows life; it is inherently practical and singular. The problem that occurs with barbarism is that the student's sensibility, her lived subjectivity, is ignored in favor of an objective equivalent. In the process, "she" becomes "it," a homogeneous phenomenon; a thing to be studied, assessed, or known, much like the genetic code. In this regard, Henry offers a scathing assessment of how the French academy has capitulated to this kind of objectification.[27]

The emphasis on the scientific method and its homogenizing tendency is buoyed by modern economics wherein workers are considered commodities, or objects, to be bought and sold. Henry calls this a "principal inadequation" whereby life is reduced to quantifiable measures—most notably, money.[28] With Capital, subjectivity becomes an object to be bought, sold, measured, exchanged, valued, organized, manipulated, and, all too often, exploited. The worker, any worker, is literally considered a commodity "worth" a certain amount: the lawyer one sum, the mechanic another. Capitalism depends on this kind of abstraction of labor as individual workers become things, or cogs, in the global industrial machine.

Each worker is measured objectively by hourly wages or future productivity. And like goods in the marketplace, they become exchangeable. Audre Lorde offers an apt description of what this looks like:

> The principal horror of any system which defines the good in terms of profit rather than in terms of human need . . . is that it robs our work of its erotic value, its erotic power and life appeal and fulfillment. Such a system reduces work to a travesty of necessities, a duty by which we earn bread or oblivion for ourselves and those we love. But this is tantamount to blinding a painter and then telling her to improve her work, and to enjoy the act of painting. It's not only next to impossible, it is also profoundly cruel.[29]

The life of workers and their singular capacities—the erotic value of painting—is deadened by the mechanism of profit required by Capital. Marx referred to this as the transformation of living labor into dead labor. Henry here draws the connection between Capital and politics: Just as Capital abstracts laborers, politics deadens individuals by reducing them to objects, or parts, in the advancement of an ideological program.

The key to Henry's analysis is that universal categories, such as money, equalize what in reality can never be measured, valued, or compared: life. Here, the distinction between the *thought of life* (or the knowledge of consciousness noted earlier) and *life itself* is tantamount. The *thought of life* offers various concepts or theories with which to think the individual: A general or universal idea is "applied" to everyone. The student, for example, is one among many of the "same" kind—students. This is evident in philosophy when it generalizes about *being* and in religion when it universalizes the category *believers*. Just as Capital rules economic life via the idea of money, politics rules social life via the "universal ideas" of justice, equality, and rights, imposing them on everyone.[30] Henry's concern is that this universalizing tendency—to consider everyone equal, for example—erases lived subjectivity. Moreover, when applying the idea of equality to everyone, politics hides the very inequalities and differences that exist among individuals. The individual becomes one empirical entity, a "generalized" thing: a unit, or number, represented by officials (be they secular or religious) and counted as data by experts. He concludes by noting that the knowledge produced on the basis of any *thought of life* is "empty" and can only "lead to impoverishment."[31] This is how the human and social sciences "miss" what is most human.

Not only does modern Western thinking objectify what should remain subjective; it also treats social entities as vitalized subjects. For Henry, modern science and Capital produce a dangerous reversal: Real individuals are devitalized as dead entities are vivified. The homogenization of life goes hand in hand with a "hypostasization" of the political.[32] Like economics, or science, politics is taken to be a *real* living entity: "It is considered as an autonomous reality and as the only true reality in which individuals can participate. Individuals draw their own being from it, to the extent that they have any being at all. This phenomenological valorization of the political—whose immediate consequence is the ontological inflation of the political essence—expresses the great deficiency of Western thought."[33] This "ontological inflation" considers politics a "natural" and "autonomous" reality that regulates all aspects of life. When this occurs, increasing bureaucracies and political machines come to dominate social life. These reified entities become the engines of all social life, imposing from the outside what one should do or be, or how one is to behave.

In addition, Henry notes that these social totalities become "objects of faith."[34] For example, we "believe" in democracy or "have faith" in the market. Political polls reveal voters' concerns with the economy and its effects on life. In other words, we accept that politics, like the economy or religion, is a real force that controls and determines life. When this occurs, politics functions just like the factory in Marx's *Capital*: We serve *it*, rather than *it* serving us. "For the political is the universal; it is motivated by and results from the negation of the singular individual."[35] Henry points to the way modern life reveals a kind of slavery to the various hypostasizations of public life, whether nation, party, market, religion, or even academia. He concludes that the same individuals that are bought and sold under Capital are manipulated by politics and organized by religious groups. Both politics and religion, like other social groups, come to be governed by the opposition of the individual to the collective. And it is the group that always takes priority. In other words, the whole is always considered bigger than the individual, who is only ever taken as "a variable in the objective functioning of an organization."[36] He is clear that all of these entities, and politics in particular, function exactly like Capital: using individuals to profit.

In the process, the individual is subsumed under any number of universal concepts: the idea of society, the concept of the people, or the community of believers. And herein lies the problem for Henry, who considers that these concepts and reified entities cannot "do" anything: "A concept is an ideal objectivity, and as such it is foreign to reality and notably to the reality of life. That is why it is stripped of all real or living properties: according to Spinoza's famous proposition, the concept of a dog does not bark."[37] For Henry, a concept—political theology, or the political, or the theological—cannot act, or live, or bark. The radical conclusion he draws, echoing Marx, is that politics as we know it, "does nothing."[38] He asks: "Who has ever seen society digging a hole or building a wall, fixing a faucet, or treating the wounded?"[39] The point is that only an individual can work in this way. His oeuvre thus exposes a curious aporia: Politics should foster individual life, but the very mechanisms that organize the public today—reified entities such as technology, science, or politics— entail a deadening of this life. Academia, too, Henry asserts, depends on these conceptualities and, as noted in the introduction, thereby misses its true subject: the human. Perhaps the question to ask here (and one that is unfortunately beyond the scope of this chapter) is how concepts function and what it might mean to reorient thinking toward living by focusing on the digging of the hole or the treating of the wounded. This would require attending to the human *qua* human and not just as a part of a social entity.

Accepting Henry's analysis leads to a critical conclusion for our purposes: Political theology participates in the minimization of life as the individual is subsumed into "the people" or "the believers" as one piece, object, or data point. Each entity, whether political or theological, takes on a life of its own and demands the allegiance of its members. These entities are also theorized by people like me—scholars who wish to understand a broader social dynamic. The problem is not just the "machine" of political theology and its dualisms that were identified by Esposito and noted earlier. Rather, it is the whole theoretical edifice insofar as it does not attend to the "real" locale of social life: the subjectivity of living labor. I suggest that the critical contribution Henry makes to political theology is to distinguish social life as determined by politics and organized technologically by objective standards from a society that promotes cultures of life and living subjectivity. Attending to the singularity of life offers a different consideration of the human—one that may be more spiritually attuned.

Conclusion: Keeping Life Living

Such a society, which would render useless an impossible justice, is a society of overabundance, not one defined by the overabundance of product, but one whose wealth would allow each to realize the potentialities of his or her own

Inese Radzins

subjectivity. It would be a world of the realization of praxis, a world of life, where the activity of life would be defined, wanted and prescribed by life.

Michel Henry, *The Michel Henry Reader*

What are we to make of political theology if one begins, as Henry does, with the premise that the modern world, and its political and academic configurations, negates life? Can political theology "work" if one considers the "human and social sciences" an obstacle to the flourishing of life and lived subjectivity? Although he criticizes politics as we know it—whether democratic, socialist, or communist—Henry affirms the spiritual capacity of *living* and the cultures that proceed from life. He is adamant that life cannot be eradicated *and* that it is neither the political nor the theological that sustains living. Rather, living subjectivities produce communities and societies. Life is its own basis and does not depend on politics, economics, concepts, or abstractions. Because Henry questions the objectifying tendencies of modern life and the corresponding reification of social totalities, his work will not offer a program or traditional solution to "fix" the problem. To do so would be to give in to barbarism and the call for experts, objective data, and social projects. Instead, what his oeuvre offers political theology is a reimagining of what constitutes life together. He calls this "material democracy," which, not surprisingly, involves an affirmation that the "real motor" of society is living labor, lived subjectivity.[40] In the process, Henry's work encourages academics and scholars of political theology to relocate their field of vision and attend to the human differently—to consider the singular capacity of each and every individual. Marx's and Lorde's work offers this possibility, as do other chapters in this volume.

The first aspect of his affirmation of Life is the need to keep subjectivity subjective and life living. Henry's radical subjectivity and Marx's idea of living labor are two sides of the same coin: Both suggest that social life should foster lived subjectivity. His affinity to Marx on this point is clear: "Just like the concept of society, the concept of the people has never been noticed in the process of laboring or of performing a surgical procedure. To do those things, as Marx said, human beings are necessary."[41] Individuals do not live to serve society. Rather, society should foster living subjectivity and, thereby, spirituality. What politics and academia often exclude is the reality of this human surgeon—singular, and unique, living subjectively. The focus, then, becomes a social life that allows each individual to realize their potentiality; in other words, their ability to labor creatively, like Lorde's painter.

Notably, this does not entail a negation of social life or a celebration of an autonomous or self-sufficient, individual.[42] It asks, instead, about the possibility of the community fostering each person's creative capacities. Gély explains: "When collective action is constructed with attention to the singularity of the life of each, when individuals are led to experience the fundamental solidarity of their life-forces, one can no longer oppose people's radically singular lives to the reality of their collective action. To the contrary, collective action permits individuals to experience and to intensify what founds the radical singularity of each, namely, the originary inventiveness of life. For participation in life increases as it is shared."[43] Social life arises with individuals and their originary inventiveness. As humans labor to meet their needs, communities arise. The key to this is another insight from Marx: attending to the needs and abilities of each human.[44] Henry's material democracy involves a society in which each life participates fully because the needs of life are prioritized and the inventiveness of each is fostered. Concerns of production, consumption, and money are displaced in favor of life. In a world of globalized Capital, in which multitudes of workers continue to be exploited and devalued and dead labor reigns supreme, Henry's attention to the individual is refreshing.

The second aspect of Henry's affirmation of Life is an emphasis on culture. For him, culture is the opposite of barbarism: It alone can attend to living subjectivities. Put simply, politics is subverted in favor of culture. Writing about the COVID-19 pandemic, the philosopher Byung-Chul Han echoes this sentiment: "Culture was the first thing to be abandoned during lockdown. What is culture? It engenders community! Without it, we come to resemble animals that want merely to survive. It is not the economy but most of all culture, namely communal life, that needs to recover from this crisis as soon as possible."[45] The critical point is that culture differs exponentially from political and economic production. It does not arise from competition; nor does it have "winners." It cannot be measured or valued according to profits or members. It is not defined by the overabundance of product or number of programs or projects. It is unconcerned with having, owning, buying, financial valuing, monetization, or objective standards of calculation. Henry refuses understanding life together in terms of these kinds of abstractions, whether political, economic, theological, or theoretical.

Instead, his oeuvre challenges traditional notions, both popular and academic, about politics by imagining a different way of situating life together: in culture. And in this, he shares Kahn's concern with *poiesis*: Are individuals able to participate in creating the cultures they inhabit? The challenge is to consider humans singularly, in their living, as providing the very roots of culture. His suggestion, to begin with Life and with living subjectivity, is both very mundane and nothing novel. We have only to consider society in his terms, as the very practical cultures of "food, shelter, work, erotic relations and relations to the dead." We are all already and always participating in producing these forms of culture. And it is here that the task of political theology lies: to rediscover and attend to the human (and not the concept of the human) in these very mundane practices. Considering culture allows for the possibility of a life together that keeps life living and subjectivity subjective and fosters spirituality by attending to cultures of creative production. When political theology puts this kind of spirituality in its field of vision, the human is no longer set aside.

Notes

Epigraphs: Henry, *From Communism to Capitalism*, 109; Henry, *Michel Henry Reader*, 163.

1 See Henry, *Marx*. His heterodox reading of Marx is rooted in a rejection of Marxism and in the assertion that Marx is a "philosopher of life."

2 See Cavanaugh and Lloyd "Why Does Political Theology Matter?"; Esposito, *Two*, introduction; Kahn, *The Future of Illusion*, introduction.

3 Esposito, *Two*, 3. He also observes how this dualism functions to determine the subject: "People are caught in a mode that escapes them but that also leads to a splitting of their lives into two spheres, one of which is subjected to the domination of the other."

4 Kahn, *The Future of Illusion*, xii, 3.

5 Kahn, *The Future of Illusion*, 20; see also 3, 22.

6 Kahn, *The Future of Illusion*, 19.

7 Kahn's specific concern is to point out how *poiesis* functioned in debates about "the Jewish question" and thereby to offer insights to consider what more recently has been called "the Muslim question": Kahn, *The Future of Illusion*, 20–22.

8 Kahn, *The Future of Illusion*, 21.

9 Henry, *Barbarism*, xv.

10 See Banerjee's chapter in this volume. Banerjee describes Ambedkar's concern as pursing "a proper religiosity based on a proper understanding of the nature of reality and the place of the solitary human self in it."

11 Henry, *Barbarism*, 102.

12 Henry, *From Communism to Capitalism*, 66.

13 Henry, *From Communism to Capitalism*, 70. For Henry's use of Marx's *living labor*, see the chapter "Being as Production" in Henry, *The Michel Henry Reader*, 143–67, esp. 153.

14 Gély, "Towards a Radical Phenomenology of Social Life," 175.

15 Henry, *Barbarism*, 10–14.

16 Henry, *Barbarism*, 11.

17 Henry, *Barbarism*, 11.

18 Henry, *Barbarism*, 125.

19 Henry, *Barbarism*, xv.

20 Henry, *Barbarism*, xv.

21 Henry, *The Michel Henry Reader*, 169.

22 Henry, *From Communism to Capitalism*, 97.

23 Henry, *From Communism to Capitalism*, 10.

24 Henry, *Barbarism*, XVI.

25 Henry, *From Communism to Capitalism*, 82, emphasis added. As such, there is nothing wrong with science. It is only when it encroaches on subjectivity that it becomes problematic.

26 Henry, *The Michel Henry Reader*, 175.

27 He offers the example of research in the social sciences that attempts to count different behaviors—the number of suicides or different types of sexual activities, for example. He asks, "Does the fact of knowing that there have been, in some time, place, and circumstance so many suicides or so many sexual acts committed add anything whatsoever to our understanding of the anxiety or vertigo that surround these 'behaviors'?": Henry, *Barbarism*, 82, 115–37 ("Destruction of the University").

28 Henry, *The Michel Henry Reader*, 163.

29 Lorde, *Sister Outsider*, 55.

30 See Henry, *The Michel Henry Reader*, 175.

31 Henry, *Barbarism*, 83–84.

32 Henry, *From Communism to Capitalism*, 102.

33 Henry, *From Communism to Capitalism*, 102.

34 Henry, *From Communism to Capitalism*, 31.

35 Henry, *From Communism to Capitalism*, 103.

36 Gély, "Towards a Radical Phenomenology of Social Life," 161. See also Henry, *From Communism to Capitalism*, 102–3.

Inese Radzins

37 Henry, *From Communism to Capitalism*, 27.

38 Henry, *From Communism to Capitalism*, 31.

39 Henry, *From Communism to Capitalism*, 31.

40 Henry, *The Michel Henry Reader*, 172; Henry, *From Communism to Capitalism*, 73.

41 Henry, *From Communism to Capitalism*, 104.

42 This point is also made by Banerjee in this volume. "According to Ambedkar, this form of individuation, without the guarantee of anything beyond the exigency and contingency of life itself, enabled critical and compassionate sociability better than did either cultural unity or individual civility."

43 Gély, "Towards a Radical Phenomenology of Social Life," 175.

44 Marx, *Selected Writings*, 321.

45 Han, "The Tiredness Virus."

Passionate Thinking

ISABELLE STENGERS
AND POLITICAL THEOLOGY

Ada S. Jaarsma

Passionate thinking brings together two areas of political theology: the refutation of the "secularity thesis" of Western modernity, in which scientific prowess unites dispassionate thinking with promises of ongoing progress, and the wide-ranging affirmation of the multiplicities of reality, perspectives, and meaning making itself. Where the first area of political theology tends to disrupt claims of transcendence, especially those invoking Nature as a causal force of all that exists, the second tends to foreground immanence, philosophically and methodologically.

As a mode of thinking, passionate thinking might seem to fit most clearly within this second area of political theology. Its first-person qualities—an existential attunement to the calls of new problems—echoes the perspectival tones of Friedrich Nietzsche and the creativity of Alfred North Whitehead and Gilles Deleuze. Indeed, given the degree to which Isabelle Stengers's elaboration of passionate thinking emerges out of close readings of these thinkers, passionate thinking holds affinity with thinkers such as William Connolly, who share this archive of texts. "Passionate thinking" refers to the entangled relations between "belief" and the dispositions by which we enact practices; trust and generosity become resources for thinking—and mistrust and belligerence keep important problems at bay, obstructed in the name of capitalist expansion.

As this chapter explores, passionate thinking offers a way to bridge this area of political theology (Deleuzian and process-based) with the first that seeks to resist secularity's claims to reason, progress, and universal reach. It provides a robust account of how to cultivate capacities for such resistance, in the first-person and in solidarity with others, while at the same time traversing lines between the religious and the nonreligious. Throughout her writing, Stengers reflects on an array of exemplars, from scientists proposing new fictions to witches invoking magic to Quakers holding clearness committees. These examples work to query overly tidy divides between those espousing secularity and those more readily called religious, poetic, fantastical, or spiritual.

Bringing passionate thinking together with political theology, I consider two problems in turn. First, which practices in our contemporary world seek to maintain the "secularization" mandates of liberalism, and how might these practices affect our own modes of thinking? I am hoping that readers might be surprised and become newly curious about the relevance of science and scientific inquiry to this problem. In the next section, I draw out a thread running throughout Stengers's work that holds import for each of us: As biomedical researchers find themselves haunted by a never fully exorcised aspect of curative work, we are all affected by this force of healing, often made recognizable by the term *placebo*. Its import for those upholding the religious-secular divide, I suggest, manifests in resentment and violence.

Second, as political theologians affirm secular-religious engagements as energizing and empowering, which practices might support such engagements?[1] Here, too, I draw on Stengers, who explains that we never resist in general, only ever as a poet, or activist, or philosopher, or theologian.[2] Passionate thinking, in other words, acts as a placeholder for vocations, lived out in the first person. Rather than any generalizable recipe, this mode of thinking involves arts of attention that are situated and sensorial.

On the one hand, passionate thinking affirms the existence of many worlds within one world.[3] This affirmation of the "pluriverse" aligns with political theologians and thinkers beyond its bounds.[4] Annemarie Mol, for example, writes that "instead of a single homogeneous universe, we inhabit different worlds."[5] By focusing on concrete practices, passionate thinking provides one way among others to reckon with this openness toward ontologies, in the plural. In the context of Stengers's writings, this holds speculative, pragmatic, and empirical significance.

On the other hand, passionate thinking involves a terrain of thinking/practice that is rarely welcome in academic circles not designated as "theological" or "art making"—terrain that has to do with being moved, even compelled, on sensorial as well as conceptual levels. At odds with norms of secularity, in which individuals consent to their own belief claims, passionate thinking re-establishes the pivotal roles of affect and disposition that thinkers such as Connolly have long acknowledged, pointing us toward an open-ended list of pragmatic suggestions. This list, which fits beautifully within "that vibrant between-space," will resonate differently with each of us because of sensorial qualities.[6] It's instructive, for example, that Jürgen

Habermas, a leading advocate for secularity as an ideal for politics, admits to a sensorial impasse when it comes to the lived experience of religiosity.[7] He confesses an inability to "hear" the musicality and tenor of religiousness, which Stengers likewise seems to name in her writing, a certain bodymind ethos that might or might not afford sniffing, tasting, or otherwise sensing the "religious" part of the secular religious. It's not that Stengers herself uses this terminology; rather, affinities emerge by reading Stengers alongside contemporary political theologians.

Passionate thinking includes the hope that we might tune in to other tonalities from those into which we've been socialized, a hope essential for affirming many worlds within one world. In the third section, I reflect on some of Stengers's pragmatic suggestions, which include practices of smelling (exemplified by Starhawk and neo-pagan witches) and of listening (exemplified by the Religious Society of Friends). My sense is that such suggestions hold relevance for those bodyminds that feel far away from the call and feel of "religiousness"—such that witches and Quakers hold meaning-making insights from and with which Stengers and others might learn.

Those of us who grew up "religious," in contrast, might require a different set of pragmatic suggestions, depending on the sensorial dispositions by which we've been formed. We might run the risk of simply endorsing one religion over another, failing to inflect our own practices with creative experimentation, and remain far from the call and feel of "secularity." For these bodyminds, I offer another suggestion: I look to the domain of placebo studies for cultivating secular-religious engagements.

Testators, or Why the Religious-Secular Divide Matters

Ontology creates obligations and commitments.[8]

This Stengerian claim provides a kind of touchstone for this chapter. Its relevance to political theology, especially cast as a method, as Alex Dubilet and Vincent Lloyd suggest in their introduction, lies in how it prompts us to notice the many ways a person's activities and vocabularies emerge out of that person's world, a world in which certain causes matter. We can attend to the first-person specificity of someone's practices, for example, while keeping space for the coexistence of other practices and other worlds.

In this chapter, I turn to Stengers's cues about method, opening the stakes of such coexistence for political theology. Rather than separating a concept from its "problematic path," Stengers suggests, we want to learn from and with a concept: We even might situate it in stories.[9] Following this suggestion, I offer two stories that each stage the religious-secular divide as a problem that matters in one ontology, in particular. What emerges from a close study of this ontology is its refusal of, even outright war on, the existence of other ontologies. To track, assess, and overturn this violence is a motivating problem for political theology, as several chapters in this collection demonstrate. David Kline looks to Sylvia Wynter, for example, and draws out "the decolonial epistemological imperative" that becomes possible as the hold of one biocentric, humanist ontology is undone. Likewise, holding space for the coexistence of relations, stories, and ontologies is a generative problem in Dana Lloyd's chapter. It can be difficult to attune ourselves to the ontology that underpins commitments to violent conquest, however, when relevant activities and vocabularies take place in domains that seem far afield from politics and from theology. As these two stories suggest, it can be in areas such as medicine and science where practices hold special import for political theology.

The first story takes place on the television screen, in a show created in the early 2000s. In this scene, President Josiah Bartlet, the fictional American leader in *The West Wing*, scoffs aloud at a request for government funding for a National Institutes of Health (NIH) study on intercessory prayer.[10] It's clear that he finds the proposal to fund a biomedical study on prayer laughable, at best, and offensive, at worst. The president's scoff suggests a risk of transgression, so the prospect of moving "prayer" into a federally sanctioned space such as the NIH must be closed. It's a slippery slope, he implies, when one messes with tidy lines between science's secularity and religious belief. "You will throw out the baby, the bathwater, and the bubbles at curtain time," he chides his advisers.

Bartlet's lack of hesitation would not be surprising to political theologians who study the presuppositions of liberalism. The issue is not with being religious; after all, the president acknowledges his own Catholicism, along with his acceptance of prayer's powers: "Well, in my faith, we've known it's worked for two thousand years. I've never known there was data available, but OK." By rejecting the funding proposal out of hand, the president is positioning religion in its own place, a "personal, often mostly private faith against which the state and the public can appear as a potentially separate, neutral, and nonsectarian sphere."[11]

While Bartlet's own religion happens to be Catholic, this understanding reflects a broader Protestantization of religion in which creeds and belief claims mark the religiosity of any or all believers, as long as believers ascribe to a set of liberal premises. As John Thatamanil argues, these include belonging to one and only one religion at a time ("I'm Catholic," the president asserts); experiencing religion as a kind of nonnegotiable identity (Catholic prayer, he intimates, has nothing to do with prayers of other faiths); and acknowledging tensions, perhaps irresolvable ones, with other religions (how laughable, in Bartlet's view, that his professed faith might be grouped with others in the name of data).[12]

Bartlet's derision toward prayer as something that might receive federally funded support reflects an asymmetry at the heart of liberalism. While religion can be looked *at*, as Kathleen Sands puts it, the secular is the perspective that moderns look *from*.[13] For some, such as the fictional President Bartlet, this relationship between secularity and religiousness holds no difficulty.

For me, as someone readying herself slowly, many years ago, to leave a church (an immigrant-inflected sectarian Calvinism), I'd felt uneasiness in the face of secularity's gaze. Rather than answering "Yes, you guessed it" when someone asked, curiously, "Are you religious?" I'd respond by naming the community I'd grown up in and hope that this would suffice.[14] I knew, without having the language for it, that pointing to beliefs as an expression of religiousness did not come close to a sufficient reflection of lived religiosity; I later discovered that this mismatch between liberalism's account and embodied experience holds great import for secular studies scholars and political theologians.[15]

I also felt, at the time, the converse side of what Bartlet seems enthusiastic about: a relational dynamic that Stengers describes as the curse of tolerance. "They are cursed," she explains, "who demand of the other that he 'express himself like everyone else.'"[16] As long as believers enact their "identities" in ways that sync well with liberal norms, tolerance offers seats at the political table. (Habermas, for example, describes this proffer as a request to translate any creedal claim into the intersubjective terms of science, a task that nonbelievers need not undertake.) Notably, this curse afflicts scientists, as well, on Stengers's accounts of scientific practices.

While I was interested in finding my own seat at the table, I had a sense that I'd be conceding too much if I adopted the terms of those who were noting my "otherness." I learned an apt description years later, coined by cultural anthropologists who study specific Protestant communities in North America: the sense of being "the culturally repugnant other."[17]

Ada S. Jaarsma

Rather than accept the curse of tolerance, I tried my best to avoid using the term *religious* at all.

In contrast with my own, long-ago feelings, Bartlet seems comfortable with what tolerance, as a mandate, requires. His Catholicism is part of a public persona that keeps "religion" in its own category. "I've never known there was data available," he quips to his advisers, "but OK." Prayer seems to conjure up a whiff of contamination, though, along with the portent of a slippery slope: If prayer is made welcome in an otherwise secular space, then "everything would be permitted," a risk too great to take.[18]

Bartlet, in this way, inhabits a specific world, which Stengers describes as "a testator ontology."[19] *Testators* is Stengers's term for modern practitioners who have acquired the skills of testing what is "real" and what is imagined, fake, or misleading. Stengers's work gets to the heart of why the stakes can seem so high when it comes to the religious-secular divide: If everything becomes permitted, then what will save us from all kinds of illusions, such as the gods of other peoples and the noisy confounds of non-valid science?[20] As this latter example suggests, scientific research often expresses "the passionate importance given to the exclusion of what cannot demonstrate its 'real' existence."[21] We can hear, in the colonizing impulses of the testators, the resonances of this line of inquiry with Kline's and Lloyd's chapters, among others.

Along these lines, the second story involves a cartoon doctor, depicted by Kate Charlesworth in terms that seem, at first glance, to share Bartlet's aversions to scientifically sanctioned prayer (see page 102). "Let it be a placebo," the doctor prays, face scrunching up and hands clasped.

While others in this control group seem engaged in intercessory prayer for patients—the activity being investigated—the doctor's prayer aims at the outcome of the trial itself. He understands full well the import of a gold-standard clinical research trial: New treatments will enter the market, but only if they differ from the "mere" placebo.[22] A sign hanging above the group suggests that this trial includes several arms or control groups. If prayer fails to be "triumphant," in Stengers's words, over its placebo counterpart, then scientists will be able to support this doctor's fervent hope: that prayer is "only" a placebo. The doctor's own treatments, produced through similar placebo-controlled trials, will also then triumph, reestablishing the credibility of evidence-based medicine.

Ontology, Stengers explains, yields obligations and commitments. There are causes that need to be defended and promoted, reflective of the world that people are inhabiting. In the case of the testator's ontology,

Placebo-controlled research trial: Is prayer an evidence-based medical treatment? Courtesy of Kate Charlesworth.

such defenses take place through carefully honed protocols. "Just like all that glitters is not gold," Stengers explains, "all what we claim to know [as testators] is not able to provide us with the firm grasp which ensures progress," precisely because of diverging beliefs and interests, illusions, and other contaminations.[23] Hence, this doctor's prayer.

Contamination, of course, poses salient risks for a doctor like the one in Charlesworth's cartoon. In fact, Stengers explains, while many researchers might find themselves working in the service of testator ontology, there is a special challenge for those in biomedicine. No matter the testator skill,

Ada S. Jaarsma

biomedicine cannot banish the workings of placebos: It's a singular feature of the living body, this "ability to be healed for the wrong reasons."[24] Unlike other objects of inquiry, called to bear witness to scientific facts, "the suffering body is not a reliable witness. It can happen that it will be cured for the 'wrong reasons.'"[25]

These are marvelous lines by Stengers, and they capture the comedic tension in Charlesworth's tale. We can't easily imagine other scientists in the plight of this cartoon doctor, since, as Stengers points out, chemists do not find themselves stalked by alchemists, nor astronomers by astrologists.[26] The doctor, however, can only try to evade "wrong" reasons—even reasons for something so wonderful as the alleviation of suffering. After all, we have not banished mesmerism, Stengers points out, or imagination and expectation.

As placebo studies researchers explain, experimenters can create placebo controls, entirely "bespoke" to each trial, as a way to filter contaminants out of the results.[27] A blue pill under investigation will receive its blue pill placebo mimic, for example, as each participant ideally receives identical attention, from those in the "real" treatment group to those in the placebo group. Pragmatically, of course, such ideals come up against the lived messiness of bodyminds in social scenarios. Affects and relational attention are, themselves, potent placebos, an aspect of biomedicine linked with systemic inequities, given the disparities in which bodyminds receive and bestow sincere attention.[28] "We all acknowledge," another placebo research team admits, "that the [placebo effect] is an immanent component of all medical (and many non-medical) interventions."[29]

For feminist science studies scholars whose causes differ from the testators', this immanence is something to explore, play with, and learn from.[30] For those upholding the testator ontology, in contrast, "any positive clinical outcomes brought about by placebo mechanisms within a clinical trial," however welcome by those who are suffering, "are seen as irrelevant to the findings of the trial."[31] Our cartoon doctor prays that this irrelevance will emerge from the prayer study so that prayer can join mesmerism in the category of non-evidence-based treatments.

Generative problems emerge here, from the intransigence of testators' longings to the refusal of placebos to go away once and for all. Perhaps, a placebo team muses, artificial intelligence will replace human clinicians in research trials, removing the messiness of affects and relational dynamics—a dream that speaks to me about the causes that matter for testators.[32] Stengers muses, in contrast, that a clinical test "does not eliminate the placebo effect, it just tries to background it by a unilateral, that is, methodological framing."[33] Feminist science studies scholars such as Elizabeth Wilson concur, drawing out the porous lines between a pill and its placebo effects.[34]

I am drawn to placebo studies research myself, I think, because I come up against my own lived experiences with meaning making. After I left the Calvinists, I began using the phrase "I grew up religious" quite freely, and while it took me longer to get there, I started adopting once unimaginable exclamations ("Oh my god!"). This line between what I'd been unable to say and what I now enjoy declaring seems to be one that is much more *bodily* than what the voluntarist logics of a Habermas or a Bartlet would suggest. I still flinch when I remember the few times I've slipped, uttering something blasphemous in a conversation with my mother or an old friend. Placebo effects express the entwined intimacy of affects and ideas. In all communities, whether religiously inclined or not, we enact our practices and our discourses in ways that bring forth embodied meanings. Lest this sound too overarching as a claim, though, we can note a multiplicity in what gets to count as a placebo, from this enactive scenario to that one.[35] This multiplicity is challenging for the testators.

Testators' Resentments

It is productive, when it comes to political theology, to take seriously the impacts and force of the testator ontology. For one, its dreams yield potent instruments and methods. It is not inevitable, though, that scientific inquiry be run or even adjudicated by testators. I first began reading Stengers's writings because they are infused with the passions and creative leaps of scientists. What is required, for scientists and for any of us seeking to affirm "many worlds" within one world, is to find ways to heed obligations and commitments from other ontologies. Summing up its devastating effects, Martin Savransky describes the testator's commitment as "modern monification of the world," a world seeking to contain only one ontology and no others.[36] "A world-destroying machine," as Stengers explains, "cannot fit with other worlds."[37]

Stengers's claim—that ontology creates obligations and commitments—resonates with an ancient word, *religare*, likely a root of our English word *religion*.[38] *Religare* means "to bind," an understanding of obligation that readily traverses the religious-secular divide. As Selden Smith explains in *The Atheist's Guide to Quaker Process*, referring to *religare*, "The nontheist

Ada S. Jaarsma

can be just as religious as anyone else—just as committed to tying up their own bundle, just as helpful to others who are trying to tie up theirs."[39] Feeling a cause, in ways that affirm one's obligations, need not manifest a "one-world-only" ontology, in other words. Quakers serve as a positive such example for Stengers, as I note in the next section.

It is not the search for truth alone that animates a testator, Stengers explains, but, rather, "the idea of a truth that should hurt and disenchant, which should go beyond illusions and destroy them."[40] As Connolly's work demonstrates fruitfully, we can examine the force of religious and secular actors by attending to the "combustible affective elements mixed into belief."[41] Affiliations become apparent that we'd otherwise miss if we focus solely on belief claims: Evangelicals, for example, share affective dispositions with cowboy capitalists when they inhabit their positions with bellicosity, revenge, or extreme entitlement.[42] More recently, Kathryn Lofton points to shared affiliations between so-called freethinking secularists such as Richard Dawkins and conservative evangelicals—affiliations that anchor "freedom" in a zero-sum message of righteousness.[43] Transphobic and sexist norms, in these scenarios, enact violence and prejudice in the name of correction, whether in the name of God ("punitheologies") or in the name of Science.[44]

As Lofton's analysis makes clear, it might be "one world" that is being invoked, but this world is not for everyone. Toward the end of the *West Wing* episode described earlier, for example, dissent from the president's perspective underscores the exclusions of Bartlet's liberalism. "You blew it," a journalist declares, referring to the foreign aid bill that would have passed had the president funded the prayer study. "We cut aid for primary education in northwest Pakistan and Egypt," he points out, "and the kids went to madrasas." In this zero-sum battle, "freedom" aligns with US American national security, imperiled by non-Christian, non-Western forms of education. Within this television world, the journalist's Islamophobia passes unremarked on. Pointing to madrasas as sites of unfreedom, the journalist secures the groundings of his own feelings and ideas in "individual free choice." In contrast, as secularism scholars such as Saba Mahmood explain, "Religious observances and rituals mark what is considered to be the coercive character of religion."[45]

As Siobhan Kelly's chapter in this volume makes clear, an additive, inclusion-based approach to redressing exclusions will not shift logics that position some as free and others as coerced. Political theology, as a project that seeks to disrupt the violence of imperialism, needs resources that resist a binary of free versus not free. This point extends to the affective realm, where I might easily indulge in feelings of freedom as superiority when I gaze backward at the natal community that I left long ago. (As this church's leaders wield successful campaigns around norms of sex, sexuality, and gender, using theology to endorse homophobia as well as what Kelly calls an "eliminationist approach to trans life," it's tempting to give in to ressentiment.[46] How satisfying to lay claim to a progress narrative in contrast to those stuck behind in pews and in bigotry. "You are evil," Nietzsche's lambs declaim, pointing to the birds of prey, "and therefore we are good."[47]) Passionate thinking offers another approach.

Witches, Quakers, and Arts of Attention

We can reclaim "thinking," Stengers writes, as a simultaneous reclaiming of feeling and imagining.[48] Recall that *religare* involves the heeding of binds, a feeling/thinking responsiveness to our ontologies. Stengers notes that our own milieu, however, so often "separates us from the possibility of honoring and feeding what makes us feel and think."[49] Even more than this distancing from our own feeling/thinking, our relations and scenarios—when shaped by testators and those who seek to profit from them—become thinned, more monoculture than multiplicities. And, as Stengers and Didier Debaise explain, "Thinned down worlds are worlds we have good reasons to mistrust and fear."[50]

One pragmatic suggestion for transforming how we feel the call of obligations concerns the activity of "reclamation" itself. Turning to Starhawk and neo-pagan witches, Stengers affirms the use of compromised words, ones that provoke derision from the testators, such as *magic*. Instead of "leaving to the testators' truth the charge of protecting us," she suggests, let's see if we might be able to feel smoke in our nostrils, reactivating our memory and imagination of witch hunting and witchery alike.[51] This suggestion hearkens back to the decolonizing ethos of Eduardo Viveiros de Castro, as Stengers herself points out.[52] The risks for thinking and feeling are high. As Viveiros de Castro writes, "The way is not the same in both directions."[53] This difference models logics that are distinctly other from the bifurcating logics of free versus not free. Such logics are only salient, however, to those who are willing to attend to what Viveiros de Castro calls "our homonymous notions."[54] The word *magic* might *sound* the same to my ears when expressed by another's mouth; if this other is truly other,

Ada S. Jaarsma

in ways that my use of words such as *truly* and *other* will always miss, this word is better assessed as a homonym, not a synonym. The perspectives, expressed by words that sound the same, cannot be made commensurate, despite the wishes of the colonizing "one world." In their chapter in this volume, Basit Kareem Iqbal and Milad Odabaei underscore the necessity for political theology to enact methods that attend to this specificity: "Concepts are not an a priori means of rendering contexts and experiences legible."

To smell burning smoke, as someone enculturated within a testator world that presumes a priori status for its concepts, might mean attuning our bodyminds to affects such as shame, according to Stengers. The triumphalism of testators, after all, requires mistrust to keep at bay "anything that could thicken the situation."[55] We might keep making cuts between what "really" exists a priori but smell smoke in the air as we do so, shamed and humbled.

We might also make our ways into more intense forms of consent, taking this term at its most literal meaning: to *feel with or together*.[56] Thus, writing with Debaise, Stengers muses, "But what of the experience of being looked at by the forest, of being aware of it as an attentive and clear-sighted presence, who knows us and can shame us?"[57] By bringing consent together with trust—which, she reminds us, "is transformative"—Stengers draws out the open-ended creativity of passionate thinking.[58] "Magic," she writes, "is one way to name what all creators know, that what empowers their creation is not theirs."[59] We might "demand," for example, "that theologians think in front of the witches, pagans, or what they call 'fetishists'" rather than seek to destroy these ways of worship.[60]

Given that such conversations require trust, it makes sense to me that Stengers turns to the Quakers. Cultivating attention and slowing down, turning toward trees or whatever unknown might look at us and express another way, she posits, involves "a rather Quaker art" of creating an occasion.[61] Trust, especially trust that a problem might be posed in better ways, "is a question of encounter, always 'here,' never in general."[62] And a culture of trust, required for passionate thinking, depends on robust means for negotiating differences. This is where Stengers, writing with Debaise, invokes the Quaker practice of gathering clearness committees, a way to build trust across conflicts: a "secular communion," in the words of a nontheist Quaker.[63] As someone who joined the Quakers some time ago, I find these references to the Friends compelling. In my own experience, the practice of meeting together in silence, with intermittent testimonies by those who might espouse Christian theology as readily as Buddhism or nontheism, speaks to a non-creedal openness that Connolly and others identify in religious life. Yet I am wary that lifting up the Friends in this way risks replacing bad religion with good (a risk that Debaise and Stengers flag, as well).[64]

Likely because of my lifelong travels within and among religious circles, I find more compelling the pragmatism of Stenger's writings on scientific practices. While we might read the cartoon doctor's prayer as a testator's prayer, as I suggested earlier, we might turn the comedy around and hear it as an "affirmation of the possibility of the coexistence of multiple and contradictory versions."[65] In medieval Europe, the opening phrase of the Vespers for the Dead, "*placebo* / I shall please," was often sung by hired mourners.[66] *Let it be a placebo* connects the Latin "it will please" with centuries-long associations of shame, even deception. Decades ago, researchers devised ways to ascertain that placebo effects are indeed "real," not imagined, establishing placebo studies.[67]

Placebos make manifest power relations; placebo effects express tacit and hard-to-articulate "beliefs" about healing. I endorse practices that we might call "placebo encounters" as instructive for political theology. Recall that what counts as "placebo" differs from one scenario to another. A prayer such as "Let it be a placebo" might awaken us to the specificity of our obligations and ontologies: How am I enacting my persona, as an instructor or researcher or activist, in ways that might elicit placebo effects in others? How, in turn, am I experiencing placebo effects, in my own bodymind, through rituals and relations? These are concrete, nongeneralizable queries, answerable in the first person. They point us to embodied processes and shared social dynamics that need not fall within the bounds of medicine at all. And given the unsteady boundary between *placebo* (what heals) and *nocebo* (what harms), a prayer such as "Let it be a placebo" might express consent for me to touch more directly those affects and activities through which I elicit harm, however unintentional, or through which I am experiencing harm or injury.[68] In secular-religious terms, the sensorial and affective registers of meaning—wonderful as well as horrifying—become just as significant for our thinking/feeling as the conceptual or epistemological. And mundane domains, such as classrooms and workshops, become endowed with meaning-making properties, perhaps for some of us more so than the chairs drawn into a circle at Quaker Meeting.

Ada S. Jaarsma

Notes

1 This description is from Keller and Crockett, "Introduction," 4.

2 Stengers, "Whitehead's Account of the Sixth Day," 45.

3 And not just many but *plus*, or more: Savransky, *Around the Day in Eighty Worlds*, 46.

4 See, e.g., Crawley, *The Lonely Letters*, 27, 29, 132, 147.

5 Mol, *The Body Multiple*, 76.

6 Keller and Crockett, "Introduction," 4.

7 Costa, "The Fragile Supremacy of Reason"; Schuller, "Foreword," 11.

8 Stengers, "The Challenge of Ontological Politics," 95.

9 Savransky and Stengers, "Relearning the Art of Paying Attention," 131.

10 Bill D'Elia, dir., "Guns Not Butter," *The West Wing*, season 4, episode 12, NBC, January 8, 2003.

11 Thiem, "Political Theology," 7.

12 Thatamanil, "How Not to Be a Religion," 59.

13 Sands, "Feminisms and Secularisms," 309.

14 Jaarsma, "Habermas' Kierkegaard and the Nature of the Secular."

15 Asad et al., *Is Critique Secular?*; Warner, "Is Liberalism a Religion?"

16 Stengers, *Cosmopolitics II*, 369–70.

17 Harding, "Representing Fundamentalism," 373–83.

18 Stengers, "The Challenge of Ontological Politics," 100.

19 Stengers, "The Challenge of Ontological Politics," 101.

20 Latour, *On the Modern Cult of the Factish Gods*, 2–7.

21 Stengers, "The Challenge of Ontological Politics," 101.

22 Stengers, *Power and Invention*, 137.

23 Stengers, "*Aude Sapere*," 406–7.

24 Stengers, *The Invention of Modern Science*, 24.

25 Stengers, "The Doctor and the Charlatan," 16.

26 Stengers, "The Doctor and the Charlatan," 12–13.

27 Locher et al., "When a Placebo Is Not a Placebo."

28 Berkhout and Jaarsma, "Trafficking in Cure and Harm"; Friesen and Blease, "Placebo Effects and Racial and Ethnic Health Disparities"; Yetman et al., "What Do Placebo and Nocebo Effects Have to Do with Health Equity?," 78, 823.

29 Enck et al., "Unsolved, Forgotten, and Ignored Features of the Placebo Response in Medicine," 462.

30   Friesen and Dionne, "'It's All in Your Head.'"

31   Friesen, "Mesmer, the Placebo Effect, and the Efficacy Paradox," 438.

32   Locher et al., "When a Placebo Is Not a Placebo."

33   Stengers, "*Aude Sapere*," 411.

34   Wilson, *Gut Feminism*, 154.

35   Mol and Jaarsma, "Empirical Philosophy and Eating in Theory."

36   Savransky, *Around the Day in Eighty Worlds*, 33.

37   Stengers, "The Challenge of Ontological Politics," 86.

38   Nongbri, *Before Religion*. See also Boundas et al., "Encounters with Deleuze," 159.

39   Smith, *The Atheist's Guide to Quaker Process*, 28.

40   Stengers, "Beyond Conversation," 245.

41   Connolly, *A World of Becoming*, 59.

42   Connolly, *Capitalism and Christianity*, 41, 57, 62.

43   Lofton, "Pulpit of Performative Reason," 454.

44   Rubenstein, "A Pantheology of Pandemic," 6; Watson, "Derrida, Stengers, Latour, and Subalternist Cosmopolitics," 87.

45   Mahmood, "Secularism, Hermeneutics, and Empire," 342.

46   Cohn, "An Elite Christian College Has Become the Latest Battleground in America's Culture Wars."

47   Deleuze, *Nietzsche and Philosophy*, 135.

48   Stengers, "*Aude Sapere*," 414.

49   Stengers, "The Challenge of Ontological Politics," 102.

50   Debaise and Stengers, "An Ecology of Trust?," 406.

51   Stengers, "The Challenge of Ontological Politics," 103, 107.

52   Savransky and Stengers, "Relearning the Art of Paying Attention," 145.

53   Viveiros de Castro, *Cannibal Metaphysics*, 115, 119; Viveiros de Castro, "Intensive Filiation and Demonic Alliance," 226.

54   Viveiros de Castro, "The Gift and the Given," 245.

55   Debaise and Stengers, "An Ecology of Trust?," 405–6.

56   Debaise and Stengers, "An Ecology of Trust?," 408.

57   Debaise and Stengers, "An Ecology of Trust?," 411.

58   Stengers, "The Challenge of Ontological Politics," 96.

59   Stengers, "Experimenting with *What Is Philosophy?*," 54.

60   Stengers, "Beyond Conversation," 238.

61 Savransky and Stengers, "Relearning the Art of Paying Attention," 136.

62 Stengers and Despret, *Women Who Make a Fuss*, 67.

63 Smith, *The Atheist's Guide to Quaker Process*, 16.

64 Debaise and Stengers, "An Ecology of Trust?," 412.

65 Despret, *Our Grateful Dead*, 81.

66 Harrington, *The Cure Within*, 62.

67 See Berkhout and Jaarsma, "Trafficking in Cure and Harm."

68 Jaarsma and Berkhout, "Nocebos and the Psychic Life of Biopower."

The Colonial, the Planetary, and the Cosmic

2

For a Historical Grammar of Concepts

THINKING ABOUT POLITICAL THEOLOGY
WITH TALAL ASAD

Basit Kareem Iqbal and Milad Odabaei

Beyond Pluralization

From their inception in interwar Germany to their more recent uptake within critical theory, debates around the term *political theology* have problematized the categorical distinction between theological and political discourses and (by consequence) the capacity of modern historiography to narrate its own arrival. Historically, these conversations about political theology were philosophical reckonings with unprecedented forms of political violence in the wake of secularization. European philosophers and jurists such as Hans Blumenberg and Carl Schmitt, brought together and divided by the experience of fascism in Germany, considered epochal transformations and translations within the *longue durée* of Christianity that had culminated in the modern age and its philosophical and juridical paradigms. As the present volume suggests, contemporary conversations about political theology are much more interdisciplinary in theoretical orientation and global in scope. Scholars now revisit and respond to early debates in the field by reflecting on colonialism, political economy, and biopolitical orders of nationalism and racialization in different contexts from diverse perspectives. Global mobility in the wake of World War II and multiple postcolonial, feminist, Black, and Indigenous interventions have pluralized and transformed the terrain of political theology and topics of consideration. Non-European histories and traditions are increasingly foregrounded in discussions of political theology.

However, these conversations—even when they are conducted in a multidisciplinary and pluralizing mode—largely remain enfolded within the universal purview of "theory." In offering the terms and rationality of debate (however reflexive or critical it may be), it is "theory" that makes it possible to cross global frames of analysis—to cross the borders of languages and worlds. We find a different engagement with political theology in the work of the anthropologist Talal Asad (b. 1932). He shows us that the academic procedure of pluralizing "political theology" occludes not just the conditions of legibility necessary for a term to be put to work as a concept but also the abstraction of concepts from their embedding in forms of life.[1] In this sense, as we explore over the course of this brief essay, Asad cautions us against hastily celebrating or heralding efforts to provincialize or globalize political theology.

Toward Defamiliarization

Political theology is not a term central to Asad's thought. Indeed, he writes critically about some of its common uses. Meanwhile, much contemporary literature in the growing, interdisciplinary field of political theology cites and engages his wide-ranging work. In this essay, we note how his writings problematize referential use of *political theology* across the many languages and grammars of life. Rather than establishing structural analogies or historical filiations between religion and politics, Asad urges attention to shifts in the grammar of concepts and practices across different situations. Rather than exposing a secret religiosity behind secular politics, his inquiries offer an anthropological defamiliarization of these terms.

Asad often frames his writing as "thinking about" a theme or a set of questions. In his practice, "thinking about" is an anthropological methodology developed through a sustained engagement with Michel Foucault and Ludwig Wittgenstein. With Foucault, Asad highlights the historical and epistemological partiality of modern discourses on religion and secularism. He relates triumphant accounts of the secular to the operation of power and to geopolitics. His genealogical inquiries do not simply recover the contested genesis of modern discourses ("anthropology") or concepts ("religion," "political theology"). Rather, they bring into focus the liberal and secular semiotic ideologies and discursive practices that provide the infrastructure for translation and theoretical debates. The aim of such genealogy is not to extend or expand conceptual categories, objectified as different or exceptional ("Islamic," "indigenous," etc.) in relation to prevailing discourses, but to come to terms with theoretical practice as an institutionally partial exercise that reproduces the asymmetries it inhabits.[2] That is, this classic anthropological gesture of defamiliarization cannot rely on a given theoretical apparatus to describe social realities, for the limits of that apparatus are continuous with the historical, geopolitical condition of the world we inhabit. This is why Asad's engagement with canonical thinkers, much like Foucault's own reading practice, is geared not toward

Iqbal and Odabaei

the reproduction or expansion of a theoretical canon but toward particular problematizations. "Thinking about" necessarily involves a confrontation with the historical specificity of language and discourse.

Likewise, with Wittgenstein, Asad notes not only the general limitation of language in understanding the world but also the embeddedness of languages as part of distinct forms of life. What matters to a concept (such as "political theology") is not the contextual determination of its linguistic or cultural meaning, or an a priori reality that precedes language and discursive practice, but the grammar that makes it legible as part of a form of life. Here Asad considers "what it means for a tradition—a poetic transmission of bodies and of language as they are bound up through the various entanglements of the senses—to disclose a form of life."[3] This broadly anthropological approach moves away from a method that makes theory the metahistorical means of comparison and translation across various cases. Concepts are not an a priori means of rendering contexts and experiences legible. Rather, they are already part of the creation of context and experience: Concepts are constitutive of embodied social relations. In similar fashion, for example, the feminist scholars Marilyn Strathern and Judith Butler move away from both naturalist and culturalist conceptualizations of gender and sex to address them as a posteriori indices of social relations.[4] Conceptual apparatuses modulate social dynamics and theoretical debates. As Veena Das has argued, following Wittgenstein, the projection of a concept into a new context brings distinct interests into contact with one another.[5] (In Wittgenstein's terms, "Concepts are the expressions of our interest, and direct our interest."[6]) Conceptual projection might lead to the reification of a concept or might reveal it to be a bad fit and, in turn, attune our interest in a different direction. Asad turns such anthropological attention to the articulation of concepts and practices in a form of life toward exploring the universal thrust of modern projects.

While Asad echoes accounts that emphasize the singular role of Christianity in the production of secular modernity, he breaks with the liberal historiography of the secular age that conceives of it as a "Judeo-Christian" achievement or the political-theological narration of secularism as an event internal to "Western Christianity."[7] Whatever their origins, universalist projects (such as capitalism and secularism, much like colonial Christianity before them) transform conditions of legibility as they transform material conditions of life at a global scale.[8] Therefore, critical attempts to pluralize our conceptual vocabularies by conceiving of multiple secularities, political theologies, or gods will necessarily (if unreflectively) participate in existing binary oppositions and the economy of signification that more generally grounds theoretical discourses.[9] Genealogical and anthropological modes of defamiliarization emerge for Asad, then, not simply as the methods of distinct disciplines but as the means necessary for observing the embodied quality of language and the location of concepts embedded in practices. These means are central to learning; they are antidotes to the elision of difference and of incommensurability in the practice of thinking and interpretation.

The Grammar of Concepts

Asad argues that the secular is "neither continuous with the religious that supposedly preceded it (that is, it is not the latest phase of a sacred origin) nor a simple break from it (that is, it is not the opposite, an essence that excludes the sacred)."[10] The relationship between the religious and the secular cannot be critically narrated in terms of mere continuity or rupture, since the conceptual differentiation of religious and secular domains already begs the question of such a narration. Nor is it enough to demonstrate the contingency of these concepts—namely, all the various and contradictory ways that "the secular" overlaps with "the religious." An inquiry into the secular must show how such contingent formations "relate to changes in the grammar of concepts—that is, how the changes in concepts articulate changes in practices."[11] On the one hand, then, Asad's anthropology of the secular explores the disjuncture between Christian and secular life that emerged in Europe and has come to bear on the emergence of new discursive grammars in the modernizing world. On the other hand, he provincializes that break and problematizes its historical expansion. The postcolonial distribution of geopolitics and the unique historicity claimed by modernity are central to Asad's wariness of the translation of different phenomena in the terms of political theology. In other words, pluralizing "political theologies" does not solve the limitation of "political theology." Pluralizing political theologies still generalizes the Western/European history and historiography of Christian and political life over and against different histories and grammars of religion and politics.

The anthropology of the secular can be read as both a response to and a critical expansion of debates on political theology, insofar as this field conceptualizes social and political phenomena in the terms of "religion." In reflecting on this approach—variously taken up with regard to such so-called political-theological forms as nationalism, Nazism and

Iqbal and Odabaei

communism, and premodern and prenationalist political organization and symbolic action—Asad also directly comments on the key reference of this field. When Carl Schmitt famously writes that "all significant concepts of the modern theory of the state are secularized theological concepts," due both to their "historical development" and their "systematic structure," Asad recommends attending to the "differential results" of secularization rather than to its "corresponding forms." There is no overarching or transhistorical essence to religion or politics, he insists. Instead, the practices that such concepts "facilitate and organize differ according to the historical formations in which they occur."[12]

Yet this does not mean that "history" is simply the ground of emergent, contingent possibilities, or that it is analytically sufficient to demonstrate the instability of meaning across different contexts. Indeed, Asad shows instability (e.g., of secularization's "corresponding forms") to be internal to the operation of modern power. When it comes to "religion," for example, he emphasizes how the "very essence of religion was differently defined" across historical moments even in premodern Europe. Along with concepts of the sacred and myth, religion was constituted as part of the modern episteme that Asad identifies as "the secular" and through the political rationality of "secularism." Consequently, Asad underscores the politics of narrative descriptions of secular modernity and interrupts genetic readings of secularism as the trace of Christianity. Across his oeuvre, whether reading Schmitt, Blumenberg, Marcel Gauchet, Jean-Luc Nancy, Jacques Derrida, Charles Taylor, or others, he avers that what is key is not the structural analogy or historical connection between religious and secular discourses but how each articulates elements of a tradition in distinct practices and embodied concepts.[13]

Two Examples: *Laïcité* and Political Fear

Over recent decades, these methodological concerns have animated Asad's queries into (among others) Christian monasticism and ritual, just war and terrorism, humanitarianism and violence, cruelty and pain, religious criticism and secular critique, Islamic reform and colonial modernity, and statistical reason and state power. In this section, we present two examples to illustrate his approach to political theology.

In our first example, Asad analyzes the French debates over schoolgirls wearing veils to discern the distinct character of French secularism. The veil becomes a site for the French state to rearticulate "conjunction and disjunction"—that is, to congeal the particular effects of universal declarations.[14] Even as French secularism claims to have inherited Christian universalism, what becomes apparent is the sheer "distance" between the two.[15] In what Asad identifies as "the political theology of laïcité," the modern state takes up the theological problem of representing an invisible deity. Just as an icon links "the presence of the divine to the cultivation of the human spirit," so, too, the Republic "realizes itself in its citizens" through deploying the right "signs." This political-theological analogy, however, dissolves the distinction between "spiritual" and "temporal" registers that had been characteristic of premodern Christian discourse. In so doing, it renders invisible the force of secular power. "By attaching the sign of sanctity to the modern concept of the abstract, de-Christianized state, it seeks to make political power exercised in the name of the nation untouchable, even as it is unspeakable."[16]

When the French Republic forbids schoolgirls from wearing headscarves, then, laïcité emerges as "the mode in which the Republic teaches the subjects in its care about what counts as real, and what they themselves really are, in order better to govern them by letting them govern themselves."[17] At stake in this public education is not only the autonomy of individual desire but what counts as knowledge of reality itself. "What seems to emerge from this discourse is not that secularism ensures equality and freedom but that particular versions of 'equality' and 'freedom' ensure laïcité." The invisibility of secular power should not be taken for granted, Asad further insists, because "the limits to the state's transcendence, as well as the excess generated by its passions, both continually undermine the clarity of its theology of signs."[18] This limit and excess together yield the traction necessary for critical anthropological inquiry into French secularism. Although secular power is made invisible through state political theology, an anthropology of the secular can yet approach its effects obliquely.[19] Against liberal theorizations of modern state/social imaginaries, for instance, Asad reminds us that secularism works by "redefin[ing] and transcend[ing] particular and differentiating practices of the self that are articulated through class, gender, and religion."[20] State transcendence is not given but needs to be constantly secured. Hence, the various means by which "representations of 'the secular' and 'the religious' . . . mediate people's identities, help shape their sensibilities, and guarantee their experiences."[21]

Our second example of Asad's thinking about political theology is drawn from his discussion of fear and suspicion around the Egyptian uprising of 2011. Political fears of the military and of Islamists were explicitly voiced in public discourse, but other kinds of fear also proliferated in the time of the revolution. In a video-recorded call for civil disobedience in January 2011, the activist Asma Mahfuz recited the Qur'anic verse 13:11: "God says that He will not change the condition of a people until they change themselves." While some Muslims invoke this verse to justify political quietism, Asad notes that, for Mahfuz, "The verse does not urge a turn to private virtue; [rather] it invites a rearrangement of emotion and attitude in order to engage more effectively in the political world. 'Never fear the government,' she ends. 'Fear only God!'"[22]

Asad's argument is not that the Egyptian revolution was actually religious rather than secular; that this was an instrumentalization of religion for political purposes; or merely that there is a vast hermeneutic range to Islamic politics. Instead, he draws attention anthropologically to the place of fear in political life. Fear is a "complex sensibility," one that "may be seen as the site at once of a fusion of the sensorium with the language and practice that help shape fear as an intention." Rather than advance a psychostructural parallel between a subject's fear of the state and fear of God, Asad observes how "language in use transcends individual intention by carrying and releasing traces"—some of which are theological, others not—"to which other speakers and listeners may connect."[23] What is key to understanding fear in this site is not its supposed structural correspondences or its moral quality but "what one makes of the feeling, how it defines the character of subjection or confrontation."[24] Fear and suspicion are bound up with the ambiguities and limitations of (political) discourse, for understanding which a clear analytic separation of "religious" (theological) fear and "secular" (political) fear will not be adequate. Nor, critically, would their conflation in a political theology of the authoritarian state. That latter approach would not account for the specific distribution and political rearrangement Mahfuz presents.

What is the referent of *political theology* or *God* in each of these examples? Beyond the function of these concepts within their given historical grammar, do they open onto an outside? In the first case, *political theology* works to disarticulate the French state from the Christian universalism that the state claims as foundational to its identity. Yet the term also signals an excess to politics and, more specifically, to the regime of visibility, intentionality, and consent that realizes the French state and the nation within each citizen (whether veiling or not). *Political theology* might be said here to name a process of political subject formation that is neither Christian nor religious in any straightforward way but defines a liberal and secular grammar of the self and the social, private and public. It does so not simply through enforcement of boundaries but by designating what is and is not real.

However, this analysis is not transposable to the second case, because what is at stake there is a different question. (Notably, Asad does not use the term *political theology* in this essay at all.) In this case, Asad writes about a relation to God in a way that provincializes what many (following Louis Althusser and Foucault) have theorized as a form of political subjectivity nested within the modern state apparatus and the biopolitical order of things. That is, his argument does not make fear of the state and fear of God transposable by underscoring the structural similarity in the subject's relation to a transcendent other (whatever it may be). This is not a theological defense against politics in somehow locating God outside history or the state form. Nor does it render the divine a political party that participates (even in the form of an interruption) in the language games that constitute secular politics. Instead, this nonequivalence is central to the performative invocation of God and its effects within Mahfuz's revolutionary politics in confrontation with the state.

The "theological" here should not be theorized simply as what lies beyond politics. Abstractions that approach God as an intractable excess to (or trace within) politics are secular theoretical exercises that render God a party to a social relation, if not a positivity or a social fact.[25] Moreover, such theorizing delimits what is legible as "politics." In this case, such a rendering would yield an anthropological frame in which multiple parties (the authoritarian Egyptian state, Muslims disavowing revolutionary politics, and Mahfuz) all reference God in their divergent political practices. Thinking with Asad instead invites us to reflect on Mahfuz's reference to God (and on political theology more generally) as part of an embodied disposition that upsets the very division between religion and politics, secular and the sacred, the real and the unreal that is attempted both by the Egyptian state and scholarly approaches beholden to these categorical distinctions.

In both of these examples, Asad's approach to political theology notes a structural correspondence (a theology of signs of the secular Republic; fear of God and of the authoritarian state) only to turn to its differential results. In doing so, he invites us to think about how embodied traditions disclose forms of life under shifting conditions of power. Notably, these inquiries do not yield a set of abstract theories about religion and politics; his formulations remain analytically close to the sites about which he is thinking.

Conclusion

In place of drawing historical filiations or structural analogies between religion and politics, Asad emphasizes how knowledge and critique are embedded in inherited and collective forms of life. Alongside his anthropology of the secular, his attention to "tradition" can also be read to decenter the debate of political theology or to reoccupy the space allotted to it in modern discourse. As an analytic term, Asad's approach to *tradition* (drawing from Foucault and Alasdair MacIntyre) foregrounds questions of authority and temporality. It traces the joining of discursivity and materiality in everyday living, in sensory experience and embodied practice. Knowledge and critique thus emerge as collective processes that are central to a living tradition. So, too, do the key themes of political theology (sovereignty, community, justice). But in place of that latter field's reliance on historical narrative and a conceptual binary between religion and the secular, Asad observes that a tradition may be refigured by secular power.[26] The secular is not the outside of tradition; rather, tradition provides an analytical point of entry to understand the work of secularization (thus, "aspects" of Islamic reform, for instance, are both the "precondition" *and* the "consequence" of "secular processes of power").[27] In this sense Asad's anthropology of the secular resonates with Walter Benjamin's attention to continuous and conflicting tensions more than with claims to disenchantment and exposure.[28]

Learning about traditions is thinking about the possibilities of common life and its forms. But it is a thinking strained when "the language we have inherited is so inadequate for our worldly experience," when *neither* "secular reason nor religious faith" can meet the "crisis generated by . . . the basic thrust of modern civilization—our institutions, our desires, our politics, and our entire form of life."[29] Rather than suspiciously asking whether politics is secretly religious or whether it should be properly secular, finally, Asad urges us to think collectively about a politics apart from the sovereign territorial state. "One might think of a plurality of groupings," he writes, "each with its institutional order and purpose but overlapping in membership or territory, and each capable of being continually readjusted through negotiation."[30] The resources for imagining such a politics are not simply given in either "secular" or "religious" domains (a division that already participates in a historical economy of state sovereignty); they do not belong to one side or the other of triumphant histories of secular progress. This gesture toward a different politics draws on given traditions but clearly is not limited by their historical forms.[31]

As one part of the effort to imagine a politics not focused on state sovereignty, for example, Asad has suggested that the Islamic tradition of *amr bi-l-maʿrūf* (enjoining good) could be "re-conceptualized as a collective moral-political project."[32] It could "find its way to collective acts of protest against excessive power."[33] It could "form an orientation of mutual care of the self, based on the principle of friendship (and therefore of responsibility to and between friends), not on the legal principle of citizenship" (or, to be clear, on a theological principle of doctrine).[34] The politics of friendship given here would not be free of power, conflict, or tension, of course, but "this sharing would be the outcome of continuous work between friends or lovers, not an expression of accomplished cultural fact."[35] Elsewhere he describes such a politics as reflecting the "ethos" of a democratic sensibility (in stark contrast to democracy as a political system). This would be a politics defined not by identity or exclusive participation within a sovereign polity that conferred rights and privileges but marked instead by a "desire for mutual care, distress at the infliction of pain and indignity, concern for the truth . . . , the ability to listen."[36] Asad implies that such an ethos is expressed in traditions (Islamic and otherwise) that insist on our essential finitude and our common vulnerability to the work of time.

The practice of such a politics of friendship would rest not on critique or communicative action but on "the capacity to experience another in a way that cannot be renounced."[37] It requires (among other passions) patience, integrity, courage, loyalty, and faithfulness, as shown when Asad reflects on E. M. Forster's famous line, "If I had to choose between betraying my country and betraying my friend, I hope I would have the guts to betray my country."[38] To be clear, this fidelity is less to an abstract principle than to an embodied friendship, which, like all such relationships, requires time to unfold and take hold.[39] Such time limits the scope of this politics, for embodied friendships depend on the coincidence of different times, including "the time of shared practice, the time of embodiment, of individual lives situated within and between traditions and even across generations."[40] Such a politics cannot be forced. Instead, its possibility emerges from the play of "numerous nonhierarchical domains of normativity," necessarily addressing "numerous overlapping bodies and territories" in our common world.[41]

This speculative exploration of an Islamic politics of friendship is not, in strict terms, a positive political theology. Nor, clearly, is it a relinquishing of tradition to the epochal division of the religious from the secular. Rather, it is part of the same broad effort at anthropological defamiliarization: "to try and unthink our language of sovereign power, its secular forms, and its progressive orientation."[42] Asad resituates embodied traditions of discourse and practice as one means of thinking about the difficulty of our present.

Notes

We thank the volume editors, the anonymous reviewers, participants in the Political Theology Reimagined virtual workshop, and Rajbir Singh Judge and Aaron Eldridge for their comments.

1   In this sense, the engagement with political theology we glean from Asad's work echoes his famous problematization of the concept of religion. He insists that "there cannot be a universal, transhistorical definition of religion, not only because its constituent elements and relationships are historically specific, but because that definition is itself the historical product of discursive processes." Commenting on Clifford Geertz's theory of religion as a symbolic system, Asad writes that the "theoretical search for an essence of religion invites us to separate it conceptually from the domain of power": Asad, *Genealogies of Religion*, 29.

2   Asad noted in 1980, "There is, after all, no guarantee that 'indigenous paradigms' [of analysis] will be any better. . . . It is not the origin of given theories, methods, and explanations which will tell us whether they are more suitable"; comment in Fahim and Helmer, "Indigenous Anthropology," 662.

3   Eldridge, "Movement in Repose," 21. This essay traces the "inseparability and mutual irreducibility" of the term *form of life* in the work of Giorgio Agamben, Wittgenstein, and Asad.

4   On reading Strathern and Asad together, see Lebner, "No Such Thing as a Concept." On reading Butler and Asad together, see Mas, "Why Critique?"

5   See Das, *Textures of the Ordinary*, particularly the chapters "Concepts Crisscrossing" and "The Life of Concepts." See also Brandel and Motta, *Living with Concepts*.

6   Wittgenstein, *Philosophical Investigations*, 570.

7   "The genealogy of secularism has to be traced through the concept of the secular—in part to the Renaissance doctrine of humanism, in part to the Enlightenment concept of nature, and in part to Hegel's philosophy of history": Asad, *Formations of the Secular*, 192.

8   Here Asad echoes Hans Blumenberg's methodological critique of secularization theories for confusing historical description for historical explanation. Just because one thing follows another does not mean that the former explains the latter; rather, the opacity of language may disguise "totally heterogeneous contents": Blumenberg, *The Legitimacy of the Modern Age*, 65.

9   See here the productive contrast with Aseel Najib's essay in this volume suggesting political theology as a method.

10   Asad, *Formations of the Secular*, 25.

11   Asad, *Formations of the Secular*, 25.

12   Asad, *Formations of the Secular*, 187–91. In *Political Theology II*, Schmitt clarified that his political theology does not imply a simple "transposition" from a religious context to a political one. Objecting to Blumenberg's reading of his argument, he insists that differences do obtain in history but offers that his political theology is indifferent to secularization, if by that is meant a periodizing foreclosure of political theology in the name of utopian peace (117). There can be no theological (or theoretical) solution to politics (126). Asad would draw attention to the objectified division of theology and politics here as already symptomatic of a certain historical-grammatical formation.

13   On Schmitt, see Asad, "Muhammad Asad Between Religion and Politics," 160, 165; Asad, "Religion, Nation-State, Secularism," 184. On Blumenberg, see Asad, "Religion, Nation-State, Secularism," 194n13; Asad, *Secular Translations*, 15–16. On Gauchet, see Asad, "Response to Gil Anidjar," 399; Asad, *On Suicide Bombing*, 10. On Nancy, see Asad, "Thinking About the Secular Body," 671–72. On Derrida, see Derrida, "'Above All, No Journalists!,'" 70, 87–89. On Taylor, see Asad, *Formations of the Secular*, 2–7; Asad, "Thinking About Religion, Belief, and Politics," 44–50 and *passim*.

14   Asad, "Trying to Understand French Secularism," 517. Focused on the so-called Islamic veil affair and the Stasi commission report, Asad here reflects on laïcité as the articulation of "organizing categories" typical of French political culture (and distinct from those of medieval Christendom). The headscarf worn by Muslim women thus comes to be understood as a "religious sign" violating the "secular personality" of the French Republic.

15   Asad, "Trying to Understand French Secularism," 518.

16   Asad, "Trying to Understand French Secularism," 520.

17   Asad, "Trying to Understand French Secularism," 521.

18   Asad, "Trying to Understand French Secularism," 522.

19   Because the secular is so much a part of modern life, Asad pursues it through its "shadows" (*Formations of the Secular*, 16): as it bears on notions of myth, embodiment, agency, pain, and cruelty, for example. This book then turns to the political doctrine of secularism (entangled in human rights, minoritization, and nationalism) and the historical process of secularization (through transformations of law and ethics in colonial Egypt).

20   Asad, *Formations of the Secular*, 5.

21   Asad, *Formations of the Secular*, 14.

22   Asad, "Fear and the Ruptured State," 292.

23 Asad, "Fear and the Ruptured State," 293.

24 Asad, "Fear and the Ruptured State," 293.

25 On some of the difficulties of thinking anthropologically about God, rather than inscribing God as a social actor "in" anthropology, see Doostdar, "God and Revolution in Iran"; Fernando, "Uncanny Ecologies"; Furani, *Redeeming Anthropology*; Mittermaier, "Beyond the Human Horizon." We remark here on the productive contrast with Carlota McAllister and Valentina Napolitano's reading of "theopolitics," for which see McAllister and Napolitano, "Political Theology/Theopolitics."

26 Moumtaz, "Refiguring Islam."

27 Asad, *Formations of the Secular*, 256.

28 Asad, *Formations of the Secular*, 62–66; Iqbal, "Asad and Benjamin."

29 Asad, "Thinking About Religion Through Wittgenstein," 431.

30 Asad, "Thinking About Tradition, Religion, and Politics in Egypt Today," 211.

31 Iqbal and Asad, "Thinking About Method," 214.

32 Anjum, "Interview with Talal Asad," 58.

33 Asad, "Thinking About Tradition, Religion, and Politics in Egypt Today," 212.

34 Anjum, "Interview with Talal Asad," 59.

35 Anjum, "Interview with Talal Asad," 59.

36 Asad, "Thinking About Religion, Belief, and Politics," 56.

37 Asad, "Thinking About Tradition, Religion, and Politics in Egypt Today," 167.

38 Bardawil, "The Solitary Analyst of Doxas," 162.

39 Such relationships are lived through the "attitudes and affects undergirding collective existence": Hirschkind, "On the Virtues of Holding Your Tongue," 473.

40 Agrama, "Friendship and Time in the Work of Talal Asad," 18.

41 Asad, "Thinking About Tradition, Religion, and Politics in Egypt Today," 212.

42 Iqbal and Asad, "Thinking About Method," 214.

7

The Political as Method

TOWARD A POSTCOLONIAL POLITICAL THEOLOGY OF ISLAM

Aseel Najib

What resources does the field of political theology offer for the study of traditions beyond European Christianity? This chapter focuses on the political. This concept was introduced by Carl Schmitt and elaborated by theorists such as Paul Ricoeur, Alain Badiou, Ernesto Laclau, Chantal Mouffe, Jean-Luc Nancy, and Philippe Lacoue-Labarthe. In France, the political was connected to a leftist Heideggerianism that sought to interrogate society's metaphysical foundation and ontological ground.[1] Here, I focus on the concept of the political advanced by Claude Lefort (1924–2010), a French political philosopher and public intellectual who theorized modern forms of politics. Recently, Lefort's work has grown popular with an English-language audience, and scholars across various fields have made use of his ideas.[2] The chapter first takes stock of developments within the field of political theology and elaborates on the subfield of postcolonial political theology. It then provides an account of the Lefortian concept of the political. Finally, it reflects on the usefulness of this concept for a postcolonial political theology of Islam.

A Postcolonial Political Theology of Islam

Throughout its history, the term *political theology* has designated different fields of intellectual activity, most prominently the field that took form in the early 2000s. As scholars sought to make sense of 9/11 and the events it unleashed—the explicit advancement of a clash-of-civilizations worldview; the wars on Afghanistan, Iraq, and terror; and the discretionary expansion of executive prerogatives—they drew on a particular conception of political theology advanced by Carl Schmitt in the early twentieth century. According to this conception, in early modern Europe, theological concepts, practices, and institutions were transposed onto the political realm.[3] Notwithstanding Schmitt's lamentation of this transposition and his call for its reversal, scholars took up Schmitt's analysis and put it to various ends. Some used it to chart the theological genealogy of political phenomena such as sovereignty, whether for the purposes of recognition or eradication. Others wielded it to interrogate the widespread assumption that secularization, understood as the cleaving of politics from religion, had taken place in early modern Euro-America and that it was only a matter of time before the rest of the world followed suit.

As the wars in Iraq and Afghanistan faded from view and the international order tended toward authoritarian and capitalist multipolarity, the field of political theology underwent two developments. First, it shifted away from the Schmittean homology between politics and theology. This is true of its object of analysis, as well as of its methodological orientation. Although current works of political theology share an interest in the relationship between religion and politics, they do not operate under a single assumption about the nature of this relationship, and to explore it, they employ diverse methods culled from literary studies, history, anthropology, and economic thought. Second, the field expanded to include traditions other than Christianity and geographical regions outside Europe.[4] Current works of political theology cover much ground; today, there are political theologies of Islam, Judaism, Confucianism, and Hinduism, as well as of India, Thailand, Latin America, Israel, and Lebanon. These developments are, of course, interrelated. As political theology expanded to include various traditions and regions, it found it necessary to account for a range of possibilities for the constitution of politics, religion, and their interrelationship.

Yet the proliferation of studies of political theology beyond European Christianity has raised a number of questions. Can this work avoid the presumption that religion and politics exist as independent, interrelated entities, a presumption that is central to European Christianity and its concomitant, secularism? How does this work conceive of the categories of religion and politics, and does it properly account for their genealogies? As Vincent Lloyd notes, "Scholars of religion have pointed to the very specific, very Protestant heritage of their object of study; Marxists and feminists have made analogous observations about politics. Yet, with the political and the theological conjoined, political theology often escapes such worries."[5] More specifically, Gil Anidjar observes that the scope of political theology grew as that of religion contracted. He asks whether political theology is at best ignorant of, and at worst fueled by, the very universalizing and imperializing dimensions of religion.[6] In light of this critique of religion, he declares: "Still, it should have been harder to find political theology—to translate it—everywhere and everywhen."[7] Even if one were to counter that political theologies beyond European Christianity do not reproduce the category of religion but empty it of its traditional content or contest it by reconstructing alternative anthropological or sociological categories, it is hard not to wonder what qualifies this work as political theology. Recalling Timothy Fitzgerald's critique of the field of religious studies, why not consider such work anthropological or sociological in the first place?[8]

The subfield of postcolonial political theology takes such questions as its point of departure. In tracing political theologies outside of European Christianity, it is guided by the notion that this form of Christianity created sites of difference—religion and politics, certainly, but no less important, race, ethnicity, and gender—and disseminated them across the globe through conquest and empire.[9] This subfield traces the itineraries of these sites to grasp their legacies for both colonizer and colonized. Not content with analyzing the entangled transplantation of religion, politics, race, and gender in the colonies, postcolonial political theology insists on bringing this analysis to bear on the metropole. For instance, Lloyd writes about political theologies of the Muslim world, "The critical tools that are sharpened as political theology expands outwards, to address Islam, or to become Islamic, are tools that will inevitably help political theology at its core, as it tells a story about post-Christian Europe that accounts for class, ethnic, and gender difference, differences just as salient at the center as at the periphery."[10] Postcolonial political theology's attention to colony and metropole is mirrored by its consideration of the past and the present. Although this subfield aims to understand, critique, and shape the present, it recognizes that the present is assembled from the precolonial and colonial past. As Lloyd puts it, "Given the inextricability of the colonial legacy from Islamic religious and political formations, Islamic political theology must necessarily probe—and push, and pull—the relationship between three domains: the Islamic tradition, regnant political structures, and the Christian religious ideas that shape postcolonial political structures."[11]

Some disclaimers are in order. While postcolonial political theology is connected through its consideration of colony and metropole, past and present, it need not center on the three domains outlined by Lloyd. A postcolonial political theology of Judaism or Thailand will inevitably proceed differently from a postcolonial political theology of Islam. Put differently, all postcolonial political theology is not Islamic political theology. Neither is all Islamic political theology postcolonial, as the recently published volume *Islamic Political Theology* makes clear. Employing a nebulous conception of Islamic political theology, the volume brings together studies of al-Farabi (d. 950), Ibn al-Tiqtaqa (d. 1309), Muhammad Abdu (d. 1905), and Ruhollah Khomeini (d. 1989).[12]

Let us return to a postcolonial political theology of Islam—specifically, to the contention that one cannot grasp the mappings of colonialism onto the Muslim world or their transmutations in the postcolonial period without understanding the precolonial Islamic tradition. In a recent study of twentieth-century Arabic-language debates about political theology, Joshua Ralston observes, "And yet, these debates, their histories, and the imaginative worlds they produce do not map directly on to the frameworks developed by figures such as Schmitt, [Giorgio] Agamben, or [Hannah] Arendt or the legacy of Augustine, [Hugo] Grotius, or [John] Locke; al-Farabi, al-Mawardi, al-Shafiʿi and Ibn Khaldun are far more formative."[13] Despite the significance and far-reaching influence of these precolonial Islamic thinkers, modern scholarship has not adequately contended with their theories of human difference, social organization, rulership, justice, and violence—theories that we would recognize as political in nature. Nor has it adequately theorized the executive spheres of caliphs and sultans—what we would recognize as the realm of politics. Bearing this in mind, the section that follows discusses a particular theoretical tool for the reconstruction of the precolonial Islamic tradition for the purposes of postcolonial political theology—namely, the concept of the political advanced by Lefort.

The Political

In theorizing the political, Lefort drew on his early influences: Maurice Merleau-Ponty, Karl Marx, and Niccolò Machiavelli. Lefort's apprenticeship with Merleau-Ponty began in secondary school. Merleau-Ponty was a philosopher and public intellectual whose theories of existentialism and phenomenology were influential in postwar France. Professionally and intellectually, Merleau-Ponty had a profound effect on Lefort.[14] He facilitated Lefort's early contributions to *Les Temps Modernes*, a prominent journal that he and Jean-Paul Sartre edited.[15] Merleau-Ponty also bequeathed to Lefort a philosophical approach that refused the notion that one could stand apart from the world as a "sovereign epistemological subject" and instead required her to apprehend her insertion into the "flesh of Being."[16] To grasp politics or history, this approach insists, one must begin from phenomenology and ontology. Lefort remained committed to this approach and to Merleau-Ponty long after his teacher's death in 1961, even posthumously publishing his teacher's writings.

Also as a young man, Lefort became a committed Marxist. He later explained, "I discovered Marx when I was eighteen. Class struggle, the proletariat—I was dazzled, and that lasted for a while."[17] In 1948, he and the philosopher Cornelius Castoriadis founded the revolutionary group Socialisme ou Barbarie. The group published a journal of the same name, which provided a leftist critique of communism and searched for a nonhierarchical socialism that could avoid the pitfalls of bureaucratization and repression. Its members believed that they had found such a socialism in Trotskyism. Yet in 1958, Lefort formally left Socialisme ou Barbarie. He had grown weary of the desire for homogeneity that he saw in the group, in Trotskyism, and, increasingly, in Marxism as an analytic and political project.[18] He later stated about the members of Socialisme ou Barbarie, "When I no longer felt compelled to constantly give them—by giving it to myself—the proof of my loyalty to the project that united us, I admitted to myself that it was pointless to compress history into the confines of a single class and to make that class the agent of society's completion. More to the point: I was surprised I ever desired that impossible completion."[19]

In subsequent years, Lefort turned his attention to the form of power that he believed animated certain regimes, the Soviet Union in particular, a power that sought to uniformize and totalize society. As he relayed, "The big novelty was the capacity of power, through the single-party rule, to be omnipresent. I say single party, but it was much more than a single party, it was a party that had tentacles all over the social body."[20] He identified this power as totalitarianism and its antithesis as democracy and devoted himself to theorizing these regimes, his work forming the seedbed from which French antitotalitarian thought later grew. In this sense, Lefort anticipated and even advanced the shift in the political and intellectual terrain of France that took place in the 1970s. James Ingram puts this succinctly when he writes that Lefort "helped pioneer a generational shift away from the radical, transformative tradition and toward reconciliation with 'normal' liberal-constitutional politics."[21] It is important to bear in mind, however, that Lefort's turn to liberalism was at least partly driven by his critique of the flattening dimensions of Marxism as an intellectual and political project.

After leaving Socialisme ou Barbarie and, as he put it, ceasing to breathe the air of Marxism, Lefort worked for almost fifteen years on a book about Machiavelli's writings, *Le travail de l'oeuvre: Machiavel.*[22] (He in fact had begun this research in 1956, shortly before he left the group.[23]) Lefort saw in Machiavelli's thought an augury of modernity, and his study of *The Prince* and *The Discourses* laid the groundwork for many of his own concepts and theories.[24] While we cannot pursue the full scope of Lefort's reading of Machiavelli here, we can nevertheless highlight one aspect that is central to the development of his notion of the political. This aspect builds on Lefort's critique of Marxism and concerns the centrality of division within society. Lefort delves into Machiavelli's insight that due to the disparate desires of social classes, conflict between them is not only inevitable but also constructive because it protects against the capture and abuse of power. Interpreting *The Discourses*, Lefort writes, "Disunion, we are to understand, has not only preserved the independence of Rome; it has established freedom within it, that is, it has established a regime such that the power can be taken over neither by a man, nor by a faction."[25] Lefort takes this one step further. Conflict is also constructive, he holds, because it binds social classes together. As Oliver Marchart explains, according to Lefort, "It is through conflict that individuals and groups posit themselves within a common world. Through their antagonism—in which the organization, the raison d'être and the goals of society are under debate—that antagonists affirm themselves as members of the same community."[26]

Drawing on these early influences, Lefort developed the notion of the political across numerous writings composed toward the middle of his career. The following analysis focuses in particular on two essays published in the early 1980s, "The Permanence of the Theologico-Political?" and "The Question of Democracy."[27] In these works, the question to which Lefort returns is about the nature of the difference among various forms of society, in particular the theologico-political, the democratic, and the totalitarian. He holds that there must be an element that determines the difference among these societies, one that is not reducible to the empirical facts of politics, such as actors, sites, and institutions.[28] He names this presocial, primordial element "the political" and expresses it in different ways: the mode of the institution of society, the principles that generate society, and the overall schema governing its configuration.[29] If we fail to identify the political, Lefort warns, we are confined to our experience of the world and deprived of the knowledge of its production. Put in practical terms, we are unable to grasp the principle that articulates social division. (Here, Lefort has in mind Marxists who grant analytical primacy to social conflict without pinpointing the origin of the social.) We are also unable to grasp that which produces the markers that order the human experience, such as the economic, the religious, and the juridical. (Here he has in mind political scientists who neglect to ask how politics was differentiated from other spheres of activity in the first place, or social scientists who study one or the other marker without apprehending them as parts of a whole.[30]) This, in turn, leaves us unable to stand apart from political regimes and critically assess them. Critiquing such approaches, Lefort writes, "By ascribing neutrality to the subject, it deprives the subject of the means to grasp an experience generated and ordered by an implicit conception of the relations between human beings and of their relations with the world."[31]

Lefort maintains that it is only by grasping the political that one gains the epistemological clarity and hermeneutic authority to analyze society. This is because it is the political that founds the social, gives it form (*mise en forme*), and shapes its social relations (*mise en sens*). It does so by representing society to itself and staging social relations (*mise en scène*).[32] Lefort assigns a high degree of importance to the staging, representational role of the political. Drawing on the theoretical framework of Merleau-Ponty, he takes for granted that each society locates its origin outside of itself, that it can only "open on to itself by being held in an opening it did not create."[33] In other words, society gains form as well as meaning by being refracted through a symbolic location. To illustrate this point, let us consider Lefort's analysis of the theologico-political, a form of society that he locates in medieval Europe. He writes that in this social form, the kings' immanent and transcendent bodies, modeled after the double nature of Christ as human and divine, served as this symbolic location. By functioning as a link between the sensible and supersensible worlds, a king's body incorporated society: It provided the form of social relations and focalized the symbols and practices through which the link between the human and the divine was staged.[34] Lefort writes of the medieval king: "His power pointed toward an unconditional otherworldly pole, while at the same time he was, in his own person, the guarantor and representative of the unity of the kingdom. The kingdom itself was represented as a body, as a substantial unity, in such a way that the hierarchy of its members, the distinction between ranks and orders appeared to rest on an unconditional basis."[35] Although Lefort mainly focuses on the symbolic, discursive aspects of the power of the medieval king, he acknowledges that these aspects reify "the horizons of real history"—from economic arrangements to military, juridical, demographic, and technological ones.[36] In other words, Lefort acknowledges that by supplying society with its symbolic representation, the political also shapes its institutions and material conditions.

Lefort suggests that grasping the political enables us to see the rise of a novel form of society from the ashes of the medieval theologico-political—namely, modern democracy.[37] To trace the rise of this novel social form, he puts forth an analysis of the relationship between modernity and religion, a term he circumscribes within the premodern experience of Christianity while acknowledging that it can also refer to a transhistorical sensibility apart from the church. For centuries, Lefort writes, the religious and the political performed concomitant functions and formed a matrix capable of withstanding any conflict that arose between their institutionalized bodies. He acknowledges that "a theologico-political formation is, logically and historically, a primary datum."[38] He maintains that this formation was destroyed in the nineteenth century, a "historical fact" to which the rise of a new form of power testifies.[39] The destruction of this theologico-political formation was neither a matter of the abolishment of religion, Lefort writes, nor of the extrication of the religious from the political. Rather, it was a novel arrangement in which an anonymous power came to provide the symbolic dimension of society, thereby stripping religion of its central function and reducing it to the realm of the imagination. Lefort's polemic is directed against various arguments: that religion did not decline in modernity; that religion was transfigured into democracy; and that modern political concepts (the people, the state) are religious at their core. He suggests that the failure of political philosophy to account for the diminishment of religion in modernity is due to its creation in religion's image and its adoption of religion's essential features—namely, the search for a singular truth and the refusal of society's self-immanence.[40]

Lefort holds that the rise of modern democracy was formally inaugurated by the democratic revolution, which disincorporated society from the king's body and dislodged it from its foundation in divine will. This is the context of his famous declaration that modern regimes are characterized by the dissolution of traditional markers of certainty and the evacuation of traditional sources of power.[41] A modern democratic regime keeps the place of power empty in both the straightforward sense that it cannot be claimed by a particular entity, and in the more laden sense that the symbolic origin of society is maintained but not filled. Unmoored from the body of the king, society can no longer be incarnated in a single body or connected to a transcendental other; it remains plural and indeterminate. Lefort insists that, despite the principle of popular sovereignty, the people do not occupy this symbolic place of power due to the ontologization of their division, as well as to the procedural constraints of democratic institutions. He writes:

> I have for a long time concentrated upon this peculiarity of modern democracy: of all the regimes of which we know, it is the only one to have represented power in such a way as to show that power is an empty place and to have thereby maintained a gap between the symbolic and the real. It does so by virtue of a discourse which reveals that power belongs to no one; that those who exercise power do not possess it; that they do not, indeed, embody it; that the exercise of power requires a periodic and repeated contest; that the authority of those vested with power is created and re-created as a result of the manifestation of the will of the people.[42]

According to Lefort, by grasping the political, we can not only trace the rise of democracy from the ashes of the medieval theologico-political but also trace the rise of totalitarianism from the ashes of democracy.[43] He explains that if a democratic society is lulled into the sedimentation of power or tempted by its substantiation, it is en route to "the totalitarian adventure," which subsumes fascism, Nazism, and certain forms of communism.[44] In these instances, social conflicts become so momentous that they cannot be resolved in the political sphere. This may be due to insecurities relating to war or economic hardship, to disputes over shared values and norms, or even to the breakdown of the authority of those who make public decisions. In these cases, Lefort writes, an entity can appear that offers to fill the empty place of power, to retrieve social identity and coherence, and to unify society in a single body.[45] He asserts, "The widespread view to the contrary notwithstanding, totalitarianism does not result from a transformation of the mode of production. . . . Modern totalitarianism arises from a political mutation, from a mutation of a symbolic order, and the change in the status of power is its clearest expression."[46] In a totalitarian regime, power is embodied in an individual or a political party. It ceases to refer to an empty place and instead refers only to itself.[47] Lefort insists that the threat of totalitarianism cannot be abolished; it endures as a latent and ineradicable response to the indeterminacy of modernity. In other words, modern democracies can "mutate" and become totalitarian. To explain this tendency, Lefort turns to Alexis de Tocqueville's analysis that at the heart of modern democracy lies a mild despotism, an equalizing yet anonymizing power that constantly seeks to expand. Yet against Tocqueville, he asserts, "We do of course have good reason to believe that the evolution of democracy has made possible the appearance of a new system of domination—be it fascism, Nazism or what is known as socialism—whose features were previously inconceivable. But we must at least recognize that the formation of that system implies the ruin of democracy."[48]

This passage elucidates the rigid distinction that Lefort draws among the various forms of society, from the theologico-political to the democratic and the totalitarian. He insists that these forms cannot coexist because each is generated by a different modality of the political. A theologico-political society is generated through the double body of the king; a democratic society is generated through the empty place of power; and a totalitarian society is generated through the body of the people as one. While Lefort concedes that vestiges of one form can exist within another—as we have seen, he acknowledges that the theologico-political can continue to haunt the democratic and that the democratic can tend toward the totalitarian—he rejects the notion that these social forms can overlap entirely.

Offerings

What can the Lefortian political, encumbered as it is, offer a postcolonial political theology of Islam? To answer this question, let us turn to an anecdote about the ninth-century Abbasid Caliph al-Maʾmun, who came to power after a brutal war with his brother al-Amin. The war lasted for several years, left no imperial province untouched, and ended with al-Amin's murder at the hands of al-Maʾmun's military commander. Recorded in a historical work, the anecdote relays an encounter between al-Maʾmun and an unnamed man, carefully documenting its details. The encounter occurred on a Tuesday during a weekly debate about law (*fiqh*) open to the public. The caliph sat atop a small carpet, and the man's robes were raised and his sandals were in his hands. He requested the caliph's permission to approach him and demanded, "Tell me about the place in which you sit; did you sit in it through the consensus of the Muslim collectivity (*ijtimaʿ al-umma*) or through force and conquest?" In his response, al-Maʾmun acknowledged the widely held norm that the Muslim community must agree on a candidate for the caliphate. Yet, he explained, "I see that when I leave [the caliphate], the rope of Islam is disturbed, [the Muslims] fight, the military affairs and pilgrimage are interrupted, and the roads shut down. So, I have taken it up out of protection for the Muslims until they can reach a consensus about a man of whom they approve and to whom I can deliver it. When they agree on a man, I will leave it to him."[49] Satisfied with the caliph's explanation, the man left, and al-Maʾmun sent one of his spies to trail him. With the spy at his heels, he headed toward a local mosque, where he relayed the caliph's explanation to a group of similarly dressed men, who subsequently disbanded. When the spy informed al-Maʾmun that his explanation had placated the group—of potential rebels, we can presume—the caliph was relieved.[50]

Applying the method of the Lefortian political enables us to enter the symbolic world of this anecdote, unlade its meanings, and examine its implications for pre- and postcolonial Islamic conceptions of difference, rulership, and law. It shifts our attention away from the analysis of ontic actors (al-Maʾmun, the rebels), sites (the caliphal throne, the mosque), and institutions (the caliphate) and toward their ontological form and function. This shift makes space for new understandings of the past and new questions for the present. If we understand the rebels as having accepted the caliph, renounced revolution, and decided to make do with difference— that is, until the ideal of consensus could be met—what insights can this yield into the recognition of difference without its ontologization? Similarly, if we understand the caliphate as the sphere not of legitimacy or sacred authority but of executive administration, how does this expand our imagination beyond notions of sovereignty and politics as salvation? And if we understand law as the site of the encounter between caliph and rebel—in other words, as the site where the caliph is put on trial by those upholding communal norms—how does this allow us to reimagine the relationship between law and politics and, indeed, the very constitution of law and politics in the first place? Such questions are a fitting starting point for postcolonial political theology, as they get at the meaning and function of Islamic politics rather than its form. They also equip us to better analyze the violence of the colonial moment, when modern political concepts and formations were imposed on those of precolonial Islam, as well as the way in which this violence continues to reverberate into the postcolonial present, thus "dwelling with and giving language to the ghosts on which sovereignty's kingdom has been built," as Alex Dubilet and Vincent W. Lloyd write in the introduction to this volume.

Yet using the method of the Lefortian political need not commit a postcolonial political theology of Islam to its content. After all, Lefort tells a particular story about modern European politics that centers on the emergence of conflict as a constructive force and its eventual domestication in modern democratic institutions. This story does not apply to pre- or postcolonial Islam. (Indeed, whether it applies to modern Europe is open to debate.) In this vein, postcolonial political theology can expand our understanding of our own societies by offering a site from which to critique the Lefortian political. Assessing the political from across the Mediterranean can bring to the surface its dematerialized nature; inattentiveness to violence and empire; and enabling of liberal, conciliatory domestic politics. Both tasks—the reconstruction of precolonial traditions, on the one hand, and the critique of colonial formations and their postcolonial afterlives, on the other—are the essential tasks of postcolonial political theology moving forward.

Notes

1   For more about the history of the political, see Marchart, *Post-Foundational Political Thought*.

2   See, e.g., the repeated references to Lefort in Arato, "Political Theology and Populism"; Ingram, *Radical Cosmopolitics*; Laclau and Mouffe, *Hegemony and Socialist Strategy*; Müller, "'The People Must Be Extracted from Within the People'"; Newman, *Political Theology*.

3   For more information, see Schmitt, *Political Theology*.

4   For an example of this expansive impulse, see Yelle, "Deprovincializing Political Theology."

5   Lloyd, *Race and Political Theology*, 7.

6   This was the product of such studies as Anidjar, "Of Globalatinology"; Asad, *Genealogies of Religion*; Masuzawa, *The Invention of World Religions*.

7   Anidjar, "Christian Interrogation."

8   Fitzgerald, *The Ideology of Religious Studies*.

9   See, e.g., Anidjar, *The Jew, the Arab*; Kwok, *Postcolonial Politics and Theology*; Scott, *Sex and Secularism*; Slabodsky, *Decolonial Judaism*; Westhelle, *After Heresy*.

10 Lloyd, "Political Theology and Islamic Studies Symposium."

11 Lloyd, "Political Theology and Islamic Studies Symposium."

12 Campanini and Di Donato, *Islamic Political Theology*.

13 Ralston, "Political Theology in Arabic," 550.

14 Lefort would later provide an account of this effect: Lefort, *"Sur une colonne absente,"* 45–104.

15 Howard, "Introducing Claude Lefort," 63.

16 I have borrowed the phrase in quotations from Flynn, *The Philosophy of Claude Lefort*, xxiii. For more information about the relationship between Lefort and Merleau-Ponty, see Dodeman, "Claude Lefort, Reader of Merleau-Ponty."

17 Rosavallon, "The Test of the Political," 11.

18 For more about Lefort's decision to leave Socialisme ou Barbarie, see Chollet, "Claude Lefort." For more about Lefort's changing orientation to Marx, see Flynn, "Lefort as Phenomenologist of the Political," 24–25. For the mature articulation of his critique of Marxism, see Lefort and Karten, "Marx."

19 Chollet, "Claude Lefort," 45.

20 Rosanvallon, "The Test of the Political," 12.

21 Ingram, "The Politics of Claude Lefort's Political," 34.

22 Chollet, "Claude Lefort," 45.

23 Bignotto, "Lefort and Machiavelli," 34.

24 Flynn, *The Philosophy of Claude Lefort*, 5.

25 Lefort, *Machiavelli in the Making*, 227–28.

26 Marchart, *Post-Foundational Political Thought*, 96–97.

27 "The Permanence of the Theologico-Political?" was originally published as "Permanence du théologico-politique?" in the journal *Le Temps de la Réflexion* in 1981, and "The Question of Democracy" was originally published as "La question de le démocratie" in an edited volume released in 1983.

28 Lefort, "The Question of Democracy," 11.

29 Lefort, "The Permanence of the Theologico-Political?," 218, 221.

30 Lefort, "The Question of Democracy," 10–12.

31 Lefort, "The Question of Democracy," 11–12.

32 Lefort, "The Permanence of the Theologico-Political?," 230.

33 Lefort, "The Permanence of the Theologico-Political?," 222.

34 Lefort, "The Question of Democracy," 16–19.

35 Lefort, "The Question of Democracy," 17.

36 Lefort, "The Permanence of the Theologico-Political?," 250. In this regard, it is helpful to remember Bernard Flynn's rejoinder that "Lefort's rejection of Marxism is not blanket and total; indeed, he retains aspects of Marxist thought which are usually ignored or marginalized. However, the idea that he rigorously rejects is the notion of alienation and the group of concepts attendant on it, namely, the primacy of productive relationships, the labor theory of value, the distinction between the base and the superstructure, and so forth": Flynn, *The Philosophy of Claude Lefort*, 89.

37 He distinguishes ancient democratic regimes from modern ones by noting that ancient democracy corresponds to the definition developed by Aristotle and Montesquieu, "a regime in which the sovereignty of the people is asserted and in which the government acts in the name of the people." By contrast, modern democracy is an "unprecedented historical adventure whose causes and effects cannot be localized within the sphere that is conventionally defined as that of government": Lefort, "Human Rights and the Welfare States," 24.

38 Lefort, "The Permanence of the Theologico-Political?," 249.

39 Lefort, "The Permanence of the Theologico-Political?," 224.

40 Lefort makes these points through a critique of the work of Jules Michelet: Lefort, "The Permanence of the Theologico-Political?," 236–54.

41 Lefort, "The Question of Democracy," 19.

42 Lefort, "The Permanence of the Theologico-Political?," 224–25.

43 Once again, Lefort distinguishes between modern and ancient totalitarianism. The distinctive feature of modern totalitarianism is that it "combines a radically artificialist ideal with a radically organicist ideal." In other words, modern totalitarianism succeeds in combining the image of the body politic with that of the machine: Lefort, "The Question of Democracy," 14.

44 Lefort, "The Permanence of the Theologico-Political?," 233.

45 It is important, however, not to mistake Lefort's totalitarian entity for the Schmittian sovereign; underlying it is a desire for the people-as-One, and not for the One. Neither is the totalitarian entity identical with the premodern king; while the former refuses the notion of a transcendental place, the latter served as a personified reference to it.

46 Lefort, "The Question of Democracy," 12–13.

47 Lefort, "The Question of Democracy," 13.

48 Lefort, "Human Rights and the Welfare States," 29.

49 Makkī, Samṭ al-nujūm al-ʿawālī fī anbāʾ al-awāʾil wa-al-tawālī, 440.

50 Makkī, Samṭ al-nujūm al-ʿawālī fī anbāʾ al-awāʾil wa-al-tawālī, 440.

8   Postsecular Philosophy and Decolonization as a Political-Theological Struggle

Rafael Vizcaíno

This chapter probes conventional demarcations of the philosophical and the theological from the perspective of epistemic decolonization to contribute to the ongoing rethinking of "political theology." Specifically, it theorizes an aspect of the modern/colonial world system as a political-theological problem by following the work of Enrique Dussel, the most notable Latin American scholar in the fields of philosophy and theology in at least the past fifty years. An early contributor to liberation theology (*teología de la liberación*) and a pioneering leader in the concurrent field of liberation philosophy (*filosofía de la liberación*), all the while being a respected historian, Dussel created a body of work that spans fields, geographies, and world history to dismantle the Eurocentric and colonialist pretensions beneath modern discourses. More specifically, I contend that a careful engagement with it helps us rethink and expand what goes by the name of political theology, in large part because Dussel's work is itself critical of the paradigm of classical political theology à la Carl Schmitt.[1]

Dussel's scholarly production dates back to the early 1960s, with the first English translations of his work beginning to circulate in the 1980s and 1990s.[2] However, it was not until the "decolonial turn" of the first two decades of the twenty-first century, to which he has been a key contributor, that his work saw a major global resurgence.[3] The critique of Eurocentrism that Dussel's variety of liberation philosophy has steadily mounted since its inception now finds itself in the halls of many universities outside Latin America, demanding the study of ignored intellectual traditions and the transformation of the methods and objectives that make up the modern university. In this regard, Dussel's work has been, and remains, at the very forefront of the task to complete the unfinished project of decolonization.[4]

This chapter begins with a brief itinerary of Dussel's work. Subsequently, I question the common dismissal of his work across the philosophy-theology disciplinary divide. Such dismissal has resulted in the reinforcement of a strict division of labor in the reception of Dussel's work that drastically separates the theological from the philosophical in a way that diminishes how such work illuminates the intersections among religion, politics, and secularization in the emergence of modernity/coloniality. It is my argument that when read in the context of *epistemic decolonization*, Dussel's work can be diverted toward overhauling political theology because it aims to go beyond the modern secular-religious complex. It does so by developing what I argue is a postsecular (and, to a certain extent, postreligious) liberation philosophy "of religion"—however paradoxical this might initially sound. The epistemic decolonization of the secular-religious complex that underpins the division of labor between the philosophical and the theological here opens up a rich "zone of indistinction" in which the entanglements among religion, politics, and secularization come together anew.[5] Such a postsecular/postreligious zone of indistinction is the "problem space" of the political-theological par excellence.[6]

Itinerant Biography

As Walter Mignolo has put it, decolonial thinking requires not only a geopolitics but also a "body-politics" of knowledge in which the biographical becomes an index for world-historical processes such as colonization, imperialism, and globalization.[7] Therefore, far from being anecdotal, this brief biographical contextualization allows us to better comprehend the scope and focus of Dussel's work, especially as I seek to illustrate how it contributes to renovating political theology—or, better yet, to renovating the analysis of the *political-theological*, a distinction that I clarify in the very unfolding of this chapter.

Dussel was born in Argentina in 1934 to a family of nineteenth-century German immigrants. His youth consisted of a strong but traditionally Eurocentric education; he was a student of Western philosophy with training in Latin, Greek, German, and French. Dussel departed Argentina as a recent college graduate in the late 1950s to pursue a doctoral degree in philosophy in Spain. This journey would mark the first stage of Dussel's career with an interest to which he would adhere: the questioning of Latin America's place in world history and the history of philosophy.

Symbolically tracing back the origins of the Conquest of the Americas, Dussel thus found himself first in Spain, and soon after in Israel, where he learned Hebrew and lived for two years while undertaking various manual labor jobs. The lived experience of the young Argentine traveler crisscrossing Europe and the Middle East embodied the search for the Western roots of "Latin" America. After completing his doctorate in Spain, Dussel relocated to France to enroll concurrently in a second licentiate (in theology) and a second doctorate (in history, at the Sorbonne). It is during this time that Dussel wrote his first series of scholarly interventions. Characterized by a phenomenological approach with a Heideggerian influence (studying, for instance, the intentional structures of consciousness while attempting to overcome the history of ontology), these books concern the colonial history of the Latin American Catholic Church and the place of Latin America in world history, as well as a comparative outline of Semitic, Hellenic, and Christian humanist traditions.[8]

The second stage of Dussel's trajectory began with his return to Argentina in the late 1960s. The tumultuous social and political atmosphere of this period elicited in Dussel an ethico-political urgency to merge his prior search for a Latin American philosophy with the ongoing popular uprisings in the region. It is in this context that liberation *theology* emerged and, soon after, liberation *philosophy*, both of which are discourses that exemplify in theory what is happening on the ground: a fight against dictatorship thus turns into a radical theoretical rupture. On the one hand, liberation theology reacts against a conservative theology that in practice justifies economic exploitation. On the other hand, liberation philosophy rejects a Eurocentric metaphilosophical narrative that invalidates most of the world's population. Notwithstanding their distinct disciplinary points of departure, both discourses diagnose social domination by way of an ethico-political commitment to a praxis of liberation.

This second period in Dussel's career was perhaps his most substantive and prolific, as it involved the consolidation of both liberatory intellectual movements. On the philosophical front, the characteristic publications of this stage are Dussel's *Método para una filosofía de la liberación* (1974) and the groundbreaking five-volume *Filosofía ética Latinoamericana*, which would be summarized most succinctly in the classic *Filosofía de la liberación* (1977).[9] It is during this period that Dussel abandoned the early Heideggerian influence to formulate the method of liberation philosophy in terms of an ethics of alterity strongly influenced by Emmanuel Levinas (with whom Dussel had studied in France).[10] Liberation philosophy would, from that point forward, idiosyncratically deploy the concepts of "totality" and "exteriority" to understand the relation between a Eurocentric modernity and its colonial "underside."

On the theological front, during these years Dussel deepened the historiographical interest in the Latin American Catholic Church. This was done primarily through the publication of his doctoral dissertation at the Sorbonne, a colossal nine-volume study of the Hispano-American episcopate and its role in evangelizing Amerindians—an inquiry that, as Eduardo Mendieta has put it, was an early influence on liberation theology's critique of European ecclesiology.[11] Correspondingly, Dussel's more systematic contributions to liberation theology during this time can be found in the two-volume *Caminos de liberación latinoamericana*, which (unlike his philosophical writings) soon appeared in English as *History and the Theology of Liberation* and *Ethics and the Theology of Liberation*.[12] As we see in the next section, it is this separation between Dussel's theological and philosophical writings that I am interested in fruitfully probing in the interests of epistemic decolonization.

This stimulating second period came to an end with the political persecution of students and professors in Argentina during the mid- to late 1970s. Thousands of people were killed or disappeared as a result. Dussel himself was placed on a list of professors to be targeted by a cell of right-wing militants. One night, a bomb detonated in his home, destroying part of his library but causing no casualties. This alarming event marked the beginning of the third major stage of Dussel's trajectory: exile. The upside of this persecution, however, would be the spread of liberationist thinking across the American continent.

Settled in Mexico by the late 1970s, Dussel turned to establishing dialogues with philosophers from various traditions all over the world. A response to his newfound exilic condition, this circumstance went on to significantly shift, once again, the conceptual framework of his work. One sees this during the 1980s, when Dussel embarked on an engagement with Marxism that produced three influential volumes on Karl Marx's economic manuscripts, as well as the publication of *Las metáforas teológicas de Marx* (1993), a landmark examination of Marx's use of theological metaphors.[13] The innovative readings of Marx developed in these four volumes ended up strengthening the analysis of material oppression in the tradition of liberation philosophy, an aspect that had been largely underdeveloped in liberation philosophy's earlier, more phenomenological and metaphysical approaches to domination.

By the early 1990s, the most important of these dialogues centered on the second generation of the Frankfurt School of critical theory, mainly the works of Karl-Otto Apel and Jürgen Habermas.[14] This dialogue reframed, for a third and last time, the core structure of Dussel's thought. In particular, the pragmatic and linguistic turns of Apel and Habermas subsumed both

Dussel's Levinasean ethics of the 1970s and Marxist critiques of capitalism of the 1980s to deliver his magnum opus, *Ética de la liberación en la edad de la globalización y de la exclusión* (1998).[15] This is a work of tremendous ambition and theoretical formality that establishes the commitment to a praxis of liberation within the aspirations of normative philosophy, all the while grounded in a non-Eurocentric world history. It is, quite simply, a potent indictment of the contemporary field of ethics, whose obsession with the formalization of norms has permitted the undertheorization of material oppression and the praxis needed to alleviate it, especially in the context of most of the world's population.

Ética de la liberación marks the last signpost of Dussel's trajectory. Coinciding with the rise of postcolonial studies in Latin America (particularly the current that would solidify into the decolonial turn) and new political struggles in the region, such as the Zapatista insurgency in Mexico and the Pink Tide in Latin America, this final stage in Dussel's work can be characterized by concern for epistemic decolonization.[16] Dussel here sought to accomplish in political philosophy what in the 1990s he had accomplished in the field of ethics. This accomplishment is evident in the three massive volumes of *Política de la liberación*, a non-Eurocentric world history, normative philosophy, and creative moment of transformation.[17]

Political Theology as Postsecular Philosophy

The fact that Dussel was a contributor to the emergence of both liberation theology and liberation philosophy has often resulted in a misguided, if not dismissive, reception of his work. On one hand, some theologians argue that his brand of liberation theology is not properly theological due to its strong Marxist influence.[18] They argue, instead, that his theological work is merely Marxist secular philosophy in disguise. On the other hand, some philosophers argue that his brand of liberation philosophy is not philosophical enough due to its close historical and theoretical relationship with liberation theology. They argue that if his philosophical work is not simply a theology in disguise, then it is at least a secular imitation of liberation theology.[19] In my view, the overly disciplinary nature of this reception has self-referentially missed the forest for the trees, as some of the most creative and critical aspects of Dussel's work take place precisely at the intersection of the theological and the philosophical. It is from such liminal space that, I contend, a careful engagement with his work can help us reconsider and broaden what we mean by *political theology*.

Rafael Vizcaíno

To be sure, because of this limited reception, Dussel has frequently found it necessary to intransigently stress the demarcation between the theological and the philosophical to preserve the integrity of his philosophical work, thereby avoiding its "ghettoization" and relegation into the "safe" area of theological studies, as Eduardo Mendieta has put it.[20] This has been a circumstance that has further disallowed a situated engagement at the intersection of these two approaches. In this arrangement, philosophy is geared toward a universal secular community of reason, whereas theology is geared toward a particular religious community of faith.[21] While such an approach might indicate, on first sight, a reification of the classical modern secular-religious divide that is often the object of critique of political-theological analysis, it is my argument that a closer examination proves the situation to be otherwise.

Elsewhere, I have sought to advance an examination concerning the idiosyncratic secularity of liberation philosophy beyond the banal assertion that liberation philosophy simply applies the methods and approaches of liberation theology to the philosophical arena, thus becoming the secular equivalent of its theological partner.[22] The banality of this formulation is that its truth is constricted hermeneutically to the modern distinction between faith and reason. What it misses is how such secularity does not prevent an engagement with its presumed other—that is, "religion." Quite to the contrary, the secularity of liberation philosophy is dialectical: It *requires* constant engagement with such a presumed other.[23] It is in this sense, I have argued, that liberation philosophy ought to be understood more as a *postsecular* philosophy, by which I mean a philosophy interested in probing the very modern secular-religious distinction that constitutes philosophy as a distinct field of inquiry.[24] And it is with this claim that we begin to approach Dussel's concrete contribution to political-theological analysis.

Dussel has come the closest to articulating this postsecular approach in his politico-*philosophical* study of Paul the Apostle.[25] This is an approach that builds on Immanuel Kant's distinction between the tasks of theology and of philosophy at the level of method. However, it does so in a way that overcomes an Enlightened secularism that treats certain texts or topics as entirely outside the scope of philosophical inquiry. So, if for Kant the theologian puts forth an interpretation at the level of ecclesiastical or institutional faith, whereas the philosopher puts forth an interpretation at the level of universal reason, then for Dussel there is basically no text or topic that is intrinsically theological and, consequently, outside the scope of a philosophical interpretation.[26] It is in this sense that one of the outstanding tasks of contemporary political philosophy (due to its inherited Enlightened secularism) is the analysis of texts or topics that traditionally have been taken to be the sole domain of theology. The *postsecularity* of Dussel's politico-philosophical approach overcomes Enlightened secularism without stepping into the ecclesiastical domain of theology.

It should be clear that this politico-philosophical approach is not "philosophical theology," either, which applies philosophical methods to elucidate theological frameworks. What is perhaps most appealing for the purposes of this chapter, however, is that, in Dussel's view, this politico-philosophical approach is likewise *not* to be confused with political theology proper. Given what we have said until now, it should not surprise us that Dussel's characterization of political theology is a "sectarian" one, following Vincent Lloyd's typology.[27] That is, for Dussel, the *theological* connotation in the category of political theology is strictly meant to represent an institutional context that delimits its validity for a particular community, as he puts it, of "believers." In other words, political theology would be the kind of inquiry that is restricted to an exploration of the political field within a strictly theological framework—whether or not it makes use of philosophical theology as a particular method. It is in this way that Dussel understands, for instance, the political thought of Thomas Hobbes, who develops a Christian theory of sovereignty and the state, rather than a universal one.[28] It is this insight that, in my view, constitutes Dussel's primary contribution to the ongoing rethinking of political-theological analysis.

Curiously, if we take the much narrower classical paradigm of political theology à la Schmitt to represent the unmasking of the theological inheritance in seemingly *nonreligious* political concepts and institutions, then we clearly see a palpable resonance of this approach in Dussel's politico-philosophical attempts to analyze topics that traditionally have been taken to be the sole domain of theology. It should not be a surprise, therefore, to find that in his analysis of Paul the Apostle, Dussel explicitly aligns himself with the general impetus of Schmitt's approach while nonetheless taking issue with the designation of this work as political *theology*. The fundamental problem with this politico-philosophical work being conceived as political *theology* is that it risks imprecision and ambiguity, as it is work not limited to the hermeneutics of a particular religious community of faith.

In short, Dussel's principal methodological contribution to the ongoing rethinking of political theology is to add theoretical precision by explicitly locating the "secular grounds" of such an inquiry.[29] For Dussel, what goes methodologically by the name "political theology" might be better understood as a politico-*philosophical* interpretation of critical categories that may very well have originated in a "religious" context but are now engaged outside the scope of a particular theological hermeneutic. This is why I argue that Dussel's type of liberation philosophy, insofar as it probes conventional demarcations of the philosophical and the theological (bound by the secular-religious complex), ought to be understood as a specifically *postsecular philosophy*. In other words, this postsecular impetus is liberation philosophy's contribution to the ongoing rethinking of "political theology."[30]

Decolonization as a Political-Theological Struggle

As a short illustration, I outline how Dussel's postsecular politico-philosophical approach reinterprets the colonial encounter that begets the modern world.[31] For this encounter is neither an exclusively theological procedure (a battle between Christians and non-Christians) nor an exclusively political conundrum (the emergence of the nation-state). But it is perhaps the exemplary modern political-theological problem. Accordingly, we arrive at the realization that all decolonial struggle takes place within the fold of the political-theological.

In the writings of key figures from the colonial encounter, such as Christopher Columbus, Hernán Cortés, and Juan Ginés de Sepúlveda, Dussel finds a shared effort to *rationalize* the moral superiority of colonization while simultaneously hiding its *irrational*, practical side.[32] Given how such claims to moral superiority substantiate the rhetoric of modernity as progress and development that culminates in the Enlightenment, such initial ambiguous and spurious effort to rationalize the irrational alludes to a fundamentally *mythical* structure of justification. This is to say that the processes that concoct modernity as the universally superior carrier of emancipatory rationality and civilization are spurious from the very start. Modernity does not overcome myth. It is, rather, an irrationally violent praxis of colonization. Thus, one of the fundamental premises of decolonial thinkers is that modernity is always already *modernity/coloniality*.[33]

This conceptual reinterpretation of modernity significantly alters the meaning of what is taken to be a "modern experience." The Renaissance humanists and the Enlightenment critics are now anticipated by the Spanish conquistador, whose practical deployment of the sword already enacts what is characteristically modern: begin an internal fracture that will slowly dismantle the theological order of medieval

Christendom. A "quasi-divine" sense of superiority of the conquistador's *ego conquiro* over his conquered victims usurped the role once prescribed for God in the theological order of medieval Christendom.[34] Consequently, the irrational violence of colonization at the root of modernity is what initiates a process of *disenchantment*, temporally and conceptually preceding the theoretical disenchantment associated with the logocentrism of the Renaissance and the Enlightenment.[35] The *ego conquiro* is thus the prior foundation of an ensuing *ego cogito*.[36]

From this perspective, certain conventional narratives of *secularization* (e.g., as religious *decline*) so often found at the center of theories of modernity now appear as ideological processes that obscure the irrationally violent process of colonization. In other words, a decolonial interpretation of modernity as modernity/coloniality undermines the classical secularization thesis that conceives of modernity as the discontinuous secularizing rupture out of medieval Christendom. On this point, we see the closest conceptual similarities with the political-theological line of investigation initiated by Schmitt, but in a way that accounts for the colonial context ignored by the German jurist in his *Political Theology*.[37] As Gil Anidjar has so powerfully put it, far from representing a clean rupture from Western Christendom, secular modernity only manages to be a kind of *reincarnation* of Western Christendom itself, as commonly exemplified in the ideological project of *secularism*.[38] Thus, decolonial theorists such as Nelson Maldonado-Torres argue that "secularism opposed itself to religion" not "because religion was imperial, but simply because it was just not imperial enough."[39]

That a substantial component of modern secularization is a colonialist and imperialist myth implies that the domain of decolonial struggle is the political-theological—a conclusion that I take to be more thorough than Schmitt's dictum that "all significant concepts of the modern theory of the state are secularized theological concepts."[40] It is in this vein that Dussel goes on to make one of his most revolutionary arguments: that *secularism*, being an *antireligious* modality of secularization, "is the false name of fetishism."[41] Elsewhere, I have argued that this formulation offers the elements to restructure political philosophy as a decolonial and postsecular philosophy "of religion."[42] This is a philosophy "of religion," however, where "religion" is broadly taken to stand for the entire field of the political-theological. Its object of analysis is therefore the forms of "fetishism" at the core of modernity that attempt to rationalize the irrational and conceal its violent colonial underside.

The task of the decolonial and postsecular philosopher is, therefore, to diagnose the fetishisms or "false names"—which is to say, the *false gods*—of the modern/colonial world that demand worship (e.g., "development" and "progress"). Presupposing a certain "anti-fetishist" atheism as its very "first thesis," this approach nevertheless preserves something like a *real* religious moment, which is what comes after the negation of the fetish: the affirmation that "Divinity is Other than any system."[43] Divinity as transcendental alterity prevents the anti-fetishist moment from self-absolutizing into yet a new fetish. It is, indeed, from this perspective that Dussel goes on to subsume the well-known Marxist critique of fetishism, but in a way that avoids the vulgarly secularist (i.e., antireligious) atheism of traditional Marxism. With a newfound capacious understanding of "religion"—which is to say, religion as the political-theological field of modernity/coloniality—the Marxist pronouncement that the critique of religion is "the premise of all criticism" takes on a new level of complexity.[44]

Conclusion

In this chapter, I have followed the work of Enrique Dussel to theorize some aspects of the modern/colonial world as a political-theological problem. In particular, I have argued that pushing Dussel's work to its ultimate conclusions helps us rethink and expand what goes by the name "political theology." This is a reconceptualization that moves from conceiving of political theology as a method to envisioning it instead as an object of study. In this instance, the political-theological refers to the always ongoing porous transitional relation between Old World Christendom and New World secular modernity. In short, "political theology" here captures the unmasking of the philosophical discourse of modernity as a colonial myth in its own right. It is for this reason that I have also argued that the task of epistemic decolonization, to which Dussel's work is deeply committed, must be regarded a political-theological struggle.[45]

But if one is hard pressed to clarify the question of method, then I would say that Dussel's work permits us to open a "zone of indistinction" where the entanglements of religion, politics, and secularization can be examined anew. This is an opening made possible by the very task of decolonization, which puts into question the traditional epistemic divisions built on the coloniality of knowledge.[46] But the method in question cannot be said to be *theological* without risking imprecision and ambiguity. Rather, it would be something like a *postsecular philosophy* that is invested in probing the modern/colonial secular-religious complex through the lens of epistemic decolonization. I have argued that this theoretical and methodological precision is the crux of Dussel's contribution to the ongoing rethinking of political theology. Such *postsecular* impetus would be, in this sense, the other side of the *post-theological* impulse that, for Mark Lewis Taylor, sets our praxis within the terrain of the *political-theological*.[47]

Future work from this perspective ought to creatively bring together the best that "theological" and "philosophical" approaches have thus far produced to expose the colonial myths of a pretendedly secular modernity.[48] However, such work must also avoid replicating the limitations of each of these two paradigms. On this point, escaping the conceptual Eurocentrism that has plagued both approaches continues to be the task where the promise of epistemic decolonization is most fertile and urgently needed. Doing so would make it possible to stage the political-theological conversation beyond the coordinates of the Christendom–New World nexus, thereby opening new decolonizing horizons—as Aimé Césaire and Sylvia Wynter would put it—"to the measure of the world."[49]

Notes

1   Schmitt, *Political Theology.*

2   See Dussel, *The Invention of the Americas*; Dussel, *Philosophy of Liberation*; Dussel, *The Underside of Modernity.*

3   Maldonado-Torres, "Enrique Dussel's Liberation Thought in the Decolonial Turn."

4   This formulation concerning the unfinished project of decolonization has been primarily advanced by M. Jacqui Alexander and Nelson Maldonado-Torres: see Alexander, *Pedagogies of Crossing*, 271; Maldonado-Torres, "Enrique Dussel's Liberation Thought in the Decolonial Turn," 3. It contrasts with the Eurocentric priority of completing the unfinished project of modernity, as advanced by someone like Jürgen Habermas: see Habermas, *The Philosophical Discourse of Modernity.* The question of modernity nonetheless remains of central importance within the decolonial turn, as seen in the nomenclatures of "modernity/coloniality" and the "modern/colonial" world system.

5   The notion of the "zone of indistinction" has been central to the revival of political-theological analysis as advanced through the work of Giorgio Agamben: see Agamben, *Homo Sacer.*

6   Kotsko, "Genealogy and Political Theology." On the notion of the "problem-space," see Scott, *Conscripts of Modernity.*

7   Mignolo, *The Darker Side of Western Modernity*, xxi–xxii.

8   See, e.g., Dussel, *El humanismo semita*.

9   Dussel, *Filosofía de la liberación*; Dussel, *Filosofía ética latinoamericana V*; Dussel, *Método para una filosofía de la liberación*; Dussel, *Philosophy of Liberation*.

10 See Levinas, *Totality and Infinity*.

11 Mendieta, "Editor's Introduction," xv.

12 Dussel, *Caminos de liberación latinoamericana*; Dussel, *Caminos de liberación latinoamericana II*. Though more needs to be said on this topic, it is a clear testament to the global influence of liberation theology that Dussel's theological writings would end up being made available in English much before his philosophical writings.

13 Dussel, *Las metáforas teológicas de Marx*. For an assessment of this intervention in light of contemporary debates in political theology and the postsecular turn across the humanities and social sciences, see my "Postsecular Philosophy as Metaphoric Theology: On Dussel's Reading of Marx."

14 A compilation of some of these dialogues can be found in Apel and Dussel, *Ética del discurso y ética de la liberación*.

15 Dussel, *Ética de la liberación en la edad de la globalización y de la exclusión*; Dussel, *Ethics of Liberation in the Age of Globalization and Exclusion*.

16 See Dussel, *Filosofías del sur*.

17 See Dussel, *Política de la liberación*; Dussel, *Política de la liberación, Volumen II*; Dussel, *Política de la liberación, Volumen III*; Dussel, *Politics of Liberation*. See also the summarized outline of the last two volumes, in Dussel, *20 tesis de política*; Dussel, *Twenty Theses on Politics*.

18 I thank Hanna Reichel for bringing this point to my attention from a theological perspective.

19 See, e.g., Schutte, *Cultural Identity and Social Liberation in Latin American Thought*, 174.

20 Mendieta, "Editor's Introduction," xiii.

21 Dussel, *Pablo de Tarso en la filosofía política actual y otros ensayos*, 11–14.

22 Vizcaíno, "Which Secular Grounds?"

23 For an outline of the dialectical theory of secularization, see Goldstein, "The Dialectical Pattern of Secularization."

24 Vizcaíno, "Which Secular Grounds?" This argument is systematically developed in my forthcoming book "Decolonizing the Postsecular."

25 Dussel, *Pablo de Tarso en la filosofía política actual y otros ensayos*.

26 Dussel, *Pablo de Tarso en la filosofía política actual y otros ensayos*, 10; Kant, *Religion and Rational Theology*, 263.

27 According to Lloyd, political theology can be characterized as three distinct modalities of inquiry: the narrow theoretical approach of Schmitt (a sociology of juristic concepts), a more general approach that seeks to understand the interactions between "religion and politics," and the sectarian approach that sees it as an applied branch of religious theology: see Lloyd, *Race and Political Theology*.

28 Dussel, *Pablo de Tarso en la filosofía política actual y otros ensayos*, 13.

29 Vizcaíno, "Which Secular Grounds?"

30 Mark Lewis Taylor has followed Dussel (among other theorists) to analyze the "political theorization of the theological." For Taylor, the theological is always already a fold within the political, a moment which he marks with the notion of the *post-theological*. My argument in this chapter can thus be seen as the mirror *postsecular* counterpart to Taylor's argument that the post-theological moment sets our praxis within the terrain of the *political-theological*: see Taylor, *The Theological and the Political*.

31 This argument is fully developed in my forthcoming book "Decolonizing the Postsecular."

32 Dussel, *The Invention of the Americas*.

33 See, e.g., Escobar, "Worlds and Knowledges Otherwise."

34 Dussel, *The Invention of the Americas*, 42.

35 This argument has been subsequently developed by Maldonado-Torres, "AAR Centennial Roundtable," 652.

36 Dussel, "Anti-Cartesian Meditations."

37 Of course, Schmitt does end up paying some attention to the colonial context at a later point in his career: see Schmitt, *The Nomos of the Earth in the International Law of the Jus Publicum Europaeum*. Contemporary scholarship has sought to establish a conversation between this late work of Schmitt and postcolonial and decolonial paradigms: see Blanco and del Valle, "Reorienting Schmitt's *Nomos*."

38 Anidjar, "Secularism."

39 Maldonado-Torres, "Secularism and Religion in the Modern/Colonial World-System," 367.

40 Schmitt, *Political Theology*, 36.

41 Dussel, *The Underside of Modernity*, 12.

42 Vizcaíno, "Liberation Philosophy, Anti-Fetishism, and Decolonization"; Vizcaíno, "Which Secular Grounds?"

43 Dussel, *Filosofía ética latinoamericana V*, 59; Dussel, *The Underside of Modernity*, 11. It is the deployment of this language that leads critics of liberation philosophy to see here nothing more than a liberation theology in disguise.

One might remember, for instance, that for Gustavo Gutiérrez, the fundamental function of theology is the liberation from forms of "fetishism and idolatry": Gutiérrez, *A Theology of Liberation*, 10.

44 Marx and Engels, *Marx and Engels Collected Works, Volume 3*, 175. I expand this formulation in my forthcoming article "Postsecular Philosophy as Metaphoric Theology." A similar reinterpretation of the Marxist critique of commodity fetishism takes place in the work of Michel Henry: see Inese Radzins's contribution to this volume.

45 For an analogous argument following Sylvia Wynter's work, see David Kline's contribution to this volume.

46 Javier Aguirre has recently argued that this decolonial agenda ought to put into question the very distinction between theology and religious studies as one dependent on belief and its lack thereof: see Aguirre, "Religiones, teologías y colonialidad."

47 Taylor, *The Theological and the Political*. See also note 30 in this chapter. From the theological side that Taylor's work explores, Dussel has most recently called for the development of a "transtheology" that can overcome the Eurocentric tendencies of Latin Christendom: see Dussel, "Epistemic Decolonization of Theology."

48 For helpful starting points, see the contributions in this volume by Basit Iqbal and Milad Odabaei, as well as that of Aseel Najib.

49 Césaire, *Discourse on Colonialism*, 73. For an assessment of Wynter's postsecular contributions, see my "Sylvia Wynter's New Science of the Word and the Autopoetics of the Flesh."

9 Political Theology and Religious Criticism

B. R. AMBEDKAR
AND HIS CONTEMPORARIES

Prathama Banerjee

Born into the untouchable Mahar caste of western India, B. R. Ambedkar (1891–1956) was, like his contemporaries W. E. B. Du Bois and Frantz Fanon, a thinker of equality. Celebrated as an anti-caste radical, he was a constitutionalist, political philosopher, social theorist, and anticolonial agitator with an oblique relationship to the reigning political ideologies of his time—namely, liberalism, nationalism, and communism. Ambedkar was also a historian and philosopher of religion, an aspect of his thought that remains relatively underdiscussed even though it has immense significance today for rethinking the provenance of the political as both concept and practice.

At about the same time as Carl Schmitt in Germany, Ambedkar in India proposed a version of what we today recognize as the political theology thesis—namely, that political society has a religious constitution at its heart. There were, of course, significant differences between Schmitt and Ambedkar. First, while Schmitt understood modern political concepts such as state, sovereignty, and law as secularized versions of older theological concepts, Ambedkar disavowed the religion-secularism binary and defined religion *qua* religion as body politic: "I take Religion to mean the propounding of an ideal scheme of divine governance the aim and object of which is to make the social order in which men live a moral order."[1] Second, unlike Schmitt, who worked with a unitary genealogy of Judeo-Christian concepts, Ambedkar thought in terms of multiple religions in critical encounter. Third, to Ambedkar the very definition of *religion* was subject to dissensus, because different traditions differently imagined religion as concept and phenomenon. And finally, to Ambedkar religion was not the source but the limit of the state imagined as a universal political form akin to a sovereign and law-giving God, an argument that he developed in conversation with contemporary Marxism.[2] Ambedkar was engaging caste as a form of social sovereignty that could effectively supersede the sovereign "decision" of the state and its laws.

In this essay, I revisit this early to mid-twentieth-century moment when Ambedkar and his contemporaries fashioned a political language via religious criticism. However, given that the very concept of religion was at stake in this debate, the preemptive use of the term *theology* might not be quite appropriate here. After all, while discussing why Christian missionary discourse failed to produce a movement for justice among untouchables in India, Ambedkar said that the theological mode of argumentation practiced by Christianity could not adequately respond to the philosophical mode of argumentation practiced by Hinduism.[3] The emancipatory desires of "broken" peoples stumbled against the Christian theological doctrine of original sin and the fall of man, which not only denigrated the species being of humans to produce the ideal of a perfect God but also, as Alex Dubilet shows in his discussion of the Gnostic challenge to Augustinian Christianity, rendered the human and the subaltern responsible for her own worldly suffering. Equally, Ambedkar argued, the theologically enjoined moral imperatives of Christian love and charity failed to respond to Brahmanical philosophies of existence that held phenomenal inequalities to be real and inevitable, even if contingent and ephemeral.[4]

Is Religious Criticism Possible?

To Ambedkar it was a "logical and historical" mistake to assume that all religions of the world, shorn of rituals, superstitions, and corruptions, are good at heart. This was not only Mahatma Gandhi's position at the time— that all religions were worthy of equal respect and must coexist peaceably— but also lay at the heart of the secular constitutional principle that, once paired down to their "essential" practices/doctrines, all religions must be juridically approached as valid, established, and an unquestionable matter of worship or faith. To Ambedkar, the right to compare and critique religions and, by implication, convert from one religion to another was an inalienable democratic right.

Ambedkar argued that religion was constitutive of human ontology because it dealt with elemental questions of birth, death, disease, and destitution. Modernity and secularism could not render religion redundant. To say this, however, was not to say that religion was universal and eternal, for religion has been repeatedly redefined through historical revolutions.[5] Of this, the most important revolution was the invention of god. The earliest forms of religion did not have god as a constituent element. Concerned as it was with death, disease, hunger, scarcity, and so on—questions of bare life and basic needs that later came to be glossed as matters of economy, ecology, and biology—religion simply propitiated the forces of nature. These were neither good nor evil but were simply there to be placated, harnessed, and battled. The idea of god emerged later from extrareligious sources, such as deference to heroes and warriors and speculations about the first cause of the world. The concept of god was thus incidental to religion.

Like god, morality was absent from early religions, Ambedkar said. Norms for human interaction did exist, as they must in all collectivities, but the moral domain was separate from the religious domain.[6] Earlier, the relationship between gods and humans was of kinship. "Political society" consisted of descendants of a common progenitor god. Consequently, competing polities had competing gods. Later, when gods became transcendent figures lying outside political society, they came to watch over the individual's conscience rather than the civic life of the community. Lineage loyalties came to be replaced by moral injunctions, and morality and religiosity came to coincide. Once god became the addressee of the individual rather than the community, it became possible to imagine a polity composed of people worshiping different gods, just as it became possible to imagine a Universal God overseeing a humanity divided into nations. A change of religion, in other words, no longer implied a change in political belonging.[7] Ambedkar was arguing against the conceptual twinning of religion and state, as had happened in Europe in the sixteenth century and in India in the nineteenth century, making necessary the general espousal of the modern doctrine of secularism.

To Ambedkar, religion evolved historically through critique and disputation. Religion(s) must be "put on trial," he insisted.[8] Clearly, Ambedkar disavowed the then hegemonic Abrahamic definition of religion as faith—that is, the precritical acceptance of a sanctified doctrine or tradition. In his *Riddles of Hinduism*, Ambedkar demonstrated how the history of Hinduism was in fact a heterogeneous history of religio-philosophical disputations based on logical and evidentiary criteria—not only about the nature of gods and anti-gods, reality and causality, epistemology and ontology, but also about competing frameworks of sociosexual norms, legal immunities, political exceptions, and spiritual expiations.[9] The result was not a secular questioning of religion by Reason but the possibility of what became unthinkable in modernity—namely, *religious criticism as a legitimate form of public ethics, constitutive of the condition of living with multiple religions and with contending imaginations of what religion was in the first place.*[10] If today religious disputes are either brushed under the carpet in the name of multicultural "tolerance" or rendered into civilizational or geopolitical disputes *among* "world religions," Ambedkar argued that in earlier times there was no religious life that was not constitutively argumentative. In fact, religious disputes were often "internal"—Sunni jurists versus Sufi mystics, Shaivas versus Vaishnavas (Siva worshippers versus Visnu worshippers), Mahayana versus Hinayana, and so on—implying that religious change was driven by relentless epistemological and ontological dissensus. Religion, in other words, was never a given or stable category.

Ambedkar was not alone in trying to mobilize a longer history of religious criticism in India. Rahul Sankrityayan (1883–1963)—Buddhist mendicant turned Marxist peasant league activist—discussed the fourth-century philosopher Asanga's text on Buddhist meditative practices, the *Yogacharbhumi*, which emphasized the virtues of "discernment and discursiveness" (*vichar* and *vitarka*) and invoked *hetuvidya* (the science of reasoned disputation).[11] The text discussed the epistemological role of argumentation, example, conceptuality, inference, experience, tradition, and correct disposition and went on to disprove sixteen religious theses—of god, soul, eternity, past-future continuity, identity through time, and, in the same paradigm, belief in the superiority, purity, and divine origin of Brahmans, as well as in cleansing ritual actions, such as bathing in the Ganga and animal sacrifice.[12] In 1918, Benimadhab Barua (1888–1948), one of the earliest historians of Buddhism in India, who was born in Chittagong, a region where many outcaste hill communities were practicing Buddhists even in the twentieth century, translated the Pali phrase *pannanvaya saddha* as "reasoned faith," cutting through the modern-day faith-reason binary, to characterize religious thought in early India.[13]

Historians have shown that in precolonial India, religious criticism was part of not just scholastic but also public life. As Vincent Eltschinger and others argue, at stake in early Indian Buddhist arguments against Brahmanical dharma was that it was impossible to "prove" one's claims of *jati* (birth) beyond reasonable doubt, human sexuality being a private and ultimately unregulated practice. Caste could not thus be sustained as a "real" or "universal" classificatory category. It was simply a convention with no ontological or epistemological basis.[14] Historians have also detailed the Mughal Emperor Akbar's *ibadatkhana* (the place of worship), which hosted the well-known sixteenth-century debate between the orthodox Abdul Qadir Badayuni and the politico Abu'l-Fazl ibn Mubarak about the relative merits of *aql* (reason) and *taqlid* (tradition).[15] Johannes Bronkhorst cites twelfth-century inscriptions in Karnataka listing Jain Digambaras, who participated in public debates, including Vimalachandra, who apparently challenged Saivas, Pasupatas, Bauddhas, Kapalikas, and Kapilas in a letter affixed to the gate of the palace of the king (an uncanny precursor to Martin Luther's legendary act in sixteenth-century Europe).[16] And so on. In non-modern times, thus, religious criticism did have a public and political life, and religion was not imagined as a domain beyond philosophical and epistemological inquiry. Ambedkar and his contemporaries drew from this older legacy.

Itinerancy, Conversion, and Community

Modern political theory, informed by the work of Max Weber and Karl Marx, understands religion to be a matter of either individual or social identity, with the term *identity* standing in for the unitary quality of both the personal and the collective being of the religious subject. Sociology and anthropology imagine religion to be the condition of possibility of society, with conceptions of symbol and structure, debt and sacrifice, ritual and the sacred—to invoke Émile Durkheim, Marcel Mauss, Claude Lévi-Strauss, René Girard, and Victor Turner in one breath—denoting not just mechanisms of being together of a people but also the boundary (call it national, social, communal or totemic) that makes possible the unity of religious being, transgressed only at the individual's peril.[17] In other words, across disciplines, modern thought tends to frame the study of religion within the binaries of identity and community, individual and society, and, by implication, private and public, convening the religion question as implicitly a friend-enemy or, at least, a kin-stranger or insider-outsider question in quasi-Schmittian terms.

Ambedkar strongly criticized the way in which religion had come to be caught up in the individual versus social, public versus private dichotomies of modern European thought.[18] He refuted the secularist definition of religion as individual/personal faith. Equally, he disputed the sociological reduction of religion to society. In fact, Ambedkar questioned the very self-evidence of society as a category. He said that India was not a society unto itself even if it was a nation, for Hinduism as a religion prohibited sociability among different castes and religions and, in resonance with Dubilet's invocation of civil war as a permanent state of being of the polity, implied that what we call Indian/Hindu society in fact subsists in a state of perpetual "general antagonism," barely tamed by the sovereign nation-state. (In fact, in Hindu cosmology, gods, anti-gods, and various "alien beings"

Prathama Banerjee

are imagined as constantly engaged in wars of ascendance, making the idea of general antagonism, in Dubilet's sense, in and by itself an organizing principle of religion.)

In his "The Annihilation of Caste," thus, Ambedkar was not only saying that religious criticism had to be constitutive of social criticism, and vice versa; he was also implying that rigorous religious criticism required a study of how different religions differently posited the horizon of sociality across diverse human collectives—a question that nationalists found redundant, because to them, religion, like caste, race, and nationality, was inherited by birth and therefore part of one's inalienable social destiny.[19] Ambedkar was also arguing, in contradistinction to Durkheimian sociology of religion, which posited society as a coherent field of immanent being, that religion had to do with relationships *among* and *across* different formations of the social. In other words, in Ambedkar's oeuvre, religion was not so much about identity or society as about the question of alternative models of sociality across difference.

As is inevitable in any multireligious context, the religion question in India was centrally animated by the issue of the relationship *among* people practicing different religions and the orientation that could be considered proper to such an interface. This was Gandhi's concern, too, as Ajay Skaria has shown in his description of Gandhi's attempt to fashion a "non-sovereign" public interface in terms of the social dispositions of dharma and *seva* (duty and service) toward the other.[20] Ambedkar, however, differed with Gandhi in that for him there was no universal or residual principle of religion that inhered in all religions of the world and made possible a foundational continuity—and amity—across them. To Ambedkar, religions were often incommensurable in their epistemological and existential approaches and, by implication, in their models of sociality. So unlike Islam or Buddhism, Hinduism prohibited interactions among individuals of different religions in the exact same way that it prohibited interactions among coreligionists of different castes—by way of proscriptions on commensality, marriage, sexuality, and touch—disabling traffic among religions and, consequently, disabling religious comparison and critique.[21]

This was why Ambedkar was so invested in the question of conversion as a defining, rather than a derivative, practice of religion.[22] The modern Indian debate around religious conversion has become a debate about competing national identities. This unhappy history may prevent us from fully sensing the place of conversion in Ambedkar's thought. To Ambedkar, potential conversion was the enabling ground for rigorous religious and social criticism. Here Ambedkar seems to intuit the longer history of religious encounters in precolonial India. Richard Eaton's work on the conversion of outcaste peasants to Islam in medieval frontier Bengal via the sanctification of agriculture and pious industry; Stephen Dale's work on the early growth of Islam in Kerala through the dynamics of travel, trade, and oceanic cosmopolitanism; and Sanal Mohan's work on the conversion of agrestic slaves to Christianity, opening up for them the possibility of conjugal family life in early colonial south India, show how earlier forms of transreligious traffic were not just about identity formation but also about the possibility of new livelihoods and new socialities.[23] Ambedkar also discussed the precolonial encounters of Islam, Jainism, Buddhism, and Brahmanism as defining events of Indian history.[24]

It seems to me, therefore, that what Ambedkar called religious conversion was in fact a mode of questing across religions, animated by a critical theory of exit, itinerancy, and arrival. Ambedkar's contemporary, the philologist, textual exegete, and historian of religion Dharmanand Kosambi (1876–1947), lived a life of spiritual and philosophical itinerancy, traveling across India, Nepal, and Sri Lanka and, later, Massachusetts and Leningrad. His autobiography details his spiritual quest, marked by penury and hardship on the road, in the course of which he became an ordained Buddhist monk. Yet at the end of his life he went on to perform the Jain ritual of *santhara* (voluntary death by fasting).[25] Rahul Sankrityayan, for his part passed, from being a Vedantic nondualist, a Vaishnav monk, an Arya Samaj reformer committed to the Vedas, and an ordained Buddhist mendicant to, finally, a Marxist. He even changed his name from Kedar to Ramodar to Rahula with each move, in an apparent simulation of "conversion." As his autobiographical fragments, tellingly titled "Waiting for Visa," bear witness, Ambedkar had already performed being a Muslim and a Parsi in early life to escape being marked out as an untouchable, performing a shadow theater of conversion, as it were.[26] In his *Ghumakkar Shastra* (The Science of Wandering), Sankrityayan argued that caste practices prevented Indians from undertaking true epistemological, spiritual, and social itinerancy. He listed religious thinkers of India in terms of their relative propensity to travel—with Buddha and Mahavira at the top because they refused to stay bound by local experience.[27] Clearly, Ambedkar and his contemporaries fashioned a form of critical religious cosmopolitanism after the precolonial itinerancy of Buddhist *parivajrakas* and Jain *yatis*, for whom "going forth" was enjoined calling.

Ambedkar structured his book *Buddha and His Dhamma* following Siddhartha's itinerary first as a seeker and then as the Buddha traveling across countries to convert kings, ministers, merchants, Brahmans, women, courtesans, untouchables, and outlaws—literally counting the miles that Buddha traveled on foot and recording his engagement with multiple schools of thought in debate and dialogue. Itinerancy across religions was therefore critical to Ambedkar and his contemporaries such that, for them, religious criticism, historical analytics, and political theory appeared to emerge out of ceaseless philosophical, spiritual, and territorial meanderings. Avishek Ray rightly points out that this longer precolonial and colonial history of wandering, contested as it was, anticipates by many years the recent theoretical turn toward "nomadology" taken by philosophers such as Gilles Deleuze, Félix Guattari, and Rosi Braidotti.[28]

If epistemological and spiritual itinerancy across multiple religions was the basis of religious comparison and critique, with conversion always already present as a horizon of possibility, then religion was *not* culture. In his manifesto, "The Annihilation of Caste," Ambedkar spoke about the limits of the modern concept of culture. He said that living in physical proximity and a "similarity of habits and customs, beliefs and thoughts" did not "constitute men into society."[29] Shared culture did not guarantee sociality. Ambedkar invoked the metaphor of mobility to describe his ideal of a sociability proper to democracy, using the organicist metaphor of "endosmosis" to describe processes of "communication," as opposed to "community," that successfully breached sociological boundaries and allowed both peoples and ideas to travel across hierarchies.[30]

Ambedkar's disavowal of the politics of community formation comes through when he explains why the Jewish question in Christian Europe was incommensurable to the untouchable question in Hindu India. He did say that the condition of the Depressed Classes in India was analogous to that of the Jews in ancient Egypt, and that untouchables, too, must embark on an exodus in search of the Promised Land.[31] Yet he also said that, while Jews self-consciously chose to be a separate community, with a separate doctrinal basis and a distinct way of life, untouchables were forced against their will to segregate themselves, even though they were culturally no different from other Indians.[32]

This was perhaps why Ambedkar was more invested in the idea of a critical *self* than in the anthropological idea of a community or culture. According to him, while Hinduism privileged social being over individual being and, worse still, *culturalized* social being as so many caste communities with distinct names, dress, and visual insignia, modern European thought privileged individual being over social being and thereby emptied civic life of religious content.[33] Ambedkar wanted to recover the ancient notion of *dhamma*, an alternative form of religious being that helped individuate those who were denied their individuality in the name of social being. *Dhamma* did not individuate through a secularization of society and a privatization of faith. Instead, by disavowing god, soul, prophet, identity, and scripture, *dhamma* left the individual with no recourse beyond her own "thrownness" in the world, to use a Heideggerian turn of phrase, which was precisely why individuals came to exist in an unmediated relationship to the other. In other words, the rise of the human subject was not predicated on the fall of god but on an originary absence of god from religion in its most archaic sense. According to Ambedkar, this form of individuation, without the guarantee of anything beyond the exigency and contingency of life itself, enabled critical and compassionate sociability better than did either cultural unity or individual civility. (Note the resonance here between Ambedkar's rendering of mortal life as being without guarantee of either god or state and the French philosopher Michel Henry's rendering of living as such, in Inese Radzin's telling in this volume, as a challenge to the objectifying tendencies of modern secular knowledge.)

Kosambi, too, discussed ethical individuation through Buddhist disciplines. He discussed *kayagata smriti* (body awareness), which led not only to the overcoming of lust, hatred, and sloth but also to an experience of the body as a structure of bones indistinguishable from other bodies, producing a phenomenological realization of equality.[34] Then followed *maitri* (friendship in ever expanding circles), with love for self, humans, quadrupeds, reptiles, and so on, eventually expanding into love for all possible species. Then came *prithivi mandal* (the Earth circle), requiring focus on the materiality of the world and surrounding objects, such as land, water, and light.[35] To Kosambi, religious being required the individual to both partake in and separate from the world in a way that led the individual to simultaneously attend to and deconstruct the apparent givenness of body, sense, language, experience, community, and society. In *Buddha and His Dhamma*, Ambedkar, too, spoke of meditative practice and cognitive purity as essential states enjoined by Buddhism, producing a form of individuation that enabled one to subject habit, custom, culture, and tradition to critical questioning. This ethical individual was the subject of principles and not of rules, Ambedkar famously said. Rules, as in religious injunctions, produced compliant and obedient bodies; principles, such as those of *dhamma* and

Prathama Banerjee

shunya (void, flux), produced autonomous agency, hermeneutic freedom, and critical activism.[36]

The critical religiosity of Ambedkar and Kosambi was very different from the devotional religiosity of Gandhi. Gandhi explicitly disavowed intellectualism and valorized manual labor to identify with common people.[37] Ambedkar, by contrast, was deeply invested in instilling an epistemological and critical stance in the untouchable, not only through modern education but also through the pursuit of a proper religiosity based on a proper understanding of the nature of reality and the place of the solitary human self in it.

State, Society, and the Existent

Religious criticism articulated with the question of the state in complex ways. Writing at the end of a long career of critical engagement with law and constitution, Ambedkar was rethinking the historical limits of the state as a form of government of people. That Brahmanism ruled through religious injunctions had recently become clear to him when his attempt as the first law minister of independent India to reform the gender and inheritance norms of the Hindu joint family came up against the putative sovereignty of the Hindu social, which seemed capable of pushing back against the sovereign law of the state. At the end of his life, therefore, Ambedkar came to argue that religion was in fact an alternative to the state because only religion helped reconstitute human society by reopening the foundational question of the nature of the world and the place of humans in it. Communists say that the state will wither away once perfect equality is achieved, but what could conceivably replace the state in this utopian future? It would be religion—not any religion, but an immanent religion such as Buddhism, which refuted the sovereignty of god and thereby the sovereignty of the state—he said.[38] To Ambedkar, thus, a rethought religion helped delimit the state's provenance rather than strengthen it.

To Ambedkar, untouchability was the *archaic* principle/command of (a-)sociality that founded the human order in South Asia. Anupama Rao captures this archaism of untouchability—a phenomenon simultaneously modern and primordial—by making an analytical distinction between juridico-political violence (the violence that ensues when Dalits assert their rights in the modern public sphere) and "ritual-archaic" violence (the violence that reenacts a kind of primordial sacrifice in the modern present). She invokes the legend of the sacrifice of the Mahars at the foundation of forts and villages in medieval western India as the instituting moment of South Asian society, analogous to the archaic moment of the social or sexual contract, for by tradition it was by this foundational sacrifice that the untouchable Mahars came to assume their liminal and outcaste aspect—given the function of guarding the village boundary, an untouchable figure was ironically charged with ensuring the integrity of caste society within the village.[39]

Ambedkar was invested in deconstructing the phenomenal archaism of untouchability but beyond the exceptional moment of the sacrifice—that is, beyond the moment of the ritual suspension of the everyday. He located the genesis of caste in an originary "decision" of Brahman enclosure—akin in conceptual status to primitive accumulation in Marxism—by which Brahmans withdrew from sociality, even accidental touch, and instituted the birth (and inheritance by birth) as the structuring principle of human order. This decision, Ambedkar argued, cannot be demonstrated as a historical or chronological event but appears and reappears in ceaseless reiterations through history, in each act of outcasting, in each act of rendering untouchable.[40] In his comparative essay "Buddha or Karl Marx," Ambedkar saw this as the shared ground between a recovered Buddhism and a revised Marxism—this recognition that inheritance by birth and withdrawal from universal sociality were the archaic principle of inequality. The difference between Buddhism and Marxism, however, was that Marxism, despite the promise of the withering away of the state, came to depend on the state as the primary agent of change (hence, "dictatorship of the proletariat"), while Buddhism spoke of self-government through ethical individuation and compassionate critique.[41] Marxism forgot its own insight that at its most archaic, inequality was about a-sociality and not about distinctions in state forms. Kosambi also imagined Buddhism as a corrective to the adversarial friend-enemy dialectic of European, including Marxist, political theory based on an a priori assumption of the sovereignty of the state.[42]

Incidentally, this imagination of immanent government before and beyond the state was also shared by several Muslim thinkers in India at this time, including Syed Abul A'la Maududi (1903–79), who critiqued state sovereignty in the name of the exclusive sovereignty of God and the consequent lack of sovereignty of man. Maududi supported Gandhi's criticism of the legislative and representational apparatus of the modern state.[43] As Faisal Devji shows, an-*archy* in this tradition of religious thought—anarchy being a derivative concept of the arche, connected but not entirely reducible to anarchism as a modern political ideology—comes through not so

Prathama Banerjee

much as a condition of chaos or disorder, the primordial "state of nature" of Hobbesian imagination, as an immanent self-governing mode of being, of both animals and humans, that conceptually precedes and supersedes the law of the state.[44]

In this conversation about the pre- and as post-state potentialities of religious being, the archaic comes through only partially as having to do with the instituting moment of state and society. More important in this debate was, in fact, the question of the *pre-social*—that is, the prior question of the constitution and distribution of bodies indistinguishable by surface markers (as in race) or biology (as in gender or species). Having to do with the very constitution of reality, causality, materiality, mortality, and corporeality, this register staged the archaic as phenomenologically prior to the institution of the state and in excess of historical and philosophical anthropology—most famously embodied in the work of European anthropologists such as Pierre Clastres—that approaches the administration of human life via a study of so-called primordial or pre-state communities.[45] It is in this presocial register that Ambedkar and his contemporaries rethought the archaic aspects of religion as entangled with metaphysical, phenomenological, and existential questions of life and mortality, finitude, and destitution—in continuity, we shall say today, with nonhumans.

Sankrityayan said that Buddhism made it easy for him to espouse Marxism because they shared ontological frameworks. (See Martin Shuster's chapter in this volume for another vision of continuity between Marxism and religion.) In his "Buddhist Dialectics," Sankrityayan argued that, like Marxism, Buddhism saw the material world as flux and helped us realize that no entity, of either the inner or the outer world, was stable, eternal, foundational. This principle of noneternity refuted both "realism" (the belief that the world was composed of immutable atoms) and "foundationalism" (the belief that the world was grounded in an ultimate reality such as the *atman* [the universal self] or elements such as fire, water, space, time, or what we today call "nature"). Buddhists believed that the world was composed not of objects (*vastus*) but events (*dharmas*) and so refuted existing theories of causality that held that causes produced effects by way of a temporal succession of necessary and sufficient, primary and secondary causes. Instead, Buddhists proposed *hetusamagrivada*, the principle that each event is the result of multiple causes coming together *uniquely*—hence, *pratitya samutpada* (dependent origination or reciprocal effect) rather than causality per se.[46] Citing the classical epistemologist Dharmakirti's theory of the "conjuncture," wherein the absence of even the most minor cause undid the possibility of an event, Sankrityayan argued that Buddhism, apparently like Marxism in his telling, disavowed historical determinism, for in Buddhist causal theories the effect is "other than" and not simply a mutation of the cause. The effect is a new, unprecedented, and underdetermined event. The Buddhist imagination of conjuncture thus made possible qualitative and revolutionary change in the world.[47]

Unsurprisingly, Marxist historians of religion in India were uncomfortable with this retreat from the history of state and society into the register of the phenomenal. Y. Balaramamoorty, for example, said that Buddhism's position that reality was "real only within limits"—that is, with no self-existence unto itself—was difficult to marry with Marxism's investment in the objective laws of history.[48] And the Marxist litterateur Ram Vilas Sharma (1912–2000) criticized Buddhism for its causal paradigm, wherein cause and effect were seen as discrete entities unrelated to each other: In Buddhism, "All existence is particular, the universal is a mental construct."[49] Buddhist particularism disabled dialectical synthesis and the subsumption of particulars under the unfolding of universal history. In Buddhism, even the human is no more than a mere "convention"—a coming together of "name and form" (*nama-rupa*)—Sharma exclaimed with incredulity.[50] But in the hands of Ambedkar and his contemporaries, it was precisely this "conventionality" of the human existent, otherwise without any enduring identity in time, that allowed total political critique and the possibility of radical equality, irrespective of the form of the state and the stage of history.

The early twentieth-century thinking together of religion and Marxism thus brought forth the question of the *archaic* in unexpected ways—in the twin connotation of the arche as having to do with the origin of the human order and as having to do with the phenomenology of the existent. As we know, classically the arche—simultaneously indexing the act of "giving grounds" to existence and the "founding" of a city or a world—relates to both ontology and politics.[51] This archaic is imagined as before and beyond history. It recurs through time in unexpected figures of "repetition and difference," to use a Deleuzian turn of phrase, and provides sense and narrative to historical unfolding. In and of itself, however, the archaic remains historically in-demonstrable. (The imagination of the point in ancient Greek philosophy as a position without magnitude or the critical place of *shunya* in Ambedkar's philosophy as the nature of being that is "neither something nor nothing" are examples of this form of historical in-demonstrability.) The importance of this question of the archaic, a question prior to the his-

Prathama Banerjee

torical question of the evolution of state and society, becomes clear only when we pay attention to modern recensions, in the work of Ambedkar and his contemporaries, of what would otherwise appear to be esoteric precolonial and nonmodern debates around metaphysical and phenomenological ideas, such as *shunya, atman, pratitya samutpada, kala* (time), and in the same breath, sociological and political concepts such as *jati* (birth), dharma (duty), *rashtra* (state), and *samaj* (society, association). These debates are usually passed over by modern scholarship because they do not combine well with modern-day historical sensibility and with the universal categories of political thought. But if read with attention, these debates actually appear to circumscribe the concept of the state and foreground the phenomenal nature of the human's mortal and finite being in the world.

Conclusion

The early to mid-twentieth-century debate that I have described here opened onto the question of state and society, on one hand, and a set of meta-questions regarding the nature of reality, materiality, causality, veracity, and temporality, on the other. Based on religious itinerancy and the comparison/criticism of multiple religions, and with Marxism as prime interlocutor, this debate concerned not only the question of just sociability but also the pre-social, archaic question of human creaturely, species condition on Earth. The basic problematic here was as follows: Religions were incommensurable in the way that they variously posited the horizon of sociability, and they variously posited the horizon of sociability because they variously imagined the nature of the world and the place of humans in it. Put otherwise, religious criticism entailed phenomenological, ontological, and existential criticism and, by implication, social criticism. It seems to me, therefore, that this paradigm of religious criticism as the ground of political critique, while operating in the neighborhood of political theology, cannot quite be reduced to it, precisely because it circumscribed the question of the state and questioned its apparent centrality to the human condition. Perhaps putting the Schmittian tradition in conversation with the Ambedkarite tradition of thinking religion may help us deemphasize the state question and mitigate the conservative, if not violent, potentials that political theology acquired in its historical association with National Socialism. Equally, perhaps, by reopening the concept of humanness and worldliness to reconsideration, this encounter might help political theology take a planetary and more-than-human turn.

Notes

This research was supported by a Senior Research Fellowship at the International Centre of Advanced Studies: Metamorphosis of the Political.

1   Ambedkar, *Philosophy of Hinduism*, 6.

2   I use "God" when referring to Abrahamic religions and "god" for other religions.

3   Ambedkar, "The Condition of the Convert," 449.

4   Ambedkar, "The Condition of the Convert," 439–40, 472. For an account of contending philosophies of existence, see the battle between Buddhists and Christians over karma as a philosophy of being unfolding across time and grace as the promise of immediate godly intervention in time, as described in Mahadev, *Karma and Grace*.

5   Ambedkar, *Philosophy of Hinduism*, 21.

6   Ambedkar, *Philosophy of Hinduism*, 10–11.

7   Ambedkar, *Philosophy of Hinduism*, 12–18.

8   Ambedkar, *Philosophy of Hinduism*, 6, 8.

9   Ambedkar, *Riddles of Hinduism*.

10 It bears mentioning here that early colonial intellectuals such as Rammohan Roy, Dayanand Saraswati, and Vidyasagar also engaged in traditional forms of religious disputation while debating contemporary social practices such as widow burning, celibate widowhood, sectarianism, and ritualism, mobilizing precolonial texts in Sanskrit, Persian, and the regional languages.

11 Kragh, *The Foundation for Yoga Practitioners*, 75; Sankrityayan, *Bauddh Darshan*.

12 Sankrityayan, *Bauddh Darshan*, 114–25.

13 Barua, *Prolegomena to a History of Buddhist Philosophy*, 24.

14 Eltschinger, *Caste and Buddhist Philosophy*; Verma, "Epistemological Foundations of Caste Identities."

15 Rezavi, "Religious Disputations and Imperial Ideology."

16 Bronkhorst, "Modes of Debate and Refutation of Adversaries in Classical and Medieval India."

17 See Durkheim, *Elementary Forms of Religious Life*; Girard, *Violence and the Sacred*; Mauss, *The Gift*; Mauss and Hubert, *Sacrifice*; Turner, *The Ritual Process*.

18 Ambedkar, *Buddha and His Dhamma*, 316.

19 Ambedkar, "The Annihilation of Caste," 50–51.

20 Skaria, *Unconditional Equality*.

21 Skaria, *Unconditional Equality*, 143.

22 Ambedkar, *Conversion as Emancipation*, 15.

23 Ambedkar, *Conversion as Emancipation*, 11, 16–17; Claerhout and De Roover, "The Question of Conversion in India"; Dale, "Trade, Conversion and the Growth of the Islamic Community of Kerala, South India"'; Eaton, *The Rise of Islam and the Bengal Frontier, 1204–1760*; Mohan, *Modernity of Slavery*.

24 Ambedkar, "The Decline and Fall of Buddhism," 236.

25 Kosambi, *Nivedan (a Narrative)*.

26 Ambedkar, "Waiting for Visa."

27 Sankrityayan, *Ghumakkar Shastra*, 2, 5, 7.

28 Ray, "Of Nomadology."

29 Ambedkar, "The Annihilation of Caste," 50–51.

30 Ambedkar, "The Annihilation of Caste," 57. See also Choudhury, "Ambedkar's Words"; Fuchs, "Reaching Out."

31 Ambedkar, "Moses and His Significance."

32 Ambedkar, *Untouchables or The Children of India's Ghetto*, 3–4. For a discussion of Ambedkar's thought in conversation of Marx's "The Jewish Question," see Skaria, "Ambedkar, Marx and the Buddhist Question."

33 Ambedkar, *India and the Prerequisites of Communism*, 99, 101.

34 Kosambi, *Buddha, Dharma, Sangha*, 264–66.

35 Kosambi, *Buddha, Dharma, Sangha*, 270.

36 Ambedkar, "The Annihilation of Caste," 44–45.

37 Gandhi, *Discourses on the Gita*.

38 Ambedkar, "Buddha or Karl Marx," 460.

39 Rao, *The Caste Question*, 259.

40 Ambedkar, "Castes in India."

41 Ambedkar, "Buddha or Karl Marx."

42 Kosambi, "Civilisation and Non-Violence," 356.

43 Devji, "A Minority of One"; Devji and Kazmi, *Islam After Liberalism*.

44 For a discussion of Catherine Malabou's retrieval of the forgotten philosophy and the concept of anarchy, see Swain et al., *Unchaining Solidarity*, 240–50.

45 Clastres, *Society Against the State*.

46 Sankrityayan, "Buddhist Dialectics."

47 Sankrityayan, "Buddhist Dialectics," 5–7.

48 Balaramamoorty, "Buddhist Philosophy," 38.

49 Sharma, "Some Aspects of the Teachings of the Buddha," 61.

50 Sharma, "Some Aspects of the Teachings of the Buddha," 62.

51 Kerényi, "Prolegomena," 6–7.

Prathama Banerjee

10

Cosmic Delegitimation

TOWARD A POLITICAL THEOLOGY
OF SCALE

Kirill Chepurin

> This thinking carries with it I know not what secret hor-
> ror; one finds oneself wandering in an immensity devoid of
> any limit or center, and therefore of any determinate place.
>
> Johannes Kepler, *De stella nova* (1606), on Giordano Bruno's
> vision of the decentered infinite universe

Political theology grapples with the structures of legitimation and delegitimation that cut across the secular-religious binary. The
production of this binary has been constitutive for Western modernity and
its modes of self-legitimation, and political theology has comprehensively
interrogated the so-called secular modern world—with one key lacuna. It
has rarely engaged with the foundational event of modernity that is the
Galilean-Copernican revolution or the transition from the hierarchized
cosmos to the decentered infinite universe.[1]

Given the post-Heideggerian suspicion toward modern science still
prevalent across critical theory, this lacuna is perhaps unsurprising, and
political theology is not alone in this. In a well-known gesture, Martin Heidegger decried the first pictures of the Earth taken from space, in which
our planet appeared, in Günther Anders's turn of phrase, as an "alien celestial body [*fremdes Gestirn*]."[2] For Heidegger, these pictures exemplified
the horror of the technological objectification of the planet instead of a
poetic terrestrial dwelling. In the guise of an environmentalist dogma represented most influentially by Bruno Latour in his call to land back on the
Earth and his dismissal of the "view from Sirius," and of the extraterrestrial
as merely an escape fantasy, the assertion of the Earth over and against the
cosmic expanse continues to live on—even in Latour's proclaimed non-
anthropocentrism.[3] Thereby, Latour's thinking reiterates the (in the strict
sense of the term) reactionary trajectory of modern geocentric thinking
represented by philosophers such as G. W. F. Hegel and Edmund Husserl,

who reacted against heliocentrism and against the affirmation of a decentered universe by insisting on the Earth as the only planet that matters philosophically and existentially. As Anders put it in 1970, "Emotionally, to this day we stand against Galileo."[4] To "stand against" Galileo is to stand on the side of his accusers—of a geocentric apparatus that unites "religious" (the church) and "secular" authority (modern philosophy).

From the outset of modernity, this persistence of the Ptolemaic over and against the Copernican generates a dichotomy between human self-assertion and the dis-ordered and decentered universe. As I argue, this dichotomy, in which the modern subject seeks to rival and subdue the cosmic, engenders the specifically modern problem of scale and what I call the process of *upscaling* at the heart of modernity. Today, this process both escalates and threatens to go off the rails as the looming climate catastrophe reveals forcefully a more-than-human planetary and cosmic scale so indifferent as to have no care for humanity's existence, and as divisions within humanity intensify again and the specter of de-globalization haunts the globe, while capitalists and states dream of life on Mars and of enclosing the last remaining commons: outer space. The present moment of crisis thus cuts across the three (temporal and spatial) scales of modernity that have been seldom thought together yet have been co-imbricated in the constitution of modernity as epoch and normative program: the global, the planetary, and the cosmic in the post-Copernican sense.

Throughout modernity, the very idea of global humanity as universal category was co-constituted with the ideas of the planetary and cosmic. Or, to put this differently, the scale on which the concept of global humanity functions was constituted over and against the planetary and cosmic scales. By "the global," I understand the idea (and ideal) of the oneness of humanity and human history across the globe as this oneness was assembled in a colonial and racialized manner following the symbolic event of 1492. As Sylvia Wynter has argued, the modern category of humanness, or of "Man," as the globally normative rational subject, was formed to mark (and to legitimate) the unequal distribution and racialization of the global in colonial modernity.[5] For my purposes in this essay, I therefore speak of "global humanity," "the human," and "the global" interchangeably. "The planetary"—a term that has gained prominence in the Anthropocene debate—indexes the deep time of the Earth's formation and its geological history, operating on a different scale from that of human history.[6] "The cosmic" points to the most measureless scale of all: the alien expanse of the universe revealed by modern astronomy. My suggestion is that "modernity"

Kirill Chepurin

itself, which consolidated as a universal epochal category in Enlightenment and Romantic thought, was from the beginning a cross-scalar category and served not least the goal of mediating among the three scales named earlier. In political-theological terms, modernity was constituted in an interplay of legitimation and delegitimation that involved playing these scales off against each other, and that continues to this day. This interplay forms the core of what can be called a political theology of scale in modernity.

In view of the current crisis as a crisis of the modern co-imbrication of the global, the planetary, and the cosmic, two speculative lines of questioning emerge for political theology. First, what would political-theological thinking proceeding from the Copernican revolution and post-Copernican cosmic immanence look like? Second, how do the operations of legitimation and delegitimation function on a post-Copernican cosmic scale?

The contemporary French philosopher Quentin Meillassoux, whose thought is usually associated with speculative realism or speculative materialism, serves in what follows as the lens through which to introduce what I call "cosmic immanence" and "cosmic delegitimation." Meillassoux's cosmic thinking is important since he is the rare philosopher to attempt to think the Copernican event immanently. However, I offer not just an exposition but a reconfiguration of Meillassoux's thinking, expanding its narrow philosophical focus. What emerges from Meillassoux once his thought is revisited from a political-theological perspective is a speculative political theology of cosmic immanence that delegitimates every claim to necessity and every transcendent legitimation, whether it is "religious" or "secular." At the same time, Meillassoux's thinking needs to be placed in the context of the ongoing "rediscovery" of the planetary and cosmic scale constitutively inscribed into modernity from the outset. Ultimately, I suggest, the cosmic scale can delegitimate the very dichotomy between human self-assertion and post-Copernican decenteredness through an embrace of universal contingency and an immanent inhabitation of the alien body of the Earth.

Cosmic Delegitimation

Meillassoux's crystalline prose in *After Finitude* (published in French in 2006) is permeated with a sense of the contingently catastrophic, opening onto a cosmic immanence that precedes and exceeds the human. This immanence is "unveiled" or "revealed" (two key verbs in Meillassoux's description of the Copernican event) in the transition from the closed world to the infinite universe—to the decentered, contingent, glacial cosmic void.

To think this inhuman cosmic immanence is to unground the standard configurations of immanence and transcendence as too human-centered. To say that the cosmic exceeds the human would seem to invoke transcendence. However, cosmic immanence precedes the human, and global modernity imposes itself transcendently on the planetary immanence of the Earth, which is one with the immanence of the universe. This immanence is what Meillassoux calls "ancestral" reality, indexing the deep geocosmic time (of the formation of the solar system) known through statements of science but unexperienceable phenomenologically—yet "diachronically" persisting alongside the time of human history and erupting in a way that is "blindly evident now."[7] While constituting the presupposition of human existence, cosmic immanence is irreducible to human immanence or divine transcendence. It impossibly exceeds what the finite subject can phenomenologically conceive, and its phenomena seem almost impossible even from a scientific perspective—and yet it is real.

The irony of the Anthropocene is that, in its demiurgic striving to control reality, modernity has come full circle, now facing the same post-Copernican scale: one that is geocosmic and inhuman, uncontrollable, and incapable of being contained within the phenomenological horizon. The shock of the Anthropocene and the shock of the Copernican event unveil the one cosmic immanence, and Meillassoux is its foremost contemporary thinker.

In the seventeenth century, this shock underlies the "horror" of which Johannes Kepler speaks, as well as John Donne's sense that, due to the astronomical disorientation, "the Sun is lost, and th'Earth," "all coherence [is] gone," and "this world's spent," or the invocation of the frightening cosmic silence in Blaise Pascal.[8] It runs likewise through eighteenth-century thought, intensifying with the rise of geological catastrophism, the discovery of deep time, and the expansion of the known universe into an endless multitude of galaxies. It gets taken up within the thermodynamic framework, lurking behind the Victorian fears of the depletion of the Earth and the heat death of the universe and underpinning the image of the blind and threatening cosmic expanse in Nikolai Fedorov, the nineteenth-century founder of Russian Cosmism whose thought provided a key inspiration for the Soviet space program. It is the same shock, too, that Anders observes in the reactions to the first real forays into space in the twentieth century. Today, this shock lives on in the discourses of transhumanism and existential risk, and in the calls to make humanity a multiplanetary species so that humanity can survive and assert itself vis-à-vis the decaying Earth and the dangers of outer space—or, in transhumanist dreams, the reality of universal death itself. But it lives on in Latour, too, through his programmatic repression of the decentered extraterrestrial expanse. These reactions to the Copernican shock, merging with the shock of the Anthropocene, amount to legitimating and recentering the human and the Earth over and against the threat of their cosmic delegitimation in a universe that no longer eternally coheres.

Meillassoux's term for this incoherence and perishability is *contingency*. In a way that resonates between the seventeenth-century and the twenty-first-century catastrophic sentiment, he writes: "Everything could actually collapse: from trees to stars, from stars to laws, from physical laws to logical laws; and this is not by virtue of some superior law whereby everything is destined to perish, but by virtue of the absence of any superior law capable of preserving anything, no matter what, from perishing."[9] Unveiled by the Copernican revolution is not just the contingency of this or that circumstance, but contingency as the absolute condition: the contingency of all invariants of the world. No law, no order is necessary. If there is an order, it is a mere fact, nothing preordained by a religious or secular authority. It could have been and could still be otherwise; nor can it be legitimately inscribed into any narrative of legitimation. Meillassoux's position is distinct from the age-old adage that everything necessarily perishes insofar as he proclaims this necessity itself to be contingent and even perishability to be a mere fact that cannot be legitimated through appeal to necessity. The Copernican event rationally discloses that everything that is is without reason, and this absence of reason, or "unreason," is the only "absolute" or "in-itself," non-metaphysical and delegitimating any appeal to a necessary entity. Cosmic contingency is thereby imbued by Meillassoux with an apocalyptic sense. It collapses any legitimation and unveils the in-itself *in* this collapse—so that, in the cosmic disorientation invoked by Donne, modernity sees the in-itself face to face. This in-itself is the infinite void of contingency, immanent only to itself, an indifferent hyper-chaos of whatever possibility and whatever fact.

For post-Copernican modernity, the infinite plenum of contingency reoccupies the position of "the veracious God."[10] The post-Copernican cosmic scale with its contingency is, in a way, omnipotent, too: "capable of destroying both things and worlds, of bringing forth monstrous absurdities, yet also of never doing anything, of realizing every dream, but also every nightmare, of engendering random and frenetic transformations, or conversely, of producing a universe that remains motionless down to its ultimate recesses."[11] This dis-orderly, eccentric omnipotence that, "far from guaranteeing order, guarantees only the possible destruction of every order," cannot but appear as menacing, underlying the Copernican shock.[12]

What this omnipotence signifies is strikingly minimal: the fact that whatever is is without reason, and thus must be thought of as *not* necessarily the way it is. It is omnipotence as delegitimation. How to think the world without justifying it? That is, I believe, a central anti-theodical question, and Meillassoux seeks both to think the conditions of possibility of the world and to delegitimate any concealing of immanent nothingness with transcendent necessity. Contra any Leibnizian attempt to stabilize the post-Copernican universe via the theodical principle of sufficient reason, Copernican immanence is to be inhabited by a reason dispossessed of its desire for sufficiency—and of its desire for universal coherence, too, another basic theodical desire. Meillassoux writes: "In reply to those metaphysical questions that ask why the world is thus and not otherwise, the response 'for no reason' is a genuine answer. Instead of laughing or smiling at questions like 'Where do we come from?,' 'Why do we exist?,' we should ponder instead the remarkable fact that the replies 'From nothing. For nothing' really *are* answers."[13] This material nothingness on a cosmic scale indexes an immanence that is decoupled from the world of human and terrestrial self-assertion and that delegitimates this world's legitimations and transcendences.

Ptolemaic versus Astro-Modernity

However, although the scientific revolution was constitutive for modernity, modernity failed to stay with the cosmic trouble revealed in the Copernican event. Meillassoux offers a critique of the trajectory of modernity, which I would recontextualize as follows.

As Hans Blumenberg argues, with the new opening of reality at the outset of modernity, the subject asserts itself *against* the groundlessness and contingency of reality, seeking to produce order out of disorder and chaos. The term *self-assertion* that I use in this essay belongs to Blumenberg and is employed by him to designate the process of the "self-assertion of [human] reason through the mastery and alteration of reality," the "existential program" that leads to what becomes modernity. Within this program, reality is seen as infinitely "open" to the subject who is supposed to "make use . . . of the possibilities" inherent in it.[14]

Modern self-assertion is a project of legitimation, too, precisely as the legitimation of the modern subject, and of the world it seeks to produce, vis-à-vis the decentered infinite real that seems to declare all human possibility futile and insignificant. Within the boundless void of what is impossible yet real, the modern subject carves out for itself a space and time—a world—of possibility, striving to master and control it, here on the Earth but also beyond it in projects such as asteroid mining or the colonization of Mars. That this project of mastery has now led to the planetary-scale eruption of the contingency that the subject set out to control is one of modernity's catastrophic ironies.

Meillassoux diagnoses this project as a *narrowing* of the cosmic and planetary to the phenomenological structure of the subject-object relationship. In the modern structure of finitude, reality appears as correlated with the subject, and this "correlationism," in various guises, characterizes especially the post-Kantian trajectory of thought. The human-world correlation is, furthermore, a structure of domination and racialization.[15] Again ironically, what Kant dubbed his own Copernican revolution constituted, as Meillassoux argues, a "Ptolemaic counter-revolution": a foreclosure of cosmic immanence.[16] In identifying the conditions of representation with the invariants of the world, the transcendental turn was, one might add, a theodical operation.

Modernity *qua* correlationism equals for Meillassoux not only "Ptolemy's revenge" but also a structure of loss, even mourning: "bereavement," "loss" of "the great outdoors."[17] Meillassoux's critique of the neediness, human-centeredness, and blind narrowness of modernity may be said to reconfigure, via cosmic immanence, Christian critiques of modernity in a way that avoids affirming either side of the secular-religious binary. That Meillassoux draws on these critiques is evident in his reference to Rémi Brague no less than in his overly simplistic view of modernity as "de-Christianization." At the same time, "de-Christianization" means for him not a secularization but a "re-ligionization." Meillassoux takes seriously Kant's claim to delimit knowledge to make room for faith. By foreclosing the in-itself and absolutizing the limits of finitude, secular skepticism and transcendental philosophy alike "abandon whatever lies beyond this limit to the rule of piety," producing a "fideism of any belief whatsoever" underwritten by faith in the necessity of the way the world is (a necessity identified with the limits of finitude themselves).[18] At this point, secular humanism becomes indistinguishable from belief in providence. Ultimately, one might say, the more the "fragility" or "mystery" of the world is emphasized, the more ironclad the world's grip becomes. What modernity calls immanence (i.e., the subject-world structure of finitude) takes for granted the (transcendent) necessity of the world, thereby mystifying it.

Meillassoux may be said to critique the coproduction of the religious and secular—which, however, I view as part of the Christian-modern apparatus of legitimation, not as de-Christianization. To regain astonishment in looking at the universe is to break through this binary apparatus and to inhabit nonhuman cosmic contingency immanently without the desire to transcend it, without the striving for mastery and control or for human self-assertion over and against cosmic immanence.

In *The Number and the Siren* (2012), Meillassoux's deciphering of Stéphane Mallarmé's *Coup de dés*, an immanent inhabitation of contingency points to the persistence of the Copernican event, despite the correlationist trajectory of modernity. As Copernican, modernity is diachronically excessive over its Ptolemaic double, ungrounding any pretense of mastery, and Meillassoux's account of this ungrounding is strikingly Christological, further complicating any de-Christianization narrative.

To give up the striving for mastery is to deliver oneself to what Meillassoux describes as "Chance, the God of the moderns." If Copernican modernity indexes the death of God and the sacrifice of transcendence, then to dispossess oneself of any attempted mastery amounts to a sacrifice of sacrifice opening onto a "divine dimension of suffering," a kenotic embrace of nothingness morphing into a kind of secular salvation—a becoming infinite by becoming Chance, a salvation voided of transcendence.[19] Importantly, while it is mathematical in character, Chance for Meillassoux cannot be reduced to probability or calculability, opposing, as "the detotalization of number," the enclosure of possibility via calculation.[20] As a result, his invocation of Chance as "the God of the moderns" may be taken to suggest, from a Blumenbergian perspective, two things: first, the reoccupation of divine infinity and the unfathomable divine will by cosmic infinity and contingency in the Copernican event; and second, the idea that, in its very attempt to tame contingency, to make it calculable and controllable, the modern subject has continued to assert itself demiurgically against the God of salvation—so that it is cosmic Chance that occupies in modernity the voided place of the *deus absconditus*.

Instead of seeking mastery, Mallarméan astro-modernity embraces Copernican immanence as crystallized in the *perhaps* (as unveiling "no longer *being*, but the *perhaps*"). Mallarmé's hypermodern poetics is an astro-poetics in which the poem—"as christic crystallization of Chance"

Kirill Chepurin

or "Christal of Nothingness"—refracts cosmic infinity, not unlike the stars in their "evanescent flickering."[21] In this, Copernican modernity promises "transfiguration" through the *perhaps*, while the Ptolemaic trajectory of modernity seeks to impose order on this *perhaps* to regain stability and control. The tension between these two poles indexes the movement of modernity, to which I now turn.

Upscaling—Or, Modernity Across Scales

In an essay from *One-Way Street* (1928) entitled "To the Planetarium," Walter Benjamin observes in World War I, with its hitherto unprecedented scale of mobilization and annihilation, a striving on the part of global humanity to attain by technological means an ecstatic unity with the cosmic scale. It was "an attempt at new and unprecedented commingling with the cosmic powers"—disrupting what Benjamin sees, repeating a traditional trope, as the absence of connection to the cosmic in modernity. Prior to the war, modernity's cosmic dimension, he posits, was either merely theoretical ("optical") or "individual, as the poetic rapture of starry nights." This time, however, things were different: "Human multitudes, gases, electrical forces were hurled into the open country, high-frequency currents coursed through the landscape, new constellations rose in the sky, aerial space and ocean depths thundered with propellers, and everywhere sacrificial shafts were dug in Mother Earth. This immense wooing of the cosmos was enacted for the first time on a planetary scale—that is, in the spirit of technology."[22] The global, the planetary, and the cosmic are the three scales that can be discerned in Benjamin's account, cutting across the ostensible division between human and nonhuman and between natural and technological or artificial. What Benjamin describes, I want to suggest, is a process of *upscaling* in which global humanity seeks to rival and "woo" the universe by elevating itself to a new massive scale, including the scale of mass annihilation and death.

It is important, I would add, that such a wooing is addressed to the post-Copernican universe of perishability. If the universe is what annihilates planets and worlds, and if annihilation is not the end but part of the processuality of the universe, and out of it new celestial formations arise, phoenix-like, then the war itself is a cosmic war, and mass annihilation is a way of being ecstatically one with the universe, a reenactment of the "cosmic power" of the void and a scaling up *to* this power. "In the nights of annihilation of the last war, the frame of mankind"—the world of the global—"was shaken by a feeling that resembled the bliss of the epileptic," Benjamin continues, "and the revolts that followed it were the first attempt of mankind to bring the new body under its control."[23] The war and the revolution constituted at once a triumph and crisis of upscaling. In its forceful transition to the new scale, global humanity found a momentary bliss (of oneness with the planetary body and with the infinite night of the universe), yet humanity could not control the scale that it attained.

The delirium of such an upscaling becomes widespread during the early twentieth century; it manifests itself likewise in Italian futurism and the Russian avant-garde or, later, in texts such as Ernst Jünger's *The Worker* (1932), for which the planetary industrial-technological scale is central. The prominence of "the masses" in twentieth-century theory and practice indexes the same upscaling, as well, and not only the leveling criticized by Friedrich Nietzsche.

At least since the industrial revolution, this upscaling forms the central movement of modernity and the precondition of the so-called Great Acceleration of the Anthropocene starting from the 1950s–1960s. As the Romantic philosopher Friedrich Schlegel speculatively proposes around 1800, during what is often considered the beginning of the Anthropocene, perhaps global humanity (and, one might add, its technology) should be viewed as an extraterrestrial outgrowth of the Earth—an image suggesting that humanity envelops the planet like a massive plant and repurposes it as humanity's own soil and resource for growth.[24] Human masses amass on the Earth, grow out of it, and remediate it, becoming a geophysical power that rivals the planet's even as it remains one with it. The current climate crisis, too, is a crisis of this process of entangled upscaling.

In fact, this process can be traced even further back, to the beginning of the modern age. While Benjamin is correct if one understands him to claim that, up to a certain point, this process was more "ideal" than "real" insofar as modern humanity still lacked the technological means and sheer mass necessary to *really* rival the planetary and the cosmic—yet, contra Benjamin, the cosmic dimension of modernity was never merely theoretical. Blumenberg points out that, within the modern logic of self-assertion, all "theory" is subordinated to the "practical" project of human mastery over reality.[25] In the late nineteenth century, Fedorov offered a critique of this project—proclaimed theoretically already by Francis Bacon and René Descartes and evident practically in the modern production of "nature" as resource—theorizing it as the ongoing attempt by the Western subject to (re)instate itself at the center of reality against the shock of the Copernican decentering.

Kirill Chepurin

For Fedorov, this impulse stands behind modern colonialism as co-imbricated with the dissolution of sacred geography (what he calls the violent "circumnavigational movement" of the modern formation of the global), as well as behind the desire to expand human mastery by colonizing the universe.[26] Both are in fact *one* movement of "circumnavigationally" remediating, through human rationality as modernity understands it, the *entirety* of the newly opened expanse of reality. Interest in exploring and mastering the depths of the Earth (a trajectory leading to modern extractive logics) and in exploring outer space, at first ideally (optically and imaginatively) but always with an eye toward real exploration, forms no less a constitutive dimension of modernity than geographical exploration and expansion, or the assembling of the globe in a Western-centric manner. Today, this cross-scalar movement continues in the remediation of the Earth and its orbit by digital networks and by the infrastructure of satellites, sensors, and cables—or, beyond the orbit, of space telescopes and probes—and it is this movement that global capitalism seeks to expand to the moon and Mars.

From this perspective, the event of 1492 and the Copernican event constitute but one event on different scales. The reality against which the modern subject asserts itself is cosmically open and contingent across all scales. The Copernican shock is engendered by the universal collapse of the idea of a proper distribution of place, and of *scala naturae* as a providential hierarchy—the collapse that occurs at the level of the global, as well. The post-1492 "shock of circumnavigation" is one with the Copernican shock.[27] Already Giordano Bruno analogizes between Columbus and himself, writing that, just as Columbus opened the globe and "unloose[d] the bonds of things," so he, Bruno, has opened the universe for "human spirit and cognition," discovering "the way to scale the skies."[28]

However, what Bruno, through his hermetic optic, views purely as liberation from cosmic prison, or as a way to inhabit the "infinite multitude" and "abundance" of the All without "ends, boundaries, limits or walls," also entails disorientation and the anxiety of decentering.[29] In the shock that reverberates between the global and the cosmic, the Christian European subject faces a cross-scalar decentered expanse over and against which the subject's assumed central position suddenly appears as contingent. In his analysis of the self-assertion of reason, Blumenberg astutely grasps the conjunction of emancipation and anxiety inherent in the project of modernity. However, he fails to see how this emancipation—which is, in modernity, subordinated to the imperative of the demiurgic production of order to stave off anxiety and to put contingency under control—itself turns subjugating. As a result, the world that the modern subject constructs serves primarily to reinstate this subject to its lost central place through mastery over all human, as well as nonhuman, reality.

One could also put it the following way: The world of possibility and mastery that the modern subject carves out for itself vis-à-vis the decentered and contingent expanse of the real does not simply remain constant. It expands and scales up in all dimensions simultaneously: around the globe but also into the depths of the Earth and into the skies. Geocosmically or geophysically, from a speculative materialist standpoint, "modernity" can be said to name the process of this expansion and upscaling, through which global humanity at once reiterates and seeks to rival and subdue the movement of the universe.

Modernity as a geophysical process of remediating the Earth and the universe has an ideal (conceptual) and a real (material) side that are inseparable. Thus, the theoretical construction of "nature" in modern thought cannot be separated from the material colonial and extractive practices, or from turning everything—and everyone who is relegated to the status of mere nature—into a resource that the subject can use. Similarly, the Romantic vision of particular national spirits as that through which global humanity is assembled forms a constitutive part of the broader modern reassembling of the globe as a network of particular national states and cultures. The Romantic ideal of synthetically assembling the universal *out of* the particular is co-imbricated with the modern architecture of a networked global world in which unity is constructed through communication among particular nodes, with the corresponding material infrastructure from telegraph and railroads to the internet. Throughout modernity, the ideal and the real, for all their tension, form one ever evolving infrastructure of remediation and upscaling—a process impossibly directed, at its limit, toward fully remediating the planetary and the cosmic scale. Contra Meillassoux, the movement of modern self-assertion is not a mere narrowing to the perspective of the subject; it is a focusing or recentering of subjectivity as a point or node *from which* to remediate and expand onto the totality of reality.

It was inevitable that at some point this process would really confront the more than human or inhuman scale—as has happened in the encounter with Gaia in the Anthropocene—and seek to upscale itself to this scale in projects such as geo-engineering, which is but another technique of rationally remediating the globe (in this case, the Earth's entire critical zone) on a planetary scale in order to put it under control. I view Meillassoux's

Kirill Chepurin

thought, and the posthuman turn across the humanities more broadly, as part of this encounter with the inhuman—the encounter that intensifies starting in the 1950s–1960s with the Great Acceleration and the rise of new more-than-human logics of remediation, such as live television, the digital, space exploration, and Earth System Science, and with the so-called "long 1968" (itself a global event) as representing the conjoined crisis of the global and the human.

On a new scale, this crisis is restaged in the present crisis of the co-imbrication of the global, planetary, and cosmic. The much discussed environmental costs of artificial intelligence and satellite systems, as real abstractions through which we navigate the globe (such as when our physical location is remediated into GPS coordinates used by Google Maps), demonstrate the oneness of abstraction and extraction within the modern process of remediation and upscaling.[30] It is as though the higher humanity, this massive plant, ascends into the skies, the deeper and vaster must its (underground and aboveground) network of roots go through which it sucks out the nutrients from the Earth and beyond it.

The ever upscaling violence and catastrophes that modernity keeps producing, too, are part of this geocosmic process. Thus understood, modernity has the structure of a catastrophic spiral, which keeps re-collecting itself as it moves from crisis to crisis and from scale to scale. Plunged into the infinite abyss by the Copernican shock, the Western subject strives to scale this abyss step by step while refusing to accept its own decentering. In the Copernican event at its most radical, the subject becomes abyssally ungrounded, seeking to assert itself *against* this event as what threatens to delegitimate the centrality of the Christian-modern world. And if the subject's ultimate desire is to become a subject free-floating in the infinite space, then it may be because modern subjectivity itself is constituted in the tension between the never-ending striving to produce, out of contingency, a world that would be fully controlled and the horror of the abyss of contingency in which this world is suspended and that is destined to consume the world of the self-assertion of "Man."[31]

A Coda: Modernity Dissolved

Short of a total climate apocalypse or nuclear annihilation, the process of upscaling is likely to continue. The programmatic return of discourses of modernity and Enlightenment in proponents of geo-engineering and planetary governance is but a symptom of that. But while this movement is unlikely to be stopped, its impasses can be rethought—which is why re-conceptualizations of the cosmic such as Meillassoux's are essential, no less than decolonial, Marxist, Russian Cosmist, and other approaches to the cosmic commons. To dismiss the extraterrestrial as an escape fantasy is as theoretically myopic as it is practically dangerous. In neglecting it, critical theory and practice abandon the cosmic—and, thus, also our planet—to the whims of billionaires acting in tandem with the state-military apparatus. It is important to oppose the escalating cosmic enclosure—and this opposition must itself be cross-scalar.

The problem originally posed by Fedorov remains central: How is one to conceive of a post-Copernican ethos of the cosmic commons so as not simply to legitimate global divisions and violence on a cosmic scale? Or, relatedly, How can one decenter and delegitimate the logics of upscaling inherent in modernity in order to rethink them? From a political-theological perspective, these questions necessitate a refusal of the theodical tendency of modernity, at least since the eighteenth century, to legitimate the global—the world as modernity has formed it—via the cosmic scale. Already Leibniz in his *Theodicy* (1710) appeals to the immensity of the universe, relative to which "our globe and its inhabitants" appear as "something incomparably less than a physical point," for the purpose of paradoxically justifying the perceived evils of human history as "almost nothingness in comparison with the good things which are in the universe."[32] In Romanticism, too, the idea of global humanity as a planetary and cosmic being is entangled with the colonial construction of universal history from a post-Enlightenment Western center.[33]

Today, many proponents of transhumanism, active evolution, geo-engineering, and Silicon Valley–style cosmism return to the idea of humanity's cosmic destiny, justifying the late-capitalist civilization as the pinnacle of planetary and cosmic evolution and arguing for the spread of this civilization onto the rest of the solar system. An often repeated sleight of hand declares technology to be the highest achievement of the human species, and even of the evolution of the Earth, to justify the current ills of the human condition as mere deviations to be rectified through increased technological agency and intensified planetary governance. This sleight of hand is dangerous because it reiterates the same old technocratic vision under the guise of a new planetary and cosmic ethos. This, too, however, is symptomatic of the widespread longing for such an ethos. What the present crisis signals is that, now that human and planetary history have become so entangled, a new configuration of the global, the planetary, and the cosmic is struggling to be born, with capitalist powers old and new seeking to control the process.

To approach the cosmic commons from the standpoint of cosmic immanence is to view all scales as equally touched by contingency and to view this world that modernity has formed as *not* having necessarily to be the way it is. Instead of proclaiming the human as it has been constructed by modernity to be the pinnacle of cosmic evolution, philosophy must embrace the immanent inhabitation of cosmic contingency and an *unknowing* that discloses the human as a contingent cosmic experiment or a manifold of experiments that all remediate the scales of reality in different ways—a cross-scalar topography of contingency foreclosed by the ever upscaling project of self-assertion. Political theology, too, must insist on the standpoint of world delegitimation and post-Copernican decenteredness. One could say that, to stay true to the Copernican event, political theology must provincialize the human and (the nomos of) the Earth in order to proceed from cosmic immanence as the otherwise to the capitalist-modern logics of transcendence concealed under the name of "this world," an otherwise that opens onto a different logic of inhabiting the cosmic. This means, among other things, that political theology must not be fixated on the political identified with the global but must take seriously the post-Copernican dimension of modernity and the constitutive modern process of upscaling to retrace the logics of world investment and (de)legitimation across scales.

The Christian-modern desire for a new world, too, must be dissolved in the bliss of inhabiting immanently the contingency of a universe in which the human, to borrow Meillassoux's expression, is but "a traveler—a *viator*—a man of the earth and not the blessed in heaven."[34] To focus on a new world, the way Meillassoux himself does, is to obscure the fact that, in its life on the Earth and its travels across scales, the human is already cosmic in the post-Copernican sense—not as the bearer of a glorious cosmic destiny or purpose, but as a cosmic attempt at intelligent life without any telos, existing in a frangible relationship with an alien planet that is itself one with the contingency and disorder of the post-Copernican universe. What post-Copernican political theology must assert is that to delegitimate this world is not to spiritually invest in a world to come—but to disclose the plenum of the Earth and the skies on which this world is transcendently imposed and that constitutes the cosmic commons that we already inhabit, yet in a way that is subordinated to the logics of profit, domination, and use. Admitting of no beyond and abolishing all investment in the world, cosmic immanence discloses the here and now of the post-Copernican universe *within* and *on* the decentered Earth, decentering and dissolving the never-ending not yet of self-assertion.

Notes

1   For one notable exception, see Taubes, *From Cult to Culture*, 98–123, 165–76. I view my essay as pointing toward a new answer to the broadly Taubesian question: How is the Gnostic logic of world delegitimation transformed from within post-Copernican cosmic immanence?

2   Anders, *Der Blick vom Mond*, 61.

3   See Latour, *Down to Earth*, 68.

4   Anders, *Der Blick vom Mond*, 61. In this regard, the Copernican revolution marks not a punctiform occurrence but a complex process that runs throughout modernity and in which the position of the human and the Earth vis-à-vis the universe keeps being recontested—but that continues to be underwritten by the shock evident in the epigraph from Kepler. This shock, together with its lasting repercussions, is what I call "the Copernican event."

5   See Wynter, "Unsettling the Coloniality of Being/Power/Truth/Freedom."

6   I build here on the distinction between *global* and *planetary* from Chakrabarty, "The Planet."

7   Meillassoux, *After Finitude*, 121.

8   Donne, *The Complete Poems*, 837–38; Pascal, *Pensées*, 64.

9   Meillassoux, *After Finitude*, 53.

10 Meillassoux, *After Finitude*, 64. On the "reoccupation" of the divine by the infinite universe in modernity, see Blumenberg, *The Legitimacy of the Modern Age*.

11 Meillassoux, *After Finitude*, 64.

12 Meillassoux, *After Finitude*, 64.

13 Meillassoux, *After Finitude*, 110.

14 Blumenberg, *The Legitimacy of the Modern Age*, 137–38, 209.

15 Wynter's work may be viewed as diagnosing this coconstitution of "human" and "world" in modernity. On correlationism and antiblackness, see also Jackson, "Sense of Things."

16 Meillassoux, *After Finitude*, 118.

17 Meillassoux, *After Finitude*, 7.

18 Meillassoux, *After Finitude*, 82.

19 Meillassoux, *The Number and the Siren*, 122–26.

Kirill Chepurin

20 Meillassoux, *The Number and the Siren*, 103.

21 Meillassoux, *The Number and the Siren*, 103, 222.

22 Benjamin, *One-Way Street*, 94.

23 Benjamin, *One-Way Street*, 95.

24 See Schlegel, *Kritische Friedrich-Schlegel-Ausgabe*, 18:151. Cf. Schlegel, *Kritische Friedrich-Schlegel-Ausgabe*, 20:329: "Humanity [is] *a massive plant*"—emphasizing the sheer (planetary) scale of global humanity.

25 Blumenberg, *The Legitimacy of the Modern Age*, 208–9.

26 Fedorov seeks to reclaim this impulse for his ideal of inhabiting the Earth and the skies in common: see Chepurin and Dubilet, "Out of the Cemetery of the Earth, a Resurrective Commons."

27 On the "shock of circumnavigation," see Sloterdijk, *Spheres, Volume 2*, 808. Jared Hickman further analyzes the event of 1492 as the disorienting cosmological clash that engenders the modern logics of racialization: Hickman, *Black Prometheus*.

28 Bruno, *The Ash Wednesday Supper*, 59–60.

29 Giordano Bruno, "On the Infinite Universe and Worlds," in Singer, *Giordano Bruno, His Life and Thought, with an Annotated Translation of His Work On the Infinite Universe and Worlds*, 245.

30 For a visualization of these costs, see Crawford and Joler, "Anatomy of an AI System." Cf. Bratton, *The Stack*, 12: "Computation is not virtual; it is a deeply physical event."

31 On the desire to be the free-floating subject, see Arendt, "Man's Conquest of Space," 535.

32 Leibniz, *Theodicy*, 135.

33 See Chepurin, *Bliss Against the World*, chap. 6; Chepurin, "Reading Novalis and the Schlegels."

34 Meillassoux, "The Immanence of the World Beyond," 473.

Race, Blackness, and Modernity

3

11

Rethinking Political Theology as Faith, Poesis, and Praxis

George Shulman

Poetic Genius, Supreme Fictions

I conceive political theology as the study of what I call *organizing faiths*. The trope of faith foregrounds how creative imagination—embodied in sentient, suffering, desiring, socially entangled bodies—is expressed in mythopoetic metaphors, images, and tales and formalized into scriptures or other genres, including the treatises now called political theology. Organizing faiths are also instantiated in ordinary, customary, ritualized social practices. Both imaginative forms and ordinary liturgies of living are (con)tested and (re)made as people struggle to make sense of their experience and address the historical and natural exigencies that shape their lives.

This conception of political theology shifts our sense of theoretical and theological practice and our sense of its political predicate. Rather than philosophically test the validity or truth of creedal arguments, I take a phenomenological approach to explore how imaginative poesis is linked to paideia and praxis, to the vernacular practices of subject formation and world building that (re)make a form of life. Rather than define the political in terms of sovereignty, or as a secular translation of theological concepts, I foreground generative and agonistic practices of popular power, expression, and action amid conditions characterized by inequality and contingency. Rather than stipulate what is or is not properly subsumed by political theology as a concept or field, I use the idea of organizing faith to embed thought and expression in historical time and lived experience, whereby suffering and aspiration are imaginatively metabolized in vernacular and literary forms and embodied by customary rituals and forms of assembly and action.

I assume that faith is inescapable and ubiquitous. It is not a philosophically bounded genre of theology but undergirds and animates every form and instance of human life, whether people worship a god or reason or invest faith in a nation or race, church or state, property and markets, political projects, personal experiments, or one another. Human beings are always enacting faith, especially as we critique another form of faith. An organizing faith is often tacit or taken for granted but always embedded in lived experience, motivated in complex ways, articulated by rhetorically resonant speech acts, and instantiated in social practices. Faith is always embodied and experiential—even when it involves disavowal or asceticism—and always open to reshaping as participants struggle to make sense of themselves and of life.

In the spirit of the Hebrew prophets, William Blake, Friedrich Nietzsche, and James Baldwin, I ground political theology not in logos but in poesis, in imaginative inventions—myths, fictions, narratives, metaphors, and images—by which human beings conjure and name, and so organize and shape, the social world and themselves. Like these mentors, I emphasize how human suffering generates what Blake calls poetic genius and Wallace Stevens calls supreme fictions—to name, explain, and express, and to protest and mobilize, our suffering; to make it endurable by making it meaningful; but also to remediate or end it. By imaginative art we also depict what is (im)possible to change or remedy "in this world," depictions at once world-defining and world-making; at once confining and generative; at once seeking hegemony, risking failure, and provoking contest.[1]

Hebrew prophets, Nietzsche, and Baldwin are linked by the premise that suffering is central in human life, and their shared question—both theological and political—is how human beings make suffering meaningful—that is, explain its causation and endow it with redemptive purpose. Each shows how faith organizes suffering into forms of idolatry as regimes of truth, promises of redemption, and fictions of race, gender, nation. For each, suffering weds people to rancor and thus to forms of poesis and practice that simplify "evil," naturalize injustice, and freeze the generativity of (their own) life. For each, suffering and meaning making are two sides of one problem, because efforts to explain and remedy suffering generate forms of meaning (myths, idols, and collective identities; metaphysics or rationalism; grammars of the rational or sovereign subject; narratives of redemption) that disavow what Nietzsche calls "the fundamental prerequisites of life," including mortal and carnal finitude, inescapable interdependence, interpretive ambiguity, and perspectival conflict. My practice of political theology thus analyzes the faiths we already (often tacitly) enact; assesses their worldly cost and impact; traces their failure or revision; and articulates alter-faiths to contest, enrich, or displace them.[2]

Against a liberal distinction between religion and politics—one denoting individual and voluntaristic creedal commitment, and the other, deliberation by public reason—I follow the Machiavellian and Gramscian premise that faiths manifest generative or constituent power as they are woven into organizing practices of congregation and festivity. Politics is thus churchlike in mobilizing constituencies and shaping forms of governance. In this sense, I reject the Pauline and Protestant distinctions between faith and works, spirit and flesh, or love and law. I see faith as intersubjectively constituted, as inseparable from social practices, as jurispathic and jurisgenerative in its lawbreaking and lawmaking capacities. Politics is not just government or state action but collective self-fashioning that forms and disturbs collective subjects, advances and displaces shared imaginaries, to (re)make social practices and regimes. Politics then names contests not only about explicit structures of power but also about rules, norms, and identifications; it names the forging, disruption, and remaking of formal rule and informal powers, modes of subjectivity, and webs of meaning.

In sum, I orient political theology toward analyzing the ways that organizing faiths are articulated, practiced, and revised, often in contests or by encounters with other forms of faith or life. Organizing faiths are thus porous, polysemic, and subject to historical exigencies and challenges. They manifest intramural contests over the meaning and practice of first principles, and they provoke or engender alter-faiths that seek to radically reconstitute or repudiate them. In Alasdair MacIntyre's terms, organizing faiths typically entail an "argumentative tradition" in which adversaries remain intelligible despite sometimes profound differences as they argue about the meaning of principles, practices, and history. Following Abraham Lincoln, I would thus construe democracy as an organizing faith and argumentative tradition, now in acute crisis.[3]

To construe theology in terms of faith is to foreground how organizing faiths—instantiated in churches, mosques, synagogues; in communities, states, or collective identities; in forms of economy, kinship, and collective action—can fail by becoming corrupt in the Machiavellian sense that collective energies are no longer adequately organized by extant social forms. As authorities, institutions, practices, or first principles lose credibility, a form of life fails to sustain its authority and vitality; as an orienting faith enters crisis—because it fails to make sense of experiences, sustain attachment, or enable flourishing—incipient voices of prophetic revelation, innovative theories, or newly resonant narratives emerge to revive or displace a once dominant political theology.

It is a commonplace among those of us who practice political theory that figures now canonized emerged in moments of crisis, and this truth is also valid for political theology. Jacob Taubes says that "theology's relation to political theory is not derivative but touches the very centers of both," not only because "there is no theology without political implication" and "no political theory without theological presuppositions," but also because he means theology not in a doctrinal or creedal sense but as connoting what he calls "mythic energies." Moments of crisis disclose both that "mythic energies cannot be ignored without peril to society" and that "they have to be formed into a nomos."[4]

In political theory terms, organizing faiths forge nomos by raising and answering three constitutive political questions. First is the question of authority: By what ideas, people, practices, or table of values are you, and should you be, oriented? Second is the question of identification: With whom do you identify and on what basis? How do you constitute a "we" that "holds these truths" to answer the first question? Third is the question of redemption: Which practices and investments can truly engender your flourishing, not only "mere life" but "more life" or "the good life," and which practices and investments that promise redemption are instead self-defeating or harmful, even to catastrophic degrees?

But in moments of crisis, theory and theology are also animated by powerful anxieties about the *danger* in politics and so also in democracy. Now canonized theories or theologies were thus forged to *secure* authority—whether of god or reason, whether by announcing law, stipulating logic, dictating scripture, producing expert knowledge and priestly castes—in ways that also cement a "we" and guarantee redemption. In avowedly antidemocratic ways, dominant theologies and canonized theories have rendered politics—ongoing contest about social forms, first principles, and shared purposes—as a pathological but fortunately containable feature of human life.[5]

In contrast, I draw on minor voices in the major traditions and fugitive elements in canonical texts, which foreground conditions—of finitude and plurality; of interpretive ambiguity and perspectival pluralism; of inequality and rivalry; of contingency, creativity, and unintended consequences—that make politics (and tragedy) *inescapable* and, indeed, generative features of a human estate that must be located east of Eden. My goal as a theorist and teacher is to affirm these conditions and the politicality they entail, for my own faith is that democratization and flourishing are linked. This faith proposes that acceptance of human finitude amid complex interdependencies, enabled by mythopoetic framing, can engender creative capacities for enlarged affiliations, self-organizing nomos, and resonant meaning making. I thus interpret political theology in poeticizing, politicizing, and democratizing ways. This focus suggests a revised canon running from Dante Alighieri and Niccolò Machiavelli to John Milton, Gerrard Winstanley, and William Blake; from Nietzsche to Franz Kafka, Walter Benjamin, and Hannah Arendt, as well as to Julia Kristeva, Luce Irigaray, Jacques Derrida, and Gilles Deleuze. In the United States, such voices include Ralph Waldo Emerson, Henry David Thoreau, and Walt Whitman, as well as William James, W. E. B. Du Bois, Allan Ginsberg, Norman O. Brown, Adrienne Rich, James Baldwin, James Cone, Audre Lorde, Hortense Spillers, and Gloria Anzaldúa.

Situating Political Theology in Liberal Modernity

I also would recontextualize *modern* political theology by bringing arguments about secularization into relation with arguments about European colonialism and the global color line, which are the two co-constituting sides of liberal modernity.

I analyze political theology and secularization in relation to Nietzsche's argument about the ascetic ideal and nihilism. He depicts the otherworldly and inner-worldly orientation of Christianity as a form of nihilism that devalues materiality, transience, and perspective to posit an unconditional truth. This faith in truth is secularized as the Enlightenment episteme he calls the ascetic ideal, which rejects theism as false or illusory. It discredits the moral order once validated by theism and entails a "devaluation of all values" because none can be unconditionally justified. If nihilism is the inability to posit values, to affirm our (poetic and political) authority as value creators, it is because modern subjects believe that values are valid only if authorized as transcendentally—objectively and universally—true in all times and places. Otherwise, they are merely subjective, lacking authority. Averse to value claims, which they reduce to "merely human" subjectivity, they will devalue their own values; despairing at the meaninglessness of life, they will focus on material well-being as the only reality, and they will produce a public world reduced to cynical self-interest and power politics, even as they long for rescue.[6]

Nietzsche thus sees himself as inhabiting the office of prophecy as he uses its characteristic tropes to announce the as yet unspoken truth of nihilism, bear witness to what it means, warn of its dangers, and seek an alternative in his own practice of life. He thus demonstrates the rhetorical problem in modern forms of political theology: In times of nihilism, how can people make fundamental claims about shared circumstances? What kinds of speech acts could engender, not believers who relinquish their own authority, but cocreators who take responsibility for value creation without extra-human validation? What kind of theory/theology can confound the skepticism and longing for unconditional truth that are nihilism's twinned symptoms?

Nietzsche's answer is exemplified by his literary practice, which includes not only prophetic utterance but also a "gay science" that shifts from epistemological arguments that validate truth to aesthetic, poetic, and existential registers of expression. He enacts an openly rhetorical and perspectival engagement with readers to shift their orientation from seeing *values* as unjustifiable nouns to seeing *valuing* as a verb, at once existential and political, both a personal action of esteeming and claim making and a social practice of commitment. In this way, moderns might again posit and enact values—to say "we hold these truths"—in rhetorically resonant ways and to invite assent to (or contest about) that *we* and those *truths*.[7]

I consider Nietzsche's experiments with prophecy and "gay science" experiments in countertheology. They model an alter-faith that affirms perspective and poesis to oppose nihilist devaluation by modern/secular regimes of truth. To use a trope of Fred Moten's, Nietzsche prompts us to ask: What forms of expression inhabit rather than disappear the twinned problem of suffering and its meaning, to hold the complexity in suffering, in the poetics of how human beings make it meaningful, and in the politics entailed by that poetics? For those who define theology via theism and transcendence, the political translates transcendence as sovereign rule. Nietzsche's radical, pluralist immanence cannot be defined in these terms. But if we conceive political theology in terms of faith, imaginative poesis, and collective self-fashioning, then he enacts countertheology. Nietzsche's thought resists the theistic substitutes (state sovereignty, race and nationalism, public reason) whereby political theology/theory tries to rescue and secure—not politicize and democratize—authority.[8]

But in ways that Nietzsche never theorized, the episteme he identified with the purportedly secularizing Enlightenment project is also the racial regime of white supremacy that establishes a global color line through colonialism, enslavement, and discourses of the human. The constitutive exclusions and systemic devaluations of the one wed liberal modernity to racial domination and violence. We thus shift a phenomenology of

Euro-Atlantic political theology from Nietzsche to Du Bois and Baldwin, each dramatizing the foundational pathologization of Blackness that, in its ideological meanings, is another name for the Dionysian threat that theist and rationalist projects would overcome. Baldwin literally casts whiteness as a "theology" that stipulates the damned (and damnation) to produce the saved. By this redemptive logic, he argues, those who come to call themselves white (and human) enact a rancorous and violent effort to secure exemption from suffering by mastering the bodies made to signify the Blackness of life.[9]

Baldwin's Nietzschean argument about whiteness as theology casts Schmittian political theology in a new light. Against Carl Schmitt's view of a proceduralist and pluralist liberalism, a focus on race suggests that the sovereignty of the liberal state is founded and renewed by violently and discursively imposing a racial state of exception that constitutes friend and enemy. American liberal nationalism weds citizenship and whiteness by a sovereign violence that makes social death, for those marked Black, the condition of life and liberty for those deemed white. Baldwin also unpacked the meaning of whiteness as theology by showing how "Blackness" is linked to the flesh, death, and transience; to irrationality and loss of self; to regressive erasure of boundaries; and, thus, to both chaos and madness. Fear of Blackness—and attraction to it—are manifest in the psychodramatic rhetoric characterizing American politics. As Sheldon Wolin later argued, democracy has been cast in proximity to Blackness by theorists and legislators from Plato to the Federalist Papers. The psychic and cultural origins of fascism, renewing both patriarchy and racial nationalism, thus appear *within* the liberal Enlightenment that, since Hobbes, authorizes itself against the primitive and regressive. Baldwin's claim that liberal modernity is a burning house—a deranged and self-destructive regime—is even more manifest sixty years later.[10]

For Americans are surely undergoing a crisis in the organizing faith that has wed whiteness, America, citizenship, possessive individualism, and patriarchy in an exceptionalist form of what must be called a *religiosity*. The civil rights movement once drew on it, but Americans across lines of race and class now display inchoate apprehensions that purportedly democratic institutions cannot represent them and that the economic growth-mass consumption model of the good life is unsustainable. The constitutive political questions of authority, identification, and redemption are contested now in terrifying but perhaps auspicious ways. Pervasive but tacit knowledge of crisis is not acknowledged in politically salient ways by mainstream media or the Democratic Party establishment but mobilized by the right's melodramatic rhetoric of civil war. Hidden in plain sight, though, Indigenous groups, young workers, resilient feminists, climate change activists, and abolitionists are prefiguring a better world. Theological terms such as *messianic, apocalyptic,* and *eschatological,* and tropes of ending and beginning, seem crucial to grasp the pathos and genres now animating American political culture.

If, as Aristotle argued, rhetoric is the study of available means of persuasion, then this moment requires rhetorically persuasive ways to amplify incipiently democratic possibilities, to recruit wider commitment among millions who are fearful of change but doubtful rather than hostile. My own faith is that imaginative poesis of an alternative futurity, allied with praxis, might enable what the Hebrew Bible calls a "turn," renewal of life that enlarges the circle of the "we." This faith is supported by a resonating historical archive of exemplary experiments and creative voices that model democratic dreams of ending one world by prefiguring another. They do not offer a new ontology to secure an emergent form of life by extrapolitical validation. Rather, they are examples of poesis, by which people in specific circumstances give themselves a future and horizon. Political theology can study different constituencies narrating what endings and beginnings mean, but also can itself be a poetic and political practice of forging countertheology in a moment of danger.

Nihilism, Race, and Countertheology

My own scholarship—on Winstanley, on Hebrew prophecy, and on the prophetic idiom in American struggles against white supremacy—recovers figures and voices who articulate countertheologies to displace the ascetic ideal, and the white supremacy, that have ruled liberal modernity. Across the theological and political frontier created by white supremacy, those marked as nonbeings are themselves called to a decision, to take exception to the racialized state of exception enabling Euro-Atlantic modernity. If Black life is lived in a violent state of racial exception; within a political structure of antagonism, not pluralism, in the wake of a slavery never overcome; in ongoing conditions of social death that characterize its afterlife, the question is: What countertheologies emerge to "take exception to exception" in existential, poetic, and political ways?[11]

By tracing how a theology of anti-Blackness linked Harriet Beecher Stowe's abolitionism to Richard Wright's protest novel in his essay "Everybody's Protest Novel," and by vividly recounting his encounter with the Nation of Islam in *The Fire Next Time*, Baldwin showed how this ongoing state of racial exception can be refused in various but also tragically self-defeating ways. Abolitionist political assumptions and the aesthetics of protest may reify, not escape, the anti-Black grammar that animates white supremacy. But he dramatized the pathology of whiteness, the meaning of Blackness, and the lived experience of people marked Black by a style of literary and political engagement that newly posited a future on different terms than the past seemed to dictate.

Baldwin narrated a catastrophic and traumatic history that foregrounded the problem of unjust suffering and the question of its meaning. He demanded acknowledgment of the past while questioning faith in historical progress. He enacted truth telling by bearing witness to ordinary human capacities not only for depravity and indifference but also for nobility and natality. He therefore situated the present in what I would call *intervals*. One is temporal, between the no longer and the not yet—a present no longer legally enslaved but not yet free. A second appears between grief over irredeemable suffering and grievances framed as demands for justice to recompense injury. A third opens between his sober sense of the depth and grip of white supremacy and his faith that resurrection—from the living death whites make for themselves, and from the social death Blacks undergo—is impossible to foreclose. Finally, Baldwin dramatized an interval between pained apprehension of irreparable harm in a world where "we are not meant to survive" and a vitalizing affirmation of life.[12]

In turn, Baldwin's countertheology inhabits another interval, between organized political engagement (not necessarily with whites) about collective responsibilities and fateful choices, and investment in Black vernacular culture and its aesthetic forms as a form of life to affirm on its own self-validating terms. One register follows the logic that leads from harm to civic remedy, from entangled history to shared fates, and requires organized public-facing action around ideas of justice; it organizes endangered, fugitive Black life into explicitly collective political projects—whether civic/national or anticolonial/diasporic is another issue. The other register doubts the efficacy of public-facing and formally organized politics; it can emphasize improvisational and collaborative practices of ordinary Black sociality but also the interiority and self-expression Kevin Quashie calls "the sovereignty of quiet." Fred Moten works with(in) these intervals.[13]

Fred Moten and Countertheology

The theological character of Moten's work appears most clearly in its relation to the Afropessimism articulated by Frank Wilderson III and Jared Sexton. They depict anti-Blackness as a political ontology that founds the human by stipulating the nonbeing, and thus social death, of those marked Black. Anti-Blackness is ontological because it defines the conditions of being by stipulating nonbeing; it is political because this historical convention could be otherwise, though only by ending the world it constitutes. Because anti-Blackness ontologically equates Blackness with nonbeing to define (human) being, Wilderson and Sexton argue, it renders self-defeating any effort by those marked Black to gain inclusion in the category of the human and the civic membership it entails. In their view, the paradigmatic structure of modernity and the utter exceptionality of Black positionality dictate the failure of coalitional or reform politics. Their narrative is thus eschatological; it seeks the end of the world but offers no praxis by which Black people could engender another world while living in this one. They thus reject Schmitt's emphasis on sovereignty but echo his structure of exceptionality: Requiring a decisive (revolutionary) event to overcome a deadening ordinary routine, they empty out the quotidian practices of Black life.[14]

Moten takes Afropessimist claims seriously, but he suggests how the "fact" or "lived experience" of ordinary Blackness, to use Frantz Fanon's phrase, can be metabolized—dramatized, resisted, and transfigured—in vitalizing ways. First, he accepts the Afropessimist view of anti-Blackness as the foundational "non-relationality" that "structures all relationality."[15] He inhabits the zone of nonbeing designated by the political ontology of anti-Blackness. Second, he echoes Baldwin's argument against Wright: "Blackness is not reducible to its social costs."[16] Moten makes catastrophic modernity generative by showing Black life as a poetic, joyous rejoinder to a regime that reduces Blackness to social death. He refuses to accept, let alone totalize, attributions of deficit or deficiency. He would "occupy nothingness in its fullness" to stand with those "who have nothing and who, in having nothing, have everything."[17] In doing so, he channels the paradox that links Jesus, Blake, the young Marx, the messianism of Benjamin, the "Dionysian Christianity" of Norman O. Brown, and the aesthetics of John Coltrane.

Seeking the generative gifts in nothingness, Moten thus rejects the negative theology of Afropessimists as a mirror of anti-Black ontology. He

George Shulman

instead transvalues the meaning of Blackness, arguing that it signifies generative energies of *life*, which include an "insistent previousness" bearing the inescapable presence of the maternal and historical, as well as the Dionysian flux of an endlessly creative and destructive becoming. Drawing on Hortense Spillers, he links Blackness to the corporeality of the "flesh," the mortal and sentient, maternal and "monstrous" materiality that is demonized by the gendered and individuated grammar of subjects and objects, but that Black people have lived otherwise. Because Blackness animates all (human) beings, Moten can say: "Everyone whom blackness claims, which is to say everyone, can claim blackness"—and so "experiment" with it.[18] The Blackness of life is "essentially fugitive" because it confounds and escapes efforts to define or capture it, including by those marked Black who stipulate what Blackness is.[19] Still, culture can be shaped to claim or affirm this excess of life as becoming.

People marked Black have drawn from dispossession "sociopoetic" practices by which they persist, thrive, and prefigure a new world. What has been refused to people marked Black—status as self-possessed subjects, citizens, and humans—must not be protested as an injustice, though it is, but refused as the grammar that stipulates subject-as-being by equating Blackness and nonbeing. The sovereign self-determination and self-possession of collective and individual subjects must also be refused because it creates a death in life for those enfranchised in such terms. How so? Because investment in the subject as sovereign means turning against the infinite indebtedness and brokenness, sensuous entanglement, and fecund multiplicity of beings that are always "more and less than one."[20]

Moten refuses the death in life created by this grammar, but he does not align "blackness" with formlessness, as the theology of anti-Blackness does. Rather, he contrasts the "logistics" of "those who run things" to the "informal form-giving" of "things that run."[21] He identifies Blackness with a "fugitive sociality" arising from a "common inhabitation" in dispossession and a "common flight" from capture, and expressing a "sociopoetic insurgency" against the rule and grammar of an anti-Black world. Naming certain features of life, but also features of a culture attuned to it, Blackness is thus "juris-generative," albeit not with respect to the nomos of modern liberalism. Those marked Black invent and sustain the colloquial practices of self-reflection and social criticism Moten and Stefano Harney call "study"; the vernacular practices of mutual aid they call "planning"; and the collaborative, improvisatory aesthetic Moten's solo work celebrates in Black music and art. "The ongoing giving of form we call the informal," in its many instantiations, thus constitutes a vitalizing, not deadening, form of life, at once insurgent and prefigurative, because it is attuned to the fractured multiplicity, opaque interiority, complex interdependence, and wayward creativity of all beings.[22]

I would put Moten's countertheology in conversation with Nietzsche, for "anti-Blackness" and "the ascetic ideal" both name the project—ontological, epistemological, moral, political, and colonial—by which Christian religiosity was modernized as a global color line. Nietzsche and Moten thus seek a critical practice that does not repeat the deepest premises, toxic affects, and disavowed drives of the object it professes to oppose. As atheist critics of Christianity retained the will to truth animating their hated object, and thereby sustained both its rancor at the injustice of life and its devaluation of plural perspectives, so abolitionist critics of anti-Blackness risk sustaining its war on life if they devalue the rich vitality of Black life to advance the unconditional truth of anti-Blackness. Moreover, as Eve Sedgwick evoked "the reparative" to address the toxic affect of "strong theory" and its "paranoid" hermeneutics of suspicion, I see Moten fashioning an alter-theology to escape the impasse between the theology of anti-Blackness and the eschatology of Afropessimism.[23]

By his practice of countertheology Moten enters the zone of nonbeing, bears witness to the life hidden in social death, and testifies to the new world it prefigures. Like a prophet, he stands with the poor and the least of us, less to protest their material deprivation and demand a reformed state than to affirm how dispossession can give access to more life; not to demand recognition and rights from the state but to affirm that stateless exile, in a Babylon doomed to self-destruction, prefigures a form of life beyond states and nations. His countertheology thus refuses the civic nationalism of the civil rights movement, even in the radically reconstructionist registers of abolition democracy, and instead claims to honor the Black radicalism that would end the nation-state as the vehicle of a colonialist modernity built on enslavement. Two features of this countertheology are notable.

First, it rejects the structure of exceptionality in political theory, Schmittian political theology, and Afropessimist eschatology that demeans the ordinary—as a site of sin, corruption, enslavement—in the name of an extraordinary (and thus miraculous) overcoming by heroic action (or divine intervention). It is exceptionality that Moten also rejects in Kantian and Aristotelian efforts to split off the properly political (as a space, activity, or orientation) from its abjected (excessive, slavish, heteronomous)

George Shulman

others. Schmitt and Arendt thus disagree about where to locate the political and the miraculous—in sovereign "decision" or non-sovereign "action in concert"—but both split it off from an ordinary life cast as devitalizing, whereas Moten embraces the ordinary by reimagining its vitalizing and form-giving character. He celebrates how subalterns create a "regenerative grammar" of life through tacit practices that are not formally organized or explicitly articulated as counter-sovereignty or formal rulemaking. Opposing the Protestant split between the sociality (and iconography) of the liturgical and individualization by creedal commitment, he invokes jazz to model how entanglement and virtuosity, indebtedness and distinction, aesthetic expression and social collaboration are inseparably bound in (Black) life. Ongoing improvisation enlivens every practice by wedding the aesthetic as form giving and the social as collaboration.

For Moten, second, the political register animating the civil rights movement worked only in the interval between grief and grievance, whereas he would inhabit the interval between "terror and beauty" or "pain and joy," as he puts it. Whereas the political reifies incalculable loss into remediable harms, posits deficiency to demand redress, and reinscribes a grammar of possession to protest denial of rights, he depicts "sociopoetic insurgency" transfiguring the meaning of traumatic history in ways animated by pleasure, not (only) grievance, and by the awe-ful sublime not (only) by justice. Black insurgency is thus an "anti-ante-extra-political party," an ongoing "jam," not a formal organization. The "socio" is "poetic" because informal form giving enacts modes of aesthetic creativity typically split off as an art apart from ordinary life. But Moten denies that the aesthetic is redemptive.

"Some may want to invoke the notion of the traumatic event and its repetition to preserve the appeal to the very idea of redress even after it is shown to be impossible. This is the *aporia* some might think I seek to fill and forget by invoking Black art," as if aesthetic practices offer the redemption that political practices (of redress) cannot. "But jazz does not disappear the problem; it is the problem." It performs "no healing [of trauma] but a perpetual undoing," an "unfolding" and "rewinding" of "rapture and wound."[24] For Moten, "the problem" is not only irremediable suffering but also how forms of poesis metabolize it. Like Nietzsche, he sees how suffering generates forms of meaning—"grammars" and critiques—that disavow the Dionysian Blackness of life *and* the perspectival and contested character of meaning making. In contrast, jazz ensemble and social improvisation, at once aesthetic and social, "hold" unspeakable suffering. Participants inhabit an impasse but transfigure it in ways that engender rather than "arrest" the generativity of life.

Conclusion

I call Moten's work a "countertheology," but in what senses does it warrant the term *theology*? By refusing any organized sense of politics as its condition of possibility, can it be called a "political" theology?

If we define *theology* as specifically theist in a transcendental sense, what do we call an orientation that makes thinkable a world in which vitality is wholly immanent? But if *theology* articulates an organizing faith or formalizes a vernacular orientation toward life, then theism is only one genre of faith, which can be conceived and practiced in wildly various ways. Moten's faith affirms the "Blackness" of life as the groundless ground of a form of life. Orientation toward this excess, fugitivity, but also self-organizing capacity enables a collaborative and improvisational sociality and thus a vitalizing, not deadening, (kind of) nomos. Radical immanence is then an alter-faith that counters "theology" in its "proper" senses.

This orientation escapes the spiritual and political impasse that domination creates for those made subordinate: to be defined either by a sense of deficiency and a quest for remedy and recognition or by a defiance that is reactively bound to its other. Turning aside from that logic and the rancorous affect it entails, Moten affirms the self-organizing life of subalterns on their own self-validating terms. Does this "faith" in radical immanence preclude critical negativity toward a world organized by systemic domination and unjust suffering? Surely not, as Baldwin demonstrated. Partly, Moten's Derridean (and Baldwinian) claim is that every inside includes an excess, remainder, or outside, hidden in plain sight, which makes "general antagonism"—contest and becoming—inescapable. Partly, this Blackness precedes and resists any world in which the few would dominate while the many seek not to be oppressed, as Machiavelli put it. Moten thus bespeaks Benjamin's "weak messianism," which aligns faith in resurrection and insurrection to imagine the everyday building of another world inside and against this one.

But the second obvious critical question appears here. For even if we grant that Moten crafts a "countertheology," its premise is the refusal of politics as conventionally practiced and of the political as canonically conceived. The premise of radical immanence is refusing the false promise of transcendence lodged in the grammar of self-determination and state-centric practices. Moten puts fugitive Black sociality in proximity to politics through the informal assembly, customary mutual aid, and improvisatory collaboration that he calls a "party," but he shifts its meaning. It bespeaks not the logic whereby harm requires a formally organized remedy but, rather, the aesthetic and libidinal registers whereby pain generates beauty and terror generates joy. Those registers of life, he insists, are necessarily devalued and inevitably endangered by people invested in representational or even radically democratic senses of politics. He thus calls his countertheology an "anti-political romance."

Moten not only abstracts from structures of inequality dividing the Black world, as if to posit a commonality long fractured, but he also disavows how institutionalized forms of power have been crucial to the vitality of historical forms of Black self-defense and struggle. It makes sense to refuse false hopes of inclusion or assimilation, and so conventional forms of both liberal politics and leftist radicalism, for the sake of fostering Black solidarity. But the complex reality is that theorists and activists in the Black radical tradition—from Du Bois to the Panthers to the Movement for Black Lives—repeatedly redefine (not only refuse) the political and radicalize (not only refuse) democracy. They have done so, moreover, by mobilizing the poetics and sociality that Moten makes only a fugitive antithesis. They have not separated the social (and aesthetic) from the political but mobilized and organized Black fugitivity into forms of organized power.[25]

It is not credible to say that generativity thrives only by refusing rule and not also through forms of structure, as parents, teachers, and organizers know. Freedom requires not only flight from rule, but flight into it, as a problem of power no one can escape but that a democratic politics must avow and "hold" to rework by participatory practices. But Moten's romance disappears rather than holds the problem of politics because it disappears rather than holds the problem of power. He makes power a demonic specter as he imagines a pastoral and, one might say, messianic escape from politics as rule. I would not discredit this messianism, but I would inflect it differently by seeking vitalizing ways to democratize power.

But it bears emphasis: Radical democrats and abolitionists need to internalize Moten's entirely persuasive critique of the anti-Blackness built into prevailing forms of politics, canonical conceptions of the properly political, and state-centered reform projects. In this sense, his anti-political theology is a necessary moment in creating an alter-political theology that thinks abolition and democracy together. Following the example of the Movement for Black Lives, an alter-political theology would not sever fugitive Black sociality from politics but would politically mobilize and organize Black fugitivity in both inward-facing and outward-facing ways. It would not separate purportedly political and purportedly aesthetic registers but, instead, would relate the pursuit of justice, one gift of Apollo, to forms of expression that transfigure trauma, another gift of Apollo. It would think the relation of radical democracy and abolition not only as a problem of justice, but also as a problem of suffering and form giving by aesthetically inspired praxis while crediting that sometimes it seems impossible to inhabit that interval.

The wager animating my faith is this: To engage the pervasive rancor in our society, a democratic counterculture must embrace not only the necessity but also the limits of the logic of harm and remedy; must affirm the abundance and goodness of life's wayward energies, despite cruel and unjust suffering; and must not only demand justice but forge democratic practices in which playful assembly and festive anger are pleasurable features of life entangled. If a democratic faith is to be saved—which means renewed and enlarged—and if fearful people are to be recruited to it, despite understandable skepticism, "political theology" must dramatize by poesis and prefigure by praxis forms of well-being beyond survival, a future with satisfactions that might justify painful sacrifices to build it.

Notes

1   On poetic fictions, see Blake, *The Marriage of Heaven and Hell*; Stevens, *The Necessary Angel*. On the "ubiquity of faith," see Connolly, *Pluralism*, chap. 1.

2   See Baldwin, *The Fire Next Time*; Nietzsche, *On the Genealogy of Morals*.

3   MacIntyre, "Epistemological Crisis, Dramatic Narrative, and the Philosophy of Science"; Stout, *Democracy and Tradition*.

4   Taubes, *From Cult to Culture*, 223. See Mazarella, *The Mana of Mass Society*.

5   See Jacobson, *Pride and Solace*.

6   See Nietzsche, *On the Genealogy of Morals*, essay 3.

7   See Nietzsche, *The Gay Science*; Nietzsche, *Thus Spoke Zarathustra*.

8   Moten, *Stolen Life*.

9   Baldwin, "Everyone's Protest Novel"; Baldwin, "Racism and World Community"; Carter, *Race*.

10 Baldwin, *The Fire Next Time*; Schmitt, *The Concept of the Political*; Schmitt, *Political Theology*; Wolin, "Fugitive Democracy."

George Shulman

11 Shulman, *American Prophecy*; Shulman, *Radicalism and Reverence*; Tranvik, "George Shulman's Letters on Political Theology."

12 Baldwin, *Notes of a Native Son*, 84. "Between grief and grievance" and "between the no-longer and the not-yet" are the brilliant phrases of Best and Hartman, "Fugitive Justice."

13 Quashie, *The Sovereignty of Quiet*.

14 See Sexton, "The Social Life of Social Death"; Wilderson, "Gramsci's Black Marx." For an elaborated reading of Afro-Pessimism, see Shulman, "Theorizing Life Against Death."

15 Moten, "Blackness and Nothingness (Mysticism in the Flesh)," 749.

16 Moten, "Blackness and Nothingness (Mysticism in the Flesh)," 774.

17 Moten, "Blackness and Nothingness (Mysticism in the Flesh)," 756.

18 Moten, "Black Op," 1746.

19 Harney and Moten, *The Undercommons*, 50.

20 Harney and Moten, *The Undercommons*, 95.

21 Harney and Moten, *The Undercommons*, 64.

22 Moten, *Stolen Life*, 189.

23 Sedgwick, *Touching Feeling*, chap. 4.

24 Moten, *Black and Blur*, xii.

25 Shulman, "Fred Moten's Refusals and Consents."

12

On Black Study and Political Theology

James Edward Ford III

> His fantasies, however unreadable they were for him, were
> inscribed in every one of his gestures, were betrayed in
> every inflection of his voice. . . . There was something
> unspoken between them, unspeakable, undone, and hid-
> eously desired. . . . It had yet to reach the threshold of
> his imagination; and it had no name, no name for him
> anyway, though for other people, so he had heard, it had
> dreadful names.
>
> James Baldwin, *Another Country*

Despite how ready-made Black lives appear for the cat-
egory of bare life, the more pressing issue is how political theology serves
as an object for Black study. Black study is a multidimensional phrase that,
for this chapter's purposes, refers to mass research and intellection that
operates within but is irreducible to the university or its credentialing
functions.[1] The university cannot do with or do without this study. Such
(in)hospitality provides unexpected ground for altering critical vocabularies, methodologies, and canons.

This chapter begins by critiquing received political theology, epitomized by Giorgio Agamben's *Homo Sacer* project carried on between 1995
and 2014. Pressing against the project's habitual avoidances, with an epigraph from James Baldwin as a hermeneutic, brings attention to missed
opportunities for intellectual exchange that might have strengthened
Agamben's inquiry into sovereignty and forms of life. Most important, this
essay identifies a theoretical aporia that troubles Agamben's *Homo Sacer*
project and Western knowledge production in general. The chapter aims to
provoke new intellectual possibilities, to stage new intellectual encounters,
and to perform Black study's rhizomatic character.

When Agamben revisited Carl Schmitt's thesis that political concepts are secularized theological concepts, he revitalized research into political theology in the US academy. This chapter restricts itself to the "sovereign" and "non-sovereign" strands of political theology closest to Agamben's work.[2] Agamben critically appropriates insights from the sovereign strand influenced by Schmitt. However, Walter Benjamin's non-sovereign political theology, encapsulated in the eighth thesis from "On the Concept of History," inspires Agamben's critical appropriation: "The tradition of the oppressed teaches us that 'the state of emergency' in which we live is not the exception but the rule. We must attain a conception of history that is commensurate with this insight. . . . It is our task to bring about a real state of emergency, and this will improve our position in the struggle against fascism."[3] Can Agamben claim to have taken Benjamin's eighth thesis seriously without addressing the vagaries of race, slavery, and colonialism in modernity?

Marcelo Svirsky and Simone Bignall, the editors of *Agamben and Colonialism* (2012), assembled a collection of scholarship that attends to the invisibility of colonialism in Agamben's analysis. Several scholars deem this invisibility stunning, since "at the beginning of the twentieth century Western colonies occupied some *85 per cent of the world's territory*" and were organized through "legal patchwork[s] and ad hoc arrangements of exceptions" composed of "foreign jurisdiction, extraterritorial jurisdiction, administrative decrees, partial annexations, combat zones, martial law and states of emergency."[4] In these instances, the exception becomes the rule, conceptually and historically preceding and modeling the catastrophes that will happen in Europe in the 1930s and 1940s. Svirsky and Bignall express shock that Agamben never discusses Italy's campaign of genocide against Libya's Cyrenaican populations in the 1920s and 1930s, through direct killings and concentration camps. Scholars examining Kenya, South Africa, Palestine, Haiti, Argentina, and postcommunist Russia, among other spaces, reveal the limits of Agamben's thought while adapting it to colonial and postcolonial research. *Agamben and Colonialism* impresses with its temporal and geographical range. Nevertheless, the volume implicitly assumes that Agamben's model is expandable to include colonialism. Bignall and Svirsky's volume does not go far enough to consider whether or not Agamben's theory is incompatible with the models of exception developed through colonialism's and chattel slavery's violence.

To go further, one can radicalize Bignall and Svirsky's observation that Agamben ignores how Greek political thought is "predicated on the fact of slavery as a condition for realization and operation of the *polis*."[5] With *The Use of Bodies* (2015), Agamben's final contribution to the *Homo Sacer* project, he replies to this criticism indirectly by offering his most extensive remarks on slavery. In the chapter "The Animate Instrument and Technology," Agamben explores the links between slavery and instrumentality in Scholastic theology. From his careful readings of Thomas Aquinas's *Summa Theologica*, Agamben concludes that the "symmetry between the slave and the machine . . . concerns the ultimate achievement of anthropogenesis, the becoming fully human of the living human being," and implies "a further symmetry" regarding "the bare life that, being situated on the threshold between *zoè* and *bios*, between *physis* and *nomos*, enables, through its inclusive exclusion, political life."[6] Agamben then asserts the necessity of "restor[ing] to the slave the decisive meaning that belongs to him in the process of anthropogenesis."[7] Agamben considers the slave not just an important instance of bare life but also the greatest example of "use" that is irreducible to the structures of law, property, and consciousness heralded in the West since Aristotle.

The Use of Bodies reaffirms the sense, among many scholars, that the slave must always have been a key instance of bare life. But this argument, which accedes the slave's originary place in the law's production of bare life, accomplishes a sleight of hand that dodges the claim's implications for the entire *Homo Sacer* project. Agamben continues by saying the "invention of slavery as a juridical institution allowed the capture of living beings and of the use of the body into productive systems, temporarily blocking the development of the technological instrument; *its abolition in modernity freed up the possibility of technology, that is of the living instrument.*"[8] This technological turn in modernity has distanced humans even more from "use," which has failed to grant humans liberation and "produc[ed] a new and unheard-of form of slavery."[9] Agamben never explains what this "new and unheard-of form of slavery" actually is. What is for sure, his thesis associates slavery with the ancient world and technology with the modern. Therefore, the "animate instrument" is not modernity's chattel slave but modernity's autonomous machine (and he finds an analogy between the two, but not their hybridity), prefigured by Aristotle's reference to "the legendary statues of Daedalus" in *Politics*.[10] Finally on the verge of becoming a key conceptual figure in thinking of bare life in modernity, the chattel slave again recedes for the sake of another concept.

Although the ancient slave receives extensive commentary in *The Use of Bodies*, one can cite Baldwin in saying that the chattel slave who provides the material basis and labor power to initiate and sustain capitalism, from the sixteenth century until today, has "no name" in the *Homo Sacer* project's textual trajectory.[11] This is ironic since almost every thinker of theology and politics that Agamben revisits, from the late Roman era into the twentieth century, is theorizing imperial formations in relation to new racial classifications of humanity that could not function without considering slavery.[12] The philosophers of late Roman and early medieval Europe, from the third to the fifth centuries, who inform Agamben's *The Kingdom and the Glory* (2011) are steeped in the rhetoric of empire that will inform later theories of sovereignty and racialization. Francisco de Vitoria's arguments for Spain's political dominion and limited land appropriation rights in the New World hinged on the indigene's openness to Christian conversion, which protected them from enslavement but infantilized them for Spain to sustain its new-found imperial holdings.[13] Francisco Suárez will argue that "while 'natural law' permitted slavery, 'human law' could positively require it."[14] Hugo Grotius's *Commentary on the Law of Prize and Booty* (1603) will justify slavery through a free labor argument allowing one to sell oneself voluntarily into slavery; a just war argument enslaving enemies defeated in war; and a moral argument, "thrust[ing]" "men of deplorable wickedness" "into a lower order . . . to the service of the virtuous, changing in a sense from persons into things."[15]

Thomas Hobbes will engage his predecessors, and especially Grotius, to place slavery firmly under the sovereign's rule and justify enslavement of those defeated in war; he will specifically imagine the Native Americans and the "Hottentots" as examples of those who cannot be included in a Western polity as anything other than slaves. These thinkers will influence Immanuel Kant's thoughts on the "unjust enemy," epitomized by people of color in Africa and the Americas who resist Europe's global economic expansion.[16] By the time Schmitt reproaches the unwieldy US imperial formation and waxes nostalgic for the *ius publicum Europaeum* in his *Nomos of the Earth*, it is safe to say that colonial domination and slavery are essential to the sovereign strand of political theology, and racial distinctions are indispensable to identifying who has become bare life and who can declare another to be bare life before the law, globally. Apparently, Agamben is the only thinker in his project who cannot see this.[17] If even Schmitt's attention to colonialism will not sway Agamben, one is left to conclude that Agamben's project is thwarted at the outset by a phobic avoidance of the racialized sites, discourses, movements, and events that most inform the sovereign strand of political theology.

Agamben does examine a modern instance of slavery, and his misreading confirms this chapter's concerns. In *State of Exception*, Agamben frames the US Civil War as a "conflict over sovereign decision."[18] He boldly contends that Abraham Lincoln "acted as an absolute dictator" by emancipating the slaves "on his authority alone," "generaliz[ing] the state of exception throughout the entire territory of the United States" and becoming "the holder of the sovereign decision on the state of exception."[19] It is extremely troubling that Agamben links the Emancipation Proclamation to a dictatorial state of exception *rather than arguing that slavery itself was already one of the boldest generalizations of the exception in nineteenth century America, if not the world*. One might counter that laws existed regulating the slaveowner's treatment of the slave. Those laws only confirm my point, being based on protecting the slave *as property* for others to own and sell, based on a racialized version of the Aristotelian ontological distinction always and already expelling the slave from civil society and legal personhood. The Western tradition contains multiple philosophical arguments, such as those from Hobbes or even John Locke, that considered the relation between master and slave to be unmediated, despite what positive law demands, and placed all right and force on the side of the master. To put it in Agamben's parlance, the master's claim to property precedes positive law and therefore places the slave under the sovereign ban.

This instance of the ban gets misunderstood because it does not create an exception out of legislative, political, or social normality. The colonized and the chattel slave enter modernity without ever inhabiting the zone of normality that provides the theoretical and historical preconditions for the modern citizen's rights and social privileges. Conceptually and historically, the United States has tended to assume that normality, property, and racial affiliation precede laws that might justify slavery or abolish it. This example reveals the limits of Agamben's emanationist treatment of the law. He, too, often makes the law the cause when it is the overdetermined effect of prior struggles—in this case, the way proslavery forces prevailed by leveraging assumptions about (and affective investments in) subjectivity, property, racialization, and legal metaphysics. As Allison Powers argues in a recent essay, legal metaphysics defined white people as civilized and Black people as barbaric.[20] By this logic, Emancipation and the granting of citizenship to freed people counts as barbarians conquering the civilized. This characterization means the desire for (increased) freedom for the half a million

James Edward Ford III

free and four million enslaved Black people in 1863 *must not* inform Lincoln's decision making. If, by this logic, Black voices for freedom do not count and proslavery voices dominate the white constituency (because white abolitionists have been bullied into silence and other whites do not care), then it produces a distorted version of the American multitude. If one judges Lincoln's Emancipation Proclamation based on this distortion, then one must conclude that he was not meeting the needs of the nation. He was a dictator carrying out his arbitrary will. This logic and its outcome is a hallmark Confederate claim. Undoubtedly, Agamben would shudder at realizing that his argument places him squarely in a Confederate perspective. That makes the shortcomings of his model even more alarming.

However, another force in opposition to chattel slavery remains illegible for Agamben. As W. E. B. Du Bois writes in *Black Reconstruction*, the enslaved had consistently undermined slavery through the Underground Railroad. When the various legal compromises meant to appease and contain slaveholding interests failed and fomented civil war, the fugitive slave used the routes of the Underground Railroad to escape en masse to the Union camps, by the dozens, hundreds, even thousands. Du Bois called this the "general strike" that destroyed the Confederacy because it removed the labor power and living infrastructure—the animate instruments—that the South needed to win. The South knew that as long as it had control of the slaves, it could win the Civil War. It was winning until the strike reached its climax, which Du Bois places at about half a million workers who joined the Union and joined every facet of the war effort to defeat the South. Most important, it is crucial that neither the Union nor the South saw this eventuality because both sides believed Black people were natural slaves who could not want freedom. Therefore, the South assumed it could fight a war that threatened to expand or end slavery and the enslaved would not intervene. Even Lincoln, the commander of the Union army, rejected the plan to arm the slaves, since he believed the slaves were so passive they would hand the guns to their masters. Even when the freed people escaped to join the camps, official policy meant they were "contraband" who must be returned to their owners. In other words, both sides bought into a version of the Aristotelian distinction between the natural free person and natural slave, altered to fit the needs of capitalism and white racial hegemony.

Yet against all these odds, the Black masses *freed themselves* from slavery. Lincoln and his cabinet belatedly realized they could exploit this plan devised by Black folk to the Union's advantage—hence, the Emancipation Proclamation. Lincoln did not act arbitrarily as a dictator. As Du Bois puts it: "Lincoln's proclamation only added possible legal sanction to an accomplished fact."[21] This is precisely the "insurrection and revolution" that Agamben mentions at the start of State of Exception, an "inverse movement" during "the state of exception, by which law is suspended and obliterated in fact."[22] Delving further into Agamben's reading of Emancipation and the Civil War in the United States was meant not to castigate his personal politics but to reveal serious limits to his model, which confuses a *real* state of exception, the primary objective of Benjamin's eighth thesis, with yet another instance of oppression.

Agamben is unable to detect this liberatory agency among the freed people because he loses sight of the first clause in Benjamin's eighth thesis: "The tradition of the oppressed teaches us." Agamben does not give enough attention to this tradition as a productive site of struggle and contestation in the *Homo Sacer* project. This is not surprising, seeing that Agamben methodologically brackets the insurrection and revolution that characterizes this tradition, and he selected primary juridical and philosophical sources that often sought to mute this tradition's impact on society. Moreover, this unreadability results from using the syntagma as a tool for "decontextualization," which allows for greater internal coherence within Agamben's theory but weakens its political implications, separated as they are from the archive giving them relevance and urgency.[23] Too often bracketed, decontextualized, and unread, the tradition of the oppressed includes a range of discontents demonstrating alternative forms of affiliation and empowerment. If the archive under discussion is the *longue durée* of Europe's formation, then it can be understood only alongside the fugitive, insurrectionary, non-sovereign politics that have also characterized modernity.

Thirty years ago, Barbara Christian critiqued European thinkers for *assuming*, rather than arguing for, the universal applicability of their theses.[24] She critiqued American institutions for following suit through curricular design, conference planning, funding, and publishing projects. In contrast, arguments from scholars of color are too often assumed to be provincial, no matter the project's global stakes. This pattern in knowledge production is an offshoot of presuppositions about some humans counting as humans and others counting as partially humans and as instruments, and about the former's ability to claim the latter's *thought*, even if it is claimed only to be disposed of. In other words, sentiment alone is not obstructing scholars from learning from the tradition of the oppressed.

James Edward Ford III

Intellectual principles quietly operating in this situation have created long-term impediments.

Now to a brief consideration of one of those impediments, located in Aristotle's ontological distinction in *Politics* between the naturally free person and natural slave or "living instrument": "[A] possession is an instrument for maintaining life. And so, in the arrangement of the family, a slave is a living possession [,] . . . an instrument which takes precedence of all other instruments"; this special instrument "obey[s] or anticipat[es] the will of others."[25] When Agamben returns to this Aristotelian distinction, he identifies a "use of bodies" that renders inoperative the distinctions enabling Western politics and producing bare life. But that "use of bodies" does not speak to the intellectual labor of the slave, which is no less appropriable than physical labor in Aristotle's account of *oikonomia*:

> For that which can foresee by the exercise of mind is by nature in-
> tended to be lord and master, and that which can with its body give
> effect to such foresight is a subject, and by nature a slave; hence master
> and slave have the same interest. . . . [F]or the part is not only a part
> of something else, but wholly belongs to it. . . . The master is only the
> master of the slave; he does not belong to him, whereas the slave is
> not only the slave of his master, but wholly belongs to him. . . . [H]e
> who is by nature not his own but another's man, is by nature a slave.[26]

Aristotle makes the slave's intellect an extension of the master's intellect: "The master and the slave have the same interest." The slave's thinking necessarily echoes the master's thoughts, even if the master could never have produced such ideas. Sometimes, the slave's ideas are deemed irrelevant. At other times, the slave's ideas are so important they magically become the master's discoveries. The outcome remains the same: The master never has to think *with* or be the object *of* the slave's thought (if one sticks to Aristotle's subject-object distinction). The slave cannot think for himself or herself; the slave can think only *for* the master's benefit. Even if that slave thinks of their own liberation, this gets misconstrued as potential theft of property: The slave could never have imagined freedom on their own; another master must have given them the idea, by this logic. Countless examples of this logic fill the freed persons' narratives across the Western Hemisphere.[27]

One should follow Frantz Fanon in *The Wretched of the Earth* by distinguishing this Aristotelian dialectic from Hegelian recognition, since this tension between master and slave cannot achieve a higher unity.[28] The master's subjectivity would dissolve if it has to recognize the slave's autonomous intellectual agency, which thwarts a dialectic of recognition at the outset. Agamben's ruminations on "contemplation" carry much promise on this matter. Agamben distinguishes contemplation from consciousness, since the latter assumes a subject divorced from its numerous individual and collaborative actions, a separation that is essential to Western ideas of sovereignty. Contemplation, in contrast, refers to a collective's fully immersive process of creating and reflecting on oneself during that process. For Agamben, contemplation belongs to a countertradition within and outside of the West's parameters. As this chapter shows, that promise gathers the greatest force within a Black studies context. In the meantime, suffice it to say the textual trajectory of the *Homo Sacer* project indicates that the aporia trapping and exploiting the slave's intellectual production does not die with the ancient world. Aristotle's thought about the slave's intellectual labor gets taken up in the late medieval and early modern eras and informs imperial *Europa*'s image of itself and of non-European peoples.[29] For instance, Grotius will revive Aristotle's arguments by stating that slaves may "partake of the rational faculty," but this partial "claim to virtue" "cannot be placed on a level with free men," since slaves lack "the deliberative faculty."[30] Grotius makes the slave the paradigmatic case for all other oppressed figures: "This same principle [of intellectual inferiority] that is applicable to slaves, may be applied to other subject persons."[31] Grotius therefore provides a basis for treating a wide range of modern colonized populations like Aristotle's slave, even with regard to their intellectual capacities.

Craig Wilder's *Ebony and Ivy: Race, Slavery, and the Troubled History of America's Universities* makes clear that when slaveholders across the Atlantic Basin invested heavily in American colleges and universities from the seventeenth to the nineteenth centuries, they set the institutional conditions to continue appropriating the intellectual labor of "subjected persons" into our present. Quite literally, these educational institutions were shaped in a master's discourse that rejects *and* appropriates the intellect of nonwhite groups in the same movement. Changes to the human sciences' curriculum and scholarship from the 1960s to the 1980s dealt a blow to this master's discourse by rendering racially homogeneous national "canons" untenable in theory. While this attack challenged that discourse's intellectual consistency, that discourse's hold on institutional power remains, such that shifts in theory remained internal to European thought, and even those gains did not always translate into new institutional openness to alternative traditions with different questions, vocabularies, methodologies, and answers. To quote Baldwin once again, the slave or the subject person's runaway intellect, as inappropriable as it is demanding, has "yet to reach the threshold" of the critical "imagination" guiding much of contemporary theory.[32]

This dearth of critical imagination is the true target of Benjamin's eighth thesis, making it a utopian and a cautionary tale that demands the undoing of the master's discourse and its retrogressive effects. One must venture into the tradition of the oppressed, into the work of subject persons and their intellectual descendants, as something other than a byproduct of European thinkers or colonial capture. As a brief case study, consider Sylvia Wynter's thrilling essay "1492: A New World View," published the same year as Agamben's *Homo Sacer*. Wynter's essay examines several texts that will figure highly in future contributions to the *Homo Sacer* project. Wynter recasts the rise of intellectual humanism so that it can be understood only through racialization. Columbus's voyages adhere to a "mercantile imperative" that "cannot be disentangled from" an "apocalyptic millenarian belief in the imminent Second Coming of Christ," and this combination unexpectedly yields what Wynter will call the "juro-theological." In late medieval and early modern Europe, a "reversal" occurs in which "the *Christian* church, of which the earlier feudal states of Latin Europe had been the temporal and military arm, would now in turn be made into the spiritual arm of these newly emergent absolute states."[33] Like Agamben's political theology, Wynter's "juro-theological" examines how Western culture once pursued "the eternal salvation of the Augustinian *civitas dei*" and then pursued the "*civitas saecularis*," the "transmuted this-worldly variant of the original feudal-Christian goal." Feudal Christian concepts took on new meanings during this transition from *civitas dei* to *civitas saecularis*, as European nation-states competed to become global powers.[34] Like Agamben in *The Kingdom and the Glory*, Wynter notes that through liturgical excesses, Latinate Europe finds a heavenly model for its earthly imperial goals.

In regard to the significance of race, however, Wynter's and Agamben's approaches could not diverge more widely. In Agamben's *The Kingdom and the Glory*, the translation of the Christian Trinitarian economy into government happens strictly within European Continental borders, though virtually every author he analyzes from the third and fifth centuries speaks in the terms of an empire that, by definition, requires expansion across the globe. *The Kingdom and the Glory* makes barely a reference to the actual effects such imperial rhetoric and restructuring of the political will have on the framing of navigation, land appropriation, and violent conquest around the globe a few centuries later. Wynter has already noted the significance of racial difference in the matter, since "glory" could not be obtained without religious conversion, economic exploitation, resource extraction, and political domination—in a word, colonialism: "Because of the specific terms on which the state transferred to its new, essentially mercantilist-political goal . . . *all non-Christian peoples and cultures became perceivable only in terms of their usefulness to the European states in securing their this-worldly goal of power and wealth.*"[35] How discomfiting is it to read Agamben speaking in *The Kingdom and the Glory* of "a field of research" "as yet unexplored" when Wynter was studying imperial glory in Black studies twelve years earlier.[36]

Wynter asserts that the year 1492 radically alters the metanarratives "*common to all human* cultures and their traditional 'forms of life.'" The "humanists," "monarchical jurists and theologians" of the day, the same class of intellectuals that fit the timeline and textual trajectory of Agamben's project, will develop new juridical principles and classifications of these forms of life.[37] Wynter once again traverses an array of scholarly sources to explain how these new classifications took shape under the broad category of race. The "apocalyptic millenarian drive" will continue to extend and set the stage for overturning the "feudal-Christian geographic accounts." As Portugal and Spain navigate the African continent and make inroads into the sub-Saharan regions and envision a lucrative triangular slave trade in the Americas, so European thinkers and politicians begin researching earlier imperial historiographies. As a result of the traffic in bodies and European study, the category of the "Indian" develops from the encounter between Europe and Indigenous populations in the Americas, while the category "black" develops from the encounter of Europe, indigenous African populations, and "medieval Islam's geographic accounts of the non-monothesistic indigenous peoples of Africa below the Sahara."[38] There, "stereotyped images" of "peoples of black Africa" played a "dual function" as the group who could be "legitimately enslaved" as well as "the extreme term that embodied the absolute lack of the optimal criterion of being as well as of rationality that defined the medieval Islamic way of life."[39] Wynter notes that the Zanj referred to indigenous African populations no longer protected through conventional kinship ties. The same stereotypes justifying the enslavement of Black Africans in the Arab slave trade would eventually be adopted by European slavers and expanded to an unprecedented scale.

In a single essay that thinks racialization and imperial expansion together, Wynter takes readers through several important themes that will show up in the *Homo Sacer* project, including empire, glory, forms of life, Christianity, and secularity. It is a serious missed opportunity for intellectual exchange that Wynter's essay had gone unmentioned at the start of the *Homo Sacer* project. That this non-exchange lasted for twenty years raises greater fears that Agamben's initial bracketing maneuvers amount to methodological foreclosure. To quote Baldwin, "There was something unspoken between them," something "unspeakable, undone," in this missed opportunity for cross-disciplinary exchange and, more pressing, to get beyond the master's discourse hearkening back to Aristotle.[40]

The question is what generativity irrupts from undoing the master's discourse as it informs the sovereign strand of political theology. The master's discourse would risk its own coherence in attending to, and not just attacking, Black life—a form of life that is not property, nor is it lacking property, as some pessimists might conclude, but *does not need* property for its coherence or vitality, save only tactically.[41] One might couple this with Fred Moten's claim that "blackness" "is not the property of black people. All that we have (and are) is what we hold in our outstretched hands."[42] David Marriott might veer from Moten's theme of the gift, but he, too, has noted through a reading of Fanon's figures of failure that Blackness "can never be a ground for self or propriety, and to that extent it cannot be thought of in terms of self-present mastery."[43] This is not simply bare life, though that is precisely what the master's discourse would prefer scholars think, because it would dodge grappling with Blackness as simultaneously negation *and surplus*. Blackness provides another way into the strand of non-sovereign political theology that places Agamben's insights into a different ensemble of concerns and approaches.

In *Seizing Freedom*, David Roediger agreed with Du Bois's calling Reconstruction a "tragedy that beggared the Greek."[44] Roediger leaves the "tragic" dimension of revolutionary time loosely defined in his fast-paced book. Evidence abounds for describing Jubilee's aftermath as tragic, if that term signals the heartbreak of liberatory objectives come to naught. But *tragedy* is one of the most loaded terms in the West, so it deserves a closer look.

Tragedy designates a particular type of narrative and a particular way to analyze narrative. When the former folds into the latter, tragedy often becomes another site of spectatorship with predetermined rises and falls. The question is how to speak to the heartbreak without easing into that pattern. While Roediger rightly references Du Bois calling the Civil War and Reconstruction a "tragedy that beggared the Greek," he does not go far enough in saying how this repeated, countered, or surpassed the Greek conceptualization. Roediger the historian need not become a literary critic. If anything, his limitation indicates that literary critics should not fixate solely on *The Souls of Black Folk* among Du Bois's prose books when his later nonfiction writings continue to reinvent long-form prose. Keep in mind that each chapter of *Black Reconstruction* concludes with stanzas of poetry from authors as varied as James Weldon Johnson, Oscar Wilde, Ralph Waldo Emerson, Fannie Stearns Davis, William Rose Benet, and Jessie Fauset. These lyric stanzas, when strung together, already encapsulate his argument and provide an avenue for tracing particular themes that play out across several chapters. The form of *Black Reconstruction*'s narrative makes contingency legible and charts an overdetermined process of collective transformation. Emancipation's history is tragic because things actually could have panned out differently, and its modernist assemblage retains that suspense as it produces new insights for attentive readers today.

Du Bois puts the tragic to multiple uses, including a reference to the Black worker's structural vulnerability in slave conditions; the "fearful tragedy" that associates the Civil War with "destiny" in Charles Sumner's speeches demanding full rights for Black people not out of goodwill, but out of urgent necessity; the Black population's role as "Nemesis" of Greek mythology who restores justice in the face of hubris; and the tragedy of monopolists and their minions seducing Andrew Johnson into betraying his beloved working-class causes.[45] These, many scholars have touched on. Fewer have attended to another instance concluding the "Back Toward Slavery" chapter, where Du Bois says, "The unending tragedy of Reconstruction is the utter inability of the American mind to grasp its real significance," amounting to "a revolution comparable to the upheavals in France in the past, and in Russia, Spain, India, and China today."[46] The master's discourse that ran the country blindly into Civil War and slaughter, that railed against Reconstruction and sabotaged it to create Jim Crow, still could not understand the meaning of these world-historical events in the 1930s, when Du Bois wrote *Black Reconstruction*. Du Bois addresses what Roediger's looser definition of tragedy misses: There is a tragic dimension to the master's discourse. It *must* deny certain truths about itself and the world and would rather lose the world then lose its phantasmatic self-image as conqueror, liberator, victim, vigilante, and moral exemplar.

Still, that form of tragedy does not exhaust Blackness. Du Bois admits "the long step backward toward slavery" after Reconstruction's sabotage has dealt "deep scars" to Black people's "soul[s]." For this reason, Du Bois places little faith in the national imagination affirming (self-)Emancipation's radical force. But he applauds Black people, who have "made withal a brave and fine fight . . . against ridicule and monstrous caricature, against every . . . cruelty and gross insult, against starvation, disease and murder." The internal movement of Black life, alongside the coalitions Black people initiated, failed in their "attempt to make black men American citizens." But it was a "splendid failure": "It did not fail where it was expected to fail. It was Athanius contra mundum . . . with all the wealth and all the opportunity, and all the world against him. *And only in his hands and heart the consciousness of a great and just cause; fighting the battle of all oppressed and despised humanity of every race and color, against the massed hirelings of Religion, Science, Education, Law, and brute force.*"[47] The Black collective is immersed in experimentation that provides a condition of possibility for sustaining diasporic belonging, alongside broader coalitions disinvesting from the being for death enshrined by sovereign political theology. These splendid experimenters do not desire the master's recognition, save to hurry the master's dissolution. They play Nemesis to the master's hirelings. This is not leisure but an acknowledgment of contemplation's role in common survival. The Black collective is immersed in experimentation that provides the condition of possibility for sustaining diasporic Black culture alongside broader coalitions disinvesting from the being for death enshrined by sovereign political theology. In this volume, George Shulman rightly claims that "freedom requires not only flight from rule, but flight into it." This claim deserves amplification. During and after the Civil War, the fugitives and free people destroyed some institutions even as they transformed others and built new ones according to a radical democratic vision, knowing that Confederates were taking every opportunity to reestablish slavery after their absolute surrender. Similarly, however much one sympathizes with today's calls to tear down current political institutions in one fell swoop, one must remember that far-right organizations also want institutional collapse so they can build new institutions dedicated to dictatorship—hence, the need for contemplation or, in other words, the poetic process of transforming oneself and one's world, including making difficult choices about what institutions to undo completely, transform from within, and invent from the ground up. The splendid experimenters mentioned in *Black Reconstruction* and those who follow in their footsteps today do not desire the master's recognition, save to hurry the master's dissolution. They play Nemesis to the master's hirelings. This is not leisure but an acknowledgment of contemplation's role in common survival.

And so, with one foray into political theology coming to a close, may this runaway intellection, long underway, continue with its study.

Notes

Material from this chapter first appeared in "On Black Study and Political Theology," *Cultural Critique* 101 (2018): 187–219.

Epigraph: Baldwin, *Another Country,* 199.

1 Jack Halberstam's foreword to *Undercommons* defines "study" as "a mode of thinking with others separate from the thinking that the [academic] institution requires of you": Harney and Moten, *The Undercommons,* 11.

2 Vatter, "The Political Theology of Carl Schmitt."

3 Benjamin, "On the Concept of History," 4:392.

4 Shenhav, "Imperialism, Exceptionalism, and the Contemporary World," 21, 23, 24, emphasis added.

5 Svirsky and Bignall, "Introduction," 1.

6 Agamben, *The Use of Bodies,* 78.

7 Agamben, *The Use of Bodies,* 78

8 Agamben, *The Use of Bodies,* 79, emphasis added.

9 Agamben, *The Use of Bodies,* 79.

10 Agamben, *The Use of Bodies,* 77.

11 Baldwin, *Another Country,* 203.

12 Blackburn, *The Making of New World Slavery,* 180; Nyquist, *Arbitrary Rule,* 20–56.

13 Judy, *(Dis)forming the American Canon,* 79–84.

14 Blackburn, *The Making of New World Slavery,* 179–80.

15 Grotius, *Commentary on the Law of Prize and Booty.*

16 Baucom, "Cicero's Ghost."

17 Hence, Agamben devotes more pages to a single sentence on Pontius Pilate in Schmitt's *Nomos* than to three sections of *Nomos* discussing the colonization of the New World and Africa.

18 Agamben, *State of Exception,* 20.

19 Agamben, *State of Exception,* 21.

20 Powers, "Tragedy Made Flesh."

21 Du Bois, *Black Reconstruction in America, 1860–1880,* 84.

22 Agamben, *State of Exception,* 29.

23 Vardoulakis, "The Ends of Stasis," 56.

24 Christian, "The Race for Theory."

25 Aristotle, *Politics*, book 1, 99.

26 Aristotle, *Politics*, book 1, 96.

27 See Moten, "Knowledge of Freedom," especially the discussion of Mary Prince.

28 "The zone where the natives live is not complementary to the zone inhabited by the settlers. The two zones are opposed, but not in the service of a higher unity. Obedient to the rules of pure Aristotelian logic, they both follow the principle of reciprocal exclusivity. No conciliation is possible, for of the two, one is superfluous": Fanon, *The Wretched of the Earth*, 38–39.

29 "The venture of transferring sub-Saharan peoples across the Atlantic correlates to the clearer articulation of the fiscal circuit (and cultural identity) 'Europe.' . . . This is to say that, paradigmatically, the 'first major consignment of slaves for the Americas was thus in every sense a European enterprise'": Barrett, *Racial Blackness*, 18–19.

30 Grotius, *Commentary on the Law of Prize and Booty*.

31 Grotius, *Commentary on the Law of Prize and Booty*.

32 Baldwin, *Another Country*, 203. This is odd considering *Black Reconstruction*'s global influence, even on Italian leftists who read it on the eve of 1968, as Ferrucio Gambino has recently stated. How might Du Bois's masterpiece have altered Agamben's reading of emancipation?

33 Wynter, "1492," 14.

34 Wynter, "1492," 13.

35 Wynter, "1492," 17, emphasis added.

36 Agamben, *The Kingdom and the Glory*, 188.

37 Wynter, "1492," 13.

38 Wynter, "1492," 20.

39 Wynter, "1492," 21.

40 Baldwin, *Another Country*, 203.

41 Robinson, *Black Marxism*, 168.

42 Moten, "The Subprime and the Beautiful," 238.

43 Marriott, "No Lords A-Leaping," 527.

44 Roediger, *Seizing Freedom*, 15; Du Bois, *Black Reconstruction in America, 1860–1880*, 727.

45 Du Bois, *Black Reconstruction in America, 1860–1880*, 10, 196, 237, 322.

46 Du Bois, *Black Reconstruction in America, 1860–1880*, 708.

47 Du Bois, *Black Reconstruction in America, 1860–1880*, 708, emphasis added.

13

The Science of the Word

SYLVIA WYNTER, POLITICAL THEOLOGY,
AND HUMAN HYBRIDITY

David Kline

Political theology and science are both complicit in the most pressing problems threatening Earthly existence today. The global challenges of racism, mass inequality, climate instability, and political stalemates are intimately linked to colonial histories of both political-theological and scientific forms of dehumanization and control. In the wake of Western colonialism and its weaponization of both religion and science, have theological and secular-scientific traditions of knowledge exhausted their capacity to contribute to human flourishing? Are other ways of thinking them possible? What place does theology have in a technocratic political order that has deflated the epistemic import of religious reflection? What bearing does science have on theological traditions grasping for political relevance in a secular frame? These are questions for both the present and the future of political theology. They are also questions called forth by the urgent necessity of new forms of knowledge and political paradigms able to face (and possibly avert) the impending "catastrophe for our species."[1]

Perhaps there is no contemporary thinker more suited to help answer questions of this magnitude than the Black studies theorist Sylvia Wynter. Over the past four decades Wynter has developed her epoch-spanning project of thinking a new account of human being beyond "Man," the colonial Christian West's "overrepresented" figure of a singular and universal form of human life that organizes the modern epistemological, political, and economic global order. Political theology and science both play central roles in Wynter's genealogy of Man, especially in her account of the racial order of colonial modernity and the Christian conceptual foundations of the secularized episteme of the contemporary global order. While there has been much recent political-theological engagement with Wynter's account of medieval and early modern Iberian Catholic theological systems of human difference, less attention has been given to the question of where political theology might fit within her constructive project of a "new science of the word" aiming to move beyond the "biocentric" framework of Man's current epistemological regime that reduces human beings to biological entities. By studying human beings' "hybrid" nature as composed of both biology and culture, or *bios/logos*, the new science of the word expands scientific knowledge to include the fullness of human forms of life against received (Western) notions of human authenticity that serve racist systems of social division and control. It also aims to recover a poetic ground for scientific inquiry oriented around self-creation (as culture) as the basis of a new human future of global solidarity. While Wynter seems reticent about religion and theology being constitutive parts of the new science of the word, turning instead to the idea of a fully realized "true secularism" of human cognitive autonomy, this chapter suggests that political theology still might have a crucial role to play in her new scientific vision. Despite her new scientific critique of the "illusions" of religious constructions as obstacles to cognitive autonomy and a fully free human agency, I suggest that religion and theology remain unavoidable functions of human self-creation, and even in Wynter's new science of the word should continue to be thought of as key modes of human storytelling and speculative thinking that will be necessary for the kind of interhuman collaborative thinking that she links to the new science.

The Autopoietic Turn

After an already brilliant intervention into cultural studies and theories of decolonial resistance spanning the years 1967–1984 and culminating with her magisterial unpublished volume *Black Metamorphosis*, Wynter turns her intellectual energy to developing a project capable of producing nothing less than a total reimagining of human life beyond the colonial order of Man.[2] This turn is marked by a vast interdisciplinary synthesis of Black studies, natural sciences, philosophy, anthropology, literature, and systems theory that positions Wynter as a truly unique thinker among her intellectual peers. Beginning with the 1984 essay "The Ceremony Must Be Found: After Humanism," and culminating with the 2015 essay "The Ceremony Found: Towards the Autopoetic Turn/Overturn, Its Autonomy of Human Agency and Extraterritoriality of (Self)Cognition," Wynter constructs a "new science of the word" inspired by Aimé Césaire's call for a new paradigm of scientific inquiry centered on human cultural production. The aim of this new science is not only a new description of human being but also an ultimate decolonial global revolution whose conceptual coordinates are laid out by, among others, Humberto Maturana and Francisco

Varela's theory of autopoiesis, Frantz Fanon's notion of "sociogenesis," and Césaire's understanding of poetic knowledge. Together, these theoretical frameworks provide Wynter a kind of scientific avant-garde capable of generating a revolutionary new form of knowledge that is both adequate to the global diversity of human forms of life and capable of overturning the current epistemic hegemony of Man.

Perhaps the theoretical framework that makes Wynter stand out most in terms of her position within Black studies is that of "autopoiesis," Maturana and Varela's neologism that describes all living entities as self-generating unities organized around specific dynamic relations and not any essence or set of component parts.[3] One of the key insights of autopoiesis for Wynter is that all human cognitive experience and knowledge is the product of a particular (i.e., embodied) point of view that is coherent only within a specific cultural mode of praxis. In autopoiesis, there is no separation between how life is lived and how the world appears to us. This insight is a crucial foundation for Wynter's understanding of "genres of being human," the multiple forms of human life grounded in different languages, stories, and religio-cultural modes of praxis that span the human species.

Autopoiesis is also the category that enables Wynter to build an epistemological bridge between the biology of human existence and sociolinguistic social formations. Human beings are a "hybrid" species made of both biology and language, or "*bios/logos*." Autopoiesis applies to both sides of the *bios/logos* dyad: Human self-creation occurs through both biological processes and narrative productions of truth and knowledge that are experienced in a social context as objective. Following Fanon's discovery that "besides phylogeny and ontogeny stands sociogeny," Wynter introduces the "sociogenic principle": Human life cannot be explained within the "biocentric" terms of the natural sciences that reduce human beings to biological entities but must be understood as a hybrid phenomenon that is "socio-situationally determined, with these determinations in turn, serving to activate their physicalist correlates."[4]

In Wynter's metahistorical framework, human autopoiesis and sociogenesis are situated in what she calls the "third event" (after the "first event" of the creation of the universe and the "second event" of the autopoietic emergence of sentient life on Earth) in which human beings first emerged as a distinctively hybrid species. The third event is marked by "the [origin] of the co-mutational emergent properties of language and narrative with the brain, themselves as the indispensable conditions of being the uniquely auto-instituting mode of living being that we are."[5] Language is the key element of the third event because of its open-ended capacity to enable diverse forms of linguistic experience and communication. It also introduces something wholly new into the history of living beings: storytelling. What makes human beings unique in relation to nonhuman animals is their ability to tell stories about their origins and environments that make possible a sense of the world in excess of their biological and genetic instincts. Like that of all other life-forms, human experience is grounded in phylogenetic and ontogenetic laws of neurobiological processes (what Wynter refers to as the "first set of instructions") that are the physical conditions of their consciousness. Unlike that of nonhuman animals, human experience is *also* set loose from these physical/biological limitations through their capacity of language that enables them to "*override*, where necessary . . . *the first set of instructions* of our own DNA."[6] As Wynter understands it, genres of being human are like a beehive in that they operate around genetically determined instincts related to biological processes and rudimentary social formations. Yet unlike bees in a beehive, human beings have the capacity to turn their genetically predetermined instincts toward an open-ended "second set of instructions" that are developed through the phenomenon of language and its expression as culture.[7] The second set of instructions is always "genre-specific," meaning that it is entirely subjective to the specific cultural stories through which each genre of being human experiences reality. Yet each genre also experiences this second set of instructions in a way analogous to the first set of instructions: The stories human beings tell about themselves and their environments are experienced *as if* they were the same as biological determination.

Autopoiesis, (Auto)Religion, and Political Theological Coding

The experience of cultural production as objective reality is precisely where religion shows up as a key (although understated) category in Wynter's thinking. The "second set of instructions" is underwritten by a particular sociogenic mechanism that emerges with the phenomenon of language. Where all living autopoietic systems operate around a "biochemical system of reward and punishment" that regulates neurological responses to physical events that happen in the system's environment (the "first set" of instructions), the sociogeny of human hybridity takes this rewards/punishment system and "transposes" it onto the *symbolic* realm of language (the "second set").[8] It is this transposition that is made possible through what Wynter identifies as "religion," which is "already presupposed with . . . the emergence of language."9 As she writes in "The Ceremony Must Be Found," "the link of continuity/discontinuity [between pre-linguistic biological processes and human language] is the shift from genetic to rhetorical-figurative systems of group bonding, with the latter carrying affective loadings from the former and the inheritable programs which determined cognition/behaviors being transferred to the governing systems of figuration called religion."10 I refer to this understanding of religion in Wynter's writing as "autoreligion," which emerges as a specifically hybrid autopoietic operation through which the prelinguistic genetic instinct of group bonding is offloaded onto a rhetorical figurative system of symbolic transcendence.11 Autoreligion is crucial to the creation and experience of a social identity grounded in a particular narrative schema of existence. Wynter describes this autoreligious mechanism as a form of storytelling that produces narrative codes of "extrahuman" order and determination, or the idea that a transcendent force outside of human beings' own self-produced narratives of origin and existence (whether articulated as divine or natural) is determinative of the ways in which human life is ordered and lived.

It is here that political-theological modes of distinction also appear as a key function of autoreligion. The production and repetition of autoreligious narratives legitimates and grounds each genre of being human's sense of self and the boundaries that separate the (self-referential) inside from the outside. Wynter's sociogenic principle understands autoreligion as the key mechanism tying the production of transcendent codes of symbolic life ("the name of what is good") and death ("the name of what is evil") to the "opiate reward and punishment biochemical implementing mechanisms of the brain."12 By linking the narratives of symbolic life/death to the neurobiological operations of the brain, each genre of being human is determined by "the imperative boundary of *psycho-affective closure*" that keeps it "*non-consciously*" subordinated to the symbolic codes governing the distinction between the "us" and the "them," or, in Carl Schmitt's famous theologico-political terms, the "friend" and the "enemy."13 These codes are made materially real through concrete practices of rewarding those who adhere to the symbolically sanctioned criterion of proper communal existence ("good") and subordinating and punishing those who do not align with or exist outside of these criterion ("evil"). Because autoreligion compels genres of being human to experience these codes as given from beyond the social community itself, they are unable to perceive that the stories told about human origins, cosmological situatedness, and ontopolitical differentiation are in fact the products of their own self-inscription.

Autoreligion and the Political Theology of Man

It is from the concept of autoreligion and its concealment of the self-generated nature of each genre of being human's sense of reality that Wynter levels her new scientific critique of Man. What is at stake in Wynter's genealogy is the figure of human being itself, which Man has hijacked under its own "secular liberal monohumanist *conception* of being."[14] While ontopolitical social hierarchization is not historically unique to Man, what is unprecedented is both the global scale on which its overdetermination of a single form of life is imposed and, as is crucial for political-theological genealogies, the secularization—or as she describes it, the "degodding"—of autoreligious codes of distinction.

In Man's genealogy, a political-theological story and life/death code emerges around the distinction between Western European Man as fully human and all others as subordinated to a sliding scale of subhumanity that ranges from not quite fully human to nonhuman. It is within this distinction that the invention of the category of race, which serves as a new kind of "life/death" code, will play an essential structural role in determining the colonial order of modernity divided along the human/subhuman distinction. To understand the origins of this globally imposed racial code, Wynter first turns to the political theology of medieval European Christendom.[15] Focusing on the theologico-political backdrop of Christopher Columbus's 1492 transatlantic journey, she locates a prototype for Man's conception of a singularly authentic figure of human life in "Latin Christian Europe's founding matrix description, Christian, which had defined the human as primarily the subject of the church."[16] In this Christian-Scholastic order of knowledge, the autoreligious life/death code is expressed through the theologico-political figure of the "True Christian self" and its "Untrue other," the latter represented paradigmatically by Jews as the most immediate "boundary-transgressive 'name of what is evil' figures, stigmatized as Christ-killing deicides."[17]

While the "descriptive statement" of the medieval Christian-Scholastic episteme underwrote a political-theological system of "vertical hierarchical order" in which the "feudal states of Latin Europe had been the temporal and military arm [of the Christian church]," beginning around the fourteenth century there occurred a massive epistemic and political-theological rupture in the European humanist revolution of the Florentine *studia humanitatis*. In this "founding heresy" of the modern world, "a new . . . ordering system of knowledge" would initiate "the secularization of the human subject—one whose mode of being would no longer be guaranteed by the 'higher system' of the divinely sanctioned *mythos* and *theologos*."[18] The European humanist revolution not only rewrites the descriptive statement of Christian Europe in terms of an emergent scientific-rational discourse of knowledge; it also fundamentally alters the divine-human relation by elevating human beings to a reciprocal relation with God, whose creation is not merely an arbitrary instrument of His (*sic*) own glory, but exists "*on behalf* and *for the sake of* humankind."[19] This theo-epistemological shift also signals a political-theological reversal in which the Christian church was "made into the spiritual arm of [the] newly emergent absolute states" of modern Europe.[20] Through these shifts, the political-theological structure of Christian Scholasticism began to unravel, ultimately being replaced by a new Cartesian secular-rationalist structure of knowledge that coincided with the citizen-subject of Western European culture as the embodied form of ideal human life.

The name Wynter gives this new subject of secularized knowledge is "Man1." While much of Man1's epistemic revolution would occur as a rupture internal to the Euro-Christian order of knowledge, it is the globally transformative event of the Christian invasion of the Americas beginning in 1492 that marked its full realization as a racialized figure of humanness. Here, political theology continued to play a crucial structural role, ultimately setting the new terms through which the complex and violent encounter with the Indigenous peoples of the Americas and the brutal inauguration of the transatlantic slave trade would take place. In the emergence of Man1, the "true Christian/untrue Other" code is structurally transformed into the Christian humanist "rational Human/subrational Other," setting the symbolic terms for the colonial racial order of modernity.

While Man1 operates explicitly within the residual political theology of Western Christendom, in the nineteenth century the human/subhuman distinction undergoes a further (and more thoroughly racialized) scientific transformation in the Darwinian-Malthusian (or "biocentric") notion of an evolutionarily "selected" white race that dominates the "dyselected" other races of the world.[21] Man2, the name Wynter gives this new conceptual mutation, represents a further intensification of the "degodded" structure of Man's descriptive statement, now grounded in the biocentric conceptual authority of the natural sciences and the bourgeois subject of liberal-capitalist political economy. If the trajectory of Man1 through Man2 is an autopoietic cognitive deterritorialization from the medieval episteme based on an increasingly secular and biocentric descriptive statement, it is also continuous with both the general hybrid-human operation of autoreligion and the historically particular Latin Christian political-theological division between the "true Christian subject" and its "untrue Others." Whether articulated in explicitly theological or secular terms, the political-theological production of a transcendent "name of what is good" against the "name of what is evil" is maintained. In this production, "race," which provided the biocentric epistemology of Man2 its most efficient and effective code of boundary enforcement, "was therefore to be, in effect, the nonsupernatural but no less 'extrahuman' ground (in the reoccupied place of the traditional ancestors/gods/God/ground) of the answer that the secularizing West would now give to the Heideggerian question as to the who, and the what we are."[22] For Wynter, understanding this specifically as an autopoietic operation of Man's specific form of life exposes and relativizes the stratifications of race, class, gender, sexuality, and so on that are posited and often *experienced* as objective simply as the self-referential product of a particular human system/genre.

The New Science of the Word

Through the theories of autopoiesis and sociogenesis, Wynter conceptualizes a new scientific method that goes beyond the biocentric model as it takes the whole hybrid human being—*bios* and *logos*—as the basis for unsettling received (Western) notions of human authenticity. The possibility of this new method emerges through the theories of meta-autopoietic origin and sociogenesis as a new "class of classes" able to "contain the magma of all 'local' origin stories/accounts and their *genre*-specific and respective autopoetic cum pseudo-speciation *member-class* representations of origin."[23] By fully incorporating the *hybrid* nature of human self-creation, the new science is undertaken from a "trans-genre-of-being-human" perspective that transcends the sociogenic limits of any one cultural perspective. In this new mode of scientific observation, Man is relativized and revealed as "but *one*, even if the first purely secular, *member class* of . . . the *class of classes*."[24]

As Wynter argues, the "breakthrough" knowledge of autopoiesis holds the potential to do what no human knowledge system has *hitherto* (a common term for Wynter) been able to accomplish: the ability to observe the self-produced and therefore subjective nature of all knowledge and thereby enable the *conscious* remaking of a new knowledge made to the full measure of our globally diverse humanity. From Wynter's systems-theoretical perspective, what began with the *studia humanitatis* and unfolded along the trajectory from Man1 to Man2 reflects the open-ended telos of perpetual human self-creation, a "process as old as life itself." Man, far from being the realization of some ideal human essence, "should be understood within the process of human evolutionary epistemology/modes of self-troping, in which the rupture of the higher system of the *theologos* implicit in the practice of the *studia* was a mutation at the level of the cognitive mechanisms."[25] While this rupture paved the way for an unprecedented human capacity to know the world through a technical secularized knowledge that no longer required recourse to explicit theological-supernatural descriptions, Man2 remains subordinated to its own autoreligious/political theological myth of "extrahuman" biocentric determination that continues to be a scourge of the Earth. However, while Man remains incapable of recognizing its own biocentric myth, its secularized and "degodded" mode of knowledge has provided the new conceptual conditions through which a genuinely new cognitive mutation might occur. For Wynter, it is the theory of autopoiesis that marks a culminating moment in Man's conceptual genealogy, and, together with the sociogenic principle, has poised a now fully integrated global humanity for a "second emergence" in which human beings might finally become *fully conscious* of the cognitive mechanisms of their own autonomous self-creation.[26]

This breakthrough is not something that is simply integrated into the current apparatus of scientific knowledge. This is not a science undertaken in the traditional labs of the modern university and its "poor and half-starved" biocentric disciplines that, as Aimé Césaire describes, have cut themselves off from the "fulfilling knowledge" of a poetics that has always been an essential element of human creativity.[27] It is here that Wynter reformulates the method of autopoiesis as an "autopoetics" that foregrounds the conscious creativity of poetics (a metonym for the creative arts and cultural production) as the vehicle of human self-creation in excess of biocentric formulations of the human. In the age of Man2, autopoetics is "born in the great silence of scientific knowledge," the "demonic grounds" beyond Man's order of knowledge.[28] The poetics of the new science of the word emerges in the social experiments of those excluded forms of life, the "Les Damnés de la Terre," hypothesizing and implementing alternative modes of being human that know Man's claim to universality is a violent fiction. Forged in the fires

David Kline

of their own theologico-political damnation (as the "name of what is evil"), this counter-praxis of the colonized is also a counter-invention in which the poet, "pregnant with the world . . . gambles all our possibilities. . . . Our first and last chance."[29] It is here that the new science of the word turns such hard-won knowledges of decolonial human resistance against Man toward the hybrid autopoietic operation in which, again in the words of Césaire, "what presides over the poem [of our being] is not the most lucid intelligence, or the most acute sensibility, but an entire experience . . . the whole weight of the body, the whole weight of the mind."[30]

Autoreligion, the New Science of the Word, and Political Theology

In Wynter's new science there is an interesting tension between autoreligion (and, by proxy, political theology) and her vision of a "second emergence" through the conscious knowledge of autopoetic invention. From its outside perspective of the "transculturally applicable constant . . . of the common reality of our varied cultural modes of being," the new science seems to necessitate moving beyond the autoreligious function of human self-creation as it realizes a new mode of collective storytelling grounded in what appears as Wynter's understanding of a "true secularity" rendered free from Man's (autoreligious) myth of biocentric secularism and its "imagined entity of race."[31] For Wynter, by recognizing the hybrid nature of our own autopoetic agency, "We will now find that we humans no longer need the illusions of our hitherto story-telling, extra-human projection of that Agency."[32] This is the decolonial epistemological imperative. As she argues, it is now crucial for the collective future of human beings and their Earthly environments to finally move beyond the illusion that human social orders are determined by forces outside human beings' own agency of self-creation. In the recognition of our own, particular autopoietic creations through the new scientific objectivity of the trans-genre common outside, the *fully conscious*—which here would mean the non-(auto)religious—construction of a new global story of human existence beyond Man is now possible.

While Wynter's references to the illusions of autoreligion are rightfully aimed at Man's overdetermination of its "substitute religion 'evolution'" and any other "extrahuman" colonial fantasy that would keep the violent story of biocentricity going, there remains the question of where other religious and theological stories of human origin and determination fit into the vision of a liberated human future.[33] While the religious sensibilities of

Afro-Caribbean traditions provide key modes of anticolonial resistance for Wynter's earlier work—especially in her novel *The Hills of Hebron* and the unpublished manuscript *Black Metamorphosis*—and while there are some references to counter-religious traditions such as Rastafarianism in her post-1984 work, it seems that her critique of Man and the implementation of a new science is premised on the idea that the specific religious nature of those examples would be irrelevant (or, at least, subservient) to the new science's imperative of cognitive autonomy. However, if, as Wynter suggests, the new science remains tied to a revelatory event achieved through an observational point of social transcendence (the "trans-genre" perspective of autopoetics), it would appear that this revelation still reflects an autoreligious operation (and therefore a political-theological foundation) that conceptually elevates autopoiesis itself as the "being of being human," the "class of classes" that determines and frees up the potential of all human cultural production.[34] This is a complex issue to think through with Wynter. Part of the difficulty is what it would actually mean to realize the twofold nature of her "new humanism," in which genres of being human are affirmed in their sociogenic autonomy while, *at the same time*, they are called to transcend that autonomy and consciously experience the "class of classes" and its meta-reality of human plurality as the basis of a new global politics of interhuman collaboration. Yet if the new science represents a kind of "second emergence" that would essentially be a "fourth event" in which human cognitive autonomy beyond autoreligion is finally fully achieved, how exactly would one know that this event has actually occurred? In other words, if the new science has positioned human beings to realize a trans-genre perspective of a true secularity in which they can now describe their own immanent productions of reality as *human* productions, how would one know if this is not still an autoreligious story of transcendence that conceptually elevates autopoiesis itself precisely as that "extrahuman" force that holds the key to human liberation?

Here is where I suggest that an affirmation of a residual political-theological operation inherent within the appeal to autopoiesis would not only challenge the new science's move away from autoreligion as a fundamental driver of human invention but also provide a basis of constructing a new political-theological imagination beyond the theologico-political legacies of Man. If contemporary academic political theology is fundamentally about challenging the modern Western assumption that religion and politics can be neatly separated, and if theology continues to remain an important source for the production of human meaning, there is an important role for political theology in the constructive decolonial task of creatively imagining new paradigms of human existence and political order.[35] Taking political-theological genealogies and the constructive power of theological imagination seriously means not shying away from what appears as the universally human need to construct (auto)religious narratives informing normative values and forms of meaning, even if these narratives appeal to what a secular perspective would call its projected "illusions." While the autoreligious projections of Man have led to disastrous effects on the global human community and the Earth it inhabits, this does not mean that all such projections are necessarily obstacles to a human future beyond Man. Wynter is clear that Man's particular forms of political theology and "secular" afterlife in no way hold a monopoly on the production of truth and that the cognitive "breakthroughs" emerging out of Man happen in the counter-poetics of forms of resistance that include religious forms.[36] However, while her political-theological genealogy is fully aware of the disrupting power of new religious and theological myths, the new science of autopoetics, even as it incorporates the sociogenic principle, ultimately discards religion and theology in a way that, as David Marriott has argued, "*presupposes* a certain fantasy of science" that does not fully interrogate its own opacity as a position of observation.[37]

The opacity of scientific observation is a key point made by other theorists of autopoiesis who emphasize the necessary "blind spots" of all cognitive frameworks of observation. Any observational perspective, including the meta-observational perspective of the "trans-genre" position Wynter advocates, will always remain self-referential and therefore cannot construct itself to include the possibility of fully observing itself. This does not necessarily mean that cognition must be blind to its own blindness, so to speak, and Wynter's new science is essentially based on this very point. As the systems theorist Niklas Luhmann, whose work is also grounded in the theory of autopoiesis, notes, "Knowledge can only know itself, although it can—as if out of the corner of its eye—determine that this is only possible if there is more than only cognition. Cognition deals with an external world that remains unknown and has to, as a result, come to see that it cannot see what it cannot see."[38] This is precisely where (auto)religion functions as the social system that steps in to fill the cognitive blind spot through the production of narratives of transcendent meaning. As Luhmann understands, it is the religion system and its code "immanence/transcendence" that resolves its observational blind spots "*through the negative value of the code, through the reflective value, and through transcendence.*"[39] By taking the side of transcendence, religion observes the unobservable—it is conscious of what cannot be accessed through consciousness.

Political theology as a constructive enterprise—which, I suggest, might be read in terms of Wynter's notion of poetics—is perhaps especially attuned to dealing with religious observation and effectively tying its moments of revelation, which by necessity remain opaque to themselves, to sociopolitical concerns in a way that has been key for historical political paradigm shifts. As Adam Kotsko argues, political theology has played an essential historical role in ushering in new paradigms of political imagination, and it has been an important tool for moving beyond the "purely diagnostic and critical" and toward "the next step into creative, constructive, and speculative theological work."[40] This is not to say that this political-theological work is beyond the risk of turning out badly. Obviously, political theology has played an oversized historical role in constructing systems of oppression. But there are also counterexamples that show that political-theological speculation has been crucial to certain revolutionary modes of praxis that usher in new paradigms of justice. For example, the political theology of white evangelicalism in the United States and its story of white nationalism inherited from the colonial legacies of Man does not do the same thing as the political theology of James Cone's anticolonial declaration that "God is Black."[41] Both are working with theological narratives of "extrahuman" transcendent determination and political order, yet both situate themselves in radically different ways in relation to the question of how that order ought to serve the interests of embodied human plurality. The point here is that political-theological and religious speculation based on an appeal to transcendence still might function as a powerful tool that human beings use to make sense of their historical situation and respond to the systems of knowledge in which they find themselves while creatively constructing new paradigms of existence. This is especially the case as the now globally unified human species struggles to create new stories about itself and the Earth adequate to the scale of challenges it now faces.[42]

I suggest that a nascent affirmation of political-theological storytelling is basically already there in Wynter, especially in her turn to the creativity of autopoetics, where I find it interesting, for example, that she still uses the language of "transcendence," "spiritual," "soul," and "reenchantment" to describe the work of the new science. The tension, however, is that her emphasis on a science without the "illusions" of autoreligion tends to overshadow the potential of theology to play an explicit role in the decolonial project. Putting Wynter's insights on autopoetics in conversation with a political theology committed to moving beyond the theologico-political legacies of Man suggests that the new human future will need to be a kind of political-theological event where creative stories of origin and existence emerge in part through theo-poetic speculation made to the full measure of global humanity. With the insights of the new science, this would be an entirely new kind of political theology that would be fully conscious of its own role in sociogenic creation but would refrain from claiming any final secular objectivity that would necessarily leave the creativity of theological storytelling behind as a human practice. In this political theology as a form of the science of the word, and the science of the word as a form of political theology, the story of our collective human life continues to open out onto a future that only we are capable of writing.

Notes

1 Wynter and McKittrick, "Unparalleled Catastrophe for Our Species?"

2 See Wynter, *We Must Learn to Sit Down Together and Talk and Talk About a Little Culture.*

3 Maturana and Varela, *Autopoiesis and Cognition.*

4 Wynter, "Towards the Sociogenic Principle," 36–37.

5 Wynter, "The Ceremony Found," 215.

6 Wynter and McKittrick, "Unparalleled Catastrophe for Our Species?," 35.

7 Wynter and McKittrick, "Unparalleled Catastrophe for Our Species?," 35.

8 Wynter and McKittrick, "Unparalleled Catastrophe for Our Species?," 211.

9 Wynter and McKittrick, "Unparalleled Catastrophe for Our Species?," 26.

10 Wynter and McKittrick, "Unparalleled Catastrophe for Our Species?," 24.

11 See Kline, "On Self-Creation."

12 Wynter, "The Ceremony Found," 218.

13 Wynter, "The Ceremony Found," 218, 220. See also Schmitt, *The Concept of the Political.*

14 Wynter and McKittrick, "Unparalleled Catastrophe for Our Species?," 31.

15 It is important to keep in mind that Wynter is not a specialist in medieval theology, drawing primarily from secondary research such as Jacques Le Goff's *The Medieval Imagination* and other late twentieth-century studies for her insights on the medieval theological foundation for the emergence of Man in early modernity. Because Wynter focuses primarily on the Iberian-Catholic context as representative of metacultural shifts within

the European theological-political imagination, significant points of the historical complexity and diversity of medieval and early modern European thought are obscured by Wynter's genealogy. Moreover, as Wynter's approach is more broadly situated within the largest historical scale possible, spanning literally the origins of the universe to the present day, I suggest she should be read as a genealogist of what David Christian calls "big history," a metahistorical view that privileges large-scale diachronic historical perspectives and whose aim is to "see if it [is] possible . . . to tell a coherent story about the past on many different scales, beginning, literally, with the origins of the universe and ending in the present day": see Christian, *Maps of Time*, 2.

16 Wynter, "Unsettling the Coloniality of Being/Power/Truth/Freedom," 265.

17 Wynter, "Unsettling the Coloniality of Being/Power/Truth/Freedom," 265.

18 Wynter, "The Ceremony Must Be Found," 21–22.

19 Wynter, "1492," 27.

20 Wynter, "1492," 13.

21 See, e.g., Wynter's discussion of Bartolome de las Casas and his famous Valladolid debate with the humanist theologian Juan Ginés de Sepúlveda over how the Indigenous peoples of the Americas would be classified within the theologico-political framework of the Spanish Catholic empire. See Wynter, "Unsettling the Coloniality of Being/Power/Truth/Freedom," 283.

22 Wynter, "Unsettling the Coloniality of Being/Power/Truth/Freedom," 263.

23 Wynter, "The Ceremony Found," 241.

24 Wynter, "The Ceremony Found," 241.

25 Wynter, "The Ceremony Must Be Found," 23.

26 Wynter, "The Ceremony Found," 223.

27 Césaire, "Poetry and Knowledge," xliii.

28 Césaire, "Poetry and Knowledge," xlii.

29 Césaire, "Poetry and Knowledge," xlix.

30 Césaire, "Poetry and Knowledge," xlvii.

31 Wynter, "Towards the Sociogenic Principle," 58; Wynter, "Unsettling the Coloniality of Being/Power/Truth/Freedom," 273.

32 Wynter, "The Ceremony Found," 245.

33 Wynter and Thomas, "Proud Flesh Inter/Views."

34 Wynter and McKittrick, "Unparalleled Catastrophe for Our Species?," 30.

35 My understanding of political theology is influenced significantly by the work of Adam Kotsko: see e.g., Kotsko, *What Is Theology?* and his chapter in this volume.

David Kline

36 See, e.g., the brief reference to Rastafarian "counter-cosmogony" in Wynter, "The Ceremony Found," 207.

37 Marriott, "Inventions of Existence," 80.

38 Luhmann, "The Cognitive Program of Constructivism and a Reality That Remains Unknown," 65.

39 Laermans and Verschraegan, "The Late Niklas Luhmann on Religion," 18; Luhmann, *A Systems Theory of Religion*, 89.

40 Kotsko, *What Is Theology?*, 22.

41 See Cone, *A Black Theology of Liberation*.

42 Many chapters in this volume are indeed doing the kind of speculative thinking I have in mind here. Beatrice Marovich's chapter on Irigaray and breathwork, for example, resonates with Wynter's *bios/mythos* framing of human life in compelling ways that point toward the necessity of reinventing our storied relationship to our own biology and environments in order "to do something with our [own body's] brilliant, breathing, power, and to do away with what blocks it."

14

Wounded or Healing?

BLACK FEMINISM AND POLITICAL THEOLOGY

Vincent W. Lloyd

The analogy between God and king seems self-evident as soon as it is spoken; so, too, with the analogy between God and father. The political is theological, and the personal is political: The concept of sovereignty orders the family, the nation, and the world. Critical engagement at any one of these three levels cannot ignore the other two—so claims feminist political theology, which is really just political theology fully thought through.

These analogies are so much a part of common sense that they are easy to overlook. Consider, for example, the 1977 short story "A Lament." The story opens with a bickering couple. Where should they eat? Whose ideas matter? And, in the opening lines, who should turn on the lights? The expectation was obvious: "He was man, and as such, the author and finisher of light. Whenever she shouted 'Oh Lord!,' he growled 'Y-e-s,' deep in his throat." The couple's quarrels are structured around the rule of the man, the rule of the divine. The woman was in "awe of him because he was handsome." He was the lord of the Hebrew Bible: awe-inspiring and full of brutal rage. "Rolling his eyes, clicking his tongue in anger and dissension, he gave an impression of decisive superiority. In those moments, he symbolically murdered the whole tribe of women."[1]

"A Lament" is a feminist story. Its narrative thrust is critical. It names the analogy of sovereignty that is familial, political, and divine, and it calls that structure of sovereignty into question. This begins in the first line. "Each one's life to the other was a conundrum: How could it be that he always groped for the light switch on the other side of the dark, familiar room, and she never did?" The story is interrogative, probing why the structures of the theo-paternal and theo-political exist as they do. There is an expectation about who should let there be light, but at the same time there is a "conundrum." Sovereignty is at once self-evident and perplexingly hollow. Indeed, the man in this opening scene, despite his abilities ("his footstep was correct," "he could see very well"), does not succeed in the simple task of illuminating the room. He takes his partner's deference as humiliating: He will have to stumble around, trying to find the switch ("collusion against his manhood?"), and she eventually takes over, letting there be light. Sovereignty continues to be put in the subjunctive: "Triumphant, she looked at him, wondering if he were ignorant and defective." There is patriarchy, there is divinity, but is its power genuine? (12).

Indeed, the feminist critique of sovereignty offered in "A Lament" is not mere curiosity; it also takes the form of reversal. In her disgust, the woman calls her partner "a small demon" (12). In these moments, he reminds her not of a powerful king but "the local devil" from her childhood, "ole Leaky," a hermit widower who was said to copulate with his dogs—and whom the woman once witnessed pleasuring himself in the weeds (13). Instead of ruler, the male protagonist takes the role of outcast, as much animal as human, leaky rather than self-contained, the opposite of divine.

"A Lament" is a feminist story. It is also a Black story, as we learn partway through the text. It is a story of Black patriarchy and Black politics, and Black religion. The man, mansplaining his views on race, "paraded around the room, looking like a Ghanaian tribal chief, being all the voices of the choir" (13). As a *Black* feminist story, the critical affect shifts. No longer is the point to pierce the precarious veneer of sovereignty, writ small and writ large. The anti-Black world has already done this; it has already made Black sovereignty an impossibility, its performance a sad parody. Instead of an optimistic challenge, the critical affect here is named by the story's title: lament. The point is not to enumerate wrongs, as if they might then be made right. The point is to name constitutive features of the world that can never be made right.

The man in this story looks like an African chief, but the message he preaches is one of militant universality. He refuses to visit the South; he states his wish to forget the poor. He believes in "universal man"; his partner "wondered who the hell the universal man was." For him, "The sacred impulse was racially neutral, and he'd stab the first sonavabitch who said anything different" (13). The couple's bickering about the mundane and domestic already slid into bickering about the theological (who will let there be light), and now it slides into bickering about the racial under the sign of the theological. The man believes in the sacred universal, disbelieves in Black particularity, in the "golden calf of race." His partner does not offer a counterpoint, only pointed questions. "Isn't universality for the black man nothing but his fear of black?" (14), she queries.

Yet the dialectic of the story does not end here. The critical point is not that Black masculinity parrots the aspirations of white sovereignty, resulting in absurd failure that contrasts unfavorably with the particularistic Black feminine. For in the story's final paragraphs, the narrator calls into question the particularism embraced by the female protagonist: "It was quite alright, she felt, that one should want inflexible identities—that one should anticipate, even demand, a consistency between depth and surface." Then the narrator intervenes, dismissing this view as "simplemindedness," describing it as the woman's "crime and passion." According to the narrator, this woman had forgotten what she was once taught: "that the human universe was not systematic"; that the sense of order is precarious, a "pitiful thing" (16).

That "pitiful thing," that commitment to order, binds together the bickering couple. As the story concludes, the woman follows her husband into the night, expecting to find him in some liaison. There he is, alone and pitiful in the rain. Then there he is again, heading into a club. A gay club. Featuring Mikki, a tall, thin, oiled dancer. "Oh God!" the woman exclaims. "This is beautiful!" (16). Finally, she realizes: Mikki is a man. Her partner. God shows up in drag.

The Black man claims impossible sovereignty, as masculine, as chieftain, as divine—as arbiter of the universal. Critique goes wrong when it seeks to usurp the position of sovereignty (the naïveté of white feminism), and it goes wrong when it refuses the universal in favor of the particular (a temptation of Black feminism). Critique succeeds, this story asserts, when it moves past the interrogative mood to one that seeks out, amidst the wounds of the world, the playful beauty of the sovereign at every level, from the personal to the political to the divine. In a story pulled forward by bickering, the final lines switch to new feelings: "The only one laughing in Tinnie's, she felt maddened. She recognized him." Laughter, madness, and recognition: This peculiar knot is, remember, not a revelation but a lament. It points to a sharpened Black feminist sensibility, one that acknowledges the precariousness of order and toys with otherwise possibilities, even as they are sharply constrained. In front of this club, Tinnie's, stand "hostile cops" who are "eyeing all the patrons" (16).

"A Lament" was written by the Black feminist literary critic Hortense Spillers, one of two short stories she published in the late 1970s.[2] In essential ways, the story parallels the concerns of Spillers's now-canonical theoretical writings, and it does so in a way that ties together her betterknown essays on Black feminism with her less well-known essays on Black religion—unified, here, by an intervention in political theology. The story also brings out the metacritical implications of Spillers's work, underscoring her emphasis on the dialectical nature of critique and the risk that criticism, even Black feminist criticism, might lose its potency when the dialectic is stilled.

At the center of all of this, and often implicit in the field of political theology more generally, is the question of how to respond to brokenness. This is the obverse of the question of sovereignty: Behind accounts of rule and order are accounts of pain and injury. How do we make them right? In a world full of violence and domination, this question, itself political-theological, is at the heart of things. Constructing and contesting accounts of sovereignty only mask the issue—so Black feminist criticism rightly teaches. But how, then, do we rightly respond to our wounds? How do we, individually and collectively, heal?

For Spillers, in "A Lament," woundedness is at the center of everything. Midway through the story we learn that the male protagonist was "martyred by a 'ruined organ,'" a "testicle shot off in war" (14). Just below the surface, then, the narrative of the story is driven by this wound, one that can never heal, one that places sovereignty permanently under erasure in the same way that Blackness does (the testicle's loss is, after all, a martyrdom). Writing at the same time that Black feminists were gravitating toward discourses of healing and eclectic spirituality as the proper framework for politics, Spillers offers an alternative response that is grounded in Black feminism but pairs it with the theological rather than the spiritual.

Wounding

After the lights finally go on, near the start of "A Lament," the male protagonist picks up Seven Types of Ambiguity, the foundational work of New Criticism, published by William Empson in 1930. "Is this heavy?" he asks. "Haven't read it," his partner responds (13). Spillers's Black man is drawn to ambiguity, curious about its possibilities; the Black woman is incurious. Neither, it seems, realizes the critical potential in ambiguity—though, in a sense, this critical potential is what Spillers herself is most known for probing.

Three years before the publication of Judith Butler's Gender Trouble, Spillers argued in "Mama's Baby, Papa's Maybe" that gender is not natural, not anchored to biological sex.[3] Spillers argued that gender is constructed, and constructed in ways that are always tied to race. But where Butler frames their argument as a polemic against theories of gender that posit a time outside of a gender binary, before or after worldly time, Spillers points to the Middle Passage as a time within not-so-distant human history when constructions of gender were erased and rewritten. This was done in the interest of white supremacy and capitalism, but remembering this moment unlocks the possibility that gender can again be radically reconfigured—this time in the direction of freedom rather than domination. The Middle Passage is ambiguous and ambivalent: In the midst of horrific violence, through a wounding that can never be undone, we also encounter the truth that gender is a lie.

Indeed, for Spillers the critical project (she takes Black criticism as criticism at its best) centers on attending to ambivalence. This comes out not only in her now canonical writings on the intersection of gender and race but also, even more clearly, in her writings on religion. Spillers's 1974 dissertation was about the Black sermon as a literary genre, and she would revisit Christianity later in her career, most extensively in her 1988 article "Moving Down the Line: Variations on the African-American Sermon." She announces the project of that article: "I regard African-American sermons as a paradigm of the structure of ambivalence that constitutes the black person's relationship to American culture and apprenticeship in it."[4] In some ways this formulation seems rather pedestrian, but when read together with Spillers's work on gender, its insight becomes clearer. Ambivalence is not a place to wallow; ambivalence is a site of potentiality, opening new horizons for those willing to attend to and struggle around that ambivalence.

Ambivalence is also the term Spillers uses to describe the relationship between Blacks and Christianity. Again, there is a pedestrian reading of this observation, with Christianity mobilized for both oppression and liberation, but there is also a more critically powerful point here. As Spillers demonstrates, the relationship in question is not two-sided but three-sided: There is a knot of ambivalence where Blacks, Christianity, and the state come together. This is political theology, but political theology reconfigured, with the focus not on sovereignty but on the fragility of sovereignty revealed from the position of the impossible subject, the Black. As Spillers points out, long before Jacques Lacan theorized the subject placed under erasure by the symbolic order, Black Americans were living this experience, their subjectivity continually rejected by the normative white order. The result of this primordial wound is an array of symptoms, some of which Spillers dramatizes in "A Lament"—the lament affixing to that wound.

Vincent W. Lloyd

From this position of woundedness, the Black subject approaches the theological conjoined with the political. In medieval Europe, art subordinated the viewer, forcing the eyes upward and the body into submission. For Spillers, the analogue in Black Christianity is the sermon, entering the ear rather than the eye and creating a culture that is horizontal rather than vertical. At its best, Spillers understands Black Christianity as the "church of the insurgent and the dispossessed," with its heart in the sermon, ritualizing and reinforcing a challenge to hierarchy and a commitment to democracy.[5] This turn from eye to ear, Spillers asserts, made Christianity a resource for the enslaved: The word—the Word—passes easily from person to person, creating spaces of democracy amid domination, whereas the visual is resource-intensive and censorable.

Spillers locates the insurgent potential of Christianity not in metaphors of liberation but in the literalness of the biblical text. The literal meaning of the Bible, read in the eighteenth, nineteenth, or twentieth century, or the twenty-first, is necessarily ambivalent. That ambivalence plays out as liberatory when it is read by those experiencing oppression. The Exodus is not *like* the Underground Railroad; the Exodus *is* the Underground Railroad. Spillers carries this sense of the literal one step further, to the material. The Word enters through the ear, sensuously, and into the mind, configuring the psyche. Switching metaphors, Spillers suggests that scripture that is embedded in ritual "bears an element of infection; everyone is compelled toward the same story."[6] And again: Spillers quotes one nineteenth-century sermon that described Blacks writing history "with the crimson ink that came from their veins."[7] The text is produced and ingested bodily, causing physical movement that becomes collective struggle.

The role of the Black church, then, is not to transmit a political message but to transmit habits of listening, of attentiveness.[8] When theology is visual and hierarchical, it involves grasping content, successfully or not; when theology is aural and democratic, when it is Black, it involves techniques of listening (and speaking)—in other words, it involves a critical sensibility. Black political theology, on this account, is not about the Black community as a collective. It is, rather, about individuals who are in impossible positions trying to understand and act in a world that tries and fails, violently, to interpellate them. As critical sensibilities develop, so, too, does the potential for social transformation, for beckoning a world organized in more just ways. The Black community, according to Spillers, is best understood as a "potentiality, an unfolding to be attended."[9]

Just as Spillers rejects the claim that metaphorical interpretation is necessary for theology to have political content, she also rejects the claim that sermons motivate political action. In her account, "The sermon not only catalyzes movement, but *embodies* it, *is movement*."[10] The story of Blackness at work here takes Blackness to mean struggle, the struggle of those dominated against forces of domination.[11] Where there is no struggle, there is no Blackness. That movement of struggle involves protest and planning, but it also involves the materiality of critique, the physical habits and psychic configurations that constitute a critical disposition. For Spillers, the sermon is first and foremost among these—or it could be. "The posture of a critical insurgency," she writes, "must be achieved. It cannot be assumed."[12] Liberatory hermeneutics takes work. Attentiveness, to text and world, is laborious.[13] Without that effort, we fall back on apolitical theology, which is really the political theology of the powers that be.

All of this sounds quite different from ambivalence as it was treated in postmodern theory (of the 1980s). For Spillers, ambivalence is not a site of ironic, joyful play, of pleasant surprise. To the contrary: She asserts that the proper way to understand ambivalence is as marking a wound, and a Black perspective underscores this. To be African and American at once is to be constitutively wounded. Spillers urges us to attend to the wound, not to heal the wound. Wounds resist closure, and they hold the potential of a "break"—in a term later elaborated by Fred Moten.[14] To say the quiet part out loud: Christianity inflects postmodernism by naming the pain of ambivalence as the crucifixion that precedes the resurrection. This, however, goes a step beyond Spillers. For her, it just happens to be that the narrative that holds the most insurgent potential is Christian. It could be anything. But could it? It is awfully convenient that, as she puts it, "The 'hermeneutic narrative' for the sermon's 'readers' matches—perfectly— the 'end' of the world; in the black community, this is Freedom, and the beginning."[15]

But, again, Spillers's conceptuality resists the easy story of preachers conjuring hopes of freedom. The image here is thoroughly horizontal, immanent: "The sermonic word does not soar; it does not leap, it never leaves the ground. It *scatters* instead."[16] Scattering is unpredictable, landing here or there, like the metaphor of infection that Spillers uses elsewhere. Political energy grows, and previously unimaginable transformations may result. This horizontality is guaranteed by Black experience: "Bound to this earth by the historical particularity of the body's wounding, the community comes face to face with the very limit of identity."[17] When the vertical register is cut off, when political theology is confined to the plane of the immanent, in the body's wounding, what results is in the register of potentiality. This is precisely what we find unfolding in "A Lament," a story that has features of a sermon.[18] The claims to particularity run against the aspirations to universality, giving rise to the unpredictable, possibly transformative, and risky: the drag show, with police guarding the doors.

Healing

Against Spillers's focus on attending to the wound, which seemingly grows out of an engagement with Christianity, let us consider another, contemporaneous strand of Black feminism. This strand is spiritual but not religious—or, at least, it puts the emphasis on the spiritual (and sometimes antagonizes the Christian). It, too, centers woundedness at the level of the personal and the political, but in this strand of Black feminist thought woundedness is eclipsed by healing.

Among the sources of this framework are the spiritual traditions of African diasporic people, particularly in the Caribbean and West Africa, traditions with one or both feet outside of Christianity. Practices such as Vodou cast Black women as privileged spiritual leaders, and they cast the role of spiritual leader as that of healer. At the heart of such practices is the need to respond to rupture, in the lives of individuals and in the communities in which they live. Practitioners mobilize rituals and objects to heal such ruptures, to reweave the fabric of lives and communities. Those rituals and objects are used pragmatically, but this is no crude pragmatism: The practices employed grow out of decades, centuries, of community practice and oral tradition, passed down from mother to daughter—relations more spiritual than biological. The healer's knowledge is embodied; its source is the ancestors; and its purpose is to restore healthy relations between individuals and their communities, both living and dead. All of this grows out of a context of oppression, slavery and its afterlives, and the healer is especially attuned to locating the effects of oppression and to the tools needed to recover from oppression. Death, which seems the ultimate tool of oppression, loses its ultimacy as the deceased return—and not just their wisdom. They take on bodies through possession, a kind of parody of the capture of bodies by worldly forces of domination and white supremacy.[19]

From Toni Cade Bambara's novel *The Salt Eaters* (1980), about a community of healers and sometimes credited as inserting healing as a key theme in this literary tradition, to fiction by Gloria Naylor, Paule Marshall, Ntozake Shange, Michelle Cliff, Sherley Anne Williams, Maya Angelou, and Toni Morrison, Black women's literary narratives over the past half-century have been driven by the cycle of trauma and healing, often as an embodied rather than abstract process.[20] Farah Jasmine Griffin locates the proliferation of such literature at a moment when books about Black healing were on the pop psychology bestseller list, including Susan Taylor's *In the Spirit* and Maya Angelou's *Wouldn't Take Nothing for My Journey*. But Griffin also points out that the 1980s and 1990s saw a proliferation of grassroots writing and thinking from Black women about healing, often growing out of religious or spiritual communities. *Jambalaya: The Natural Woman's Book of Personal Charms and Practical Rituals* (1985) recommends cleansing baths for survivors of gendered violence. The National Black Women's Health Project published *Body and Soul: The Black Women's Guide to Physical Health and Emotional Well-Being* (1994), aimed at healing both Black individuals and communities. It features a foreword by Angela Davis and June Jordan, who laud the book as marking a turn away from the Civil Rights Movement framework. The book makes the personal political with its focus on healing through "learning to fearlessly love and respect our individual and collective bodies and souls."[21]

The three preeminent Black feminists of the 1980s each championed healing and placed it at the center of their political vision. In 1980, Audre Lorde wrote movingly about her experience with cancer and with the medical apparatus around it, arguing that healing must be understood beyond scientistic terms and that the personal and the political must be thought together at the site of the wounded and healing body. In 1982, Alice Walker rose to literary superstardom, and won the Pulitzer Prize, with *The Color Purple*, an account of Black women's trauma and the journey to healing through the affirmation of the sensuous Black body, in itself and in community with other Black women. While bell hooks began as a Marxist theorist unpacking the connections between class, race, and gender, in the late 1980s and early 1990s her work turned toward the sensual and affective, with love and healing taking center stage. Indeed, hooks famously asserts that, in her youth, she embraced theory in order to heal and that she has come to think of healing as "an act of communion."[22]

Today, the discourse of healing has proliferated in political movements inspired by Black feminist thought. In the 2016 policy platform put forward by the Movement for Black Lives, growing out of consultation between grassroots organizing collectives, reparations is framed as a practice of heal-

Vincent W. Lloyd

ing. The platform demands "reparations for the wealth extracted from our communities through environmental racism, slavery, food apartheid, housing discrimination and racialized capitalism in the form of corporate and government reparations focused on healing ongoing physical and mental trauma, and ensuring our access and control of food sources, housing and land."[23] Several groups organizing under the umbrella of Black Lives Matter have designated individuals within them as healing justice coordinators, tasked with calling the group's attention to the work of healing internally. Prentis Hemphill, who served in such a role for the Black Lives Matter Global Network, describes healing work as a prerequisite for political work. Black people are gripped by trauma, individually and collectively. That trauma pulls them toward death. Even before political organizing can happen, survival is necessary, and survival requires healing—even as trauma is ongoing. Hemphill names "healing justice" as the framework responsive to this condition, calling it "the how of our movements," "the texture, the experience and the vision that guides us."[24]

What is the theory of healing that Black feminists endorse? Framing a question in this way runs against the account of healing circulating in movement spaces, as ad hoc, drawing on a repertoire of practices as required by a particular instance, addressing a particular need. In other words, healing is not the sort of thing that can be theorized—or, at least, not in the way we conventionally understand theory. We may be tempted to think that the language of healing, especially around a political movement, implies an initial state of perfection, or at least stability that went wrong, and to which we can now return. But such a view is firmly rejected by the Black feminist tradition. As Mariame Kaba pointedly puts it, "Healed is not a destination. You're just always in process."[25] Griffin expands on this point, synthesizing the literary and grassroots healing frameworks: "Healing does not pre-suppose notions of a coherent and whole subject, . . . [T]he healing is never permanent: it requires constant attention and effort."[26] There is no sense of wholeness from which we came or to which we are going. Yet we are called to persist in the work of healing, addressing sites of brokenness in ourselves and our world.

The first step in healing, in both activist and theoretical discourse, is to acknowledge the need for healing—that is to say, to acknowledge scars, wounds, harms, or, in the fashionable language of today, traumas. Black women's literature models what such acknowledgment looks like, offering language for brokenness that has often gone unnamed and unnoticed. As Griffin puts it, healing involves "claiming the body, scars and all, in a narrative of love and care."[27] Once all of us are acknowledged, instead of just the pristine or polished parts of us, we are able to imagine ourselves differently and to work on ourselves to achieve that new vision.[28]

In Hemphill's explicitly political formulation, urging a pivot away from feel-good pop psychology, "We don't heal only for the sake of feeling good. We heal so that we can act and organize. We heal so that we can use the lessons gained through the wounds of our trauma to make necessary change in our world."[29] There is no end state of contentment in the world. There is injustice in the world. We are better able to address that injustice when we are engaged in the work of healing. But healing need not be so melancholy. The Black Youth Project 100's Healing and Safety Council sees healing as necessarily mixing the acknowledgment and working of traumas with the embrace of joy. Indeed, the council aims to cultivate healing spaces within its organizations as "incubators of Black joy."[30]

It seems hard to explain what would motivate the work of healing if there is no hope of being healed, of reaching a state where healing is no longer necessary. Joy, if it is part of healing, provides an explanation. But why would joy result from attending to trauma and from working through the knots of feeling and flesh that result from trauma? The answer is often connected with spirituality. The activist and women's studies scholar K. Marshall Green reflects:

> We are all on a journey, and we are all given divine lessons and medicine along the way. We must discover that medicine and share it. The medicine that is for you is not for everyone, but there are some who might have the same or similar diagnoses, which is why we need everyone to heal themselves and share their stories to unleash the healing potential that every individual possesses. It is a communal act though, this kind of healing, because it is about you being able to experience love and joy to the fullest this lifetime. Once you are able to cultivate that *God-love* in yourself, and tap into it at all times as if you and love are breathing as one, then everyone who encounters you has the opportunity to encounter *God-love*. What a great power to be unleashed![31]

According to Green, the work of healing attunes one to the divine, aligning an individual's breathing and being with God's, presumably understood in an expansive, New Age sense. This, supposedly, results in a sense of fullness, and of joy.

Vincent W. Lloyd

Dialectics

In all its variations, the way that healing circulates around Black feminism has clear affinities with the discourse of the spiritual but not religious. That label does not necessarily mean what those who identify with it intend: Religious studies scholars have been very good at demonstrating the particularly Christian background of contemporary spirituality.[32] The gambit of political theology is that there is something more powerful about probing the repressed or sublimated politics of Christianity than there is in probing the surface-level politics of (secularized Christian) spirituality. As Spillers puts it, "Christianity identifies the cultural ground upon which one stands and for that reason, precisely, is not always immediately visible."[33] Making visible the invisible transforms the horizon of possibility.

One important task of political theology—perhaps the most important—is to critically engage with ostensibly secular political discourse. Once upon a time, that always meant the discourse of the state. Today, more often than not, it means critically engaging with discourse of social movements. It means probing how secularized theological concepts circulate in social movements, unpacking the political implications of those repressions and sublimations. A movement that, on the surface, seems oriented toward justice may, in fact, be disoriented if it is fueled by unacknowledged theological commitments. The task of the critic, then, is not to compare a particular social movement discourse against some objective measure of justice. Nor is it to unveil hidden theological knots in the belief that, unconcealed, they will lose their power and allow for social movements to run their natural course. Rather, the task of the critic is to make explicit the normative commitments found in the theological background of a social movement discourse so that those commitments can be evaluated to see whether they fit with the struggle for justice animating a particular movement.

In some ways, the political spirituality of healing and the political theology of woundedness are closely aligned.[34] In both cases, it is essential to acknowledge sites of brokenness. It is essential to work those sites. And there is a sense that this work is unending. Yet in the political spirituality of healing, there is a sense that we can rightly identify sites of rupture, of trauma, on a small scale and on a grand scale. In the political theology of woundedness, sites of rupture are sites of ambivalence. They resist having their descriptions fixed, and in this resides their transformative potential. (Here there are echoes of the fundamental and unresolvable Christian paradox, of divine and human in one, a paradox that may hold more political potential than the analogical identification of Jesus with the downtrodden.) Further, in the political spirituality of healing, while the work of healing may be never-ending, it brings power and joy to the individual and to the community. In the political theology of woundedness, attending to sites of ambivalence, tending to wounds, has unpredictable results. At its best, such attention will align those involved with struggle, but that is far from a guarantee of joy.

Most significant, the political theology of woundedness acknowledges the necessity and power of texts and practices not of our choosing, that are of no substantial use to us: the Bible, for example. It is not a tool to be applied to a problem; it is part of the normative world that constitutes who we are. The point—and this is the point of political theology in general—is to acknowledge that we are embedded in a world of norms not of our choosing, and our task is to figure out how to be disposed to those norms in such a way that they, whatever they are, will lead to freedom, to a new world after the end of this world. The political spirituality of healing ignores that constitutive normative world and so is stuck in a reformist paradigm, one that ultimately secures the hold of the powers that be.

Realizing that we must focus on what constitutes us rather than what momentarily ails us changes the temporality of politics. The political spirituality of healing involves a long-term process of identifying ruptures, accumulating tools to respond, seeing what works, identifying new traumas, and repeating. In contrast, Spillers's account of the wound is at once more urgent and more patient. The position occupied by Blacks is one of instability, ambivalence, wound—neither African nor American. Spillers recommends attending to woundedness in a posture that involves "hearing, listening, waiting, meditating." Out of this patience comes "a pregnancy of attentiveness."[35] Here Spillers actually invokes the language of healing, suggesting that her view may not, in fact, be so distant from the political spirituality of healing—it may be a gentle corrective to that view. The pathway from attention to transformation is underdetermined, according to Spillers. It necessarily involves "faith" in the unseen. This is the case for healing, as well. Associating meditation with medicine, Spillers reflects, "Even though from our current point of view the sciences of medicine designate a more or less apodictic certainty, the profession seems to adhere—in its deepest motivations—to the optimism of the cure, the stochastic game of healing."[36] In other words, the language of healing tempts us to think of a clear path from here to there, from wound present to wound fixed, but, in fact, we must reject the pragmatic if we want to realize the political potential of healing. In brief, healing has political potential only if it is coupled with uncomfortable faith—faith that requires belief beyond the evidence, not faith that embraces what we already find comfortable.

Just as Spillers pushes from the political theology of woundedness toward a more critical account of healing, there are some who push from a political spirituality of healing in the direction of woundedness. Mariame Kaba, a Black Muslim activist who has become the leading exponent of restorative justice and prison abolition, asks, "How are we going to create in our communities spaces that allow people real opportunity to heal?"[37] But Kaba is also very careful to separate the need for processes that address harm from healing. Such processes create the possibility for healing, but they themselves do not heal. Accountability is the focus of such processes. Rather than make one who has been harmed feel healed, in fact, such processes "often feel terrible to the people while they're in it," as an incident of harm is revisited in the charged atmosphere of a circle where the individual harmed sits together with the one who harmed.[38] In that space, deep work is necessary to process feelings of fear and anger and a desire for vengeance. What survivors of interpersonal violence need, Kaba asserts, is acknowledgment of that harm and assurance that it will not happen again, achieved through individual and collective processing of feeling. And even then, the results are unpredictable, requiring a certain faith.

Notes

1   Spillers, "A Lament," 12. Hereafter, page numbers are cited in parentheses in the text. I reflect on these interlocking registers of sovereignty in Lloyd, "From the Theopaternal to the Theopolitical."

2   The other, centering on a wounded protester, is Spillers, "A Day in the Life of Civil Rights."

3   Spillers, "Mama's Baby, Papa's Maybe."

4   Spillers, "Moving on Down the Line," 254.

5   Spillers, "Moving on Down the Line," 252.

6   Spillers, "Moving on Down the Line," 264.

7   Spillers, "Moving on Down the Line," 276.

8   Compare the similar argument made about democratic citizenship, as spectatorship, in Green, *The Eyes of the People.*

9   Spillers, "Moving on Down the Line," 258.

10 Spillers, "Moving on Down the Line," 254.

11 Spillers writes of a Black version of struggle that she describes as paralleling Hegel's philosophy of history: Spillers, "Moving on Down the Line," 269–70. I develop these themes in Lloyd, *Black Dignity*.

12 Spillers, "Moving on Down the Line," 262.

13 An anonymous reviewer helpfully suggested that we should read Spillers's short stories as pedagogical in this sense, rather like the sermon.

14 Spillers, "Moving on Down the Line," 262; Moten, *In the Break*.

15 Spillers, "Moving on Down the Line," 264.

16 Spillers, "Moving on Down the Line," 276.

17 Spillers, "Moving on Down the Line," 276.

18 An anonymous reviewer helpfully writes, "There is a deep coherence in Spillers's work so that her writing on religion and her short stories, along with her theorizing, are all of one piece."

19 See, e.g., the Black feminist theorist M. Jacqui Alexander's account of how African-derived religious traditions inspire her theorizing in *Pedagogies of Crossing*.

20 Davies, "Mothering and Healing in Recent Black Women's Fiction"; Griffin, "Textual Healing"; Johnson, *We Testify with Our Lives*, chap. 1.

21 Quoted in Griffin, "Textual Healing," 523.

22 hooks, *All About Love*, 215.

23 These are demanded for both Native and Black people: see Movement for Black Lives, "Vision for Black Lives," n.d., https://m4bl.org/policy-platforms.

24 Hemphill, "Healing Justice Is How We Can Sustain Black Lives." See also Woodly, "Black Feminist Visions and the Politics of Healing in the Movement for Black Lives."

25 Kaba, *We Do This 'til We Free Us*, 145.

26 Griffin, "Textual Healing," 524.

27 Griffin, "Textual Healing," 524.

28 See also Jennifer Nash's explication of Black feminist love politics, which she closely relates to the discourse of healing, and that she suggests—in quite Christian terms—involves continuous, difficult work on the self: Nash, "Practicing Love."

29 Hemphill, "Healing Justice Is How We Can Sustain Black Lives."

30 Green et al., "#BlackHealingMatters in the Time of #BlackLivesMatter," 932.

31 Green et al., "#BlackHealingMatters in the Time of #BlackLivesMatter," 921.

32 See, e.g., Schmidt, *Restless Souls*.

33 Spillers, "Moving on Down the Line," 262.

34 My presentation here is necessarily simplifying the complex issues at the interface of wounding and healing. For example, healing requires the grievability of a wound, which is unevenly distributed: see Butler, *Frames of War*. Or consider processes of lamentation that attend to but do not precisely heal a wound: see Seremetakis, *The Last Word*.

35 Spillers, "Moving on Down the Line," 275.

36 Spillers, "Moving on Down the Line," 275.

37 Kaba, *We Do This 'til We Free Us*, 76.

38 Kaba, *We Do This 'til We Free Us*, 167.

Itineraries in Feminism
and Gender

4

15 Finding Air

BIOMYTHOLOGIES OF BREATH

Beatrice Marovich

In the beginning there was a word. Of course, in the beginning there were many words. Too many words. An infinite plurality of possible words. But for the time being, let us concern ourselves with just one word and its very particular emergence. So in the beginning there was a word, and the word was רוּחַ. With this word in the mouth, or the mind, people invoked the breath of the creator of all things. But because breath is a sign of life that animates, this word also described the spirited power of this creator and phenomena that issued forth from it, such as those terrible winds that sweep across the Earth and even rip out trees by their roots as if they were garden weeds. These forces that move and animate—breath, wind, air—are not different from the creator's spirit. Instead, these phenomena are caught up in a kind of natural-spiritual convergence. We might call this a biomythology of sorts—a form of storytelling that weaves together the biological and the mythological. It is a biomythology of breathing that makes breath feel like a divine thing.

I never thought so much about breathing as I did once the COVID-19 pandemic began in 2020. I never spent so much time thinking about how good it feels to breathe deeply, without coughing or wheezing. Or about how blissful it can feel to just link one breath to the next, smoothing them out like wrinkles on a bedspread, without thinking of anything else. Or how a very rapid breath—breathing as if I'm starting a fire—can feel almost like a high if you sustain it long enough. Breathing feels more like having a spirit, or being a spirit, than anything else I've ever tried. So it makes sense to think about breath theologically, doesn't it? Breath feels like it could be a divine thing.

What if theology—that storehouse of theories on divine things—has only ever been an elaborate story about the wind? About where the wind came from, and how it came to animate everything? About how, and what, and why we breathe? It's a nice thing to imagine: that theology has only ever been creating biomythologies that link us to the powerful bliss of our own breath. But, of course, this would discount thousands of years of other competing biomythologies—the ones about that cosmic patriarch, and his management team on Earth, who restricted breathing, making it difficult, even impossible, for so many to breathe at all. For thinkers such as the feminist philosopher Luce Irigaray, this cosmic creator who animates all things with his breath is appropriating breath. He is working with stolen breath. She reminds us that a fetus, before birth, receives oxygen from a mother's body. To suggest that we were created, nurtured, and sustained by the breath of a great cosmic man is an erasure or appropriation of the creative power of mothers. It is a story about birth, about origin, in which the powers of mothers are appropriated by a patriarchal deity who will come to hold authority over reproduction itself and to legislate the laws that regulate it. He will pass his authority (so the story often goes) on to those who are made in his manly image. For Irigaray, this biomythology is an appropriation of breath, for use in a patriarchal reproductive politics.[1]

Breath also offers a counterpolitics for Irigaray: a site through which we can seize or sense a form of spiritual autonomy. Irigaray suggests that we, as humans, are created with our own "first gesture of autonomy," which is that initial breath we each take by ourselves as we emerge from the birth canal.[2] "To become aware of the fact that our life exists thanks to our own breathing is essential for making us autonomous living persons," she argues.[3] This is not a secularization of breath, because—for Irigaray—breath still serves as a natural-spiritual confluence that infuses us with something we could even call divine. Instead, as I would describe it, she offers another biomythology of breath: one that resists the infusion of life, and breath, into the reproductive politics driven by the patriarchal history of theology. As Alex Dubilet and Vincent Lloyd argue, in the introduction to this volume, "The past is not past but persists in violent fragmentation, never easily sublated or superseded." Perhaps our breath bears witness to this.

I think, here, in a biomythical mode, about breathing. I also call this thinking, the writing that follows this thinking (or the writing that draws this thinking out) *political theology*. I have argued, elsewhere, that political theology is characterized by "the simultaneous erasure and endurance of the theological." Political theology is distinct from the work of theology in the sense that there is some attempt to "absent" the divine, conceptually. But the work of political theology is something other than a secularization. Instead, in a political theology, "The experience of this attempted absentia remains shadowed by the theological."[4] What I am doing here might be a form of strategic absenting: I want to grab hold of that biomythical live wire that might otherwise be used to appropriate breath for those figures of a reproductive politics. I want to explore where (and how) it might, instead, feed into a natural-spiritual sense of our own body's brilliant, breathing, power.

Breathwork

While it is the case that the COVID-19 pandemic made breath—and the importance of breathwork—more obvious to me, it is also the case that breathwork as a form of counterpolitics predates the natural-spiritual chaos of the pandemic. It's long been true, of course, that we live on a planet where the burning of fossil fuels makes the air less and less breathable all the time. But more to the point, in the United States, "I can't breathe!" has become a political rallying cry. Thinkers in Black studies have made breathwork into a social, cultural, political project. And this breathwork—resistant, powerful—has inspired the sort of breathwork I am trying to think about here.

Ashon Crawley has explored the social, cultural, and political dimensions of breath, arguing that the phrase "I can't breathe" expresses not simply the lament or protest of a single person (Eric Garner or George Floyd) but something more collective. It has become, writes Crawley, "a rupture, a disruption, an ethical plea regarding the ethical crisis that has been the grounds for producing this moment, our time, this modern world."[5] This rupture is also a form of desire "for otherwise air than what is and has been given."[6] This struggle for otherwise breath, and otherwise air, is an act of resistance against "white supremacist capitalist heteropatriarchy"; against "a violence that cannot conceive of black flesh feeling pain."[7] In the face of this social and political violence, says Crawley, breath (and the air on which it feeds) becomes "not just a sign of life" but also "an irreducibly irruptive critique of the normative world."[8] Cultivating this breath, then, is the cultivation of a critique and another way of seeing, thinking, feeling. Crawley's work creates a narrative, or storytelling, framework around breath that illuminates and amplifies the social, cultural, and political dimensions of breathwork.

Alexis Pauline Gumbs describes breath as a transitional, transformative power. In her poetic project *M Archive*, Gumbs imagines what it is that ends the world and what it is that helps some survive this end. Gumbs describes the work itself as a "speculative documentary" written "from and with the perspective of a researcher, a post-scientist sorting artifacts after the end of the world."[9] This end does not have one source but is tied to a force: a "suicidal form of genocide" that made the planet "unbreathable." This suicidal form of genocide is also a form of anti-Blackness—a quest to escape "the dark feminine."[10] On the other side of the end of the world, those who survive and emerge into something new are the ones that Gumbs calls "the black oceanists," those who "trained themselves and each other not to be afraid of going black (that was what they called it) for days at a time. they were not afraid to slow and evolve their breathing. they were not afraid of their kinship with bottom crawlers who could or could not glow."[11] Breath (finding air in changed conditions, learning to breathe differently) is what helps them evolve, transform, and survive. Breath, for Gumbs, is a Black feminist project. It unfolds from within the space of what Gumbs calls "the dark feminine." The breathwork that Gumbs is doing in *M Archive* is not used to reify this figure of the dark feminine or assert its sovereignty. Rather, Gumbs illuminates the ways in which this power (these sets of powers) might be worked with, communicated with, to facilitate a transformative breathwork that enables survival in a world wracked by extreme alteration and change.

As I read them, Crawley and Gumbs are both thinkers whose work is, in part, inspired by inspiration (breath) itself. They each highlight the social, political, and cultural functions of breath in a way that exceeds or pushes beyond a conversation about breath as physiology. For Crawley and Gumbs, breath is cultivated to disrupt or disturb the world as it exists. But breath is also sourced, or cultivated, to see the world otherwise or to facilitate transitions and survival. Breath brings about disruptions, shifts, and changes. Yet it also serves as a source of stability in the midst of change. Breath and breathing, in their work, is a physiological function that—I would argue—is biomythically described to disrupt the world as it is and to transform it.

On Biomythology

Biomythology is a term that sometimes functions as a cognate for *pseudoscience*. Susan Greenhalgh, for instance, describes the body mass index (BMI) as a biomyth. The BMI is a working assumption about our bodies, weight, and health that guides both medical professionals and everyday behavior merely because it's a biomyth that's accepted as common sense, despite the theory's "contested status in the scientific community."[12] The BMI tells us a story about bodies, and fatness, that obscures (rather than illuminates) elements of our biological reality. The story that the BMI tells us cultivates a particular (often antagonistic) relation to our physical, bio-logical bodies detached from other key markers of well-being. This points to troubling dimensions in the fictionalizing, or storytelling, dimensions of biomythologies.

And yet *mythology* is a contested term with many meanings. Does it gesture toward a false understanding? Toward a story about origins? Or toward a drive that we have, as storytelling creatures, to create narrative structures that can animate the facts and data we gather? How can we use a word such as this—*mythology*—when there is so little agreement about what it actually means? I think we often make recourse to the term *myth* when we are struggling to find language for something large, grand, cosmic, or colossal and we realize that there is a dimension of narrative, fiction, or storytelling in the descriptive work that we are doing. A myth is what steps in when we need a captivating narrative to illuminate a source of power.

Reflecting on her decision to call her book *Zami: A New Spelling of My Name* a "biomythography," Audre Lorde admits that she created this term because she had "found no other word to really coin what I was trying to do."[13] The work is a blend of autobiography, psychology, and fiction. But it also makes use of mythology. Lorde reflects on the fact that she has noted, in her own life experience, a series of patterns in how women of African descent raise their children—in different times and different places. This reflects and illuminates, she observes, a "source of our power." African American women "need to know that this [power] is part of our tradi-tion," she argues. And this is why she finds it necessary "to weave myths into our world."[14] There have to be captivating narratives to illuminate these sources of power within these cultural patterns. Sylvia Wynter has suggested that the very idea that we—as humans—are (first and foremost) simply biological beings is itself a mythology. While several other authors in this volume are turning to Wynter as a source for political theology, I turn to her here as (also) a source on mythology. Humans, Wynter reflects, are "storytellers who now storytellingly invent themselves as purely bio-logical."[15] This makes us, she suggests, hybrid beings that are defined by both our *bios* and our *mythoi*. Even when we believe that we are speaking purely about our human biology, we are engaging in dimensions of *mythoi*, acts of storytelling.

Biomythology, as I use it here, gestures toward these storytelling, nar-rative dimensions of our humanness—especially the ways in which we tell stories about our biology and physiology. Biomythology is a form of theoretical imagination that takes nature and the natural into account but also refuses to forget that how we narrate or describe this nature (the stories we tell about bodies and how we tell these stories) also shapes the life of these bodies. Breath is part of our physiology, our biology. But it's also a dimension of our social, cultural, and political existence. The stories we tell about breath, and breathing, shape how we use that breath and how we cultivate our breathing. It is because we cultivate our breath in these ways that it can become a resource for a political theology that is after both the erasure and also the endurance of more ancient biomythological narratives.

Sex and Breath

The biomythologies that animate Western culture's reproductive politics receive their life breath from the figure of a divine patriarch who has, himself, appropriated the breath of birthing mothers, Irigaray's work suggests to us. With this in mind, Irigaray argues that, to stop infusing these reproductive politics with life, our relationship between sex and breath must be differently understood.

In Westernized cultures, Irigaray suggests, we develop in a context that serves as something of a substitute for the kinship network of the family. We see this evidenced in the figure of a divine patriarch, representing the father writ large across social, cultural, and political landscapes. But to flourish as "sexuate, and a human being," as someone who "must fulfill his or her desire in order to flourish," we have to learn how to exist—how to find ourselves and know ourselves—beyond the reproductive politics of this familial unit.[16] Irigaray argues that this separation or independence becomes possible by "cultivating our breathing." This allows for a separation from this reproductive creative structure—from fathers, but also from mothers—without demanding that we also "renounce our natural belonging."[17]

Through breath, by cultivating our breath, we find another way to situate (and sexuate) ourselves, naturally and spiritually. The term *sexuate*, for Irigaray, serves as a kind of cognate for desire. It is "neither neuter nor indifferent to our bodily constitution." But being sexuate is not always aimed at sexual intercourse. Sexuate energy is what she calls "an important living source and reserve" that marks a mode of inhabiting our bodies.[18] This energy gestures toward a path beyond the reproductive politics that, for so long, has been spiritually authorized by a patriarchal religious tradition. But this is not a path beyond either the natural or the spiritual.

Instead, breath remains a figure that sexuates and situates as it weaves nature and spirit together.

To the extent that Irigaray has an origin story, or a theory about the emergence of religion as such, it is structured by breath. The name *God*, she suggests, is a word that exists to describe a more than human form of breath. "In the history of humanity, the one we name God and those who enjoy spiritual powers demonstrate their strength through a creative breath." They act "through the domination of winds" by setting in motion "that which was motionless, rigid, dead."[19] But in her work she gestures toward a breath that is more primal than (and so, often shrouded by) the legacy of a tradition such as Christianity. Religion (which, for Irigaray, tends to serve as a cognate for Christianity) "remembers something about the importance of breath," she observes. "But it grants the privilege and responsibility of it to God more than to humans. God would create them with his breath, redeem them with his spirit."[20] In the West, breath comes from, and belongs to, God.

This theological situation is a problem for Irigaray because of that cosmic patriarch—the old Man of the West. "Before our birth, our mother provided us with oxygen through her blood," she writes. But "we scarcely remember this first gift of life," instead "transferring it onto God himself." We misattribute what gives life. After we are born, "air is that which gives us first autonomy as living beings." But we also "forget that most of the time." In attributing our breath, our spirit, to this patriarchal divine, we not only lose this elemental bond, but we also "lose our autonomy."[21] For Irigaray, it is crucial for humans—especially women—to move beyond this old Man of the West. And the way to do this, she argues, is by cultivating our own breath rather than outsourcing it.[22] This amounts to an act of casting aside this old Man of the West (absenting this figure of God) to find another divinity in what used to be his shadows. This is a form of political theology that disrupts a stable theological narrative to displace it. But from what hovered in the shadows of that troubling theological figure she pulls something that is both old and new.

This political theology shifts the center of divine gravity: It changes where we might understand the divine to be located: "The gods are far from us, it is said." But, Irigaray writes, "We forget that they already dwell in us and that often we prevent them from speaking." If the gods—the divine— could be heard, she argues, we would understand that "what is most divine in them" is "related to breathing and, through the breath, they can communicate with the earth and mortals, dwell in them and among them. The gods are far away—in us."[23] The point is not to determine whether or not these gods actually exist, she argues, but instead to realize that "in the intimate of ourselves" there is "a dwelling place [that] must be safeguarded for them."[24] The practice of breathing and of cultivating breath is, in essence, a practice of absenting one form of the divine to inspire or amplify another.

Against the sexual monoculture that Irigaray argues was established for Man, she calls for women to build (to breathe) a space for themselves. This monosexual culture (the world of, and for, Man) has become the standard against which all things are measured and from which other identities (such as woman) are shaped and formed. Irigaray argues that sexual difference is important, and the construction of a culture of difference (beyond this sexual monoculture) is also a spiritual task. Thinking about what it means to be a woman, and how women inhabit the world differently, is a central task for her—one that relies on air and breath. "Once we have left the *waters* of the womb," she writes, "we have to construct a space for ourselves in the *air* for the rest of our time on earth—air in which we can breathe and sing freely. Once we were fishes. It seems that we are destined to become birds."[25] This airy space is essential, she argues, because it is "the space of bodily autonomy, of free breath."[26] This airy space, and breath, offers a site where women can begin to feel the divinity within themselves.

Sexual difference is related to differences that are both natural and cultural for Irigaray. So she believes that sexual difference is a prime site for reflecting on the natural and cultural habitats of ethics. But she also recognizes that the figure of nature, in sexual difference, is dangerous. We must avoid *both* nature's "annihilation" *and* its "over-valorization," she suggests.[27] This is especially true in our cultural context, where the family (often understood as the home of our intimate lives, our "so-called private life") is often naturalized as a form. Each member of the family "alienates their own identity" to cultivate a sense of self shaped around this reproductive unit, around "what it can contribute to the family."[28] These identities support reproductive politics and reduce identities to their reproductive functions.

For Irigaray, an ethics of sexual difference works against this. At the heart of sexual difference is what Irigaray calls the "mystery" of difference. The ethics of sexual difference is a "negative pathway" or a "nocturnal approach" that seeks to keep alive the mystery, alterity, and freedom of others as sexually different.[29] In essence, we cannot know the sexuality or the sexuate identity of another. Perhaps we cannot even completely know our own—although we should seek to describe it. The ethics of sexual difference are a renunciation of "all possession, all appropriation, in order to respect, in the relation, two subjects, without ever reducing one to the other."[30] Breath is a dimension of this negative—of this nocturnal ethical approach toward sexual difference—because negation for Irigaray is a practice. The negative is "the step back" that allows for "listening and silence" for "the necessary alternation of doing and letting be, toward self and other."[31] Breathing in and out, cultivating the breath that sustains our own, unique embodiment and is the foundation of our autonomy is what allows this negative space of mystery to exist between us. When we cultivate our breath, we create space for sexual difference. It is unethical, says Irigaray, to be a "mere consumer of nature"—to simply take and take. But the cultivation of breath is done with the intention of creating space and sharing. Our breath "must be nourished and enrich our respective incarnations" so that "we might engender together not only natural children but the becoming of humanity."[32] Here breath works against reproductive politics without becoming disconnected from sexuality or creativity.

Restricted Breathing

Irigaray reads her own breathwork as emancipatory. But are there ways in which the convergence of sex and breath—in her work—can make breathing restricted for others? Are there ways in which she, like the patriarchal reproductive politics she critiques, also restricts or appropriates breath? The nature of sexual difference, in Irigaray's work, has been extremely controversial, especially because she believes that sexual difference is not merely cultural but also natural. Her work has long been critiqued as an "essentialist" project that reduces women to a state of nature. Her work on sexual difference has also been preoccupied with the man-woman gender binary, a fixation that could read as exclusionary or anti-trans.

I maintain concerns about the potentially reductive dimensions of Irigaray's work. I also tend to agree with Danielle Poe, who argues that Irigaray's aim is for a "flourishing of difference" against the difference-destroying sexual monoculture established by, and for, Man.[33] Irigaray's natural (or idea of nature), as Poe reads it, is not something to be accepted but is instead (like breath) something to be cultivated. While we are born with a "natural" body, our spirit can tell us "different stories of who one is." Our body's nature can be *cultivated* to bring body and spirit in line.[34] This might be one way of thinking about gender transition as a natural-spiritual practice.

While Jules Gill-Peterson recognizes that Irigaray is one of the most "infamously anti-trans feminists," she actually finds an "unlikely trans feminism" in Irigaray. Encountering Irigaray at a workshop as a graduate student, and before gender transition, Gill-Peterson asked Irigaray about how trans people fit into sexual difference. Irigaray replied that she "never meant that there can only be two sexes," but there should be "at least two sexes," and there is only "a single sex [(Man)] at this time." Ultimately, Gill-Peterson found in Irigaray's ethics of sexual difference an "autonomy and a legitimation in my search for a livable self." Gill-Peterson's commentary on Irigaray is moving, and I will not try to reduce it into any simple formula here. I will only note that this essay made me take another, closer, differently skeptical look at Irigaray's theory of sexual difference.[35]

One point of critique that Gill-Peterson does make of Irigaray's work is one that I agree is problematic. Irigaray is not, says Gill-Peterson, "known for thoughtfully and expansively acknowledging Western Europe's colonial relation to the rest of the world." Gill-Peterson notes that Irigaray's interest in yoga, developed in work such as *Between East and West,* can read as "embarrassingly naive."[36] Irigaray's discussion of breath in later work emerges in conversation with her discussion of the practice of yoga. But she is working with a caricature of "the East" in these discussions. When she writes about or reflects on yoga, she speaks only of ancient texts or her own yoga practice and never of contemporary critical scholarship that contextualizes this tradition (or its appropriation in Western contexts). While Irigaray does, at points, acknowledge that Western appropriations of the practice of yoga are problematic, she does not appear to see any issue with her own, uncritical appropriation of ancient texts from a cultural context that she does not understand.

I see this problem as related to, and of a piece with, what I would describe as a latent and subcritical christocentrism in Irigaray's work. Despite her arguments that the theological cosmology she actively critiques is a Judeo-Christian worldview, her work displays little to no knowledge of Judaism or Jewish intellectual traditions. Instead, she is fixated on a set of problems derived from a Western European intellectual tradition that has been deeply shaped by Christianity. While she seeks to free thinking itself from the burdens placed on it by the reproductive politics that support this tradition's patriarchal structure and form, it is nevertheless the case that she sometimes fails to see all the subtle ways in which she nevertheless remains embedded within its structure and its form.

Despite this, I still see in Irigaray's breathwork a disruptive potential that speaks to our breathless time and place. She argues that theological and philosophical thought—in the West—has been founded on breath and air. We can see this in the biomythologies of the early tradition (in a creator god whose breath is also his spirit). But she also argues that these spiritual resources remain unthought by philosophers in the sexual mono-culture built by, and for, the reproductive politics of this patriarchal tradi-tion. Against this, the cultivation of breath is a work of political-theological transformation to counter what has been repressed by Man's sexual mono-culture. "Transforming our natural energy without dispensing it" is, Iri-garay writes, "indispensable." This is particularly true in relationships of desire and attraction. "Attraction, especially sexual attraction is the largest resource of energy for humans," she argues. "Repressing it instead of cul-tivating it deprives us of the energetic resources that we need in order to live as humans and to share our humanity."[37]

Finding Air

In a recent conversation with several of my students about the fetal poli-tics that Jennifer Holland lays out in *Tiny You: A Western History of the Anti-Abortion Movement,* one student described to us her political nihil-ism that has been taking shape since *Roe v. Wade* was overturned. Politics feel, as she described it, freshly pointless, and she feels disenfranchised in new ways. I can't help but think of this student now, as I wax eloquent on this political-theological breathwork. That is to say, I can't help but think of the arrogance in suggesting, as I might seem to be, that in in the face of a changed political landscape, and in the evaporation of reproductive choices, one should *just breathe.*

This reminds me of the advice that seemed to be everywhere on my Twitter feed for most of 2020: *just breathe.* In the face of incredible anxiety about an unfolding pandemic with severe respiratory symptoms, social media spaces were full of injunctions to *just breathe.* If the intent was to say something soothing, the effect was often contrary, and inflammatory. Many people I know felt patronized by this advice to *just breathe*—as if one's anxiety and anger were out of place and just needed to be smoothed out.

It reminded me, at the time, of being pregnant and being taught—in a comically brief childbirth course in the basement of my local hospital—about the Lamaze breathing technique. While I was already aware of the effects that various forms of controlled breathing can have on symptoms of pain and anxiety, something about Lamaze felt off—even comical, perhaps too staged—to me. Our discussion of it, in that context, felt perfunctory: simply an item on the agenda to check off. I filed it away, in some forgettable mind folder, along with the bath that we were asked to give a plastic doll in a very small pink tub that they let us take home at the end of the class. It all felt patronizing, as if I could be tricked into believing that I was ready to mother after bathing a plastic doll or that I could work through the pain of labor with a very specific breathing technique that I might also easily forget. During labor I did not think about Lamaze once. But, of course, I did breathe. And breathe and breathe. Working through the incredible crush of labor pains, I had to feel my way in. There were times when the only thing my body felt like doing was screaming, which is its own kind of breathwork. It's difficult for me to imagine that a practice of breathwork can be helpful when it's prescribed or imposed. Instead, if it works, it has to be something that we find or feel our way into. Perhaps it's a strategy we were once taught and are driven to recover or remember. Or perhaps it's something we invent specifically for the demands of the moment. Once you find it, once you strike on a movement or a pattern that feels right, breathwork can sustain you through change and transition. But even so, the external injunction to *just breathe* can feel worthless and empty.

As we face into the uncertain waves of repressive reproductive politics—the evaporation of reproductive choices, anti-trans legislation and politics—I feel what my student feels. I understand the sense of nihilism. Although I'm not sure that the nihilism I feel isn't older and more enduring—something that was seeded years and years ago. I also wonder if this nihilism, a desire to do something with this nihilism, wasn't part of what drew me to breathwork in the first place. Irigaray describes air itself as an elemental negativity. Something about this has always felt right to me. There is something in the practice of breathwork that is itself like working with the negative—the negative made into a form of sustenance.

In *The Forgetting of Air in Martin Heidegger*, Irigaray claimed that air is the "arch-mediation" for philosophical thinking.[38] It enables philosophy itself. And yet, said Irigaray, air remains unthought by philosophers of Being, such as Heidegger. For Irigaray, air is the greatest "unthought" resource for Being itself.[39] Her task in this project was to remember this air that has been forgotten. And she finds in air a dimension of the negative. The philosophers, she argues, created nothingness so they might "prevail over an emptiness which was not."[40] But this emptiness—the nothingness of the philosophers—was actually air: "reduction to nothingness without destruction, at least without any apparent destruction."[41] What we breathe—air—is a material form of nothing that is also everywhere and in everything.

Beatrice Marovich

Breathwork, perhaps, is one of the gestures we can make to cope with nihilism or to help us transform it into something else. Working with breath, or air, is like working with and within nothingness or emptiness. One could make the argument that this is of absolutely no political value. And it might be true. At the same time, I think, there is also something nourishing in learning how to cope with nothing, with that ever present sense of emptiness—not to try and prevail over it or to erase it, but to work with it, to be filled by it, to see what we might make of it: what we might make of our own body's brilliant, breathing, power. To see how it is that emptiness, perhaps more than we might have imagined, can also animate. That desire—to do something with our brilliant, breathing, power and to do away with what blocks it—is political theology.

Notes

1   Irigaray, *Sexes and Genealogies*, 16.

2   Irigaray, *A New Culture of Energy*, 19.

3   Irigaray, *A New Culture of Energy*, 20.

4   Marovich, "Hearing Nothing," 334.

5   Crawley, *Blackpentecostal Breath*, 1.

6   Crawley, *Blackpentecostal Breath*, 2.

7   Crawley, *Blackpentecostal Breath*, 2.

8   Crawley, *Blackpentecostal Breath*, 42.

9   Gumbs, *M Archive*, xi.

10 Gumbs, *M Archive*, 7.

11 Gumbs, *M Archive*, 10.

12 Greenhalgh, *Fat-Talk Nation*, 30.

13 Lorde, *Conversations with Audre Lorde*, 110.

14 Lorde, *Conversations with Audre Lorde*, 149.

15 Wynter and McKittrick, "Unparalleled Catastrophe for Our Species?," 11.

16 Irigaray, *A New Culture of Energy*, 16.

17 Irigaray, "To Begin with Breathing Anew," 218.

18 Irigaray and Marder, *Through Vegetal Being*, 96.

19 Irigaray, *Between East and West*, 166.

20 Irigaray, "To Begin with Breathing Anew," 223.

21 Irigaray in conversation with Judith Still, in Irigaray and Still, "'Towards a Wisdom of Love,'" 28.

22 Irigaray, *To Be Born*.

23 Irigaray, *The Way of Love*, 51.

24 Irigaray, *The Way of Love*, 51.

25 Irigaray, *Sexes and Genealogies*, 66.

26 Irigaray, *Sexes and Genealogies*, 66.

27 Irigaray, "Spiritual Tasks for Our Age," 176.

28 Irigaray, "Spiritual Tasks for Our Age," 179.

29 Irigaray, "Spiritual Tasks for Our Age," 183.

30 Irigaray, *Between East and West*, 128.

31 Irigaray, *Between East and West*, xi.

32 Irigaray, *A New Culture of Energy*, 26.

33 Poe, "Can Luce Irigaray's Notion of Sexual Difference Be Applied to Transsexual and Transgender Narratives?," 124.

34 Poe, "Can Luce Irigaray's Notion of Sexual Difference Be Applied to Transsexual and Transgender Narratives?," 126.

35 Gill-Peterson, "The Miseducation of a French Feminist."

36 Gill-Peterson, "The Miseducation of a French Feminist."

37 Irigaray, *A New Culture of Energy*, 15.

38 Irigaray, *The Forgetting of Air in Martin Heidegger*, 12.

39 Irigaray, *The Forgetting of Air in Martin Heidegger*, 14.

40 Irigaray, *The Forgetting of Air in Martin Heidegger*, 164.

41 Irigaray, *The Forgetting of Air in Martin Heidegger*, 162.

16

Sovereign Storytelling

A POLITICAL THEOLOGY OF
BAD INTENTIONS

Dana Lloyd

This essay brings into dialogue European feminist theory and Indigenous feminism to push political theology forward on two fronts: one methodological and one theoretical. The methodological contribution, coming from the Italian philosopher Adriana Cavarero, asks political theology to approach its foundational concepts with irony or, in Cavarero's words, "with bad intentions."[1] Recognizing sovereignty as a (perhaps *the*) foundational theoretical concept of political theology, Indigenous feminists demonstrate what it looks like to approach Schmittian sovereignty with bad intentions. Cavarero herself is not interested in settler colonialism or in indigeneity, and she hasn't written much about race at all until her most recent book, *Surging Democracy* (2021). So I am also hoping the encounter between Cavarero and Indigenous feminists can demonstrate what Indigenous feminist theorists have to offer European feminist philosophers for whom Cavarero's work has been formative. If Cavarero's bad intentions can help political theology feminize Schmittian sovereignty, Indigenous feminists will approach, in turn, European feminism with bad intentions to decolonize sovereignty, as well.

A Political Theology of Bad Intentions

Adriana Cavarero is a contemporary Italian feminist thinker and an honorary professor of political philosophy at the University of Verona. Emerging as a feminist scholar in the 1980s, she was among the founders of the Diotima philosophical community in Verona, which is considered one of the most important Italian political expressions of the philosophy of sexual difference. The feminist communities in which she took part sought not to be included in existing man-dominated institutions but to form their own spaces. Thus, in addition to establishing Diotima in Verona, they created the Women's Bookstore Collective in Milan and founded the journal *DonnaWomanFemme* in Rome.

Cavarero's voluminous body of work mostly ignored religion until she wrote the essay "The Archeology of Homicide," which was published in English in 2015 as part of her political and theological dialogue with Angelo Scola, titled *Thou Shalt Not Kill*. The essay is the most obvious point of entry into her work if you are interested in political theology, and I certainly plan to get there in this essay. But I also want to find the kind of advice, or critical theoretical tools, she might give theopolitical thinkers in other writings that are not explicitly about religion.

Cavarero's critique of philosophy, or of theory more broadly, begins with her reading of the philosophical canon as too masculine and too passive. Political theory is an oxymoron, she tells us in the article "Politicizing Theory," because politics calls us to action while theory calls for mere contemplation.[2] However, if in the 1980s Cavarero and her feminist collaborators sought to separate themselves from political spaces dominated by men, in her academic career she remained part of the philosophical disciplinary world (perhaps because Italian universities do not have Gender, Women's, and Sexuality Studies Departments), and she has spent this career trying to dismantle the master's house using the master's tools. In a 2008 interview, she says she treats the traditional terms of philosophy—*ontology*, *essence*, and *substance*—ironically, or "with bad intentions."[3] This is the only way, she says, to liberate ontology from the sacred truth that has been imposed on it by traditional philosophical perspectives. If one merely questions or deconstructs ontology, seeking in this way to avoid it, then ontology itself has not been transformed.

Cavarero elaborates on this project in a recent essay: "Rather than in the undoing of critical theory—whatever this label could mean—I am interested in the positive task of redirecting the questions of ontology, politics, and ethics toward a framework of altruism and peace capable of capturing our imagination and mobilizing our actions."[4] Liberating ontology from the sacred truth that has been imposed on it, so it seems, has to do with redirecting ontology toward altruism and peace. What can Cavarero help us find when we are looking for critical theoretical tools for political theology? How can we be inspired by her bad intentions, by her irony, when we think about the sacred cows of political theology—sovereignty, for example? And how can bad intentions redirect our political theology toward altruism and peace?

I came to Cavarero almost by accident. I usually work on Indigenous law and Indigenous religion, and Cavarero helps me see what Indigenous studies, and especially their theorization of sovereignty, can bring to

Dana Lloyd

political theology. What is new here is not approaching sovereignty with bad intentions: Carl Schmitt himself came to sovereignty with bad intentions when he wrote that "all significant concepts of the modern theory of the state are secularized theological concepts."[5] To do political theology is to approach modern political theory (perhaps also theology) with bad intentions. But the sovereignty that political theology inherited from Schmitt is violent and authoritarian, and, most important to Indigenous theorists, it has nothing to do with land. As the literary scholar Scott Richard Lyons (Ojibwe/Dakota) reminds us, US Supreme Court Chief Justice John Marshall approached Indigenous sovereignty with "good intentions," with devastating results.[6] What, then, does Indigenous sovereignty do for political theology when it comes to Schmittian sovereignty with bad intentions?

In their introductory chapter on sovereignty in the collection *Native Studies Keywords*, Stephanie Nohelani Teves (Kanaka Maoli), Andrea Smith, and Michelle H. Raheja (Seneca) ask: "Can Native peoples rearticulate sovereignty given its ideological baggage?"[7] I think their answer is, ultimately, yes, though not all Indigenous scholars and activists agree. For the political theorist Joan Cocks, sovereign power (or "sovereignal freedom") is not only a modern invention but also a delusion, and one that poses political dangers, as well, especially when it is democratized.[8] Cocks casts doubt with regard to the aspiration to Indigenous sovereignty, asking about "the tendency of those oppressed by sovereign power to make counter-sovereignty bids to save themselves."[9] "Human rights advocates and other progressives condemn the sovereign power of xenophobic majorities and defend the aspirations to sovereign power of vulnerable peoples," Cocks writes, "but what exactly makes the exclusivism of privileged citizenship a minus in the ledger of democracy, and the exclusivism of penetrated indigeneity a plus?"[10] This doubt is in line with the political theorist Taiaiake Alfred's (Kahnawà:ke Mohawk) assertion that "sovereignty is not an appropriate political objective for Indigenous peoples, as the concept itself is essentially western, and has served as a tool in colonizing Indigenous peoples."[11] With the anthropologist Audra Simpson (Kahnawà:ke Mohawk) we can think about sovereignty through the method of refusal: "An ethnographic calculus of what you need to know and what I refuse to write. This is not because of the centrality of esoteric and sacred knowledge. Rather, the deep context of dispossession, of containment, of a skewed authoritative axis and the ongoing structure of both settler colonialism and its disavowal make writing and analysis a careful, complex instantiation of jurisdiction and authority, what Robert Warrior has called 'literary sovereignty.'"[12]

Others still work with the idea of sovereignty. As Teves, Smith, and Raheja write, "Many Native activists are envisioning what sovereignty would look like if it were based on principles of justice for all peoples and care for all of creation."[13] I'd say with them that the first step toward reenvisioning sovereignty has been to establish Native studies as a discipline, since "Native peoples historically had been relegated to the status of ethnographic objects who could be theorized about but who could not theorize on their own behalf."[14] More on this in the next section.

How can we liberate sovereignty from the sacred truth that has been imposed on it by Schmitt and his disciples? How can we redirect it toward peace? What alternative can Cavarero offer us to the sovereign who decides on the exception? And then, what can Indigenous feminists offer Cavarero, or European feminist theory more broadly, and political theology?

A Plurality of Voices

Western philosophy and politics respond to universals, not to unique personalities, and Cavarero, following Hannah Arendt, wants to do theory that would respond to the unique person, a theory that would care *who* someone is. She finds such theory in the "feminine art" of narration, and instead of partaking in Emmanuel Levinas's obsession with the face, she asks to center the voice. Cavarero's interest in the uniqueness of the person (in the "who" instead of the "what") does not mean she is interested in individualistic politics. Such politics flattens the uniqueness of each person and makes us all into individuals who are bearing universal, equal rights. The most important thing about the "unique existent" at the center of Cavarero's philosophy is that it is in a constitutive relation with others. In Judith Butler's reading of Cavarero, the only question that is truly nonviolent is "Who are you?": "This question assumes that there is an other before us whom we do not know and cannot fully apprehend, one whose uniqueness and nonsubstitutability set a limit to the [Hegelian] model of reciprocal recognition."[15] Once I stop asking "Who are you?," once I assume I know you, I am violent toward you.

The voice is political because we are constitutively exposed to one another through our bodily senses. This is an Arendtian sentiment, but Cavarero adds that we are narratable by the other; that we are dependent on others for the narration of our life stories. The narratable self is defined by a desire for the story of her own birth from the mouth of another. The voice expresses the uniqueness of the speaker, regardless of the content of the speaker's words. "A voice means this: there is a living person, throat, chest, feelings, who sends into the air this voice, different from all other voices," she quotes Italo Calvino.[16] And her fascination with literature is not limited to Calvino. Engaging with literature that ranges from Greek mythology, through Gertrude Stein and Karen Blixen, and all the way to Elena Ferrante, Cavarero insists that "symptomatically only literature, only narration can show us this *concreteness of the relationship to the other*."[17] And so if Cavarero's first piece of advice to us was that we approach our sacred concepts—sovereignty—with bad intentions, her second must be that we do it while reading and listening to stories.[18] In this way, the sovereign can become relational, vulnerable, dependent on another. Maybe then the sovereign won't have to declare war; maybe we'll get closer to the peaceful world Cavarero envisions.

Storytelling and sovereignty are tightly related in what Lyons called "rhetorical sovereignty." This relationship formed throughout the nineteenth century, in boarding schools, when Native children were forced to learn English (and unlearn their Indigenous languages) and to take settler names instead of their own Indigenous names. It was formed in the hundreds of treaties that were signed but not ratified. It was reinforced in court cases, especially in what came to be known as the "Marshall Trilogy," in which US Supreme Court Chief Justice John Marshall referred to Indigenous peoples as "savages" and as "domestic dependent nations," thus writing them out of their sovereign status.[19] Lyons calls it "rhetorical imperialism": "the ability of dominant powers to assert control of others by setting the terms of debate."[20] By contrast, rhetorical sovereignty "is the inherent right and ability of *peoples* to determine their own communicative needs and desires in this pursuit, to decide for themselves the goals, modes, styles, and languages of public discourse."[21]

Just as sovereignty is a foundational term for political theology, it is foundational to US-Native relations. "From the early moments of first contact on this continent, the construction of Indian and non-Indian senses of sovereignty was a contested and contradictory process," Lyons writes.[22] But he looks to the history of the Western idea of sovereignty to recover its relational meaning: "As modern nations and states underwent their various forms of development, the concept was consistently deployed to address not only domestic authority at home but a state's relative independence from *and among* other states; thus, sovereignty came to mean something systemic and relational."[23] If Western sovereignty is already relational, what can feminist "bad intentions" bring to it? Perhaps it is this relationality that we should approach with bad intentions: Ironically, Western sovereignty in the way Lyons reads it is only relational in the sense that it needs another, as audience, in front of which to declare its authority and independence. Cavarero thinks about relationality more substantively—a relationship in which you and I are constituted by each other. Indigenous feminists will bring a similar idea of relationality to sovereignty itself.

The literary scholar Robert Warrior (Osage) has coined the term "intellectual sovereignty," which is committed to revitalization through attention to Native intellectual traditions.[24] According to Lyons, the power of this idea lies in its "refusal to dissociate culture, identity, and power from the *land*."[25] The artist, scholar, and activist Leanne Betasamosake Simpson (Anishinaabe) advanced this idea when she wrote about "land as pedagogy," explaining that learning happens in the context of family and community, including land.[26] As Maile Arvin, Eve Tuck, and Angie Morrill explain, "within Indigenous contexts land is not property, as in settler colonialism, but rather land is knowing and knowledge."[27]

But when we talk about storytelling, we need to remember that one of the most harmful stereotypes about Indigenous peoples is that they are essentially oral creatures and that they are vanishing or have already died off. According to this myth, "A writing Indian is no Indian at all."[28] Cavarero insists on the voice, on the oral, as central to her relational philosophy, but she does not think about indigeneity and its struggles against what Lyons calls the "oral-literate binary." Bringing the Indigenous voice—indeed, a plurality of Indigenous voices—into this insistence on storytelling may change our understanding of sovereignty: "Rhetorical sovereignty requires above all the presence of an Indian voice, speaking or writing in an ongoing context of colonization and setting at least some of the terms of debate. Ideally, that voice would often employ a Native language."[29] With Cavarero I'll add that ideally this story would include a plurality of voices— after all, not all Indigenous peoples want the same thing or think of sovereignty in the same way—and a plurality of languages that are still alive and are being revitalized. Sovereignty would mean that Indigenous voices are present and that the stories they tell (and the languages they speak) matter. The plurality of Indigenous voices, languages, and stories would remind us, too, that settler law is also just that: a story.

Stories are also always about relationships—to one another, to land, and to the nation-state. As the political theorist Heidi Kiiwetinepinesiik Stark (Anishinaabe) writes, it is through stories that "we can unearth the approaches and principles that enabled the development or restoration of proper relationships with others," including the land itself and the nation-state.[30] The author Thomas King says more than that: "The truth about stories is that that's all we are."[31] I think what Indigenous scholars are telling us is that sovereignty is enacted, lived, practiced through storytelling. And it is through practice that sovereignty is liberated from the sacred truths imposed on it by traditional political theology. This is a lesson for a political theology of bad intentions: Approach your sacred concepts as lived and practiced, not as mere theories. And if Cavarero told us that political theory is an oxymoron because politics calls us to action and theory is no more than contemplation, then for political theology to make sense, both the political and the theological should be about action, practice, living. Storytelling is part of that because it is not theoretical. It is a way of living and impacting the world. "Once a story is told," King writes, "it cannot be called back. Once told, it is loose in the world."[32] Once loose in the world, these stories, according to the literary scholar Cheryl Suzack (Anishinaabe), intervene in the "collective social imaginary" and allow us to visualize justice anew.[33] And this justice is always gender justice, according to Suzack, which ties together sovereignty and storytelling and takes us back to Cavarero.

A Feminist Philosophy of Nonviolence

We are finally arriving at *Thou Shalt Not Kill*. Cavarero opens her essay with the question whether the sixth commandment, you shall not kill, is "an unconditional principle that holds forever and in every circumstance," as Levinas interpreted it.[34] History makes this interpretation seem absurd, Cavarero writes. In fact, the opposite interpretation seems true: In some cases, such as legitimate defense, punishment of murder, or in war—all those states of emergency our sovereign may declare—"killing is just and necessary."[35] Cavarero's feminist theory of nonviolence takes as its starting point a biblical commandment, one that is ethical (it is about one's relationships with others) and religious (it is about one's relationship with God), but also political (without it, political communities cannot exist).

An interpretation of the sixth commandment as meaning "You shall *never* kill" is exemplified in the Roman Catholic thesis that "the destruction of frozen embryos constitutes homicide" or, perhaps, in the recent US Supreme Court decision in *Dobbs v. Jackson Women's Health Organization* (2022), which overturned *Roe v. Wade* (1973).[36] And so Cavarero asks what conception of the human is invoked in these examples.[37] What she concludes is that the object of the prohibition is not the individual person but life itself (the "what" rather than the "who," if you will). When we look at modern politics—in Auschwitz, New York, Afghanistan—the inconsistency of "You shall not kill" is obvious. I'd add that it is the same when you look at the involvement of the church in Indigenous genocide. But Cavarero tells us that, "according to the purest style of philosophy, . . . the challenge is precisely to problematize the obvious."[38] We understand "Thou shalt not kill" to prohibit homicide (the original Hebrew is best translated as "You shall not murder"), and homicide is understood as a private crime. The category does not include war or killing that is geographically distant from us. We are still outraged by the former, but we are mostly indifferent to the latter, and this is what Cavarero asks to problematize. Why is homicide, and even abortion, more troubling than distant killings?

One possible explanation might take us back to Levinas and his focus on the face as the foundation of ethics. In an earlier work, *Inclination: A Critique of Rectitude* (2016), Cavarero embraced, albeit critically, Levinas's face-to-face ethics, writing, "In the 'face-to-face' encounter . . . there is no longer an I characterized by the *conatus essendi*, a selfish and possessive I, but an I, a *me*, that already has been dispossessed by the 'thou shalt not kill' that is expressed by the face of the other, which precisely constitutes me through this 'thou.'"[39] But, then, what do we do when the killing is distant and the defenseless face of the other is not right there to dispossess me of my selfish, possessive I? And bringing indigeneity back into the picture, what do we do when the other is not considered human at all; when she is considered just a savage to be domesticated? "Precisely when butchery spreads on the global scene on a large scale," Cavarero writes in "The Archeology of Homicide," "the commandment 'you shall not kill' discovers old and new reasons to suspend itself."[40] Going back to Schmitt, we may say that homicide is more troubling than war precisely because war is in the realm of the exceptional state declared by the sovereign and suspending the rule to never kill. One may ask whether settler colonialism and genocide are also in the realm of the exception and therefore acceptable and about the dehumanization of Native Americans (writing them into savagery, as Chief Justice John Marshall did in his infamous 1823 decision in *Johnson v. M'Intosh*) that has gone hand in hand with this exception. If this is the case, then revisiting sovereignty, treating it with bad intentions, is necessary if we want to liberate political theology of its commitment to settler colonialism. With Suzack and King we need to let the story of Indig-

Dana Lloyd

enous sovereignty loose into the world, and, along with it, lived, practiced, Indigenous sovereignty.

Cavarero goes in a different direction, and this direction is not surprising if you know her work. Her answer has to do with sexual difference and gender stereotypes. "To a real man, at least in certain circumstances, 'You shall not kill' sounds unvirile, womanish, false."[41] But for women, Cavarero writes, the sixth commandment is almost trivial. "Experts in the drama of birth rather than of death, women know that no one arrives in the world alone and that existence is structurally dependent, often off balance, and in need of care."[42] And so perhaps Antigone (who makes earlier appearances in Cavarero's work, most notably in her 2002 book *Stately Bodies*) is a better model for us than Cain. The problem that even Levinas has not escaped is that murder—or the temptation to murder— is at the center of Western origin stories. Instead, what if the infant is the "you" who constitutes the "I" and strips it off its narcissism? I'd say this is Cavarero's third piece of advice to us. Indigenous scholars may want to center Mother Earth as this "you."

Cavarero offers us a feminist philosophy of nonviolence. Indigenous feminists argue that a feminist philosophy of nonviolence must also be decolonial or anticolonial. Maile Arvin (Kanaka Maoli), Eve Tuck (Unangax̂), and Angie Morrill (Klamath) ask "how feminist theories can imagine and realize different modes of nationalism and alliances in the future."[43] The answer has to do with realizing that both settler colonialism and patriarchy are structures rather than events and centering settler colonialism within gender studies and within ethnic studies. So if Schmitt approached political theory with bad intentions when he declared sovereignty as a secularized theological concept, and European feminism approached Schmittian sovereignty with bad intentions when it relied on principles of justice and care rather than violence and authoritarianism, then Indigenous feminist theorists do even more than that when they insist that sovereignty depends on gender justice. But by gender justice, Indigenous feminists do not mean inclusion or representation, because "the project of inclusion can serve to control and absorb dissent rather than allow institutions like feminism and the nation-state to be radically transformed by differing perspectives and goals" (one might say that Indigenous feminists approach the foundational terms of white feminism with bad intentions, as well).[44] Gender justice must mean that women are safe and that our relationships—to one another, to the land, to our kin—are centered in politics and, for political theologians, in theology. Women's safety and relationships should be centered when we debate the personhood of a fetus, the pollution of bodies of water, the need to go to war to defend the nation-state. A plurality of women's voices—as mothers, as aunties, as elders, as religious leaders, as workers—must be heard if we want a just and peaceful world.

Sovereign Kinship

In what follows, I try to recover ideas of Indigenous feminist sovereignty and then connect them back to Cavarero's advice for political theologians who want to be liberated from the sacred truths that have been imposed on them (on us) by Schmittian sovereignty. Arvin, Tuck, and Morrill connect "bad intentions" with rewriting when they argue that the feminist project needs to be rewritten to include not only the dismantling of heteropatriarchy but also of the settler colonial nation-state. Feminism's end goal, they claim, should be not only gender parity but decolonization.[45] So what do Indigenous feminists want from sovereignty? Leanne Simpson explains that "Indigenous thought, which is as diverse as the land itself, roots sovereignty in good relationships, responsibilities, a deep respect for individual and collective self-determination, and honoring diversity."[46] Simpson's understanding of Indigenous sovereignty is inspired by the midwife Katsi Cook (Mohawk), which is something I think Cavarero would like:

> Sovereignty means not only the freedom to make decisions about our land but also the freedom to make decisions about our bodies. Sovereignty is the ability to keep our bodies safe from violence; to use the best of both indigenous and Western medicine to care for ourselves; to define and identify our bodies, sexualities, and relationships the way we see fit; and the capacity to express those identities freely without fear of violence or reprisal. It means the freedom to decide if we want to give birth and when and how. It means we must have the support to breastfeed and that our breast milk is free of contamination, which means that our land and water must also be free of contamination. It means the freedom and support to raise our children with the support of our families and communities, with free access to our lands, our Elders, our languages, and all aspects of our cultures.[47]

Cavarero's mother-infant dyad is expanded here into a whole community. In fact, kinship is fundamental to Indigenous feminist theories about sovereignty. As colonization and dispossession of Indigenous peoples was done through the disruption of kinship relations (some of the most terrifying, genocidal policies and strategies of the federal government targeted the Indigenous family: kidnapping Indigenous children, sexual assault, and regulating and criminalizing marriage practices, as well as tearing Indigenous communities and individuals from their lands), resistance should come from this sphere, as well. "The continuation of strong and dynamic kinship relations between Indigenous women, their families, communities and their land has . . . been the source of growing forms of resistance against cultural destruction," the Indigenous studies scholars Patricia Dudgeon (Bardi) and Abigail Bray write.[48]

As the literary scholar Mark Rifkin writes, "The coordinated assault on native social formations that has characterized U.S. policy since its inception, conducted in the name of 'civilization,' [can] be understood as an organized effort to make heterosexuality compulsory as a key part of breaking up indigenous landholdings, 'detribalizing' native peoples, and/or translating native territoriality and governance into the terms of U.S. liberalism and legal geography."[49] Therefore, resistance, or decolonization, also has to come from kinship. If "US-Indian policy . . . translates place-based indigeneity into a matter of lineage," decolonial kinship reinforces the place-based identity of Indigenous peoples: "A certain attachment results from knowing that some of your relatives are the life-forms that share your place with you. This belief influences one's sense of identity and thought/language."[50] If the "representation of Indigenous peoples as if they were extended families, and therefore necessarily something other than full polities," is designed to dismiss Indigenous sovereignty, then practices of kinship importantly insist on tribal sovereignty. [51]

What this means for political theologians is that we should take kinship seriously. If settler colonialism reduces Indigenous relationships (to one another, to land) to things (as commodity, as resources), then a political theology that is liberated from its commitment to settler colonialism would treat kinship with bad intentions. It would remap our relationships in a way that would center kinship both in religion and in politics. The literary scholar Daniel Heath Justice (Cherokee) argues that "kinship is best thought of as a verb, rather than a noun, because kinship, in most indigenous contexts, is something that's *done* more than something that simply *is*"; similarly, Indigenous nationhood can be understood as based less on a logic of jurisdiction than "an understanding of common social interdependence within the community . . . that link[s] the People, the land, and the cosmos together in an ongoing and dynamic system of mutually affecting relationships."[52] David Delgado Shorter similarly asks for an ontological shift toward Indigenous intersubjectivity. He asks to replace the language of spirituality, a settler colonial language that portrays Indigenous subjects as incapable of knowing themselves, with a notion of relationships.[53] And Dudgeon and Bray connect this relationality with Indigenous law: "The law comes from the land, is the land. . . . For many Indigenous cultures, this law is a worldview, an ethics, which is governed by *responsibility* and *reciprocity* toward humans and more-than-human kin."[54] Treating natural entities as more than human, as kin, as rights-bearing persons can be thought of as approaching theology—especially theologies that see only humans as persons, who were created in the image of God—with bad intentions.

Ultimately, what Cavarero, Simpson, and others offer us is sovereignty that is not an abstract political concept but an intimate, lived concept. Sovereignty can be about sharing, nurturing, kindness. Leanne Simpson tells us about territories in which more than one Indigenous nation exercises sovereignty, and so sovereignty can be about a plurality of voices who all care about and for the land. Cavarero's feminist philosophy of nonviolence depends on centering the mother-infant dyad, and Indigenous feminists take this foundational kinship relationship as a model for sovereignty itself, what I call here "sovereign kinship." When sovereignty is approached with bad intentions and when we refuse to think about it as a divine right to rule, when we think of it instead as a responsibility, stemming from our kinship relations with the human and more-than-human world, to care for one another and to let the land care for us, then sovereignty is liberated from the sacred truth imposed on it by Schmitt. A political theology that centers stories of such relationship, of responsibility, of justice, may be liberated from its commitment to settler colonialism and to violence.

By way of concluding, I'd like to demonstrate how Cavarero herself is following the advice I find in her work. The book *For More Than One Voice* (2005) opens with a chapter on the voice of Jacob. Even though Cavarero begins her exploration of "the primacy of voice with respect to speech" with a biblical story, her epigraph for the chapter comes from Grace Paley. (See Cavarero's second piece of advice earlier in the chapter: Listen to stories; use literature.)[55] Here is the epigraph: "The word which comes out of the mouth is a sound made in the echo of God."[56] She goes on to tell us that in the Hebrew Bible both creation and revelation are associated with God's voice rather than with the content of his words. It was the Christian interpretation of the Hebrew Bible that misled us to believe that *logos* is what matters. Instead of abandoning the sovereign, Cavarero liberates it from the sacred truth imposed on it by Christianity (Cavarero's first piece of advice: Approach theopolitical concepts with bad intentions). Finally, the book may open with Jacob, but it ends with the mother-child dyad (Cavarero's third piece of advice): "The voice is always *for* the ear, it is always relational; but it is never as relational as it is in the first cry of the infant—an invoking life that unknowingly entrusts itself to a voice that responds."[57] Cavarero's move is a feminist one because, traditionally, man has been equated with the mind, while woman has been "represented under the sign of a body that only comes to speech through idle chatter."[58] Yet for Cavarero, the mother-child relationship is the foundation of the political.

What might our political theology look like if we take Cavarero's advice seriously? What might we learn if we took Indigenous feminism seriously and set feminist stories of Indigenous sovereignty loose into the world? I think that the most important thing we might get is a political theology that is not an oxymoron, one that calls us to action and not only to contemplation, to gender justice but also to decolonization, one that is committed to doing—to living—sovereignty differently, with one another and with the land, oriented toward altruism and peace.

Notes

1   Bertolino, "Beyond Ontology and Sexual Difference," 132.

2   Cavarero, "Politicizing Theory," 506.

3   Bertolino, "Beyond Ontology and Sexual Difference," 132.

4   Cavarero et al., *Toward a Feminist Ethics of Nonviolence*, 179.

5   Schmitt, *Political Theology*, 36. Some might have the urge to distinguish Schmitt's bad intentions from Cavarero's, saying that Schmitt was a Nazi, and thus his bad intentions were *really* bad, whereas Cavarero's intentions are actually good. But my point here is that both approach their object of inquiry *ironically*. The critique of Schmitt presented in this volume by Adam Kotsko—that Schmitt's approach to political theology is too narrow; that he thinks of sovereignty only in the context of Christianity and the state— seems more relevant to me to explaining the violence of Schmittian political theology.

6   Lyons, "Rhetorical Sovereignty," 459.

7   Teves et al., "Sovereignty," 3.

8   Sovereign freedom, Cocks writes, is "quintessentially modern, along with the idea of the sovereign individual, ethnonational sovereignty, popular sovereignty, and the dream that the human race might rule the earth and eventually even the universe": Cocks, *On Sovereignty and Other Political Delusions*, 4.

9   Cocks, *On Sovereignty and Other Political Delusions*, 9.

10 Cocks, *On Sovereignty and Other Political Delusions*, 24.

11 Alfred, "Sovereignty," 38.

12 Simpson, *Mohawk Interruptus*, 105. On the relevance of refusal to political theology, see Chi, "Refusal."

13 Teves et al., "Sovereignty," 15.

14 Teves et al., "Sovereignty," 4–5.

15 Butler, *Giving an Account of Oneself*, 31.

16 Cavarero, *For More Than One Voice*, 4.

17 Pinto and Milkova, "Storytelling Philosophy and Self Writing," 240.

18 Other essays in this volume also see storytelling as essential to political theology: see, e.g., David Kline's and Beatrice Marovich's readings of Sylvia Wynter.

19 Lyons, "Rhetorical Sovereignty," 449, 452.

20 Lyons, "Rhetorical Sovereignty," 452.

21 Lyons, "Rhetorical Sovereignty," 449–50.

22 Lyons, "Rhetorical Sovereignty," 450.

23 Lyons, "Rhetorical Sovereignty," 450.

24 Warrior, *Tribal Secrets*, chap. 3.

25 Lyons, "Rhetorical Sovereignty," 457.

26 Simpson, "Land as Pedagogy," 7.

27 Arvin et al., "Decolonizing Feminism," 21.

28 Lyons, "Rhetorical Sovereignty," 459.

29 Lyons, "Rhetorical Sovereignty," 462.

30 Stark, "Stories as Law," 254.

31 King, *The Truth About Stories*, 2.

32 King, *The Truth About Stories*, 10.

33 Suzack, *Indigenous Women Writers and the Cultural Study of Law*, 100.

34 Cavarero and Scola, *Thou Shalt Not Kill*, 49.

35 Cavarero and Scola, *Thou Shalt Not Kill*, 50.

36 *Dobbs v. Jackson Women's Health Organization*, 597 U.S. 215 (2022).

37 Cavarero and Scola, *Thou Shalt Not Kill*, 52.

38 Cavarero and Scola, *Thou Shalt Not Kill*, 60.

39 Cavarero, *Inclination*, 163.

40 Cavarero and Scola, *Thou Shalt Not Kill*, 65.

41 Cavarero and Scola, *Thou Shalt Not Kill*, 107.

42 Cavarero and Scola, *Thou Shalt Not Kill*, 109.

43 Arvin et al., "Decolonizing Feminism," 9.

44 Arvin et al., "Decolonizing Feminism," 17.

45 Arvin et al., "Decolonizing Feminism," 28.

46 Simpson, "The Place Where We All Live and Work Together," 19.

47 Simpson, "The Place Where We All Live and Work Together," 20.

48 Dudgeon and Bray, "Indigenous Relationality," 24.

49 Rifkin, *When Did Indians Become Straight?*, 5–6.

50 Rifkin, "Around 1978," 172; Salmón, "Kincentric Ecology," 1329.

51 Rifkin, "Around 1978," 172.

52 Justice, "Go Away Water!," 151–52.

53 Shorter, "Spirituality."

54 Dudgeon and Bray, "Indigenous Relationality," 3.

55 Cavarero, *For More Than One Voice*, 19.

56 Cavarero, *For More Than One Voice*, 19.

57 Cavarero, *For More Than One Voice*, 169.

58 Cavarero, *For More Than One Voice*, 207.

17

Toward an Intersectional Genealogical Method

SILVIA FEDERICI AS A PARADIGM
FOR POLITICAL THEOLOGY

Adam Kotsko

The Problematic Genealogy of Genealogical Political Theology

As the editors of this volume remind us in their introduction, *political theology* is said in many ways. Broadly speaking, we can group the field into three approaches, based on the emphasis that is placed on the two constituent terms. The first and most common inflection is political *theology*, in the sense of politically engaged theological reflection or theologically informed activism. We can also reverse the stress and speak of *political* theology in the sense of political movements that inspire a religion-like fervor. Finally, there is the less intuitive mode that aims to investigate the relationship between the political and the theological, ideally without presupposing a relationship of subordination or reducibility of one to the other.

This last variation on the field has been one of the most exciting and dynamic in recent decades. Beginning with questions surrounding sovereignty in the early 2000s—a topic of obvious and urgent relevance during the George W. Bush administration's War on Terror—the field slowly but surely came to embrace every important aspect of social life, demonstrating that the afterlife of theology in our ostensibly secular era is not limited to the state's deployment of emergency powers. The literature has achieved arguably its greatest depth and maturity on questions relating to economics and race, but political-theological inquiries of the third kind have come to engage every major political question and axis of oppression, promising the emergence of a truly intersectional approach to political theology.

The common trait of all these investigations is a genealogical approach. Broadly speaking, they all seek to trace the theological roots of ostensibly secular modern power structures. While recognizing the importance of politically engaged theologies and critiques of theologically charged political phenomena such as "cults of personality," I believe that political theology in the genealogical style has a special role to play in helping us get to the bottom of the destructive dynamics of our culture. Genealogical political theology has the advantage that it does not require any specific faith commitment, as politically engaged theology most often does; nor does it presuppose, like the critiques of politics as religion, that politics and theology are two distinct realms that must remain separate. It invites in people with secular backgrounds and those, like me, who have become alienated from religion and gives them tools to reflect on a theological heritage that belongs to all of us—if only in the sense of being a *problem* for all of us.

Of course, this branch of the field brings with it considerable genealogical baggage of its own—namely, its founder, Carl Schmitt, who was a Nazi and coined the term as part of an argument for the necessity of sovereign dictatorship. His destructive agenda is obviously shared by no one in the field today, but it has shaped the definition of *political theology*, creating a conceptual straitjacket that later investigators have struggled to get out of. To put it briefly, Schmitt defines the political very narrowly, as having to do with state sovereignty and the friend-enemy distinction. Similarly, he seems to view monotheistic and specifically Christian theology as the only legitimate representative of the theological. These narrower definitions must be kept in mind when we recall Schmitt's famous methodological dictum: "All significant concepts of the modern theory of the state are secularized theological concepts, not only because of their historical development—in which they were transferred from theology to the theory of the state, whereby, for example, the omnipotent God became the omnipotent lawgiver—but also because of their systematic structure, the recognition of which is necessary for a sociological consideration of these concepts."[1] As I have argued elsewhere, this parallel structure grows out of the two spheres' profound existential stakes and their claim to govern every aspect of life— traits that are not necessarily shared by every sphere of human interest.[2]

From this perspective, both economics and race, so central to the contemporary field of genealogical political theology, are a poor fit for the style of genealogical inquiry Schmitt has inspired. While recognizing that Communist Parties have successfully politicized the economic question of class, Schmitt clearly views economic questions as incompatible with the high dignity of the political. Everything can, in principle, become the basis for a decision on friend and enemy, but at the same time he can declare in *Concept of the Political*: "To demand seriously of human beings that they kill others or be prepared to die themselves so that trade and industry may flourish for the survivors or that the purchasing power of grandchildren may grow is sinister and crazy."[3] Hence, when Giorgio Agamben attempts, in *The Kingdom and the Glory*, to integrate questions of economics into the basically Schmittian analysis of Western political institutions, he introduces "economic theology" as a second paradigm existing alongside "political theology" proper; the relationship between them is never specified.[4]

A Schmittian approach to race is even less promising, if only because of his deep personal racism. On a more conceptual level, too, his concept of politics would allow for the relevance of race only insofar as it is taken up into a friend-enemy distinction that could potentially lead to war—not as an ongoing structuring principle of society. Perhaps recognizing this problem, Gil Anidjar, in his study of the Christian origins of modern concepts of race, gestures toward Schmitt's famous dictum by proclaiming, "All significant concepts of the history of the modern world are liquidated theological concepts," but largely follows his own genealogical course.[5]

None of this is to say that anyone is under any obligation to use Schmitt or justify their work in his terms. Indeed, Anidjar's half-ironic nod toward Schmitt may display the most appropriate attitude toward political theology's problematic founder. But given that the genealogical, diagnostic mode of political theology does trace its origins to Schmitt, the difficulty of expanding his analysis to include the key questions of economics and race—much less topics such as gender and sexuality, which would seem to be all but absent from his work—does raise methodological questions. Those questions are, of course, not unanswerable. In *Neoliberalism's Demons*, for instance, I attempt to offer a Schmittian way out of Schmitt, laying the foundations for the much more capacious concept of political theology demanded by contemporary research by reinterpreting the field as a general study of systems of legitimacy so that any institutional form or power structure (including non-state-centered ones) could count as "political" and any foundational value commitments (including non-monotheistic or even nontheistic ones) could count as "theological."

Yet no matter how broadly I was able to define the field in principle, I was forced to reach outside the field of political theology "proper." And looking back, what most guided my choice of interlocutors was not only the focus or rigor of their research, but a sense that their approach was broadly compatible with political theology. In that respect, there was no single figure who seemed to be a better fit than Silvia Federici.[6] Particularly in her pathbreaking work *Caliban and the Witch* (2014), she provides an account of the transition to modernity—a perennial concern of the genealogical form of political theology—that analyzes political, theological, economic, gender, racial, and colonial dynamics as part of a single articulated strategy of power.[7] And though I "officially" maintained continuity with Schmitt through my reconceptualization of political theology, Federici provided much more concrete inspiration for my approach.

In this essay, I want to put forth a provocation and argue that the genealogical strain of contemporary political theology should take a step further and completely revise its methodology with Federici, rather than Schmitt, as the central methodological point of reference. Focusing primarily on *Caliban and the Witch*, I isolate three key ways that Federici takes up and develops key political-theological concerns: her rejection of conventional binaries, which echoes and radicalizes political theology's approach; her historical method, which brings together the synchronic and diachronic elements of genealogical investigation in an exemplary way; and her strategic presentism, which mines the past for lost histories and alternative models to respond to contemporary problems. There are other thinkers who fit this basic pattern—Michel Foucault and Agamben most prominent among them. What recommends Federici's approach—aside from her radical and anticlerical perspective, which contrasts sharply with Schmitt's reactionary Catholicism—is that she engages in a fully intersectional analysis at every step, a concern that is largely absent from Agamben and arguably is underdeveloped in Foucault, particularly on questions of race. Having established what Federici has to offer to contemporary political theology, I then consider ways that two common critiques of her project can be productively recontextualized if her work is taken as part of the field of political theology. Overall, my goal is to show that whether or not Federici would identify as a political theologian, political theologians would do well to take her as a model for the kinds of intersectional genealogies that increasingly define the field.

Political Theology and the Federician Paradigm

Questioning conventional binaries has always been the stock in trade of political theology. The very name of the field reflects Schmitt's forceful rejection of the secular-religious binary that has been so foundational for modernity. More recent studies have pushed beyond that to reject other, equally foundational binaries: political-economic, class-identity, public-private, metropole-colony, and so on. What makes Federici's approach so productive is that she challenges all these binaries simultaneously by showing how they were all constructed together as part of a cohesive strategy of power.

Federici's holistic method is evident in the first main chapter of *Caliban and the Witch*, "All the World Needs a Jolt: Social Movements and Political Crisis in Medieval Europe." Breaking with modern stereotypes, she portrays medieval Europe as a site of intense political struggle that took in every major area of life—most notably, economics, gender relations, and religion. In a move that at once connects her to genealogical political theology and shows her resonance with politically engaged theologies, Federici characterizes millenarian and other so-called heretical religious movements as modes of political resistance that aimed to radically reorganize the whole of social life. If they had succeeded, she suggests, it "might have spared us the immense destruction of lives and the natural environment that has marked the advance of capitalist relations worldwide" because, "at their best, they called for an egalitarian social order based on the sharing of wealth and the refusal of hierarchies and authoritarian rule." Unfortunately, however, "These were to remain utopias" (22)—though *not* because they were doomed by their religious illusions. These movements do not merely foreshadow a "properly" political modern workers' movement, nor are their religious claims purely "symbolic" of political "implications." Their theology was political, and their politics were theological, inseparably and without remainder—and far from being representatives of medieval backwardness, they are avatars of a lost future that we should wish to rejoin.

In her analysis of the modern period, too, Federici rejects the religious-secular dyad. For instance, at one point she claims that, in the effort to discipline the working class and prevent collective working-class power from emerging, "Even the individual's relation with God was privatized" (84)—putting the conventional secular-religious (and public-private) binaries in a broader context. Admittedly, though, theology narrowly defined is not a major focus of her analysis. But if we adopt my broader definition of the "theological" element in political theology, we can see that she practices the same kind of nonreductive search for homologies between the dominant ideas and political institutions of a given era that political theology carries out. This is clearest in her analysis of the intellectual struggle between René Descartes and Thomas Hobbes. While disclaiming any direct causal influence between these philosophers' ideas and the political and economic developments she decries, she sees both as resonating with a broader strategy aimed at mechanizing the body. Here she is not espousing a vulgar-Marxist technological determinism. As she clarifies, "These

Adam Kotsko

mechanical metaphors reflect not the influence of technology per se, but the fact that the *machine was becoming the model of social behavior*" (145). This shift in attitudes toward the body "did not remain at a purely ideological level. Many practices began to appear in daily life to signal the deep transformation occurring in this domain: the use of cutlery, the development of shame with respect to nakedness, the advent of 'manners'" (153). This kind of fine-grained analysis of personal behavior, so foreign to the Schmittian perspective, comes naturally to Federici as a feminist for whom "the personal is the political."

More central to Federici's concerns than the political-theological (or practical-ideological) dyads are gender, racial, and colonial hierarchies. In contrast to a Schmittian perspective, which would view those concerns as irrelevant unless "politicized" in some limited context, or a vulgar Marxist perspective, which would dismiss them as epiphenomenal to the reality of class struggle, Federici persistently characterizes the development of such hierarchies as strategies to divide and conquer the working class— providing short-term privileges to one group (men, white people, residents of the metropole) over against another (women, Black people, colonized subjects) in ways that wound up reinforcing the power of the capitalist class in the long term. This is perhaps clearest in the gradual development of a racial hierarchy centered on the dyad of Black and white. In the early days of colonialism, Federici argues, slaves were drawn from all racial groups, but once the enslaved started to band together to resist the masters' demands, racial hierarchy emerged as a ready way to divide and conquer the lower classes. As she points out, though, it "was not an automatic process. . . . [R]acism had to be legislated and enforced" (108). Federici's reminder that "a segregated, racist society was instituted from above" (108) is particularly relevant in an era when racism, sexism, and other prejudices are presented as the spontaneous attitudes of everyday people and equality is, paradoxically, supposedly an "elite" concern. In reality, the binaries that appear so natural to most modern subjects are part of a complex, mutually reinforcing strategy of power.

While Federici's analysis touches on every area of life, at its center is an account of the construction of modern gender roles that takes the form of a daring reinterpretation of the phenomenon of witch hunting in early modern Europe and the colonial world. Where interpreters traditionally have viewed the wave of witch hunting as one last outburst of medieval superstition in a world that had not yet become fully modern, Federici argues that we need to see the witch hunts as integral to what is euphemistically called "the transition to capitalism." Far from an anachronistic holdover, in Federici's account the witch hunts were the most extreme and vicious outgrowth of a broader campaign to discipline female bodies, and particularly their reproductive power, in ways that would support the demands of capitalist accumulation.

Crucial to her argument here is a perhaps unexpected connection between the witch hunts and the enclosure of the commons, which deprived peasants of access to shared means of subsistence and forced them into the emerging regime of wage labor. For Federici, women have traditionally had a special relationship with the commons, a phenomenon that she detects in premodern Europe as well as in contemporary Africa and Latin America.[8] Shared control over the commons went hand in hand with shared control over social reproduction as well as biological reproduction. Hence the destruction of an economic regime centered on the commons necessarily entailed the destruction of women's social and reproductive autonomy. More than that, though, the historical connection between women and the commons continued in a perverse form as *"every woman (other than those privatized by bourgeois men) became a communal good,* for once women's activities were defined as nonwork, women's labor began to appear as a natural resource, available to all, no less than the air we breathe or the water we drink" (97). Once again, we are forced to upend our stereotypes of the medieval period as repressive and backward: "In pre-capitalist Europe women's subordination to men had been tempered by the fact that they had access to the commons and other communal assets, while in the new capitalist regime *women themselves became the commons,* as their work was defined as a natural resource, laying outside the sphere of market relations" (97).

Here we come to the second feature of political theology that Federici both exemplifies and extends: genealogy. As the example of the witch hunt shows, the strategies that enforced the "transition to capitalism" did not emerge in a vacuum. Federici acknowledges that the theological doctrines and folk beliefs that came together in the phenomenon of witch hunting were already present in medieval culture. Yet she emphasizes throughout that the demands of the emergent capitalist order determined which preexisting beliefs were highlighted and how they were articulated together.

Particularly intriguing are Federici's suggestions that witch-hunting ideology was decisively shaped by the conquest of the Americas because "the charge of devil-worshipping played a key function also in the colonization of the American aboriginal population" (220). Once again, though, the historical root of a political strategy is less important than its ongoing relevance in modernity, as Federici demonstrates a "growing exchange, in the course of the seventeenth century, between the ideology of witchcraft and the racist ideology that developed on the soil of the Conquest and the slave trade. The Devil was portrayed as a black man and black people were increasingly treated like devils" (198).

This demonization, Federici repeatedly emphasizes, was not a "left-over" element of medieval superstition but integral to the modern strategy of power. And the reason that the emerging capitalist class drew on religious ideology to strengthen its claims was not simply because it wanted to borrow that ideology's authority for its own purposes. More than that, the emerging capitalist class was responding to the fact that religion—in the form of millenarian and heretical movements—had been a powerful site of resistance and alternative community building throughout the medieval period. In other words, Federici goes beyond conventional political theology, and even many contemporary versions, in her awareness of the dynamism and conflict within the medieval period itself, which effectively decenters the medieval-modern dyad by inscribing both within a broader lineage of struggle and reaction.

As Federici makes clear in both her preface and the book's final lines, the struggle she outlines in *Caliban and the Witch* is ongoing. She relates her experience as a visiting professor in Nigeria in 1984–86, when the country was undergoing "structural adjustment" at the behest of the International Monetary Fund and World Bank. What she witnessed seemed to recapitulate her research on the origins of capitalism, as state authorities waged a "War Against Indiscipline" that included misogynistic attempts to discipline women and control their reproductive power (9). For Federici, though, the very fact that such a vicious campaign was necessary was a source of unexpected hope, "as it proved that, worldwide, formidable forces still contrast the imposition of a way of life conceived only in capitalist terms" (9).

Hence, at the same time that she contextualizes her work with references to the brutal imposition of neoliberalism, Federici also, more importantly, bookends it with accounts of resistance movements—in many cases led by women—that reject capitalist hegemony. Where one might be tempted to indulge in fatalism in light of the reiteration of similar dynamics in the birth of capitalism and in its contemporary rearticulation in neoliberalism, Federici aims to help us see that there were and are real alternatives.

In this respect, Federici's strategic presentism could be seen as clearly in line with the practice of political theology, which—even in its more strictly diagnostic mode, which is primarily what I have in mind here—has always marshaled its genealogical narratives and conceptual homologies in response to contemporary problems. Yet it has often done so in a way that could be characterized as passive-aggressive. This tendency is clearly present in Schmitt's foundational text itself, which invents the discipline of political theology as part of an indirect argument for the necessity of dictatorship. Subsequent practitioners have often had subterranean agendas of their own—for instance, purging illegitimate religious accretions from secular politics.

Viewing Federici's approach as a form of political theology not only provides a model for clarifying the relevance and stakes of any particular work of political theology. It also points to the deeper methodological difference between political theology and more conventional history. Political theology, even in its most purely diagnostic or genealogical versions, aims not simply to relate what happened in the past, but to transform our vision of the past to make it usable for the transformation of the present.

Reading Federici as a Political Theologian

At this point, then, I have established a clear structural homology between Federici's methodology and that of political theology in the genealogical mode. As a political theologian, my next instinct is to seek out the genealogical roots of this remarkable correspondence. Does it arise from the influence of Foucault, so decisive for the work of Agamben and the political-theological investigations that follow after him? Does it result from a shared rejection of vulgar Marxist reductionism? Or does the convergence simply reflect the broad path that anyone would wind up going down if they reject the progressive medieval-to-modern narrative, along with the religious-secular dyad that is so central to the West's self-congratulation?

These questions are fertile ground for further investigation, but for now I leave them aside in favor of more future-oriented considerations. Specifically, now that I have shown that Federici's approach is potentially very fruitful for a contemporary political theology, I want to approach this relationship from the other direction and ask: How would we read her work differently in the context of the contemporary enterprise of genealogical political theology? More pointedly, what would Federici have to gain, conceptually, from this alliance? I suggest that the recontextualization I propose would allow Federici to respond more effectively to two critiques of her work, one long-standing and one more recent.

Adam Kotsko

The first critique is that Federici vastly overstates the death toll, and thus the importance, of the witch hunts. As far as I have been able to determine, Federici was in fact drawing on the most reputable scholarship available at the time she was writing. Yet later scholars have most often proposed much lower casualty rates, and in a review of all her published essays, I have yet to find any text in which she walks back or even nuances her empirical claims about the scale of the witch hunts. This doubling down arguably reflects the centrality of the witch hunts to her investigation. They form the nodal point of all the disparate threads of her argument, allowing her to tie together the enclosure of the commons, the invention of the housewife, and the development of race-based chattel slavery for life in a single narrative. If she is wrong about the witch hunt, that seems to pose a real threat of vitiating her analysis.

Here the distinction between genealogical inquiry and conventional history may be helpful in insulating Federici from a simplistic empirical "disproof." If we view her investigation as a genealogical one, then I would propose that Federici is effectively treating the witch hunts as what Agamben, drawing on both Foucault and Thomas Kuhn, calls a "paradigm." Agamben developed this concept in response to similar critiques of his own work—namely, that he was exaggerating or misrepresenting the empirical importance of certain key examples, above all the (in)famous Roman legal figure of the *homo sacer*, who can be killed but not sacrificed. In *The Signature of All Things*, he seeks to clarify the stakes of such exemplary figures: "While [they] are all actual historical phenomena, I nonetheless treated them as paradigms whose role was to constitute and make intelligible a broader historical-problematic context."[9] Referring to Kuhn's well-known account of scientific practice, Agamben notes that, for Kuhn, a paradigm designates both the full "disciplinary matrix" and "an example, a single case that by its repeatability acquires the capacity to model tacitly the behavior and research practices of scientists."[10] For Kuhn, then, a paradigmatic experiment—whose outcome, far from being empirically common, is most often highly counterintuitive and therefore striking and memorable—comes to ground an entire scientific research project.

In Agamben's account, Foucault radicalizes Kuhn's approach in his use of particular historical examples to capture the character of an entire regime of thought. For instance, "The panopticon functions as a paradigm in the strict sense: it is a singular object that, standing equally for all others of the same class, defines the intelligibility of the group of which it is a part and which, at the same time, it constitutes."[11] We know that very few literal panopticons on Jeremy Bentham's model were built, but the very fact that it could be proposed and considered is nonetheless revelatory. Though Agamben does not respond directly to his critics, we could say the same of the *homo sacer*. Even if the legal category was seldom deployed in practice, the fact that it was on the books reflects something about the structure of legal reasoning in the Roman world, as in the later Western legal systems that take up the Roman legacy.

Similarly, even if the scholarly consensus on the scale of the witch hunts at the time Federici wrote *Caliban and the Witch* may have *suggested* their importance for understanding the underlying dynamics of the "transition to capitalism," what really makes her argument productive is the conceptual connections she is able to make using the witch hunt as her lens—connections that would still exist even if the witch hunt were carried out on a much smaller scale than she claims. What really seals her argument on the witch hunts' influence is not the sheer body count, but striking and unexpected moments such as Hobbes's declaration that witches deserve to die for *falsely believing* they have magical powers: "Even the materialist Hobbes, while keeping his distance, gave his approval [to the witch hunts]. 'As for witches,' he wrote, 'I think not that their witchcraft is any real power; but yet that they are justly punished, for the false belief they have that they can do such mischief, joined with their purpose to do it if they can.' He added that if these superstitions were eliminated, 'men would be much more fitted than they are for civil obedience'" (143–44). One could also mention the repeated patterns of persecution and resistance on both sides of the Atlantic, reinforced by the carefully selected illustrations. Such observations demonstrate that witches were paradigmatic *for early modern Europeans*, from the most revered philosopher all the way down to the most debased propagandist for colonialism. And they are paradigmatic precisely because they serve as a nodal point for anxieties—conscious, explicitly articulated anxieties—around disciplining the body under early capitalism.

The second critique centers on Federici's most recent book as of this writing, *Beyond the Periphery of the Skin* (2020), which addresses trans issues in a way that is, if not outright transphobic, deeply thoughtless and insensitive.[12] I have no desire to defend or explain away these remarks, though I do believe they can serve as a teachable moment for contemporary genealogical political theology. Nevertheless, it seems fair to point out that this development, along with being profoundly disappointing on an ethical level, is somewhat surprising in that it seems to contradict some of her earlier writings. In the concluding essay of *Re-Enchanting the World* (2019),

Federici lists several signs of resistance to the capitalist disciplining of the body, including "the preference for *androgynous* models of gender identity, the rise of the transsexual and intersex movements and the queer rejection of gender, with its implied rejection of the sexual division of labor." In her account, these trends point to "a profound desire for a remolding of our humanity in ways different from, in fact the opposite to, those that centuries of capitalist industrial discipline have tried to impose on us."[13] To put it simply, all of this sounds like a very good thing from Federici's perspective. By contrast, in *Beyond the Periphery of the Skin*, "body remakes"—which include but are not explicitly limited to transition surgeries—represent an attempt to fight back against "an experience of devaluation" but "remain individual solutions and add to the process of social stratification and exclusion."[14] Together with the rise of surrogate pregnancy, these "body remakes" become evidence of a world that wants to capture and destroy "the magic of life" that occurs in pregnancy and childbirth.[15]

What happened? As reviewers have pointed out, Federici seems to be indulging in a kind of gender essentialism that links womanhood to the "magic" of pregnancy and childbirth.[16] Though most commentators attempt to dissociate these anti-trans sentiments from her earlier masterwork, already in *Caliban and the Witch* there are hints that Federici may not view "magic" as solely a metaphor. In her account of the mechanization of the body, for instance, she claims, "The body had to die so that labor-power could live" and then immediately clarifies, "What died was the concept of the body as a receptacle of magical powers that had prevailed in the medieval world. In reality, it was destroyed" (141). After describing some of the magical practices that early modern thinkers found most troubling, she makes a seemingly unmotivated statement: "It would not be fruitful to investigate whether these powers were real or imaginary. It can be said that all precapitalist societies have believed in them and, in recent times, we have witnessed a revaluation of practices that, at the time we refer to, would have been condemned as witchcraft" (142), such as parapsychology or astrology.

This agnosticism could represent an attempt to get inside the worldview of the people Federici is studying. They were not sure whether magic was real or not, so for the sake of her analysis, it is best to leave the question undecided. When we read this passage in light of *Beyond the Periphery of the Skin*, however, it is difficult to avoid concluding that Federici believes magic was real in some sense—and was all but wiped out by capitalism. From this perspective, the tragedy would, in a way, be even more profound than if the victims of the witch hunts had been killed through ignorance and superstition. The powers that the persecutors attributed to the women really did exist, the world really was alive and magical in a sense we can no longer fully grasp, and capitalism destroyed it and replaced it with a dead machine.

If this really is Federici's viewpoint, then I obviously suspect that she is mistaken—but what a productive mistake! Federici's idiosyncratic standpoint gives her the ability to make a uniquely thoroughgoing critique of a gendered order that puts itself forward as natural but that is in reality a product of extreme and ongoing violence. We do not need to get on board with the romantic style of second-wave feminism that apparently underlies her work to admire and use her radical critique of modern gender relations and their embeddedness in capitalism.

In other words, if Federici really does believe in magic, then we can number her among the many productive cranks in the political theology pantheon—scholars with idiosyncratic obsessions that sent them down paths of inquiry no one else would have discovered. From this perspective, there is no need to explain away or excuse her trans-exclusionary rhetoric any more than we need to justify Schmitt's Nazism or the deeply questionable politics of other foundational figures such as Friedrich Nietzsche and Ernst Kantorowicz. What makes them valuable is not their "positive" opinions but the radical critiques that their idiosyncratic views enable. In a field accustomed to reading figures "against the grain," we can certainly embrace Federici's critique without accepting her apparent gender essentialism or the anti-trans position she has recently embraced—thinking with and beyond her, using the tools she has given us.

This methodological reserve, which values a thinker's critical, genealogical insights over their positive, prescriptive views, also illustrates the value of the genealogical mode of political theology for politically engaged theologies. From that perspective, an aspect of Federici's thought that might appear particularly appealing is her insistence on the primacy of the commons over any mode of property or possession. This conviction resonates deeply with much contemporary theological reflection on the environmental crisis (and, of course, many other issues). Yet for Federici, it is also deeply connected to her gender essentialism insofar as she posits a special relationship between women and the commons. A politically engaged theologian who simply took up Federici's ideas about the commons as they stand would have much to explain away—unless they first investigated her arguments in the mode of a genealogical political theologian. Then they might ask whether Federici is simply inverting the plight of women as the collective commons of all men in capitalist modernity to project a more positive connection between women and the commons into the precapitalist past, and whether we might need to take the step—deeply Federician in spirit, if not in letter—of dispensing with the gender binary to think a truly redemptive vision of the commons that does not idealize the past but seeks in it the fragments of a yet unrealized future.

Notes

1   Schmitt, *Political Theology*, 36.

2   See Kotsko, *Neoliberalism's Demons*, chap. 1.

3   Schmitt, *The Concept of the Political*, 48.

4   Agamben, *The Kingdom and the Glory*, 1.

5   Anidjar, *Blood*, viii.

6   Her nearest competitor would be Sylvia Wynter, who was a crucial interlocutor for several of the essays in my *What Is Theology?* and whose potential contribution to political theology is ably charted in David Kline's contribution to this volume.

7   Federici, *Caliban and the Witch*. Hereafter, page numbers are cited in parentheses in the text.

8   Her research into contemporary commoning is best represented by the essays collected in Federici, *Re-Enchanting the World*.

9   Agamben, *The Signature of All Things*, 9.

10 Agamben, *The Signature of All Things*, 11; Kuhn, *The Structure of Scientific Revolutions*.

11 Agamben, *The Signature of All Things*, 17.

12 Federici, *Beyond the Periphery of the Skin*.

13 Federici, *Re-Enchanting the World*, 195.

14 Federici, *Beyond the Periphery of the Skin*, 54–55.

15 Federici, *Beyond the Periphery of the Skin*, 38.

16 Boast, "The Doctor's Knife."

Siobhan Kelly

In political theology we encounter the millennial Judith Butler. This is not a bad messianism joke—that will come later—but a commentary on reception history. Butler's writings prior to the late 1990s are referred to only in passing in the work of political theologians, usually to situate gender as outside the field's domain. Political-theological engagement with Butler's scholarship bypasses arguably their two best-known works: *Gender Trouble: Feminism and the Subversion of Identity* (1990) and *Bodies That Matter: On the Discursive Limits of "Sex"* (1993). This selective reading is a symptom of a larger, fieldwide inability—what I understand as a psychic refusal—to take gender seriously as a key term for political theology. I call this the degendering of political theology; I aim to identify this degendering to clear the ground so other kinds of political theology, such as the kinds on display in this volume, can flourish.

Butler's millennial work is crucial to political theology, to be sure. Their 2012 *Parting Ways: Jewishness and the Critique of Zionism* received a roundtable in *Political Theology*, a journal for which Butler serves as a board member. Butler's output in the past twenty years—including the coauthored collections *Is Critique Secular?* (2009) and *The Power of Religion in the Public Sphere* (2011), alongside their trenchant critique of Zionism in *Parting Ways* and work on precarity and nonviolence—reveals deep critical engagement with key terms and theorists of political theology.[1] Their work emerges from one particular vein of political-theological thought running through Franz Rosenzweig, Walter Benjamin, Emmanuel Levinas, Mahmoud Darwish, Hannah Arendt, and Jacques Derrida, a largely Jewish lineage, in contrast to the long-standing (and oft-contested) Schmittian norm. Examining how Butler's work is treated in the field reveals a curious, gender-size gap. This gap is not *only* encountered in political theology when Butler is at hand; it may, in fact, constitute the field itself.

Degendered Political Theology

Gender is rarely a central analytic in political theology. Authors are quick to identify this issue and hope for future research that might fix this problem. The 2004 *Blackwell Companion to Political Theology* includes a section, "Political Theologies: Survey," featuring essays meant to do just that. Ten men receive chapters of their own, and all but one—Gustavo Gutiérrez, founder of liberation theology—are white and from Europe or the United States. An additional five essays in this section are organized on themes: "Eastern Orthodox Thought," "Feminist Theology, Southern," "Feminist Theology, Northern," "Political Theologies in Asia," and "Black Political Theologies." In feminist theology's Northern iteration, Elaine Graham notes an undertheorization of gender in the field, where feminism is reduced to identity with "woman": "While the politics of gender provides a shared framework for woman-centered politics and theorizing, the common bonds of 'women's experience' are complicated by other indices of power and difference, such as class, sexual orientation, race, and nationality.... Despite—perhaps because of—its emphasis on the crucial impact of the category of 'women's experience,' for example, Latina, womanist, and feminist theologies have tended to be somewhat undertheorized in terms of critical theories of gender."[2] As Graham articulates, political theology tends to equate feminism with womanhood alone, and differences among women already complicate any such easy equation. She connects political theology's inattention to gender to the flatness of concepts such as subjectivity and agency in feminist theology, pointing specifically to the early work of Butler as a potential corrective—the volume's only reference to Butler. Graham argues, "No feminist theologian has yet to come to terms with the radical complications of agency, subjectivity, and identity represented by feminist scholars such as Donna Haraway and Judith Butler."[3] Critiques of subjectivity confound theological inquiry and thus tend to be ignored, mirroring the absence of gender in the same discourses. Through this absence, *The Blackwell Companion* places Butler's work on gender—as well as work on gender in general—outside the purview of political theology.

The *Blackwell Companion* is indicative of a fieldwide trend. Whether or not the millennial Butler appears, political theology fails to treat *gender* as a crucial term of analysis. In the 2015 *Cambridge Companion to Christian Political Theology*, published after Butler began engaging political theology and was taken up in the field, such an analysis of gender still did not surface, and Butler's work is completely absent from that volume. Feminist thought remains peripheral, at best, to political theology. The editors, Craig Hovey and Elizabeth Phillips, offer the following mea culpa: "Due to the length of this volume, thinkers, movements, and topics that deserve attention in their own right are dealt with in relation to one another. Black theology and feminist theology in particular deserve their own chapters."[4] Interested in "political theology as a focus of Christian theology—an inquiry carried out by Christian theologians in relation to the political, where *the political* is defined broadly to include the various ways in which humans order common life"—the editors note the absence of Black thought and feminist analytics from the volume alongside geographic limitations.[5] "Africa, Southeast Asia, [and] the political theologies of Eastern Orthodoxy" are also not investigated here, and such constraints allow this volume to provide a nuanced view of "the English-speaking West," as they describe their primary focus.[6] After all this situating, Hovey and Phillips insist questions about "oversights and unintentional exclusions" including and beyond those named "are the conversations that keep scholarship moving forward and that make Christian theology a living tradition."[7] While analytics such as gender and race may make the tradition a living one, they apparently do not enliven it enough to warrant inclusion in the volume.

Feminism does make a brief appearance in Susan Abraham's contribution on postcolonial theology in *The Cambridge Companion*, where the language of feminism is quickly replaced by the language of "woman." Abraham writes, in a discussion of Gayatri Spivak's work:

> A feminist perspective on freedom is strongly critical of masculinist political theory, which can afford these occlusions in which the freedom for "woman" is subsumed into a general category of freedom. Woman as the subject and object of ethics infinitely complicates philosophy, politics, and cultural theory. Rhetorical and discursive strategies in context are better able to illuminate how freedom for women is inseparable from freedom for anyone else. This point is also made in [the Botswanan postcolonial feminist theologian Musa] Dube's work; gendered oppression, its domestic and global face, can only be met by careful attention to the way in which culturally influential texts construct women. Neither Dube nor Spivak is invested in identity politics. The force of their rhetorical analyses of freedom is aimed at dissolving binary metaphysics of Self and not-Self with a view to decolonization.[8]

Siobhan Kelly

Abraham here is attuned to the dangers of binary modes of thought, particularly as articulated by postcolonial thought against the history of philosophy. However, this critical attention short-circuits when the terms of gender appear, such that binary thinking about "women" (alongside its unspoken but obvious pair, "men") is not treated to critical scrutiny but allowed to proliferate. Graham's diagnosis of the undertheorization of gender in feminist political theology still holds true.

Saul Newman's *Political Theology: A Critical Introduction* (2019) upends the terms of argument set forth in Graham's work. Rather than being interested in the critiques of subjectivity that spring from the critical-theoretical interventions of Butler and others, Newman sees feminist thinking only in the context of identity politics, which, he argues, is equally misguided on the left and the right: "In both cases, the identity being promoted is associated with a certain moral position. . . . One's identity becomes the only basis upon which one is authorised to speak and upon which other non-identifying voices are automatically delegitimised."[9] For Newman, political theology must position itself against such identitarian discourses, as any attempt launched within its terms will fail. He uses transness as exemplar to communicate this: "Even 'trans' identities, of which we have been hearing so much these days, do not necessarily break with the essentialism of identity but, on the contrary, insist even more fervently on the 'truth' of one's gender, to which one's physical body must be made to conform."[10] This understanding of transness is eerily identical to that forwarded by the Catholic ethicist, student of Mary Daly, and transphobe extraordinaire Janice Raymond in her polemic *The Transsexual Empire* (1979), representing the lowest common denominator of regurgitated transphobic laziness. Trans identity (unattached from trans people) appears as marker only—a hollow shell without content merely distracting "us" from the "real" work of political theology. Incapable of doing political theology, irrelevant to the discourses of political theology, the trans figure is somehow punished without even appearing. Butler, along with a host of other queer and trans theorists, shows us how understanding gender as "mere" identity will always be incomplete and misleading, and how an analysis of gendered subject formation can instead serve as a crucial backbone of political theology moving forward.

In April 2021, the journal *Political Theology* published a call for papers for the special issue "(How to Do) Political Theology Without Men?" that seeks to address the degendering of political theology made apparent in these previous texts.[11] The editors assert, "Despite its flexibility and self-reflective character, political theology remains a field which is unquestionably dominated by men," noting that two *Political Theology* issues featured articles *only* by men. To compensate for this imbalance, "No men will be involved in this special issue—there will be no male authors, no male peer reviewers, no male book reviewers, no male-authored books reviewed, and so on."[12] Before I can begin asking a series of increasingly petulant questions about the gap between "men" and "male" and what their elision *does* (Butler's rallying cry that sex reveals itself to always already be gender ringing in my ears), the editors add a third term by stating, "The only strict criterion we have is that the authors are non-men." The specific terms of gender taken up are multiple, a mix of invocations speaking of gender in the negative ("no men," "no males," "non-men"), on one hand, and ones that use positive or including logics on the other ("We invite proposals from scholars of political theology who identify as women or gender nonbinary"). While this rhetoric means to communicate inclusion and a worldview that is broader than sexual dimorphism, it fails to move beyond the woman-centric, additive approach to feminist thought questioned by Graham in 2004.

To be sure, Karma Ben Johanan and Brandy Daniels, the editors of the special issue, provide a necessary diagnosis of a long-standing and damning issue: the overrepresentation of men in political theology. They recognize a problem as old as the field itself that may be worsening over time. However, their solution of additive, inclusion-based metrics over and above the development of a robust analysis of gender cannot fully ameliorate the issue. Attempts at "inclusive" gender complementarianism serve only to reify the existing paradigm of gender while stifling critical work that attends to gender. They mistake a theoretical issue for the demographic inequality that follows from it. An attempt to counter the oppressive force of scholarly normativity and patriarchy ends up replicating and solidifying the conditions of gender as they exist today, shutting down the possibility of those who refuse the terms of identity or take more complex approaches to the issue even *existing* in the same scholarly milieu, much like Newman. Analyses of the gendered contours of subject formation in and through political theology are rendered anathema, even in a special issue that would seem most conducive to it. Rendered anathema, too, are scholars who refuse these terms; who do not fit into this complementarian worldview; whose desires and solidarities confound such elisions; and who, to bring us into Butlerian territory, are perhaps illegibly precarious.

Siobhan Kelly

Covering the past nearly two decades in political-theological thought, this analysis reveals uneven engagement with Butler alongside a generalized inattention to gender. There is no progress narrative to be found here: The problems in thinking gender, including the failure to take seriously the work of Butler, endure.

Perhaps an obvious point, but one worth stating, is that gender and political theology are not separable. Reading across Butler's corpus reveals gender's very political-theological constitution, giving rise to a broader vision of ethics useful for those thinking in and with political theology; in the process, it calls into question some of the field's assumptions.[13] An account of gendered subject formation is necessary for justice-oriented projects of political theology that do not wish to replicate the very harms they seek to ameliorate.

Butler's Work as Political Theology

I hope for a political theology that seeks not to solve a discrete and identifiable problem through inclusion but to rearticulate the questions being asked and the forms of the subject they demand. Tarrying with Butler's work—reading their trenchant critique of gender subjectivation in *Gender Trouble* (1990) and *Bodies That Matter* (1993) in conversation with their later, more obviously political-theological, work—may be a place to start. What happens when we *miss* gender, and what might instead become possible when gender's role in subject formation is seen, not as outside of or, at best, incidental to political theology but as the necessary ground from which to launch what Julia Reinhard Lupton and Graham Hamill call "political theology"?

Hammill and Lupton name political theology "the condition for a range of modern political positions and socio-poetic experiments" that examine "the exchanges, pacts, and contests that obtain between religious and political life, especially the use of sacred narratives, motifs, and liturgical forms to establish, legitimate, and reflect upon the sovereignty of monarchs, corporations, and parliaments" (and, I would add, gender—though it is also worth recognizing once more that the authors crucially do *not*).[14] They distinguish between political theology$_1$ as "inveterate, entrenched, phantasmatic, and reactionary, the stuff of Nazism, racial panic, and the *arcana imperii*," and political theology$_2$ as that which "would rework and refigure those disturbing anchors of psychic life, not only in order to create an easement from their tenacious claim, but also to recover and repurpose whatever it is that makes them so resilient."[15] A turn away from Schmittian political theology and toward the term's resignification as a strategy for reworking field assumptions can help us think more capaciously and critically about gender's place in political theology. Butler's own engagement with political theology operates not through recourse to Schmitt but via a different, predominantly Jewish and Palestinian field genealogy. This genealogy contains immense resources for critiques of sovereignty, which Butler uses to great effect to dismantle Zionist ideology. Beyond orienting the field away from fascistic modes of thinking and desiring, then, a reconsideration of Butler for political theology$_2$ can give us a model of analysis connecting gender subjectivation to Palestinian oppression, enmeshed sites where claims to sovereignty undergird immense political violence. This can also illustrate the type of intervention the field should prioritize at this time of reinvigoration. A broader understanding of political theology$_2$ refuses to focus solely on Western Christendom, turning to alternative genealogies of thought, where Butler's work is situated.

Butler's Gender for Political Theology

Butler's ideas in *Gender Trouble* and its follow-up *Bodies That Matter*, crucial texts in the development of queer and trans theory, have played an outsize role in the seismic shifts in public perceptions of gender since 1990, though sometimes Butler's most insightful contributions are lost along the way.[16] Misreadings are plentiful.[17] In *Gender Trouble*, Butler explores "gender as an enactment that performatively constitutes the appearance of its own interior fixity."[18] Gender is not something one *is* or *has*; rather, it is what one *does*—and the doing is not a single, fixed moment denoting completion or stability, or even necessarily a conscious process. Gender is produced through the repetition and citation of modes of being that themselves do not chart back to any original, stably gendered position; "the essence or identity" our gendered actions "purport to express are *fabrications* manufactured and sustained through corporeal signs and other discursive means."[19] Gender appears fixed and stable only by the accretion of these signs into a "matrix of intelligibility," and the contemporary (and perduring) iteration Butler analyzes is the heterosexual matrix, which they later call the "gender matrix."[20] Butler appeals to a future feminist politics *not* beholden to the stable subject "woman" to make political claims, which could thus operate outside the confines of not only heterosexuality but also the binary gender and sex system. Butler elucidates a coalitional feminist politics without recourse to any stable notion of identity—a crucial argument of *Gender Trouble* that falls out of its reception when there is an exclusive focus on Butler's theory of performativity.

For Butler, gender and sexuality together create "a hegemonic discursive/epistemic model of gender intelligibility that assumes that for bodies to cohere and make sense there must be a stable sex expressed through a stable gender (masculine expresses male, feminine expresses female) that is oppositionally and hierarchically defined through the compulsory practice of heterosexuality."[21] Gender only "makes sense" as a culturally imposed dyad because it is meant to instantiate the heterosexual, reproductive unit. Gender (along with its naturalizing name, "sex") and sexuality cannot be easily separated; rather, they come to define and reify each other through cultural operations meant to corral difference through appeals to intelligibility, discursive and material processes Butler calls "naturalization." These processes of naturalization, of being rendered intelligible (or not), are central to what Butler, after Michel Foucault, calls subjectivation, the process of becoming a subject and simultaneously of delimiting what kinds of subjects are possible.[22]

Butler's concern with the discursive led to harsh criticism by some for a seeming failure to address material concerns by keeping their analysis at the level of "mere" discourse. This critique is addressed in *Gender Trouble*'s follow-up, *Bodies That Matter*, in which Butler shows how such intelligibility calls into question the very material-discursive split. Butler argues, against those who claim sex to be (only) a discrete, identifiable, material condition (and who consider material bodily being "most real, most pressing, most undeniable"), that sex is instead "an ideal construct which is forcibly materialized through time. It is not a simple fact or static condition of a body, but a process whereby regulatory norms materialized 'sex' and achieve this materialization through a forcible reiteration of those norms," with that forcible reiteration being precisely what Butler means by gender performativity.[23] Gender performativity names the reiterative processes by which the ideal construct of binary sex is enforced and materialized—a process of discursive materialization that radically questions any sense that the material predates or can exist separately from the discursive. Performativity, then, cannot be separated from either the discursive or the material—and the latter inevitably collapses into the former. Butler calls attention here to how these linguistic operations actually *shape* what we know, think, and feel about bodies. It is our discursive terrain that animates the materiality of (as well as our structures of knowledge and feeling for) sex, gender, and sexuality.

Butler's work is an unfolding articulation of ethics without identity. Their attention to *subjectivation*, the process through which a subject becomes and the matrices of power that constrain how, where, and to what ends a subject *can* become, is key. In *Giving an Account of Oneself*, Butler offers: "There is no making of oneself (*poiesis*) outside of a mode of subjectivation (*assujettisement*) and, hence, no self-making outside of the norms that orchestrate the possible forms that a subject may take. The practice of critique then exposes the limits of the historical scheme of things, the epistemological and ontological horizon within which subjects come to be at all."[24] *Giving an Account of Oneself*, then, makes clear that Butler applies a critique to the processes of subjectivation that create, rely on, and reinforce the heterosexual (or gender) matrix. *Gender Trouble* and *Bodies That Matter* show gender's role in subjectivation—what forms of gender are accessible to the becoming subject; what is precluded; and how the demand for legible gender reifies heteronormativity and a biologistic understanding of gender as sex simultaneously. This also opens avenues to critique forms of power intent on constraining available modes of gender subjectivation and to proliferate blocks to seamless subjectivation in and to gender.

Butler makes this connection explicit in *Excitable Speech*, where the power of resignification is described through anti-queer hate speech and queer reappropriation of slurs. However, it is equally present in works where gender is not the central analytic. Butler's later conceptualization of "grievability" argues that grief is determined within the heterosexual or gender matrix (which itself is a deeply Christian phenomenon). Communities form in resistance to heteronormativity, where shared ideas that counter the refusal of gender's centrality can take shape. Mourning during the AIDS crisis and trans memorialization against familial rejection are two key examples. The gendered contours of subject formation inflect Butler's later work even when gender is not the central concern, and a failure to see this earlier intervention still at play in, say, *Precarious Life* or *Parting Ways*, flattens their contributions and limits their applicability. Reading *Parting Ways* in light of Butler's work on gender calls Zionism's reproductive ideals to account, particularly given the cooptation of the language of queer inclusion by Israel as a defense against claims of state violence and genocide.[25] There, the assimilation of normative forms of homosexuality that still prioritize reproduction are revealed as the operation of the gender matrix, intent on securing identifiable forms of the subject through nominal inclusion that will not overturn the system.[26]

Millennial Butler in Political Theology

While Graham argued in 2004 that feminist theology has failed to account for the critique of subjectivity levied by scholars such as Butler, in *Judith Butler and Theology* Anna Maria Riedl aims to incorporate that critique of subjectivity by divorcing it from the context in which it arose—namely, in work attending to gender. Riedl identifies *gender* as the impediment to theology taking up Butler's critique of subjectivation: "It is perhaps precisely this debate on Butler's gender theory that is blocking the view of [their] wider work, and in particular of the fact that [Butler] has since turned to a range of different issues, such as hate speech, American politics after 9/11, and a critique of Zionism."[27] While true, a reading of this work without the paradigm of gender subjectivation will fail to cohere; those who cannot abide Butler's work on gender, including the Catholic Church, will invariably have incommensurate understandings of subject formation. *To accept Butler's paradigm of gendered subject formation and the performative constitution of the subject is to accept that binary sexual difference and gender complementarity cannot hold.* Without attending to Butler's work on gender, we end up, at best, with a theoretical paradigm that is unevenly applied and, at worst, with a complete misapprehension of Butler's work that prevents interrogation at the level of the subject *or* at the level of gender. Riedl writes, "Without wishing to diminish [Butler's] contribution to gender theory, or to deny its significance to [their] work as a whole. . . . I want to shift attention away from [their] roots in gender theory, and towards [their] reflections on ethics, politics, and the theory of recognition."[28]

Riedl goes on to leverage Butler's work for what she calls a "theology of vulnerability," to specifically Christian ends. She argues, "A reading of Butler's texts from the perspective of Christian theology should be aware of where Butler positions [themself], since this would prevent our rashly appropriating [their] claims to bolster Christian positions."[29] After this chiding, Riedl proceeds to do exactly what she just expressed trepidation about doing: "At the same time, though, Butler's religious origins can serve as a basis for a theological reading of [their] work, since it is apparent that [their] texts are at least partially rooted in a theological soil."[30] Absenting queers might be theologically useful—but only if the theology constitutively requires binary sexual difference. And if it does, I ask, *for whom* is this useful?

Riedl's refusal of Butler's attention to gender in subject formation reveals a supersessionist framework at play. Language of "origins" and "theological soil" rhetorically enforces Judaism as the forebear of Christianity, a developmental model in which Christianity is the holy flower emerging from Judaism's useful dirt. For Riedl, the flower is a Christian theology of vulnerability that both draws from Butler and purposefully obfuscates the question of gender. As "the Catholic Church in particular finds it difficult to deal with gender theories, and its representatives often speak of gender as an ideology, with Butler frequently being made into the figurehead of this 'ideology,'" Riedl chooses to sidestep the issue.[31] She is perhaps unaware of, or unwilling to note, the cruel irony of casting aside gender as an analytic in the context of the harm caused by Catholic attacks on so-called gender ideology. Butler's recent work on this topic responds to these transphobic invocations and connects them to other forms of political violence, including white nationalism and racism. Butler also identifies such forms of violence in the rising tides of militant Zionism in Israel and among evangelical Christians in the United States.[32] A critique of Zionism and a critique of the Christian naturalization of the gender matrix are interlocking and central to Butler's work, revealing the shared aspects of their constitution and the precarity such political-theological paradigms offload onto gender minorities and Palestinians alike. In *Parting Ways*, Butler argues that "religion often functions as a set of practices and, indeed, as a matrix of subject formation."[33] Subject formation occurs through imbricated matrices of religion and gender working together to demand heteronormative binary sexual difference from subjects in formation. Any attempt to articulate the vicissitudes of subject formation must be responsive to the mutual constitution and reinforcement of religion and gender; attempting to think one without the other will always prove insufficient.

Evacuating Butler's attention to gender in subject formation to do Christian theology with their work not only prevents these crucial connections from being made but risks making the enmeshed theological and political consequences of Zionism and the movement against "gender ideology" harder to recognize. It also allows for theologies undergirded by binary sexual difference to continue unmarked and unimpeded. One cannot control the proliferations of discourse that emerge from a given text or scholar. Though one cannot preclude future (bad) readings, bad readings are nevertheless instructive. They reveal the political-theological work being done by certain scholars, traditions, and discourses through their strategic silences.

Conclusion: Don't Miss Gender

Apprehension of gender (or Butler) does not alone make for good political theology. Where better to turn for an example than Pope Benedict XVI? In the anthology *Political Theologies: Public Religions in a Post-Secular World* (2006), edited by Hent de Vries and Lawrence E. Sullivan, Benedict XVI appears in conversation with Jürgen Habermas a few dozen pages after Butler performs a close reading of Walter Benjamin's work. The volume was published two years after Benedict, as Cardinal Joseph Ratzinger and leader of the Congregation for the Doctrine of the Faith, released his "Letter to the Bishops of the Catholic Church on the Collaboration of Men and Women in the Church and in the World."[34] The letter decries any blurring of binary sexual difference, taking aim at Butler in particular.[35] Mary Anne Case demonstrates that Catholic anti-gender positions appeared in Ratzinger's work as early as the 1980s, and "trans rights claims were, together with feminist claims, thus a foundational component, not a recent addition, to the Vatican's sphere of concern around 'gender' and to the focusing of that concern on developments in secular law."[36] While the particular issue of gender goes unstated in Benedict's contribution to this volume on political theology, he hints at it through a critique of "the temptation now to construct the proper human being" that aligns transness with medical developments inimical to Catholic theological anthropology, including gene editing, human cloning, and test tube babies.[37]

What does it *do* to include Butler alongside Benedict XVI in a collection shortly after the latter made clear the former was an enemy of the church? Can political theology₂, explicitly oriented toward social justice, engage in conversations that demand a gender-size hole? Butler has recently written about the backlash they have witnessed to their work, connecting Catholic anti-trans ideology, trans-exclusionary radical feminists (TERFs), and fascist political formations.[38] All three are committed to the eradication of transness and trans people, to the impossibilization of trans life. Should political theology aspire to be useful for such projects?

A similarly eliminationist worldview animates Zionism's approach to Palestinian life. Butler's work in *Parting Ways* and activism in support of the Palestinian struggle has brought attention to the Boycott, Divestment, and Sanctions (BDS) movement. More than five hundred religious studies scholars have signed on to a statement organized by Religious Studies Scholars for BDS, a movement whose political urgency is made crystalline by the tens of thousands of Palestinians murdered since October 7, 2023. While the field of political theology flirts with Butler's writings on Zionism, is the field prepared to take their implications seriously and support BDS—implications made clear once Butler's work on Zionism is contextualized by their work on gender?

Should the Catholic Church's anti-trans eugenic policies be met with boycotts, divestment, and sanctions?[39] Butler can appear alongside Benedict only if we defang Butler's work on gender and simultaneously ignore the full force of Benedict's (and the Vatican's) anti-trans position and the damage it continues to cause.

I wonder, too, if anti-trans political theology, like that of Benedict XVI, and its tacit support in our field impacts our demographic unevenness more than any ill-described special issue could possibly correct. What if we let our theoretical paradigms and political commitments lead? What if we were to leave those fangs in and bite down?

Notes

1   Vincent Lloyd and David True argue that one "way to approach the question of canon, one that underscores our aspirations for the journal [*Political Theology*], is to reflect on the scholarship of our distinguished editorial board members," pointing specifically to Butler as a scholar who recovers "resources from the Jewish political tradition for thinking subtly about diaspora, foregrounding questions of justice": Lloyd and True, "What Is the Political Theology Canon?" 540. While descriptive of Butler's contemporaneous work, Butler's prominence as a theorist of gender notably goes unmentioned here.

2   Graham, "Feminist Theology, Northern," 211, 221.

3   Graham, "Feminist Theology, Northern," 222.

4   Hovey and Phillips, *The Cambridge Companion to Christian Political Theology*, xii.

5   Hovey and Phillips, *The Cambridge Companion to Christian Political Theology*, xi–xii.

6   Hovey and Phillips, *The Cambridge Companion to Christian Political Theology*, xii.

7   Hovey and Phillips, *The Cambridge Companion to Christian Political Theology*, xii.

8   Abraham, "Postcolonial Theology," 150.

9   Newman, *Political Theology*, 57.

10 Newman, *Political Theology*, 57.

11 Political Theology Network, "CFP."

12 Ben Johanan and Daniels here echo Raymond's mentor Mary Daly and myriad other (often transphobic) feminist thinkers in finding power in separatism; one may be moved to ask, as many feminists and queers have: Who decides and polices these boundaries?

13 Basit Kareem Iqbal and Milad Odabaei's essay in this collection shows how critiquing field assumptions reveals necessary new directions for political theology, particularly their nuanced caution "against hastily celebrating or heralding efforts to provincialize or globalize political theology."

14 Hammill and Lupton, "Introduction," 1, 5.

15 Hammill and Lupton, "Introduction," 5.

16 In Butler's first monograph, *Subjects of Desire*, they investigate how "desire" is formulated by Hegel and his French interlocutors and critics, while attending to varying conceptions of subjectivity. When we miss Butler's (early) critiques of gender, we often also lose Butler's earlier engagement with Hegel and French Hegelianism. The attention to the discursive terrain of subjectivation and the role of desire therein, in *Subjects of Desire*, reveals the motivating questions concretized in *Gender Trouble* that remain at the center of Butler's philosophical project, showing just how intertwined these supposedly distinct projects are. Losing gender always involves losing more than simply gender.

17 Jay Prosser's *Second Skins* both critiques Butler and analyzes the proliferating misreading's of *Gender Trouble*. While Prosser reveals weaknesses in Butler's treatment of race and transness, his project solidifies gender normativity in ways Butler's theoretical paradigm refuses. Even analyses of how easy it is to misread Butler may, themselves, misread Butler.

18 Butler, *Gender Trouble*, 70.

19 Butler, *Gender Trouble*, 136. I find this comment particularly useful as a rejoinder to Newman's understanding of transness.

20 Butler, *Gender Trouble*, 17.

21 Butler, *Gender Trouble*, 151.

22 In Butler's recent publications, the language of "subject-formation" supplants that of "subjectivation." In an attempt to think across Butler's oeuvre, I try to use *subjectivation* when discussing works in which Butler explicitly uses that term, and I defer to *subject-formation* when engaging Butler's work as a whole: see Butler, *Senses of the Subject*.

23 Butler, *Bodies That Matter*, ix, xii.

24 Butler, *Giving an Account of Oneself*, 17.

25 See Puar, *Terrorist Assemblages*.

26 See Lafleur, "Heterosexuality Without Women."

27 Riedl, *Judith Butler and Theology*, ix.

28 Riedl, *Judith Butler and Theology*, ix.

29 Riedl, *Judith Butler and Theology*, ix.

30 Riedl, *Judith Butler and Theology*, ix.

31 Riedl, *Judith Butler and Theology*, ix.

32 Butler, "Anti-Gender Ideology and Mahmood's Critique of the Secular Age"; Butler, "What Threat?"

33 Butler, *Parting Ways*, 22, 116.

34 Ratzinger and Amato, "Letter to the Bishops of the Catholic Church on the Collaboration of Men and Women in the Church and in the World."

35 Fassin, "Gender and the Problem of Universals," 176. On the Catholic attack on "gender ideology," see the 2016 special issue of *Religion and Gender* in which Fassin's piece appears, as well as Perreau, *Queer Theory*; Robcis, "Catholics, the 'Theory of Gender,' and the Turn to the Human in France."

36 Case, "Trans Formations in the Vatican's War on 'Gender Ideology,'" 640.

37 Pope Benedict XVI, "Prepolitical Moral Foundations of a Free Republic."

38 Butler, "Why Is the Idea of 'Gender' Provoking Backlash the World Over?" Butler was notably burned in effigy in Brazil in a protest led by far-right Christians. The effigy featured a witch's hat, replaying a formative motif in the scholarship of Silvia Federici, whose importance for political theology (and recent transphobic confusion) is investigated in Adam Kotsko's contribution to this volume. See also Jaschik, "Judith Butler on Being Attacked in Brazil."

39 Recent developments seem to show the Catholic Church as at a moment of transformation, with trans people now eligible to be baptized, witness weddings, and be godparents at Catholic baptisms—news that emerged alongside stories of Pope Francis having lunch with a group of trans women (and stands at odds with his earlier comparisons between trans people and nuclear proliferation for failure to "recognize the order of creation"). Regardless, dimorphic sexual complementarianism remains Catholic doctrine: see Boselli et al., "Italy's Transgender Women Thank Pope for Making Them Feel 'More Human'"; McElwee, "Francis Strongly Criticizes Gender Theory, Comparing It to Nuclear Arms."

Tabitha's Trauma

CHRISTIAN NATIONALISM, CENTRIST
JEREMIAD, AND THE RECONSTRUCTION
OF THE AMERICAN FAMILY

Lucia Hulsether

Spectacles of national sentimentality hit fever pitch in the aftermath of the attempted coup at the US Capitol on January 6, 2021. In his remarks during the second impeachment trial of Donald Trump, Representative Jamie Raskin of Maryland testified about his experience of that day. Raskin had come to Washington to certify the election results just a week after his son's suicide. His daughter had tagged along. Neither expected that, hours later, she and Raskin's staff members would be barricaded in an office, composing goodbye text messages to their families, fearing murder by the mob storming the building. Raskin described their reunion after the immediate crisis passed: "I hugged them and I apologized. And I told my daughter Tabitha, who is 24 and a brilliant algebra teacher in Teach for America now—I told her how sorry I was. And I promised her that it would not be like this again the next time she came back to the Capitol with me. And you know what she said? She said, 'Dad, I don't want to come back to the Capitol.'"

What did this response by his daughter have to do with the coup or the impeachment trial? Raskin's next sentences discovered the connection, "Of all the terrible, brutal things I saw and heard on that day . . . , that one hit me the hardest, that and watching someone use an American flag pole, with the flag still on it, to spear and pummel one of our police officers ruthlessly, mercilessly—tortured by a pole with a flag on it that he was defending with his very life." Raskin's voice broke, and he collected himself before continuing: "People died that day. Officers ended up with head damage and brain damage. People's eyes were gouged. An officer had a heart attack. An officer lost three fingers that day. Two officers have taken their own lives. Senators, this cannot be our future."[1]

As will become apparent when we unpack this performance of rhetoric and affect, we will need to break with Raskin's habits of the heart or the future could indeed be quite bleak. Our interruption of sentiment will require critical reading of a scholarly tradition around civil religion and nationalism, as well as skepticism about the ways that scholars have been recruited to reproduce liberal-centrist distinctions between good and bad religion and good and bad nationalism. In the moment that I write, this discourse is often framed through descriptions of supposedly rising "Christian nationalism" that threatens the vital center of pluralist tolerance and republican virtue.

But I get ahead of myself. For the moment, the point belongs to Raskin. Weeping, he drilled his takeaway message: To prevent the Capitol raid from presaging "the future of America," the Senate must convict Donald Trump of his crimes. The ex-president had perpetrated something beyond mere violation of federal law; he had desecrated core symbols of US identity. Raskin's rendition of what scholars call the "American jeremiad" stood out in a chorus of similar speeches. While Trump headed toward acquittal, the establishment press coronated Raskin as a preeminent "defender of democracy." He landed a book deal and media tour in which he made his deceased son and grieving family interlocking metonyms for a national democratic reckoning.[2] Although Raskin did not use the term *Christian nationalism* in his impeachment remarks, he soon adopted it for his repertoire. Within months he was urging his audiences to "hang tough against the forces of white Christian nationalism that arrayed against us on January 6, alongside the Proud Boys and Oath Keepers."[3]

Apart from what Raskin is or is not expressing, liberal and leftist anxiety over a right-wing theocratic advance continues to mount in the United States, to say nothing of concern over the global right-wing religious and ethnonationalist movements in Israel, South Africa, India, Nigeria, Brazil, and beyond.[4] This anxiety is justifiable, and one can only fear how these movements might have reshaped geopolitical landscapes by the time you are reading this chapter. Raskin's discourse around January 6 merits scrutiny less because the coup is a decisive historical turning point—to me, this seems like an open question—than because of how a culture industry of public intellectuals has elevated it as the centerpiece of narratives about Christian nationalists who threaten to upend US democracy, unless and until everyday people stand up for centrist (in my mind, center-right) liberalism. Whether such warnings come from pundits or scholars or a combination of the two, they repeat tropes that have been used to legitimate US empire and manage dissent to it for a least a century. Interrupting this pattern will require stronger vocabularies for addressing the status of the religious and the secular in sociopolitical movements, as well as greater concern about the historical contingencies and dynamics of institutional power that have shaped our methods of scholarship. Rather than recirculating these tropes—filling in the same old structure of the American jeremiad with updated content—students of religion and politics should attend to how and when these forms recur, with what stock characters, toward what structures of feeling, with what probable consequences.

Raskin's viral monologue is an opportunity to experiment with this approach. I begin by analyzing the post-2016 embrace of Christian nationalism as a privileged framework for discussing the political right. After a brief overview of public scholarship on Christian nationalism, I situate the term's circulation within a history of majoritarian discourses that have been deployed to manage contradictions of American hegemony and empire, especially by stoking feelings of grief for a lost "vital center" that audiences are called to reclaim. This context helps get leverage on some of the questions evoked by the spectacle around Trump's second impeachment: By what logic does it seem natural that a security breach at the Capitol was renarrated through a framing story about a politician's dead son and grieving daughter? What is the history of this sort of lament? How did it become compelling? What political and intellectual horizons does it enable, or foreclose? Ultimately, not unlike Tabitha, I am unimpressed by the promises of liberalism's spokespeople. Better to get out.

The Ticker Tape of (Public Scholarship on) "Christian Nationalism"

An alliance of public scholarship on Christian nationalism and secularist political punditry on right-wing religious threats to US democracy could have been the theme of the 2023 Summit for Religious Freedom, sponsored by advocacy group Americans United for the Separation of Church and State (AU). The event at the Washington Plaza Hotel kicked off with a videoed message from Raskin and proceeded with a lineup of keynotes and workshops designed, per the official press release, to equip more than three hundred attendees "with the information they need to oppose Christian nationalism."[5] The first speaker, Bradley Onishi, a scholar of religion and co-host of the popular *Straight White American Jesus* podcast, spoke as a self-identified "former Christian nationalist" raised in evangelical circles. His personal experience informed his grim predictions about an "authoritarian turn in American politics" spearheaded by Christian nationalists whose "goal is to go backward" from 1960s democratic gains. His testimony of deconversion from this worldview animated his ultimate call to action.

"What I realize now is those who are supposedly not the real Americans are the ones trying to save the nation," he announced, "What I realized is that those who told me they were the ones who cared about God and country are the ones willing to turn their backs on this republic."[6] The featured cast at this event—which, besides Raskin and Onishi, included the secularist lawyer Andrew Seidel; the journalist Kathleen Stewart; and Kierra Johnson, then the executive director of the National LGBT Task Force—indexed the concerted effort to construct Christian nationalism as an extremist force against which "real Americans" should define themselves. This push was made possible by a combination of social-science scholarship and historical writing that refined the concept for wider use.

Much of the conversation on Christian nationalism is animated by social scientists who have done quantitative studies on the phenomenon. Led by the sociologists Andrew Whitehead and Samuel Perry, studies of "Christian nationalist beliefs" are the basis for dozens of publications that expose racist, authoritarian, patriarchal, and theocratic leanings among populations who fall under its umbrella. From the first academic monographs to come out of Whitehead and Perry's studies to editorials in legacy media, policy briefs with congressional committees, and conferences of church lobby groups, a cottage industry has jumped to document the Christian nationalist threat.[7] The situation is at once familiar and maximally urgent. "Christian nationalism is one of the oldest and most powerful currents in American politics," declare Perry and his collaborator Philip Gorski, "but until the insurrection it was invisible to most Americans." The literature on Christian nationalism aims to restore clarity to the uninformed majority and, in so doing, rally "real Americans" to "save the nation."[8]

Turning to arguments informed by Whitehead and his colleagues and produced by a larger cohort of collaborators, one articulation stands out for how it presented the threat of Christian nationalism to lay audiences. The twenty-six-page *Christian Nationalism and the January 6, 2021 Insurrection* report arose from a collaboration among the Baptist Joint Committee for Religious Liberty (BJC) and the Freedom from Religion Foundation (FFRF), with contributions from the leadership of AU. They released the report in February 2022 as an educational resource for legislators and mainline churches. They saw it as part of a bigger campaign to expose the role of Christian imagery, symbolism, and ideology in far-right political activity in the United States. An introductory note by the BJC's executive director defines Christian nationalism as "a political ideology and cultural framework that seeks to merge American and Christian identities, distorting

Lucia Hulsether

both the Christian faith and American constitutional democracy."[9] From the start, concerns about Christian nationalism were framed by an implied call to defend American secularism and civil religion against supposedly fact-starved and anachronistic opponents.

The report's first article, "What Is Christian Nationalism?," finds a gap in intelligence between its assumed readers and the populations under its spotlight. "Christian nationalist ideology," explain Whitehead and Perry, is associated with "conspiratorial thinking—such as QAnon—and white supremacist ideology."[10] These sociologists' own quantitative studies expose correlation between "Christian nationalism" and other disturbing political ideas. The authors analyzed a survey in which individual respondents rated their agreement with two key indicators of "Christian nationalist ideology": "believing the founding documents of the United States are divinely inspired" and "[believing] that the federal government should declare the United States a 'Christian nation.'"[11] They found that people who self-reported strong agreement with these statements were more likely to self-report agreement with "other conspiratorial views." Seventy-three percent of Americans who "strongly embrace Christian nationalism . . . agree with the QAnon conspiracy."[12] They "distrust science and scientists," "participate[d] in incautious behaviors during the pandemic," "endorse 'traditional' gender roles where men lead and women follow," "oppose interracial marriage and transracial adoption," "want[ed] to protect the economy and liberty over the vulnerable during the pandemic," "fear immigrants," and believe that "Black Americans deserve whatever violence they receive from police."[13] Here and in their book-length publications, this list of correlate views appears without any substantial historical or ethnographic contextualization, reading like a confirmation of cliché culture war positions that the intended audience of the report already feared.

The second article, "What Is White Christian Nationalism?" defines Christian nationalism in terms of its framework for interpreting US history. "White Christian nationalism has worked as a unifying theme for a particular type of narrative about America," writes the historian Anthea Butler. The narrative has five features:

1 America is a divinely appointed nation by God that is Christian.

2 America's founders, rather than wanting to disestablish religion as a unifier for the nation, were in fact establishing a nation based on Christian principles, with white men as the leaders.

3   Others (Native Americans, enslaved Africans, and immigrants) would accept and cede to this narrative of America as a Christian nation, and accept their leadership.

4   America has a special place not only in world history, but in biblical scripture, especially concerning the return of Christ.

5   There is no separation between church and state.[14]

From these themes Butler constructs a strategic counternarrative of US history. She retains the idea that the United States is a white patriarchal Christian nation, but rather than glorifying it, she excoriates its violence, from the transatlantic slave trade to the "Lost Cause" of the post–Civil War south, Jim Crow terror, and the massacre of people attending a Bible study at Mother Emmanuel African Methodist Episcopal (AME) Church in Charleston, South Carolina, in 2015.[15] Together, the chronology seems like an inverse affirmation of a conviction that the author associates with Christian nationalism: White Protestant supremacy is the dominant force in US history. The primary difference between Butler's critical narrative and the narrative she ascribes to Christian nationalism is ethical.

These two articles—Whitehead and Perry's sociology and Butler's history—point to a methodological tension that is also latent within literatures on Christian nationalism. Whereas sociologists such as Gorski, Whitehead, and Perry massively understate historical complexity in the process of reducing Christian white supremacy to private beliefs, Butler, as a historian, is interested in analyzing its manifestations in social, religious, and political movements over time. This approach enables her to address entanglements of white and Christian nationalisms, against many social-science and journalistic accounts that address race as either a stable demographic identifier or a dynamic primarily or exclusively related to the experiences of people of color. Despite these differences, however, these scholars approach Christian nationalism as a clear phenomenon open to identification and analysis by those who are trained to recognize it. This reification of phenomena that are not monolithic but, on the contrary, full of internal fissures and complexities leaves many threads hanging. Pull those threads, and parts of the larger analysis may start to unravel.

Suppose that after hearing Raskin's speech or encountering one of these educational publications you feel motivated to keep reading, even to join a study group, to gain clarity about the issues. You may find your questions interrupted by a shock-and-awe tour of the threats you failed to learn about before.[16] Here is a "JESUS IS MY SAVIOR, TRUMP IS MY PRESIDENT" banner on the Capitol steps! There is a pastor invoking the Battle of Jericho as an allegory for the Christian mission today! There is the mob invoking the name of Christ beneath the Confederate flag and lynching gallows for Mike Pence and Nancy Pelosi! There is the QAnon Shaman praying in the congressional chambers! All this represents *one of the oldest and most powerful currents in American politics.*

Another approach might lean into the latent contradictions and strategic ambiguities in how documents such as this report frame their umbrella concept. What, if anything, is the difference between describing Christian nationalism as a set of beliefs about state power versus as a lens for articulating what Michael Rogin called the countersubversive tradition in American history?[17] The report does not achieve the level of self-awareness that would be required to address such questions. Butler's history lesson has barely begun when—*squirrel!*—the reports of Make America Great Again (MAGA) demonstrations resume: Here is the QAnon Shaman again in his fur costume! There is a cross looming over the entire spectacle! There they are praying right before they desecrate our sacred national symbols!

Not All Christian Nationalism?

To witness the proliferation of a new concept for explaining social phenomena and defining civic life may also be to witness the attempted manufacture or repristination of common sense—and this is even more likely when the concept in question has shown up before. Prior to the 2016 presidential election, one might have been more likely to find the idea of Christian nationalism in sources on the *Black* Christian nationalism of Albert Cleage and the Shrine of the Black Madonna, and the term would have been placed in the context of other forms of Pan-African cultural nationalism.[18] Likewise, limited articulations of white Christian nationalism seem to have developed in studies of Afrikaner organizing for and theological defenses of South African apartheid in the first half of the twentieth century.[19] These contexts, as far as I can gather, are largely absent from most scholarship on the Christian nationalism of the Trump era. Despite this intellectual shakiness, the term has gained traction in and beyond the academy as a none-too-precise trope for gesturing simultaneously at numerous factions of the right. Under what historical conditions did Christian nationalism become so compelling as cultural and political diagnostic? How might those conditions illuminate the effects of this term on our political imaginations?

It turns out that right-wing ideologues with ugly signs are not the only people trafficking in nationalisms undergirded by secularized theological tropes. The flurry of scholarship on Christian nationalism (and the funding and media infrastructure that supports it) can be situated in the wake of other concepts that traveled from contexts of well-supported intellectual production, including and especially among scholars who work on religion and politics, and began to appear regularly in public conversations about civic life, state security, and national futures. These terms include, but are not limited to, *interfaith cooperation, religious pluralism,* and *civil religion,* all of which have been subject to critique for how they append discourse of American liberal exceptionalism and manage crises posed to US global hegemony.[20] The decade that followed September 11, 2001, witnessed a wave of interfaith organizations and service initiatives, described by their backers as soft antiterrorism programming, since they would engage adolescents who might otherwise fall prey to Islamic extremism. Their leadership harped on how the "American experiment" gave unique support to religious diversity and participated in Bush and Obama administration foreign policy initiatives.[21] The key organizations pushing for "interfaith dialogue" themselves were riffing on curriculum developed a generation earlier by Harvard University's Pluralism Project, which was founded in 1991 to document American religious diversity, with an emphasis on "new" associations of Buddhists, Hindus, Sikhs, and Muslims that were allegedly outpacing white mainline Protestantism.[22] As free trade opened borders to international capital while closing them to the racialized poor fleeing economic catastrophe, Harvard's new center naturalized a kind of religious multiculturalism that could at once reject the overt xenophobia of that generation's "clash of civilizations" hawks while continuing to project confidence in US exceptionalism.[23] Going back even further, we can sense how this narrative of liberal pluralism resonates with, and borrows from, 1960s and 1970s appeals to "civil religion" that transcend the particularities of any one tradition and forge collective identification from the multitude of individual difference.[24]

With respect to the scale of its application and ideological work, the more recent discourse around Christian nationalism is comparable to, and an extension of, these prior formulations. No doubt, there are differences between narratives that begin with positive celebration of an exceptional American civic multiculturalism and those that start with a negative vilification of the far-right takeover. Yet the two emphases—national pluralism that vanquishes extremism and Christian nationalist extremism that liberalism must defeat—are often mutually reinforcing to a point of codependence. Looking at moments when appeals to civic pluralism gained potency by mobilizing a crisis of liberal consensus, we can discern how jeremiads on Christian nationalism invert the constituent elements of a longer-running discourse. At the turn of the twenty-first century, scholars exclaimed about how "a supposedly Christian country became the most religiously diverse nation on earth."[25] Two decades on, scholars lament how this same pluralist polity is existentially imperiled by religious authoritarians. These arguments share a covert, endemic failure to problematize a more palatable brand of empire—one that is multicultural instead of monolithic, secular instead of theocratic, and pluralist instead of exclusivist.[26]

This dynamic is most apparent in discussions of how Christian nationalism differs from moderate, faith-based patriotism. In *The Flag and the Cross*, Gorski and Perry assert that while US history contains a destructive throughline of Christian nationalism, it also holds a constructive promise of democratic equality, available for recuperation by citizens who are willing to protect it. "Is it possible for a Christian to be a patriot?" the sociologists ask rhetorically. "Certainly," they answer, "so long as patriotism is understood in terms of constitutional ideals and democratic institutions and citizenship is not based on racial, ethnic, or religious identity."[27] They nominate Black evangelicals—a notable statistical outlier in their studies—as an object lesson for what it would mean to have virtuous Christian faith in the American nation. When Black respondents score high on the Christian nationalism scale, they explain, their answers usually do not predict racist, anti-history, or anti-science attitudes.[28] They thus differentiate white Christian nationalism from Black evangelical patriotism.

The evangelical scholar and writer Jemar Tisby speaks to this difference in the *Christian Nationalism* report. He notes that, although "public attention often turns to the absurdities and indignities promulgated by white Christian nationalism," it is also true that "Black Christians throughout US history have often hearkened back to the nation's stated commitment to freedom and democracy to fight for greater inclusion." For them, activism to make the American nation better was "a coherent, integrated expression of their Christian faith."[29] Tisby lists Frederick Douglass, Martin Luther King Jr., and Fannie Lou Hamer as exemplars of this kind of Christian patriotism; Gorski and Perry mention the writing of James Baldwin and the upbeat political messaging of the 2008 campaign of Barack Obama. Glossing over the substance of these examples, they effectively construct varied instances of strategic speech to specific audiences as a perennial truth of Black Christian suffering, forbearance, and struggle to "save the soul of the nation."[30]

Meanwhile, if we inquire into which parts of this discourse are most potent in the commentaries on Christian nationalism, it is clearly the heavy stress on white grievance, with or without the continual recourse to trauma and loss.[31] Even as these works depict Christian nationalism as a subterranean force in US politics, Gorski and Perry suggest that its "eruption" in January 2021 was driven by the grievances of white people who resented being outnumbered by people of color in a "majority-minority" nation.[32] This soft demographic displacement narrative conceives contemporary political movements in terms of a felt loss of status, legitimacy, and influence, effectively recycling a backlash argument roundly rejected by historians of conservatism.[33] As Gillian Hart has argued, this "liberal thrust of recent efforts to understand Trumpism in terms of Christian nationalism" impedes conjectural analysis of "articulations of race, religion, and nationalism with capitalism and class—and hence the profound contradictions through which these interconnected forces play out in practice."[34] The elision of context in favor of scaremongering—there is the mob trampling a cop!—enables the polemical resolution: Often consciously, sometimes inadvertently, they fall back on calls to reinvest in a "vital center" that will rescue American democracy from threats on both the right and the left.

We could say that the public scholarship on Christian nationalism is updating tradition of the American jeremiad with two new editions. A first version—the one that pundits on Christian nationalism seek to quantify with opinion polls—laments the crumbling hegemony of white heteropatriarchal masculinity and revives under the banner of theocratic authoritarianism. A second version—the one that pundits on Christian nationalism perform without interrogating its mixed benefits—mourns the drift of liberal republicanism toward Christian fascism. Although they champion different visions of American identity, these ritual rhetorical acts share a common form. They begin from a premise of national exceptionalism, itself derived either from a divine promise (for literalists) or from virtuous precedents set down by a Protestant dominant culture (for Christian historicists) or, for those who scoff at the Christian nationalism of such ideas, from mythologized founding texts that center on the separation of church and state. This basic exceptionalist premise is followed by a declensionist assertion that the people who should be carrying forward the original ideals are betraying them. After chronicling the people's failures, the jeremiad

Lucia Hulsether

concludes in a prophecy that citizens will take responsibility for their errors and rededicate themselves to building a society that lives up to the original charge to make a "city on a hill." The literary theorist Sacvan Bercovitch argued famously that this rhetorical form has pervaded US cultural discourse since the Puritans established its key coordinates—covenant, exodus, sin, and renewal—four hundred years ago.[35]

These liberal (Protestant) nationalisms are difficult to address, and to critique, as long as our analyses of the right are invested in distinctions between rational, liberal, secular actors and the irrational, illiberal, and antisocial ones.[36] Besides producing overly simple answers to underthought questions, this approach reifies imperialisms both hard and soft while circumscribing its analyses of emergent social formations.

This Cannot Be Our Future: Refusing National Sentimentality

Earlier I posed this question: What do the images of Raskin's late son and grieving daughter have to do with the Trump impeachment proceedings? Now we are getting closer to an answer. If the lingua franca of liberal democratic revival is indeed a political-theological discourse of innocence lost and a promise revived, who better than children to serve as symbolic stakes? Scholars across disciplines have observed the central role that children have played in constructions of social and political imaginaries.[37] From the practice of calculating war atrocities in reference to the deaths of children to the celebrity status of child activists in social movements and the clichéd invocation of "the next generation" to justify any and all policy positions, the specter of childhood—its innocence, optimism, and vulnerability—is consistently present in attempts to motivate adults to civic action. Little surprise, then, that public grief about lost children has also been mobilized toward liberal nationalism and state building.

Raskin's rehearsal of his conversation with Tabitha following the January 6 raid captures this problematic. He claimed that "of all the terrible, brutal things" he witnessed on that day, what "hit [him] the hardest" was Tabitha's aversion to returning to the Capitol. On its face, this interaction stretches the limits of plausibility. Is Raskin really asking his audience to believe that, amid all that happened that day, the most troubling part was his adult daughter's assertion of personal boundaries? Also, of everything Raskin could have said to his child in that moment, he chose to focus on what would happen when she came to his unhinged workplace "the next time"? Even if he did not think or say any of this, what failure of self-awareness would lead a parent to confess such ineptitude on primetime television?

Of course, anyone encountering this speech as a factual portrayal of events has missed the key point, which lies in the allegory between the child and the nation. Although a skeptic might be incredulous about the gaps in this narrative, when it is considered literally, a preferred listener—the believer—would fill those gaps by finding their symbolic significance.[38] For this latter listener, Tabitha was never legible as fully grown adult. She was a vulnerable girl who needed protection from her parent. Or, we could say, she was a prototype of what Lauren Berlant terms the "infantile citizen" that has become dominant in modern US political culture. Berlant argues that the prototypical citizen-subject is constructed not as a civically engaged adult person but as an infantile subject who remains endearingly naïve to the perversions of political and economic life. Her naïveté helps to reproduce a set of fantasies about equal justice under representative democracy, family values, and social mobility made possible by a meritocratic system. Berlant suggests that, if appeals to the innocence of children land as apolitical, they have political effects. In evoking "the children" who still believe in national promises, they teach their adult audiences to reinvest in the broken promises of the American dream: If we can guard these children's optimism until they take the reins of power, maybe the nation will still live up to its potential.

Raskin was an authoritative spokesperson for the impeachment because he knew what it meant to fail to deliver a child's idealism to its adulthood. "Tommy loved the Constitution," he told anyone who would listen, sometimes suggesting in the same breath that his son's empathic streak rendered him too fragile to survive independently.[39] Tommy Raskin was a Harvard Law student living at home, where he left a suicide note that asked his survivors to "watch after the animals and the global poor for me"; his biographers interpret the theme of his life as a kind of unreconstructed idealism that his caregivers failed to keep safe.[40] Such qualities, and the apparent shame of Raskin's insufficient vigilance, mirror Raskin's point about the US nation-state in crisis. "The private and public traumas of suicide and violent insurrection . . . demolished all the core assumptions I carried around with me each day—that my children would be healthy and alive, that they would let [my spouse] and me know if they needed anything, that no political party or power elite would try to overthrow our constitutional democracy."[41] Figuring his son's suicidal depression as a metaphor for democratic crisis and his paternal grief journey as a

Lucia Hulsether

metaphor for national renewal, Raskin urges his readers to do likewise: "If a person can grow through unthinkable trauma and loss, perhaps a nation may, too."[42]

Raskin was a slam-dunk impeachment prosecutor because he metabolized his loss toward reattachment to the normative conventions of US political liberalism.[43] Key to this centrist liberal grief work is an exemplary (if unconscious) reinvestment in the endemic anti-feminist tradition of situating the private nuclear family as a building block of and metaphor for the nation.[44]

Which brings us to Tabitha. She was like her elder brother, except that her survival made her available for symbolic saving.[45] This made it even more troubling when she expressed doubts about returning to the Capitol. Raskin was so disturbed about daughter's lost desire to return to the physical center of the national fantasy—the same one into which he had just conscripted her as a plot point—that he compared it to watching "someone use an American flag pole, with the flag still on it, to spear and pummel one of our police officers ruthlessly, mercilessly."[46] The seamless transition from Tabitha's preference to a graphic depiction of a cop penetrated by "an American flag pole" trusts that listeners will infer the scandalous implication: The attack on the Capitol is tantamount to rape. This is as much a lament over nation's (child's) lost innocence as it is a condemnation of the paternal authorities who failed to protect their dependents.

Raskin confesses his paternal failures because it is one way to entreat his colleagues—and, by extension, his fellow citizens—to return the national fantasy to safety. "This cannot be our future," Raskin urges, where his *this* is ambiguous enough that it could be at once reference to a white supremacist coup, a dearth of police power, a disappointed fantasy about functional democracy, and the differentiation of daughters from their fathers. The extent of the vagueness is also the extent of the speech's rhetorical effectiveness: Each of these threats becomes more disturbing, considering the ones combined with it.

Luckily, liberals have plans to solve all of them at the same time: Convict the lecherous demagogue of his high crimes. Urge principled conservatives and the principled social democrats to make common cause. Revive American civil religion. Deputize the bereft patriarch—if not this one, then another will come along—and let his lament for his children bleed into the lament for democracy. Jump on what seems like the best available train, at least going in a better direction than outright fascism, and ride the rails of the search for the most just and reasoned common good.[47] Deploy rationality and constitutional expertise to rescue Tabitha and other girls, women, and queers from the monsters (rapists) who invaded the house of democracy.[48] Talk about innocent children who might have grown up and "been there" committing sedition had they not been delivered into true Christian patriotism, or about the children of statesmen whose optimism was crushed when their fathers didn't secure the gates. Pretty soon, you might not be able to be able to tell the difference between the traumas befalling the family and the traumas befalling the nation. When this happens, celebrate: You are reattaching to the national fantasy and its founding myths, and because of this, we are one step closer to restoration.

Still, mastering the performance is not the same as controlling its effects. Listen again, this time with an ear tuned to the unresolved, the loss that makes an opening, the refusal of a toxic promise: *I don't want to go back to the Capitol.*

What if you stayed with this? What if there was no need to read on, no complementary and competing jeremiad to announce in response? You could walk out the door with her. If you had to say something, you could shout over your shoulder that the patriarchy is lying and that rallying to defend the vital center has been tried and shown to fail over and over. There will be no rehabilitation today, especially not if it is in the warmed-over rhetorical rituals of Puritans and youth ministers pointing down long-standing ruts misrecognized as redemptive potential.

If you decide this is a dead end, you get to imagine a different route altogether. Where could you go? What could you make? What could you learn to want, or to lose, instead? Deferring those questions—whether in relation to one person's dreams for their future or a mass academic investment in the renewed vitality of the American nation-state—is how so many of us even learned to want these deferred and privatized horizons, as opposed to finding something more alive in the collective present.

Notes

1   Raskin, "Closing Remarks at the Second Impeachment Trial of Donald Trump."

2   Deahl, "Harper Buys Raskin Memoir."

3   Raskin, "Remarks to the Freedom from Religion Foundation, 45th Annual National Convention, San Antonio."

4   On Christian nationalism scholarship in global contexts, see Hart, "Why Did It Take so Long?"

5   Boston, "Scaling the Summit."

6   Onishi, quoted in Boston, "Scaling the Summit." Onishi makes a longer version of this article in Onishi, *Preparing for War*.

7   The first book was Perry and Whitehead, *Taking America Back for God*. The subsequent public-facing redaction of that study is Gorski and Perry, *The Flag and the Cross*.

8   Gorski and Perry, *The Flag and the Cross*, 1.

9   Whitehead and Perry, "What Is Christian Nationalism?," 1.

10   Whitehead and Perry, "What Is Christian Nationalism?," 1.

11   Other publications by these authors have six or seven different indicators of Christian nationalism. Perry and Whitehead's *Taking America Back for God* codes the following six statements:

    1   The federal government should declare the United States a Christian nation.

    2   The federal government should advocate Christian values.

    3   The federal government should enforce a strict separation of church and state (reverse coded).

    4   The federal government should allow the display of religious symbols in public places.

    5   The success of the United States is part of God's plan.

    6   The federal government should allow prayer in public schools.

Note that the "divine inspiration" indicator was not in the original analysis. Such inconsistency and variability in use of indicators—and the vagueness of key terms—has led other sociologists to worry that this work "makes stronger and more diffuse claims about the conceptual scope, centrality, and pervasiveness of Christian nationalism than the results from the [quantitative] analyses can plausibly sustain": Smith and Adler, "What *Isn't* Christian Nationalism?"

12   Whitehead and Perry, "What Is Christian Nationalism?," 2.

13   Whitehead and Perry, "What Is Christian Nationalism?," 3.

14   Butler, "What Is White Christian Nationalism?" These points resonate with ones that Butler addresses more in Butler, *White Evangelical Racism*.

15   Jakobsen and Pellegrini, *Secularisms*, 4–5.

16   See, e.g., Altman and Copulsky, *Uncivil Religion*.

17   Rogin, *Ronald Reagan, The Movie*, xiii–xvii.

18 Cleage, *Black Christian Nationalism*.

19 Bloomberg, *Christian Nationalism and the Rise of the Afrikaner Broederbond in South Africa, 1918–1958*.

20 See especially Ferguson, *The Reorder of Things*; Hicks, "Between Lived Religion and the Law."

21 I elaborate this point in Hulsether, "Out of Incorporation, Pluralism."

22 Eck, *A New Religious America*, 2–5.

23 Hulsether, "The Grammar of Racism."

24 Noble, "Robert Bellah, Civil Religion, and the American Jeremiad."

25 Eck, *A New Religious America*, 1.

26 Singh, "Culture/Wars."

27 Gorski and Perry, *The Flag and the Cross*, 10

28 Gorski and Perry, *The Flag and the Cross*, 19–28.

29 Tisby, "The Patriotic Witness of Black Christians."

30 On the contradictions of Black intellectual formations in relation to liberal nationalism, see Gaines, *Uplifting the Race*; Singh, *Black Is a Country*.

31 On the politics of white grievance, especially in relationship to Black grief and trauma, see Hooker, *Black Grief/White Grievance*. Missing from Hooker's otherwise helpful analysis is analysis of how seemingly apolitical instances of private, white, and elite grief are mobilized for liberal state-building and nationalist mythmaking.

32 Gorski and Perry, *The Flag and the Cross*, 2.

33 Hart, "Why Did It Take so Long?"

34 Hart, "Decoding 'The Base,'" 63–64.

35 Bercovitch, *The American Jeremiad*.

36 Fessenden, *Culture and Redemption*, 2.

37 On centering children in thinking about religion and politics, see Lloyd, "Why Political Theology Needs Children." On childhood and cultural politics, see Bernstein, *Racial Innocence*, 1–29.

38 Harding, *The Book of Jerry Falwell*, 1–27.

39 Tomasky, "Jamie Raskin, Democracy's Defender." See also Gross, "After His Son's Suicide and the Jan. 6 Attack, Rep. Jamie Raskin Is Not Giving Up."

40 Raskin, *Unthinkable*, 19.

41 Raskin, *Unthinkable*, 16.

42 Raskin, *Unthinkable*, 22.

43 I take the language of "metabolization of loss" from Gabriel Winant's writing on the uses of loss and trauma to establish Zionist politics. I also am inspired

by how Barbara Sostaita has helped me connect this notion of metabolized loss to my own interest in critiquing the itineraries of US racial capitalism. Winant, "On Mourning and Statehood," and Sostaita, "On Grief and Capitalist Humanitarianism."

44 See Cooper, *Family Values*, 1–24.

45 Tabitha might also be read through the tradition of captivity narratives, which, literary scholars argue, play an important role in American jeremiad: see Fitzpatrick, "The Figure of Captivity."

46 Raskin, *Unthinkable*.

47 Arguably the most alarming aspect of the mainstream scholarship on Christian nationalism that I have cited is the silence on generations of feminist and queer critiques that have called into question much of the Habermasian conversation on the public sphere. This absence could go a long way to explain how and why figureheads such as Raskin and Seidel and the various public scholars who ally with their projects end up reenacting tropes of the rational (masculine) champion of constitutional law who saves vulnerable children and women from lawless threats to their bodily autonomy.

48 Puar and Rai, "Monster, Terrorist, Fag."

Bibliography

Abraham, Susan. "Postcolonial Theology." In *The Cambridge Companion to Christian Political Theology*, edited by Craig Hovey and Elizabeth Phillips, 133–54. Cambridge University Press, 2015.

The Accused of Tarnac. "Spread Anarchy, Live Communism." In *The Anarchist Turn*, edited by Jacob Blumenfeld, Chiara Bottici, and Simon Critchley, 224–34. Pluto, 2013.

Adorno, Theodor W. *Minima Moralia: Reflections on a Damaged Life*. Translated by E. F. N. Jephcott. Verso, 2005.

Adorno, Theodor W. *Minima Moralia: Reflexionen aus dem beschädigten Leben*. Suhrkamp, 1951.

Adorno, Theodor W. *Negative Dialectics*. Translated by E. B. Ashton. Routledge, 2004.

Adorno, Theodor W. *Notes to Literature, Volume 2*. Translated by Shierry Weber Nicholsen. Columbia University Press, 1992.

Adorno, Theodor W. "Vernunft und Offenbarung." In *Stichworte: Kritische Modelle 2*. Suhrkamp, 1969.

Adorno, Theodor W., and Walter Benjamin. *The Complete Correspondence, 1928–1940*. Translated by Nicholas Walke and edited by Henri Lonitz. Harvard University Press, 2001.

Adorno Theodor W., and Gershom Scholem. *Der liebe Gott wohnt im Detail: Briefwechsel 1949–1969*. Edited by Asaf Angermann. Suhrkamp, 2015.

Agamben, Giorgio. *Homo Sacer: Sovereign Power and Bare Life*. Translated by Daniel Heller-Roazen. Stanford University Press, 1998.

Agamben, Giorgio. *The Kingdom and the Glory: For a Theological Genealogy of Economy and Government*. Translated by Lorenzo Chiesa and Mattero Mandarini. Stanford University Press, 2011.

Agamben, Giorgio. *The Signature of All Things: On Method*. Translated by Luca D'Isanto with Kevin Attell. Zone, 2009.

Agamben, Giorgio. *Stasis: Civil War as a Political Paradigm*. Translated by Nicholas Heron. Stanford University Press, 2015.

Agamben, Giorgio. *State of Exception*. Translated by Kevin Attell. University of Chicago Press, 2003.

Agamben, Giorgio. *The Use of Bodies*. Translated by Adam Kotsko. Stanford University Press, 2015.

Agamben, Giorgio. *Where Are We Now? The Epidemic as Politics*. Translated by Valeria Dani. Rowman and Littlefield, 2021.

Agrama, Hussein Ali. "Friendship and Time in the Work of Talal Asad." *Religion and Society* 11 (2020): 16–19.

Agrama, Hussein Ali. *Questioning Secularism: Islam, Sovereignty, and the Rule of Law in Modern Egypt*. University of Chicago Press, 2012.

Aguirre, Javier. "Religiones, teologías y colonialidad: Hacia la decolonización de los estudios académicos de las religiones y las teologías." *Revista de Estudios Sociales* 77 (2021): 76–92.

Ahmed, Siraj. *Archaeology of Babel: The Colonial Foundation of the Humanities*. Stanford University Press, 2017.

Aland, Barbara. "Was ist Gnosis? Wie wurde sie überwunden? Versuch einer Kurzdefinition." In *Religionstheorie und Politische Theologie*, edited by Jacob Taubes, 54–65. Fink, 1984.

Albernaz, Joseph. "Impossible Freedom: Gnostic Retrievals." Paper presented at the Annual Meeting of the American Comparative Literature Association, Washington, DC, 2019.

Albernaz, Joseph, and Kirill Chepurin. "The Sovereignty of the World: Towards a Political Theology of Modernity (After Blumenberg)." In *Interrogating Modernity: Debates with Hans Blumenberg*, edited by Agata Bielik-Robson and Daniel Whistler, 83–107. Palgrave Macmillan, 2020.

Alexander, M. Jacqui. *Pedagogies of Crossing: Meditations on Feminism, Sexual Politics, Memory, and the Sacred*. Duke University Press, 2005.

Alfred, Taiaiake. "Sovereignty." In *Sovereignty Matters: Locations of Contestation and Possibility in Indigenous Struggles for Self-Determination*, edited by Joanne Barker, 33–50. University of Nebraska Press, 2005.

Altman, Michael J., and Jerome Copulsky. *Uncivil Religion: January 6, 2021*. Uncivil Religion, n.d. Accessed February 2, 2024. https://uncivilreligion.org /home/index.

Ambedkar, B. R. "The Annihilation of Caste." In *Babasaheb Ambedkar: Writings and Speeches*, 17 vols., edited by Vasant Moon, 1:23–97. Ambedkar Foundation, 2020.

Ambedkar, B. R. *Buddha and His Dhamma*. In *Babasaheb Ambedkar: Writings and Speeches*, vol. 11, edited by Vasant Moon. Ambedkar Foundation, 2020.

Ambedkar, B. R. "Buddha or Karl Marx." In *Babasaheb Ambedkar: Writings and Speeches*, 17 vols., edited by Vasant Moon, 3:441–62. Ambedkar Foundation, 2020.

Ambedkar, B. R. "Castes in India: Their Mechanism, Genesis and Development." In *Babasaheb Ambedkar: Writings and Speeches*, 17 vols., edited by Vasant Moon, 1:3–22. Ambedkar Foundation, 2020.

Ambedkar, B. R. "The Condition of the Convert." In *Babasaheb Ambedkar: Writings and Speeches*, 17 vols., edited by Vasant Moon, 5:445–76. Ambedkar Foundation, 2020.

Ambedkar, B. R. *Conversion as Emancipation*. Siddharth, [1935] 2019.

Ambedkar, B. R. "The Decline and Fall of Buddhism," chap. 9 of *Revolution and Counter-Revolution in Ancient India*. In *Babasaheb Ambedkar: Writings and Speeches*, 17 vols., edited by Vasant Moon, 3:229–338. Ambedkar Foundation, 2020.

Ambedkar, B. R. *India and the Prerequisites of Communism*. In *Babasaheb Ambedkar: Writings and Speeches*, 17 vols., edited by Vasant Moon, 3:95–149. Ambedkar Foundation, 2020.

Ambedkar, B. R. "Moses and His Significance." In *Babasaheb Ambedkar: Writings and Speeches*, 17 vols., edited by Vasant Moon, 17:342–44. Ambedkar Foundation, 2020.

Ambedkar, B. R. *Philosophy of Hinduism*. In *Babasaheb Ambedkar: Writings and Speeches*, vol. 3, edited by Vasant Moon. Ambedkar Foundation, 2020.

Ambedkar, B. R. *Riddles of Hinduism*. In *Babasaheb Ambedkar: Writings and Speeches*, vol. 4, edited by Vasant Moon. Ambedkar Foundation, 2020.

Ambedkar, B. R. *Untouchables or The Children of India's Ghetto*. In *Babasaheb Ambedkar: Writings and Speeches*, vol. 5, edited by Vasant Moon. Ambedkar Foundation, 2020.

Ambedkar, B. R. "Waiting for Visa." In *Babasaheb Ambedkar: Writings and Speeches*, 17 vols., edited by Vasant Moon, 12:661–91. Ambedkar Foundation, 2020.

An, Yountae. *The Coloniality of the Secular: Race, Religion, and Poetics of World-Making*. Duke University Press, 2023.

Anders, Günther. *Der Blick vom Mond: Reflexionen über Weltraumflüge*. Beck, 1970.

Anderson, Kevin. *Marx at the Margins: On Nationalism, Ethnicity, and Non-Western Societies*. University of Chicago Press, 2016.

Anidjar, Gil. *Blood: A Critique of Christianity*. Columbia University Press, 2014.

Anidjar, Gil. "Christian Interrogation." *Political Theology Network*, September 3, 2019. https://politicaltheology.com/christian-interrogation.

Anidjar, Gil. "Of Globalatinology." *Derrida Today* 6, no. 1 (2013): 11–22.

Anidjar, Gil. *The Jew, the Arab: A History of the Enemy*. Stanford University Press, 2003.

Anidjar, Gil. "Secularism." *Critical Inquiry* 33, no. 1 (2005): 52–77.

Anidjar, Gil. *Semites: Race, Religion, Literature*. Stanford University Press, 2008.

Anjum, Ovamir. "Interview with Talal Asad." *American Journal of Islamic Social Sciences* 35, no. 1 (2018): 55–90.

Apel, Karl-Otto, and Enrique Dussel. *Ética del discurso y ética de la liberación*. Trotta, 2004.

Arato, Andrew. "Political Theology and Populism." *Social Research* 80, no. 1 (2013): 143–72.

Arendt, Hannah. "Man's Conquest of Space." *American Scholar* 32, no. 4 (1963): 527–40.

Arendt, Hannah. *On Revolution*. Penguin, 1963.

Aristotle. *Politics*. Translated by Benjamin Jowett. Accessed December 14, 2016. http://classics.mit.edu/Aristotle/politics.1.one.html.

Armstrong, Amaryah. "Losing Salvation: Notes Toward a Wayward Black Theology." *Critical Times* 6, no. 2 (2023): 324–44.

Arvin, Maile, Eve Tuck, and Angie Morrill. "Decolonizing Feminism: Challenging Connections Between Settler Colonialism and Heteropatriarchy." *Feminist Formations* 25, no. 1 (2013): 8–34.

Asad, Talal. "Fear and the Ruptured State: Reflections on Egypt After Mubarak." *Social Research* 79, no. 2 (2012): 271–98.

Asad, Talal. *Formations of the Secular: Christianity, Islam, Modernity*. Stanford University Press, 2003.

Asad, Talal. *Genealogies of Religion: Discipline and Reasons of Power in Christianity and Islam*. Johns Hopkins University Press, 1993.

Asad, Talal. "The Idea of an Anthropology of Islam." *Qui Parle* 17, no. 2 ([1986] 2009): 1–30.

Asad, Talal. "Muhammad Asad Between Religion and Politics." *İnsan ve Toplum* 1, no. 2 (2011): 155–66.

Asad, Talal. *On Suicide Bombing*. Columbia University Press, 2007.

Asad, Talal. "Religion, Nation-State, Secularism." In *Nation and Religion: Perspectives on Europe and Asia*, edited by Peter van der Veer and Hartmut Lehmann, 178–96. Princeton University Press, 1999.

Asad, Talal. "Response to Gil Anidjar." *Interventions* 11, no. 3 (2009): 394–99.

Asad, Talal. *Secular Translations: Nation-State, Modern Self, and Calculative Reason*. Columbia University Press, 2018.

Asad, Talal. "Thinking About Religion, Belief, and Politics in Egypt Today." In *The Cambridge Companion to Religious Studies*, edited by Robert A. Orsi, 36–57. Cambridge University Press, 2012.

Asad, Talal. "Thinking About Religion Through Wittgenstein." *Critical Times* 3, no. 3 (2020): 403–42.

Asad, Talal. "Thinking About the Secular Body, Pain, and Liberal Politics." *Cultural Anthropology* 26, no. 4 (2011): 657–75.

Asad, Talal. "Thinking About Tradition, Religion, and Politics in Egypt Today." *Critical Inquiry* 42, no. 1 (2015): 166–214.

Asad, Talal. "Trying to Understand French Secularism." In *Political Theologies: Public Religions in a Post-Secular World*, edited by Hent de Vries and Lawrence E. Sullivan, 494–526. Fordham University Press, 2006.

Asad, Talal, Wendy Brown, Judith Butler, and Saba Mahmood. *Is Critique Secular? Blasphemy, Injury, and Free Speech*. University of California Press, 2009.

Assmann, Jan. *Herrschaft und Heil: Politische Theologie in Altägypten, Israel und Europa*. Fischer, 2002.

Augustine. *The De Haeresibus of Saint Augustine: A Translation with an Introduction and Commentary*. Translated by Liguori G. Müller. Catholic University of America Press, 1956.

Balaramamoorty, Y. "Buddhist Philosophy." In Rahul Sankrityayan, *Buddhism: A Marxist Approach*, edited by Debiprasad Chattopadhyay, Y. Balaramamoorty,

Ram Vilas Sharma, and Mulk Raj Anand, 37–53. People's Publishing House, 1970.

Baldwin, James. *Another Country*. Dial, 1962.

Baldwin, James. "Everyone's Protest Novel." In *James Baldwin: Collected Essays*. Library of America, 1998.

Baldwin, James. *The Fire Next Time*. Penguin Random House, 1963.

Baldwin, James. *Notes of a Native Son*. Beacon, 2012.

Baldwin, James. "Racism and World Community." In *The Price of the Ticket*. St. Martin's, 1985.

Balibar, Étienne. "The Nation Form: History and Ideology." In *Race, Nation, Class: Ambiguous Identities*, edited by Étienne Balibar and Immanuel Wallerstein, 86–106. Verso, 1991.

Banerjee, Milinda. "In Memoriam Ranajit Guha—Anticolonial Political Theologian." *Political Theology Network*, May 19, 2023. https://politicaltheology .com/in-memoriam-ranajit-guha-anticolonial-political-theologian.

Barber, Daniel Colucciello. *On Diaspora: Christianity, Religion, and Secularity*. Cascade, 2011

Barber, Daniel Colucciello. "Unpossessed Knowledge." In *Speculation, Heresy, and Gnosis in Contemporary Philosophy of Religion: The Enigmatic Absolute*, edited by Joshua Ramey and Matthew S. Haar Farris, 221–31. Rowman and Littlefield, 2016.

Bardawil, Fadi. "The Solitary Analyst of Doxas: An Interview with Talal Asad." *Comparative Studies of South Asia, Africa, and the Middle East* 36, no. 1 (2016): 152–73.

Barrett, Lindon. *Racial Blackness and the Discontinuity of Western Modernity*. University of Illinois Press, 2013.

Barua, Benimadhab M. *Prolegomena to a History of Buddhist Philosophy*. University of Calcutta, 1918.

Baucom, Ian. "Cicero's Ghost: The Atlantic, the Enemy, and the Laws of War." In *States of Emergency: The Object of American Studies*, edited by Russ Castronovo and Susan Gillman, 124–42. University of North Carolina Press, 2009.

Belcourt, Billy-Ray. *This Wound Is a World*. University of Minnesota Press, 2017.

Benjamin, Walter. "Karl Kraus." In *Reflections: Essays, Aphorisms, Autobiographical Writings*. Translated by E. Jephcott, 239–73. Schocken, 1978.

Benjamin, Walter. "On the Concept of History." In *Selected Writings, Volume 4: 1938–1940*, edited by Howard Eiland and Michael W. Jennings, 389–400. Harvard University Press, 2006.

Benjamin, Walter. *One-Way Street*. Translated by Edmund Jephcott. Harvard University Press, 2016.

Bercovitch, Sacvan. *The American Jeremiad*. University of Wisconsin Press, [1978] 2012.

Berkhout, Suze G., and Ada S. Jaarsma. "Trafficking in Cure and Harm: Placebos, Nocebos and the Curative Imaginary." *Disability Studies Quarterly* 38, no. 4 (2018). https://doi.org/10.18061/dsq.v38i4.6369.

Bernstein, Robin. *Racial Innocence: Imagining Childhood from Slavery to Civil Rights*. New York University Press, 2011.

Bertolino, Elizabetta. "Beyond Ontology and Sexual Difference: An Interview with the Italian Feminist Philosopher Adriana Cavarero." *Differences* 19, no. 1 (2008): 128–67.

Best, Stephen, and Saidiya Hartman. "Fugitive Justice." *Representations* 92, no. 1 (2005): 1–15.

Bignotto, Newton. "Lefort and Machiavelli." In *Claude Lefort: Thinker of the Political*, edited by Martín Plot, 34–50. Palgrave Macmillan, 2013.

Blackburn, Robin. *The Making of New World Slavery: From the Baroque to the Modern, 1492–1800*. Verso, 1997.

Blake, William. *The Marriage of Heaven and Hell*. Oxford University Press, 1790.

Blanco, John D., and Ivonne del Valle. "Reorienting Schmitt's *Nomos*: Political Theology, and Colonial (and Other) Exceptions in the Creation of Modern and Global Worlds." *Política Común* 5 (2014). https://doi.org/10.3998/pc.12322227.0005.001.

Bloomberg, Charles. *Christian Nationalism and the Rise of the Afrikaner Broederbond in South Africa, 1918–1958*. Edited by Saul Dubow. Indiana University Press, 1989.

Blumenberg, Hans. *The Legitimacy of the Modern Age*. Translated by Robert M. Wallace. MIT Press, 1983.

Blumenberg, Hans. *Work on Myth*. Translated by Robert M. Wallace. MIT Press, 1985.

Boast, Hannah. "The Doctor's Knife." *Radical Philosophy* 2, no. 10 (2021): 106–9.

Bonney, Sean. *Letters Against the Firmament*. Enitharmon, 2015.

Bonney, Sean. *Our Death*. Commune, 2019.

Boselli, Oriana, Antonio Denti, and Philip Pullella. "Italy's Transgender Women Thank Pope for Making Them Feel 'More Human.'" *Reuters*, November 20, 2023. https://www.reuters.com/world/europe/italys-transgender-women-thank-pope-making-them-feel-more-human-2023-11-19.

Boston, Rob. "Scaling the Summit: At Summit for Religious Freedom, AU Exposes the Dangers of Christian Nationalism—and Urges Americans to Pledge Support for Church-State Separation." *Church and State* 76, no. 5 (2023). https://www.au.org/the-latest/church-and-state/articles/scaling-the-summit-at-summit-for-religious-freedom-au-exposes-the-dangers-of-christian-nationalism-and-urges-americans-to-pledge-support-for-church-state-separation/.

Boundas, Constantin, Daniel W. Smith, and Ada S. Jaarsma. "Encounters with Deleuze." *Symposium* 24, no. 1 (2020): 139–74.

Brandel, Andrew, and Marco Motta, eds. *Living with Concepts: Anthropology in the Grip of Reality*. Fordham University Press, 2021.

Bratton, Benjamin. *The Stack: On Software and Sovereignty*. MIT Press, 2015.

Bronkhorst, Johannes. "Modes of Debate and Refutation of Adversaries in Classical and Medieval India: A Preliminary Investigation." *Antiquorum Philosophia* 1 (2007): 269–80.

Bruno, Giordano. *The Ash Wednesday Supper*. Translated by Stanley L. Jaki. Mouton, 1975.

Butler, Anthea. "What Is White Christian Nationalism?" In *Christian Nationalism and the January 6, 2021 Insurrection*, 4–6. Baptist Joint Committee for Religious Liberty and the Freedom from Religion Foundation, February 9, 2022. https://bjconline.org/wp-content/uploads/2022/02/Christian _Nationalism_and_the_Jan6_Insurrection-2-9-22.pdf.

Butler, Anthea. *White Evangelical Racism: The Politics of Morality in America*. University of North Carolina Press, 2021.

Butler, Judith. "Anti-Gender Ideology and Mahmood's Critique of the Secular Age." *Journal of the American Academy of Religion* 87, no. 4 (2019): 955–67.

Butler, Judith. *Bodies That Matter: On the Discursive Limits of "Sex."* Routledge, 1993.

Butler, Judith. *Frames of War: When Is Life Grievable?* Verso, 2009.

Butler, Judith. *Gender Trouble: Feminism and the Subversion of Identity*. Routledge, 1990.

Butler, Judith. *Giving an Account of Oneself*. Fordham University Press, 2003.

Butler, Judith. *Parting Ways: Jewishness and the Critique of Zionism*. Columbia University Press, 2012.

Butler, Judith. *Senses of the Subject*. Fordham University Press, 2015.

Butler, Judith. *Subjects of Desire: Hegelian Reflections in Twentieth-Century France*. Columbia University Press, 1987.

Butler, Judith. "What Threat? The Campaign Against 'Gender Ideology.'" *Localism* 3 (2019): 1–12.

Butler, Judith. *What World Is This? A Pandemic Phenomenology*. Columbia University Press, 2022.

Butler, Judith. "Why Is the Idea of 'Gender' Provoking Backlash the World Over?" *The Guardian*, October 23, 2021. https://www.theguardian.com/us-news /commentisfree/2021/oct/23/judith-butler-gender-ideology-backlash.

Campanini, Massimo, and Marco Di Donato, eds. *Islamic Political Theology*. Lexington, 2021.

Carter, J. Kameron. *Race: A Theological Account*. Oxford University Press, 2008.

Case, Mary Anne. "Trans Formations in the Vatican's War on 'Gender Ideology.'" *Signs* 44, no. 3 (2019): 639–64.

Cavanaugh, William, and Vincent Lloyd. "Why Does Political Theology Matter?" *Political Theology Network*, November 2, 2022. https://politicaltheology .com/what-is-the-state-of-political-theology-today-a-conversation-with -paul-heck-william-cavanaugh-and-vincent-lloyd.

Cavarero, Adriana. *For More Than One Voice: Toward a Philosophy of Vocal Expression*. Translated by Paul A. Kottman. Stanford University Press, 2005.

Cavarero, Adriana. *Inclination: A Critique of Rectitude*. Translated by Amanda Minervini and Adam Sitze. Stanford University Press, 2016.

Cavarero, Adriana. "Politicizing Theory." *Political Theory* 30, no. 4 (2002): 506–32.

Cavarero, Adriana. *Surging Democracy: Notes on Hannah Arendt's Political Thought.* Translated by Matthew Gervase. Stanford University Press, 2021.

Cavarero, Adriana, Judith Butler, and Bonnie Honig. *Toward a Feminist Ethics of Nonviolence.* Edited by Timothy J. Huzar and Clare Woodford. Fordham University Press, 2021.

Cavarero, Adriana, and Angelo Scola. *Thou Shalt Not Kill: A Political and Theological Dialogue.* Translated by Margaret Adams Groesbeck and Adam Sitze. Fordham University Press, 2015.

Césaire, Aimé. *Discourse on Colonialism.* Translated by Joan Pinkham. Monthly Review Press, [1955] 2000.

Césaire, Aimé. "Poetry and Knowledge." In *Lyric and Drama Poetry, 1946–82,* xlii–lvi. University of Virginia Press, 1990.

Chakrabarty, Dipesh. "The Planet: An Emergent Humanist Category." *Critical Inquiry* 46, no. 1 (2019): 1–31.

Chakrabarty, Dipesh. *Provincializing Europe: Postcolonial Thought and Historical Difference.* Princeton University Press, 2000.

Chepurin, Kirill. *Bliss Against the World: Schelling, Theodicy, and the Crisis of Modernity.* Oxford University Press, 2024.

Chepurin, Kirill. "Reading Novalis and the Schlegels." In *The Palgrave Handbook of German Idealism and Poststructuralism,* edited by Tilottama Rajan and Daniel Whistler, 59–81. Palgrave Macmillan, 2023.

Chepurin, Kirill, and Alex Dubilet, eds. *Nothing Absolute: German Idealism and the Question of Political Theology.* Fordham University Press, 2021.

Chepurin, Kirill, and Alex Dubilet. "Out of the Cemetery of the Earth, a Resurrective Commons: Nikolai Fedorov's Common Task Against the Biopolitics of Modernity." CR: *New Centennial Review* 23, no. 2 (2023): 259–94.

Chi, Elisha. "Refusal." *Political Theology Network,* November 15, 2022. https://politicaltheology.com/refusal.

Chollet, Antoine. "Claude Lefort: An Intruder in *Socialisme ou Barbarie?*" Translated by Allyn Hardyck. *Journal of the Collège International de Philosophie* 96, no. 2 (2019): 46–52.

Choudhury, Soumyabrata. "Ambedkar's Words: Elements of a Sentence-to-Come." *Social Scientist* 45, nos. 1–2 (2017): 3–18.

Christian, Barbara. "The Race for Theory." *Cultural Critique* 6 (1987): 51–63. https://doi.org/10.2307/1354255.

Christian, David. *Maps of Time: An Introduction to Big History.* University of California Press, 2004.

Claerhout, Sarah, and Jakob De Roover. "The Question of Conversion in India." *Economic and Political Weekly* 40, no. 28 (2015): 3048–55.

Clastres, Pierre. *Society Against the State: Essays in Political Anthropology.* Translated by Robert Hurley and Abe Stein. Zone, 1989.

Cleage, Albert. *Black Christian Nationalism: New Directions for the Black Church.* William Morrow, 1972.

Clover, Joshua. *Riot, Strike, Riot: The New Era of Uprisings*. Verso, 2016.

Cocks, Joan. *On Sovereignty and Other Political Delusions*. Bloomsbury, 2014.

Cohn, Jonathan. "An Elite Christian College Has Become the Latest Battleground in America's Culture Wars." *HuffPost*, June 19, 2022. https://www.huffpost.com/entry/calvin-university-professor-joe-kuilema-gay-marriage-lgbtq_n_62aca02de4b06169ca988191.

Cone, James. *A Black Theology of Liberation*. Orbis, 2010.

Connolly, William. *Capitalism and Christianity, American Style*. Duke University Press, 2008.

Connolly, William. *Pluralism*. Duke University Press, 2005.

Connolly, William. *A World of Becoming*. Duke University Press, 2011.

Cook, Deborah. "Through a Glass Darkly: Adorno's Inverse Theology." *Adorno Studies* 1, no. 1 (2017): 66–78.

Cooper, Melinda. *Family Values: Between Neoliberalism and the New Social Conservatism*. Zone, 2019.

Costa, Paolo. "The Fragile Supremacy of Reason: Jürgen Habermas and the Concept of Post-Secularity." In *The Post-Secular City*, 121–52. E. J. Brill, 2022.

Crawford, Kate, and Vladan Joler. "Anatomy of an AI System: The Amazon Echo as an Anatomical Map of Human Labor, Data and Planetary Resources." AI Now Institute and Share Lab, September 7, 2018. https://anatomyof.ai.

Crawley, Ashon. *Blackpentecostal Breath: The Aesthetics of Possibility*. Fordham University Press, 2016.

Crawley, Ashon. *The Lonely Letters*. Duke University Press, 2020.

Dale, Stephen F. "Trade, Conversion and the Growth of the Islamic Community of Kerala, South India." *Studia Islamica* 71 (1990): 155–75.

Das, Veena. *Textures of the Ordinary: Doing Anthropology After Wittgenstein*. Fordham University Press, 2020.

Davies, Carole Boyce. "Mothering and Healing in Recent Black Women's Fiction." *Sage* 2, no. 1 (1985): 41–43.

Davis, Heather, and Paige Sarlin. "'On the Risk of a New Relationality': An Interview with Lauren Berlant and Michael Hardt." *Reviews in Cultural Theory* 2, no. 3 (2012). Accessed January 15, 2023. http://reviewsinculture.com/2012/10/15/on-the-risk-of-a-new-relationality-an-interview-with-lauren-berlant-and-michael-hardt.

Davis, Kathleen. *Periodization and Sovereignty: How Ideas of Feudalism and Secularization Govern the Politics of Time*. University of Pennsylvania Press, 2008.

Deahl, Rachel. "Harper Buys Raskin Memoir." *Publisher's Weekly*, September 3, 2021.

Debaise, Didier, and Isabelle Stengers. "An Ecology of Trust? Consenting to a Pluralist Universe." *Sociological Review* 70, no. 2 (2022). doi.org/10.1177/00380261221084.

Deleuze, Gilles. *Nietzsche and Philosophy*. Translated by Hugh Tomlinson. Columbia University Press, 2006.

Derrida, Jacques. "Above All, No Journalists!" In *Religion and Media*, edited by Hent de Vries and Samuel Weber, 56–94. Translated by Samuel Weber. Stanford University Press, 2001.

Despret, Vinciane. *Our Grateful Dead: Stories of Those Left Behind*. Translated by Stephen Muecke. University of Minnesota Press, 2021.

Devji, Faisal. "A Minority of One." *Global Intellectual History* 7, no. 6 (2022): 1058–64.

Devji, Faisal, and Zahir Kazmi. *Islam After Liberalism*. Oxford University Press, 2017.

De Vries, Hent. "Inverse Versus Dialectical Theology: The Two Faces of Negativity and the Miracle of Faith." In *Paul and the Philosophers*, edited by Hent de Vries and Ward Blanton, 466–511. Fordham University Press, 2013.

De Vries, Hent, and Lawrence E. Sullivan. *Political Theologies: Public Religions in a Post-Secular World*. Fordham University Press, 2006.

Dodeman, Claire. "Claude Lefort, Reader of Merleau-Ponty: From 'The Proletarian Experience' to the 'Flesh of the Social.'" Translated by Jackson B. Smith. *Journal of the Collège international de Philosophie* 96, no. 2 (2019): 108–16.

Donne, John. *The Complete Poems*. Edited by Robin Robbins. Pearson, 2010.

Doostdar, Alireza. "God and Revolution in Iran." *Comparative Studies of South Asia, Africa, and the Middle East* 45, no. 1 (2025): 91–104.

Du Bois, W. E. B. *Black Reconstruction in America, 1860–1880*. Free Press, 1998.

Dubilet, Alex. "An Immanence Without the World: On Dispossession, Nothingness, and Secularity." *Qui Parle* 30, no. 1 (2021): 51–86.

Dubilet, Alex. "The Just Without Justification: On Meister Eckhart and Political Theology." *Postmedieval* 13, nos. 1–2 (2022): 5–28. https://doi.org/10.1057/s41280-022-00222-6.

Dubilet, Alex. "On the General Secular Contradiction: Secularization, Christianity, and Political Theology." In *Nothing Absolute: German Idealism and the Question of Political Theology*, edited by Kirill Chepurin and Alex Dubilet, 240–55. Fordham University Press, 2021.

Dubilet, Alex. "A Political Theology of Interpellation: On Subjection, Individuation, and Becoming Nothing." *Cultural Critique* 122 (2024): 132–61.

Dudgeon, Patricia, and Abigail Bray. "Indigenous Relationality: Women, Kinship and the Law." *Genealogy* 3, no. 2 (2019): 23–34.

Durkheim, Émile. *Elementary Forms of Religious Life*. George Allen and Unwin, 1915.

Dussel, Enrique. "Anti-Cartesian Meditations: On the Origin of the Philosophical Anti-Discourse of Modernity." *Journal for Cultural and Religious Theory* 13, no. 1 (2014): 11–52.

Dussel, Enrique. *Caminos de liberación latinoamericana: Interpretación histórico-teológica de nuestro continente latinoamericano*. Latinoamerica Libros, 1972.

Dussel, Enrique. *Caminos de liberación latinoamericana II: Teología de la liberación y ética*. Latinoamerica Libros, 1974.

Dussel, Enrique. *El humanismo semita: Estructuras intencionales radicales del pueblo de Israel y otros semitas*. Editorial Universitaria de Buenos Aires, 1969.

Dussel, Enrique. "Epistemic Decolonization of Theology." In *Decolonial Christianities: Latinx and Latin American Perspectives*, edited by Raimundo Barreto and Roberto Sirvent, 25–42. Palgrave Macmillan, 2019.

Dussel, Enrique. *Ethics of Liberation in the Age of Globalization and Exclusion*. Translated by Eduardo Mendieta, Camilo Pérez Bustillo, Yolanda Angulo and Nelson Maldonado-Torres. Edited by Alejandro Vallega. Duke University Press, [1998] 2013.

Dussel, Enrique. *Ética de la liberación en la edad de la globalización y de la exclusión*. Trotta, 1998.

Dussel, Enrique. *Filosofía de la liberación*. Fondo de Cultura Económica, [1977] 2011.

Dussel, Enrique. *Filosofía ética latinoamericana V: Arqueológica latinoamericana: Una filosofía de la religión antifetichista*. Universidad Santo Tomás, 1980.

Dussel, Enrique. *Filosofías del sur: Descolonización y transmodernidad*. Akal, 2017.

Dussel, Enrique. *The Invention of the Americas: Eclipse of "the Other" and the Myth of Modernity*. Translated by Michael D. Barber. Continuum, 1995.

Dussel, Enrique. *Las metáforas teológicas de Marx*. Verbo Divino, 1993.

Dussel, Enrique. *Método para una filosofía de la liberación: Superación analéctica de la dialéctica hegeliana*. Sígueme, 1974.

Dussel, Enrique. *Pablo de Tarso en la filosofía política actual y otros ensayos*. San Pablo, 2012.

Dussel, Enrique. *Philosophy of Liberation*. Translated by Aquilina Martinez and Christine Morkovsky. Orbis, [1977] 1985.

Dussel, Enrique. *Política de la liberación: Historia mundial y crítica*. Trotta, 2007.

Dussel, Enrique, *Política de la liberación, Volumen II: La arquitectónica*. Trotta, 2009.

Dussel, Enrique, ed. *Política de la liberación, Volumen III: Crítica creadora*. Trotta, 2022.

Dussel, Enrique. *Politics of Liberation: A Critical World History*. Translated by Thia Cooper. SCM, [2007] 2011.

Dussel, Enrique. *Twenty Theses on Politics*. Translated by George Ciccariello-Maher. Duke University Press, [2006] 2008.

Dussel, Enrique. *The Underside of Modernity: Apel, Ricoeur, Rorty, Taylor, and the Philosophy of Liberation*. Edited and translated by Eduardo Mendieta. Humanities, 1996.

Dussel, Enrique. *20 Tesis de política*. Siglo XXI, 2006.

Eaton, Richard. *The Rise of Islam and the Bengal Frontier, 1204–1760*. University of California Press, 1996.

Eck, Diana. *A New Religious America: How a "Christian Country" Has Now Become the World's Most Religiously Diverse Nation*. Harper San Francisco, 2001.

Eldridge, Aaron Frederick. "Movement in Repose: Notes on Form of Life." *Qui Parle* 30, no. 1 (2021): 19–49.

Eltschinger, Vincent. *Caste and Buddhist Philosophy: Continuity of Some Buddhist Arguments Against the Realist Interpretation of Social Denominations.* Translated by Raynald Prevereau. Motilal Banarsidass, 2012.

Enck, Paul, Sibylle Klosterhalfen, and Katja Weimer. "Unsolved, Forgotten, and Ignored Features of the Placebo Response in Medicine." *Clinical Therapeutics* 39, no. 3 (2017): 458–68.

Escobar, Arturo. "Worlds and Knowledges Otherwise: The Latin American Modernity/Coloniality Research Program." In *Globalization and the Decolonial Option*, edited by Walter D. Mignolo and Arturo Escobar, 33–64. Routledge, 2010.

Esposito, Roberto. *Two: The Machine of Political Theology and the Place of Thought.* Translated by Zakiya Hanafi. Fordham University Press, 2015.

Fahim, Hussein, and Katherine Helmer. "Indigenous Anthropology in Non-Western Countries: A Further Elaboration." *Current Anthropology* 21, no. 5 (1980): 644–63.

Falk, Francesca. "Hobbes' Leviathan und die aus dem Blick gefallenen Schnabelmasken." *Leviathan* 39 (2011): 247–66.

Fallon, Francis T. "The Gnostics: The Undominated Race." *Novum Testamentum* 21, no. 3 (1979): 271–88.

Fanon, Frantz. *The Wretched of the Earth.* Translated by Constance Farrington. Grove, 1963.

Fassin, Éric. "Gender and the Problem of Universals: Catholic Mobilizations and Sexual Democracy in France." *Religion and Gender* 6, no. 2 (2016): 173–86.

Federici, Silvia. *Beyond the Periphery of the Skin: Rethinking, Remaking, and Reclaiming the Body in Contemporary Capitalism.* PM, 2020.

Federici, Silvia. *Caliban and the Witch: Women, the Body, and Primitive Accumulation.* Autonomedia, 2014.

Federici, Silvia. *Re-Enchanting the World: Feminism and the Politics of the Commons.* PM, 2019.

Ferguson, Roderick. *The Reorder of Things: The University and Its Pedagogies of Minority Difference.* University of Minnesota Press, 2011.

Fernando, Mayanthi. *The Republic Unsettled: Muslim French and the Contradiction of Secularism.* Duke University Press, 2014.

Fernando, Mayanthi. "Uncanny Ecologies: More-than-Natural, More-than-Human, More-than-Secular." *Comparative Studies of South Asia, Africa and the Middle East* 42, no. 3 (2022): 568–83.

Fessenden, Tracy. *Culture and Redemption: Religion, the Secular, and American Literature.* Princeton University Press, 2005.

Firestone, Shulamith. *The Dialectic of Sex: The Case for Feminist Revolution.* Bantam, 2003.

Fitzgerald, Timothy. *The Ideology of Religious Studies.* Oxford University Press, 2000.

Fitzpatrick, Tara. "The Figure of Captivity: The Cultural Work of the Puritan Captivity Narrative." *American Literary History* 3, no. 1 (1991): 1–26.

Flynn, Bernard. "Lefort as Phenomenologist of the Political." In *Claude Lefort: Thinker of the Political*, edited by Martín Plot, 23–33. Palgrave Macmillan, 2013.

Flynn, Bernard. *The Philosophy of Claude Lefort: Interpreting the Political*. Northwestern University Press, 2005.

Foucault, Michel. *Discipline and Punish: The Birth of the Prison*. Translated by Alan Sheridan. Vintage, 1977.

Foucault, Michel. *The Punitive Society: Lectures at the Collège de France, 1972–1973*. Translated by Graham Burchell. Palgrave Macmillan, 2015.

Friesen, Phoebe. "Mesmer, the Placebo Effect, and the Efficacy Paradox." *Critical Public Health* 29, no. 4 (2019): 435–47.

Friesen, Phoebe, and Charlotte Blease. "Placebo Effects and Racial and Ethnic Health Disparities." *Journal of Medical Ethics* 44, no. 11 (2018): 774–81.

Friesen, Phoebe, and Émilie Dionne. "'It's All in Your Head': Magic and Misdirection in Medicine." *Science and Technology Studies* 35, no. 2 (2022): 72–96.

Fuchs, Martin. "Reaching Out; or, Nobody Exists in One Context Only: Society as Translation." *Translation Studies* 2, no. 1 (2019): 21–40.

Furani, Khaled. *Redeeming Anthropology: A Theological Critique of a Modern Science*. Oxford University Press, 2019.

Gaines, Kevin. *Uplifting the Race: Black Leadership, Politics, and Culture in the Twentieth Century*. University of North Carolina Press, 1996.

Gandhi, M. K. *Discourses on the Gita: Lectures at the Ashram in 1926–27*. Navajivan, [1933] 2016.

Gellner, Ernest. *Nations and Nationalism*. Cornell University Press, 2008.

Gély, Raphaël. "Towards a Radical Phenomenology of Social Life: Reflections from the Work of Michel Henry." In *Michel Henry: The Affects of Thought*, edited by Jeffrey Hanson and Michael R. Kelly, 155–77. Continuum, 2012.

Gill-Peterson, Jules. "The Miseducation of a French Feminist." *e-flux*, no. 117 (2021). https://www.e-flux.com/journal/117/382426/the-miseducation-of-a-french-feminist/.

Gilmore, Ruth Wilson. "Race and Globalization." In *Geographies of Global Change: Remapping the World*, edited by R. J. Johnston, Peter J. Taylor, and Michael Watts, 261–72. Wiley-Blackwell, 2002.

Girard, René. *Violence and the Sacred*. Johns Hopkins University Press, 1977.

Goldstein, Warren S. "The Dialectical Pattern of Secularization: A Comparative-Historical Approach." In *Religion, Öffentlichkeit, Moderne: Transdisziplinäre Perspektiven*, edited by Judith Könemann and Saskia Wendel, 18–42. Transcript, 2016.

Gordon, Avery. *The Hawthorn Archive: Letters from the Utopian Margins*. Fordham University Press, 2018.

Gordon, Peter E. *Migrants in the Profane: Critical Theory and the Question of Secularization*. Yale University Press, 2020.

Gordon, Peter E. "Secularization, Genealogy, and the Legitimacy of the Modern Age: Remarks on the Löwith-Blumenberg Debate." *Journal of the History of Ideas* 80, no. 1 (2019): 147–70.

Gorski, Philip, and Samuel Perry. *The Flag and the Cross: White Christian Nationalism and the Threat to American Democracy*. Oxford University Press, 2022.

Graham, Elaine. "Feminist Theology, Northern." In *The Blackwell Companion to Political Theology*, edited by Peter Scott and William T. Cavanaugh, 210–26. Blackwell, 2004.

Green, Jeffrey E. *The Eyes of the People: Democracy in an Age of Spectatorship*. Oxford University Press, 2010.

Green, Kai M. [now K. Marshall], Je Naé Taylor, Pascale Ifé Williams, and Christopher Roberts. "#BlackHealingMatters in the Time of #BlackLivesMatter." *Biography* 41, no. 4 (2018): 909–41.

Greenhalgh, Susan. *Fat-Talk Nation: The Human Costs of America's War on Fat*. Cornell University Press, 2015.

Grelet, Gilles. "Proletarian Gnosis." Translated by Anthony Paul Smith. *Angelaki* 19, no. 2 (2014): 93–98.

Griffin, Farah Jasmine. "Textual Healing: Claiming Black Women's Bodies, the Erotic and Resistance in Contemporary Novels of Slavery." *Callaloo* 19, no. 2 (1996): 519–36.

Gross, Terri. "After His Son's Suicide and the Jan. 6 Attack, Rep. Jamie Raskin Is Not Giving Up." *Fresh Air*, National Public Radio, January 4, 2022.

Grotius, Hugo. *Commentary on the Law of Prize and Booty*. Edited by Martine Julia van Ittersum. Liberty Fund, 2005.

Guénoun, Denis. *About Europe: Philosophical Hypotheses*. Translated by Christine Irizarry. Stanford University Press, 2013.

Guha, Ranajit. "Prose of Counter-Insurgency." In *Selected Subaltern Studies*, edited by Ranajit Guha and Gayatri Chakravorty Spivak, 45–84. Oxford University Press, 1988.

Gumbs, Alexis Pauline. *M Archive: After the End of the World*. Duke University Press, 2018.

Gutiérrez, Gustavo. *A Theology of Liberation: History, Politics, and Salvation*. Orbis, [1971] 1973.

Habermas, Jürgen. *The Philosophical Discourse of Modernity*. Translated by Fredrick G. Lawrence. MIT Press, 1990.

Hammill, Graham, and Julia Reinhard Lupton. "Introduction." In *Political Theology and Early Modernity*, 1–22. University of Chicago Press, 2012.

Han, Byung-Chul. "The Tiredness Virus." *The Nation*, April 12, 2021. www .thenation.com/article/society/pandemic-burnout-society.

Harding, Susan. *The Book of Jerry Falwell: Fundamentalist Language and Politics*. Princeton University Press, 1994.

Harding, Susan. "Representing Fundamentalism: The Problem of the Repugnant Cultural Other." *Social Research* 58, no. 2 (1991): 373–93.

Harney, Stefano, and Fred Moten. *All Incomplete*. Autonomedia, 2021.

Harney, Stefano, and Fred Moten. *The Undercommons: Fugitive Planning and Black Study*. Autonomedia, 2013.

Harney, Stefano, and Fred Moten. "Wildcat the Totality." *Millennials Are Kill-ing Capitalism* (podcast), July 4, 2020. Accessed January 16, 2022. https://millennialsarekillingcapitalism.libsyn.com/wildcat-the-totality-fred-moten-and-stefano-harney-revisit-the-undercommons-in-a-time-of-pandemic-and-rebellion-part-1.

Harrington, Anne. *The Cure Within: A History of Mind-Body Medicine.* W. W. Norton, 2008.

Hart, Gillian. "Decoding 'The Base': White Evangelicals or Christian National-ists." *Studies in Political Economy* 102, no. 1 (2021): 61–76.

Hart, Gillian. "Why Did It Take so Long? Trump-Bannonism in a Global Con-jectural Frame." *Geografiska Annaler: Series B, Human Geography* 102, no. 3 (2020): 239–66.

Hartman, Saidiya. "The Anarchy of Colored Girls Assembled in a Riotous Man-ner." *South Atlantic Quarterly* 117, no. 3 (2018): 465–90.

Hegel, G. W. F. *Philosophy of Right.* Translated by S. W. Dyde. Batoche, 2001.

Hegel, G. W. F. *Science of Logic.* Translated by A. V. Miller. Allen and Unwin, 1969.

Hemphill, Prentis. "Healing Justice Is How We Can Sustain Black Lives." *Huff-ington Post,* February 7, 2017. https://www.huffpost.com/entry/healing-justice_b_5899e8ade4b0c1284f282ffe.

Henry, Michel. *Barbarism.* Translated by Scott Davidson. Continuum, 2012.

Henry, Michel. *From Communism to Capitalism: Theory of a Catastrophe.* Trans-lated by Scott Davidson. Bloomsbury Academic, 2014.

Henry, Michel. *Marx: A Philosophy of Human Reality.* Translated by Kathleen McLaughlin. Indiana University Press, 1983.

Henry, Michel. *The Michel Henry Reader.* Edited by Scott Davidson and Frederic Seyler. Northwestern University Press, 2019

Hickman, Jared. *Black Prometheus: Race and Radicalism in the Age of Atlantic Slavery.* Oxford University Press, 2017.

Hicks, Rosemary. "Between Lived Religion and the Law: Power, Empire, and Expansion in American Religious Studies." *Religion* 42, no. 3 (2012): 409–24.

Hill, Christopher. *The World Turned Upside Down: Radical Ideas During the English Revolution.* Penguin, 1972.

Hirschkind, Charles. "On the Virtues of Holding Your Tongue." *Critical Times* 3, no. 2 (2020): 471–77.

Hollywood, Amy. "Introduction." In *The Cambridge Companion to Christian Mysticism,* edited by Amy Hollywood and Patricia Z. Beckman, 1–33. Cam-bridge University Press, 2012.

Hooker, Juliet. *Black Grief/White Grievance: The Politics of Loss.* Princeton Uni-versity Press, 2023.

hooks, bell. *All About Love: New Visions.* HarperCollins, 2000.

Hovey, Craig, and Elizabeth Phillips, eds. *The Cambridge Companion to Christian Political Theology.* Cambridge University Press, 2015.

Howard, Dick. "Introducing Claude Lefort: From the Critique of Totalitarian-ism to the Politics of Democracy." *Democratiya* 11 (2007): 61–66.

Hulsether, Lucia. "The Grammar of Racism: Religious Pluralism and the Birth of the Interdisciplines." *Journal of the American Academy of Religion* 86, no. 1 (2018): 1–41.

Hulsether, Lucia. "Out of Incorporation, Pluralism." *Journal of Interreligious Studies* 17 (2015): 45–53.

Ingram, James D. "The Politics of Claude Lefort's Political: Between Liberalism and Democracy." *Thesis Eleven* 87 (2006): 33–50.

Ingram, James D. *Radical Cosmopolitics: The Ethics and Politics of Democratic Universalism*. Columbia University Press, 2013.

Invisible Committee. *Now*. Translated by Robert Hurley. Semiotext(e), 2017.

Iqbal, Basit Kareem. "Asad and Benjamin: Chronopolitics of Tragedy in the Anthropology of Secularism." *Anthropological Theory* 20, no. 1 (2020): 77–96.

Iqbal, Basit Kareem, and Talal Asad. "Thinking About Method: A Conversation with Talal Asad." *Qui Parle* 26, no. 1 (2017): 195–218.

Irigaray, Luce. *Between East and West: From Singularity to Community*. Translated by Stephen Pluháček. Columbia University Press, 2003.

Irigaray, Luce. *The Forgetting of Air in Martin Heidegger*. Translated by Mary Beth Mader. University of Texas Press, 1999.

Irigaray, Luce. *A New Culture of Energy: Beyond East and West*. Columbia University Press, 2021.

Irigaray, Luce. *Sexes and Genealogies*. Translated by Gillian C. Gill. Columbia University Press, 1993.

Irigaray, Luce. "Spiritual Tasks for Our Age." In *Key Writings*, edited by Luce Irigaray, 171–85. Continuum, 2004.

Irigaray, Luce. *To Be Born: Genesis of a New Human Being*. Palgrave Macmillan, 2017.

Irigaray, Luce. "To Begin with Breathing Anew." In *Breathing with Luce Irigaray*, edited by Emily A. Holmes and Lenart Škof, 217–26. Bloomsbury, 2013.

Irigaray, Luce. *The Way of Love*. Translated by Heidi Bostic and Stephen Pluháček. Continuum, 2002.

Irigaray, Luce, and Michael Marder. *Through Vegetal Being: Two Philosophical Perspectives*. Columbia University Press, 2016.

Irigaray, Luce, and Judith Still. "'Towards a Wisdom of Love': Conversation between Luce Irigaray and Judith Still." In *Conversations*, by Luce Irigaray, 21–36. Translated by Stephen Pluháček. Routledge, 2008.

Jaarsma, Ada S. "Habermas' Kierkegaard and the Nature of the Secular." *Constellations* 17, no. 2 (2010): 271–92.

Jaarsma, Ada S., and Suze G. Berkhout. "Nocebos and the Psychic Life of Biopower." *Symposium* 23, no. 2 (2019): 67–93.

Jackson, Zakiyyah Iman. "Sense of Things." *Catalyst* 2, no. 2 (2016): 1–48.

Jacobson, Norman. *Pride and Solace*. University of California Press, 1978.

Jakobsen, Janet, and Ann Pellegrini. *Secularisms*. Duke University Press, 2008.

Jaschik, Scott. "Judith Butler on Being Attacked in Brazil." *Inside Higher Ed*, November 12, 2017. https://www.insidehighered.com/news/2017/11/13/judith-butler-discusses-being-burned-effigy-and-protested-brazil.

Jay, Martin. *The Dialectical Imagination: A History of the Frankfurt School and the Institute of Social Research, 1923–1950*. University of California Press, 1973.

Johnson, Terrence L. *We Testify with Our Lives: How Religion Transformed Radical Thought from Black Power to Black Lives Matter*. Columbia University Press, 2021.

Jonas, Hans. *Gnostic Religion: The Message of the Alien God and the Beginnings of Christianity*. Beacon, 1963.

Judy, Ronald. (*Dis*)*Forming the American Canon*. University of Minnesota Press, 1993.

Justice, Daniel Heath. "'Go Away Water!': Kinship Criticism and the Decolonization Imperative." In *Reasoning Together: The Native Critics Collection*, 147–68. University of Oklahoma Press, 2008.

Kaba, Mariame. *We Do This 'til We Free Us: Abolitionist Organizing and Transforming Justice*. Haymarket, 2021.

Kahn, Victoria. *The Future of Illusion: Political Theology and Early Modern Texts*. University of Chicago Press, 2014.

Kant, Immanuel. *Religion and Rational Theology*. Edited and translated by Allen W. Wood and George Di Giovanni. Cambridge University Press, 1996.

Kantorowicz, Ernst. *The King's Two Bodies: A Study in Medieval Political Theology*. Princeton University Press, 2016.

Kaplan, Andrew Santana. "Notes Toward (Inhabiting) the Black Messianic in Afro-Pessimism's Apocalyptic Thought." *The Comparatist* 43 (2019): 68–89.

Karatani, Kōjin. "Beyond Capital-Nation-State." *Rethinking Marxism* 20, no. 4 (2008): 569–95.

Karatani, Kōjin. *The Structure of World History: From Modes of Production to Modes of Exchange*. Duke University Press, 2014.

Karatani, Kōjin. *Transcritique: On Kant and Marx*. MIT Press, 2005.

Karatani, Kōjin, and Joel Wainwright. "'Critique Is Impossible Without Moves': An Interview of Kojin Karatani by Joel Wainwright." *Dialogues in Human Geography* 2, no. 1 (2012): 30–52.

Keller, Catherine, and Clayton Crockett. "Introduction: Political Theology on Edge." In *Political Theology on Edge: Ruptures of Justice and Belief in the Anthropocene*, edited by Clayton Crockett and Catherine Keller, 1–16. Fordham University Press, 2022.

Kerényi, K. "Prolegomena." In C. G. Jung and K. Kerényi, *Essays on a Science of Mythology*, translated by R. F. C. Hull, 1–24. Princeton University Press, [1941] 1969.

King, Karen L. *What Is Gnosticism?* Harvard University Press, 2003.

King, Thomas. *The Truth About Stories: A Native Narrative*. University of Minnesota Press, 2003.

Kline, David. "On Self-Creation: Autopoiesis and Autoreligion." In *Words Made Flesh: Sylvia Wynter and Religion*, edited by David Kline and Justine Bakker, 21–43. Fordham University Press, 2025.

Kohlenbach, Margarete. "Kafka, Critical Theory, Dialectical Theology: Adorno's Case Against Hans-Joachim Schoeps." *German Life and Letters* 63, no. 2 (2010): 146–65.

Kosambi, Dharmanand. *Buddha, Dharma, Sangha.* In *Dharmanand Kosambi: The Essential Writings,* edited and translated by Meera Kosambi, 243–311. Permanent Black, [1910] 2013.

Kosambi, Dharmanand. "Civilisation and Non-Violence." In *Dharmanand Kosambi: The Essential Writings,* edited and translated by Meera Kosambi, 327–57. Permanent Black, [1910] 2013.

Kosambi, Dharmanand. *Nivedan (a Narrative). Reprinted as 'Nivedan—1912–1924.'* In *Dharmanand Kosambi: The Essential Writings,* edited and translated by Meera Kosambi, 53–205. Permanent Black, [1924] 2013.

Koselleck, Reinhart. *Critique and Crisis: Enlightenment and the Pathogenesis of Modern Society.* MIT Press, 1988.

Kotsko, Adam. "Genealogy and Political Theology: On Method in Agamben's *The Kingdom and the Glory.*" *Political Theology* 14, no. 1 (2013): 107–14.

Kotsko, Adam. *Neoliberalism's Demons: On the Political Theology of Late Capital.* Stanford University Press, 2018.

Kotsko, Adam. *What Is Theology? Christian Thought and Contemporary Life.* Fordham University Press, 2021.

Kragh, Ulrich Timme, ed. *The Foundation for Yoga Practitioners: The Buddhist Yogacarabhumi Treatise and Its Adaptation in India, East Asia, and Tibet.* Harvard Oriental Series, 75. Harvard University, Department of South Asian Studies, 2013.

Kuhn, Thomas. *The Structure of Scientific Revolutions.* University of Chicago Press, 2012.

Kwok, Pui-lan. *Postcolonial Politics and Theology: Unraveling Empire for a Global World.* Westminster John Knox Press, 2021.

Laclau, Ernesto, and Chantal Mouffe. *Hegemony and Socialist Strategy: Toward a Radical Democratic Politics.* Translated by Winston Moore and Paul Cammack. Verso, 1985.

Laermans, Rudy, and Gert Verschraegen. "The Late Niklas Luhmann on Religion: An Overview." *Social Compass* 48, no. 1 (2001): 7–20.

Lafleur, Greta. "Heterosexuality Without Women." *Los Angeles Review of Books,* May 20, 2019. https://blog.lareviewofbooks.org/essays/heterosexuality-without-women.

Laruelle, François. *A Biography of Ordinary Man: On Authorities and Minorities.* Translated by Jessie Hock and Alex Dubilet. Polity, 2018.

Laruelle, François. *Future Christ: A Lesson in Heresy.* Translated by Anthony Paul Smith. Continuum, 2010.

Latour, Bruno. *Down to Earth: Politics in the New Climatic Regime.* Translated by Catherine Porter. Polity, 2018.

Latour, Bruno. *On the Modern Cult of the Factish Gods.* Duke University Press, 2010.

Lebner, Ashley. "No Such Thing as a Concept: A Radical Tradition from Malinowski to Asad and Strathern." *Anthropological Theory* 20, no. 1 (2020): 3–28.

Lefort, Claude. "Human Rights and the Welfare States." In *Democracy and Political Theory*, translated by David Macey, 21–44. Polity, 1988.

Lefort, Claude. *Machiavelli in the Making*. Translated by Michael B. Smith. Northwestern University Press, 2012.

Lefort, Claude. "The Permanence of the Theologico-Political?" In *Democracy and Political Theory*, translated by David Macey, 213–55. Polity, 1988.

Lefort, Claude. "The Question of Democracy." In *Democracy and Political Theory*, translated by David Macey, 9–20. Polity, 1988.

Lefort, Claude. *"Sur une colonne absente": Écrits autour de Merleau-Ponty*. Gallimard, 1978.

Lefort, Claude, and Terry Karten. "Marx: From One Vision of History to Another." *Social Research* 45, no. 4 (1978): 615–66.

Le Goff, Jacques. *The Medieval Imagination*. University of Chicago Press, 1992.

Leibniz, G. W. F. *Theodicy*. Translated by E. M. Huggard. Edited by Austin Farrer. Open Court, 1985.

Levinas, Emmanuel. *Totality and Infinity: An Essay on Exteriority*. Translated by Alphonso Lingis. Duquesne University Press, 1969.

Lloyd, Dana, ed. "Why Political Theology Needs Children." *Political Theology Network*, September 19, 2023. Accessed March 21, 2024. https://politicaltheology.com/symposium/why-political-theology-needs-children.

Lloyd, Vincent. *Black Dignity: The Struggle Against Domination*. Yale University Press, 2022.

Lloyd, Vincent. "From the Theopaternal to the Theopolitical: On Barack Obama." In *Common Goods: Economy, Ecology, and Political Theology*, edited by Elias Ortega-Aponte, Catherine Keller, and Melanie Johnson-DeBaufre, 326–43. Fordham University Press, 2015.

Lloyd, Vincent. "Political Theology and Islamic Studies Symposium: What Is Islamic Political Theology?" *Political Theology Network*, July 24, 2013. https://politicaltheology.com/political-theology-and-islamic-studies-symposium-what-is-islamic-political-theology.

Lloyd, Vincent, ed. *Race and Political Theology*. Stanford University Press, 2012.

Lloyd, Vincent, and David True. "What Is the Political Theology Canon?" *Political Theology* 18, no. 7 (2017): 539–41.

Locher, Cosima, Jens Gaab, and Charlotte Blease. "When a Placebo Is Not a Placebo." *Frontiers in Psychology* 9 (2018): 2317. https://doi.org/10.3389/fpsyg.2018.02317.

Lofton, Kathryn. "Pulpit of Performative Reason." *TSQ* 9, no. 3 (2022): 443–59.

Loraux, Nicole. *The Divided City: On Memory and Forgetting in Ancient Athens*. Translated by Corinne Pache with Jeff Fort. Zone, 2006.

Lorde, Audre. *Conversations with Audre Lorde*. Edited by Joan Wylie Hall. University Press of Mississippi, 2004.

Lorde, Audre. *Sister Outsider: Essays and Speeches*. Crossing, 2007.

Losurdo, Domenico. *War and Revolution: Rethinking the Twentieth Century.* Verso, 2015.

Luhmann, Niklas. "The Cognitive Program of Constructivism and a Reality That Remains Unknown." In *Selforganization: Portrait of a Scientific Revolution,* edited by Wolfgang Krohn, Gunter Kuppers, and Helga Nowatny, 64–85. Springer Science + Business Media, 1990.

Luhmann, Niklas. *A Systems Theory of Religion.* Stanford University Press, 2013.

Lyons, Scott Richard. "Rhetorical Sovereignty: What Do American Indians Want from Writing?" *College Composition and Communication* 51, no. 3 (2000): 447–68.

MacIntyre, Alasdair. *After Virtue: A Study in Moral Theory.* University of Notre Dame Press, 2007.

MacIntyre, Alasdair. "Epistemological Crisis, Dramatic Narrative, and the Philosophy of Science." *The Monist* 60, no. 2 (1977): 453–72.

Magid, Shaul. *Meir Kahane: The Public Life and Political Thought of an American Jewish Radical.* Princeton University Press, 2021.

Mahadev, Neena. *Karma and Grace: Religious Difference in Millennial Sri Lanka.* Columbia University Press, 2023.

Mahmood, Saba. *Politics of Piety: The Islamic Revival and the Feminist Subject.* Princeton University Press, 2005.

Mahmood, Saba. "Secularism, Hermeneutics, and Empire: The Politics of Islamic Reformation." *Public Culture* 18, no. 2 (2006): 323–47.

Makkī, ʿAbd al-Malik al-. *Samṭ al-nujūm al-ʿawālī fī anbāʾ al-awāʾil wa-al-tawālī.* Edited by ʿĀdil Aḥmad ʿAbd al-Waḥīd and ʿAlī Mūḥammad Mūʿawwiḍ. Dār al-Kutub al-ʿIlmiyya, 1998.

Maldonado-Torres, Nelson. "AAR Centennial Roundtable: Religion, Conquest, and Race in the Foundations of the Modern/Colonial World." *Journal of the American Academy of Religion* 82, no. 3 (2014): 636–65.

Maldonado-Torres, Nelson. "Enrique Dussel's Liberation Thought in the Decolonial Turn." *Transmodernity* 1, no. 1 (2011): 1–30.

Maldonado-Torres, Nelson. "Secularism and Religion in the Modern/Colonial World-System: From Secular Postcoloniality to Postsecular Transmodernity." In *Coloniality at Large: Latin America and the Postcolonial Debate,* edited by Mabel Moraña, Enrique Dussel, and Carlos A. Jáuregui, 360–84. Duke University Press, 2008.

Marchart, Oliver. *Post-Foundational Political Thought: Political Difference in Nancy, Lefort, Badiou and Laclau.* Edinburgh University Press, 2007.

Marovich, Beatrice. "Hearing Nothing: A More Than Human Silence." *Political Theology* 24, no. 3 (2023): 321–37. doi:10.1080/1462317X.2022.2035957.

Marriott, David. "Inventions of Existence: Sylvia Wynter, Frantz Fanon, Sociogeny, and 'the Damned.'" *CR: New Centennial Review* 11, no. 3 (2011): 45–89.

Marriott, David. "No Lords A-Leaping: Fanon, C. L. R. James, and the Politics of Invention." *Humanities* 3, no. 4 (2014): 517–45. https://doi.org/10.3390/h3040517.

Martel, James. *Anarchist Prophets: Disappointing Vision and the Power of Collective Sight*. Duke University Press, 2022.

Martins, Ansgar. *Adorno und Kabbalah*. Universitätsverlag Potsdam, 2016.

Marx, Karl. "Letter to A. Ruge, September 1843." In *Karl Marx: Early Writings*, edited by Lucio Colletti and translated by Rodney Livingstone and Gregor Benton, 206–9. Penguin, 1975.

Marx, Karl. *Selected Writings*. Edited by Lawrence H. Simon. Hackett, 1994.

Marx, Karl, and Frederick Engels. "Manifesto of the Communist Party." In *Marx and Engels Collected Works, Volume 6: Marx and Engels, 1845–1848*. Lawrence and Wishart, 1976.

Marx, Karl, and Frederick Engels. *Marx and Engels Collected Works, Volume 3: Karl Marx—March 1843–August 1844*. Lawrence and Wishart, 1975.

Mas, Ruth. "Why Critique?" *Method and Theory in the Study of Religion* 24 (2012): 389–407.

Masuzawa, Tomoko. *The Invention of World Religions: Or, How European Universalism Was Preserved in the Language of Pluralism*. University of Chicago Press, 2005.

Maturana, Humberto R., and Francisco J. Varela. *Autopoiesis and Cognition: The Realization of the Living*. D. Reidel, 1980.

Mauss, Marcel. *The Gift: The Form and Reason for Exchange in Archaic Societies*. Routledge, 2002.

Mauss, Marcel, and Henri Hubert. *Sacrifice: Its Nature and Functions*. University of Chicago Press, [1898] 1981.

Mazarella, William. *The Mana of Mass Society*. University of Chicago Press, 2018.

McAllister, Carlota, and Valentina Napolitano. "Political Theology/Theopolitics: Thresholds and Vulnerabilities of Sovereignty." *Annual Review of Anthropology* 50 (2021): 109–24.

McElwee, Joshua J. "Francis Strongly Criticizes Gender Theory, Comparing It to Nuclear Arms." *National Catholic Reporter*, February 13, 2015. https://www.ncronline.org/news/vatican/francis-strongly-criticizes-gender-theory-comparing-it-nuclear-arms.

Meillassoux, Quentin. *After Finitude: An Essay on the Necessity of Contingency*. Translated by Ray Brassier. Continuum, 2008.

Meillassoux, Quentin. "The Immanence of the World Beyond." Translated by Peter M. Candler. In *The Grandeur of Reason*, edited by Peter M. Candler and Conor Cunningham, 444–78. SCM, 2010.

Meillassoux, Quentin. *The Number and the Siren: A Decipherment of Mallarmé's Coup de dés*. Translated by Robin Mackay. Urbanomic, 2012.

Meister, Robert. *After Evil: A Politics of Human Rights*. Columbia University Press, 2011.

Mendieta, Eduardo. "Editor's Introduction." In *The Underside of Modernity: Apel, Ricoeur, Rorty, Taylor, and the Philosophy of Liberation*, edited and translated by Eduardo Mendieta, xiii–xxxi. Humanities Press, 1996.

Mignolo, Walter D. *The Darker Side of Western Modernity: Global Futures, Decolonial Options.* Duke University Press, 2011.

Milbank, John. *Theology and Social Theory.* Blackwell, 2006.

Mittermaier, Amira. "Beyond the Human Horizon." *Religion and Society: Advances in Research* 12 (2021): 21–38.

Mohan, P. Sanal. *Modernity of Slavery: Struggles Against Caste Inequality in Colonial Kerala.* Oxford University Press, 2015.

Moin, A. Azfar, and Alan Strathern. *Sacred Kingship in World History: Between Immanence and Transcendence.* Columbia University Press, 2022.

Mol, Annemarie, and Ada S. Jaarsma. "Empirical Philosophy and Eating in Theory: An Interview with Annemarie Mol." *Symposium* 27, no. 1 (2023): 189–211.

Mol, Ashon. *The Body Multiple: Ontology in Medical Practice.* Duke University Press, 2002.

Moten, Fred. *Black and Blur.* Duke University Press, 2017.

Moten, Fred. "Blackness and Nothingness (Mysticism in the Flesh)." *South Atlantic Quarterly* 112, no. 4 (2013): 737–80. https://doi.org/10.1215/00382876-2345261.

Moten, Fred. "Black Op." *Modern Language Association of America* 123, no. 5 (2008): 1743–47. https://doi.org/10.1632/pmla.2008.123.5.1743.

Moten, Fred. *In the Break: The Aesthetics of the Black Radical Tradition.* University of Minnesota Press, 2003.

Moten, Fred. "Knowledge of Freedom." CR: *New Centennial Review* 4, no. 2 (2004): 269–310.

Moten, Fred. *Stolen Life.* Duke University Press, 2018.

Moten, Fred. "The Subprime and the Beautiful." *African Identities* 11, no. 2 (2013): 237–45.

Moumtaz, Nada. "Refiguring Islam." In *A Companion to the Anthropology of the Middle East,* edited by Soraya Altorki, 125–50. Wiley-Blackwell, 2015.

Müller, Jan-Werner. "'The People Must Be Extracted from Within the People': Reflections on Populism." *Constellations* 21, no. 4 (2014): 483–93.

Nash, Jennifer. "Practicing Love: Black Feminism, Love-Politics, and Post-Intersectionality." *Meridians* 11, no. 2 (2011): 1–24.

Newheiser, David. *Hope in a Secular Age: Deconstruction, Negative Theology, and the Future of Faith.* Cambridge University Press, 2019.

Newman, Saul. *Political Theology: A Critical Introduction.* Polity, 2019.

Nietzsche, Friedrich. *The Gay Science.* Translated by Walter Kauffman. Vintage, 1974.

Nietzsche, Friedrich. *On the Genealogy of Morals.* Translated by Michael A. Scarpitti. Penguin Random House, 2014.

Nietzsche, Friedrich. *Thus Spoke Zarathustra: A Book for Everyone and No One.* Translated by R. J. Hollingdale. Penguin Random House, 1961.

Nietzsche, Friedrich. *Twilight of the Idols.* In *The Anti-Christ, Ecce Homo, Twilight of the Idols,* translated by Judith Norman. Cambridge University Press, 2005.

Noble, David W. "Robert Bellah, Civil Religion, and the American Jeremiad." *Soundings* 65, no. 1 (1982): 88–102.

Nongbri, Brent. *Before Religion: A History of a Modern Concept.* Yale University Press, 2013.

Nyquist, Mary. *Arbitrary Rule: Slavery, Tyranny, and the Power of Life and Death.* University of Chicago Press, 2013.

Onishi, Bradley. *Preparing for War: The Extremist History of Christian Nationalism—And What Comes Next.* Broadleaf, 2023.

Owens, Patricia. "Decolonizing Civil War." *Critical Analysis of Law* 4, no. 2 (2017): 160–69.

Pandolfo, Stefania. *Knot of the Soul: Madness, Psychoanalysis, Islam.* University of Chicago Press, 2018.

Pascal, Blaise. *Pensées.* Translated and edited by Roger Ariew. Hackett, 2004.

Perreau, Bruno. *Queer Theory: The French Response.* Stanford University Press, 2016.

Perry, Samuel, and Andrew Whitehead. *Taking America Back for God: Christian Nationalism in the United States.* Oxford University Press, 2020.

Peters, Edward. "What Was God Doing Before He Created the Heavens and the Earth?" *Augustiana* 34, nos. 1–2 (1984): 53–74.

Pinto, Isabela, and Stiliana Milkova. "Storytelling Philosophy and Self Writing—Preliminary Notes on Elena Ferrante: An Interview with Adriana Cavarero." *Narrative* 28, no. 2 (2020): 236–49.

Plato. *The Republic.* Edited by G. R. F. Ferrari. Translated by Tom Griffith. Cambridge University Press, 2000.

Poe, Danielle. "Can Luce Irigaray's Notion of Sexual Difference Be Applied to Transsexual and Transgender Narratives?" In *Thinking with Irigaray*, edited by Mary C. Rawlinson, Sabrina L. Hom, and Serene J. Khader, 111–28. State University of New York Press, 2011.

Political Theology Network. "CFP—(How to Do) Political Theology Without Men?" April 21, 2021. https://politicaltheology.com/cfp-how-to-do -political-theology-without-men.

Pope Benedict XVI. "Prepolitical Moral Foundations of a Free Republic." In *Political Theologies: Public Religions in a Post-Secular World*, edited by Hent de Vries and Lawrence E. Sullivan, 261–68. Fordham University Press, 2006.

Powers, Allison. "Tragedy Made Flesh: Constitutional Lawlessness in Du Bois's *Black Reconstruction*." *Comparative Studies of South Asia, Africa and the Middle East* 34, no. 1 (2014): 106–25.

Pritchard, Elizabeth. "Bilderverbot Meets Body in Theodor W. Adorno's Inverse Theology." *Harvard Theological Review* 95, no. 3 (2002): 291–318.

Prosser, Jay. *Second Skins: The Body Narratives of Transsexuality.* Columbia University Press, 1998.

Puar, Jasbir. *Terrorist Assemblages: Homonationalism in Queer Times.* Duke University Press, 2007.

Puar, Jasbir, and Amit Rai. "Monster, Terrorist, Fag: The War on Terrorism and the Production of Docile Patriots." *Social Text* 72, no. 3 (2002): 117–48.

Quashie, Kevin. *The Sovereignty of Quiet: Beyond Resistance in Black Culture.* Rutgers University Press, 2012.

Ralston, Joshua. "Political Theology in Arabic." *Political Theology* 19, no. 7 (2018): 549–52.

Rao, Anupama. *The Caste Question: Dalits and the Politics of Modern India*. University of California Press, 2009.

Raskin, Jamie. "Closing Remarks at the Second Impeachment Trial of Donald Trump." *Democracy Now!*, February 10, 2021. Accessed March 10, 2023. https://www.democracynow.org/2021/2/10/jamie_raskin_impeachment _trial_capitol_insurrection.

Raskin, Jamie. "Remarks to the Freedom from Religion Foundation, 45th Annual National Convention, San Antonio." *Freedom from Religion Foundation*, November 3, 2022. Accessed December 1, 2023. https://ffrf.org/news/news -releases/item/41558-rep-raskin-remarks-to-ffrf-convention-call-out-white -christian-nationalism.

Raskin, Jamie. *Unthinkable: Trauma, Truth, and the Trials of American Democracy*. Harper, 2022.

Ratzinger, Cardinal Joseph, and Archbishop Angelo Amato. "Letter to the Bishops of the Catholic Church on the Collaboration of Men and Women in the Church and in the World." *Congregation for the Doctrine of the Faith*, May 31, 2004. https://www.vatican.va/roman_curia/congregations/cfaith /documents/rc_con_cfaith_doc_20040731_collaboration_en.html.

Ray, Avishek. "Of Nomadology: A Requiem for India(n-ness)." *Crossings* 10, no. 2 (2019): 281–92.

Rezavi, Syed Ali Nadeem. "Religious Disputations and Imperial Ideology: The Purpose and Location of Akbar's *Ibadatkhana*." *Studies in History* 24, no. 2 (2008): 195–209.

Riedl, Ann Maria. *Judith Butler and Theology*. Brill, 2021.

Rifkin, Mark. "Around 1978: Family, Culture, and Race in the Federal Production of Indianness." In *Critically Sovereign: Indigenous Gender, Sexuality, and Feminist Studies*, edited by Joanne Barker, 169–206. Duke University Press, 2017.

Rifkin, Mark. *When Did Indians Become Straight? Kinship, the History of Sexuality, and Native Sovereignty*. Oxford University Press, 2011.

Robcis, Camille. "Catholics, the 'Theory of Gender', and the Turn to the Human in France: A New Dreyfus Affair?" *Journal of Modern History* 87, no. 4 (2015): 892–923.

Robinson, Cedric. *An Anthropology of Marxism*. University of North Carolina Press, 2019.

Robinson, Cedric. *Black Marxism: The Making of the Black Radical Tradition*. 3rd ed. University of North Carolina Press, 2020.

Robinson, Cedric. *The Terms of Order: Political Science and the Myth of Leadership*. University of North Carolina Press, 2016.

Roediger, David R. *Seizing Freedom: Slave Emancipation and Liberty for All*. Verso, 2014.

Rogin, Michael. *Ronald Reagan, The Movie: And Other Episodes in Political Demonology*. University of California Press, 1988.

Rosanvallon, Pierre. "The Test of the Political: A Conversation with Claude Lefort." *Constellations* 19, no. 1 (2012): 4–15.

Rubenstein, Mary-Jane. "A Pantheology of Pandemic: Sex, Race, Nature, and the Virus." *American Journal of Theology and Philosophy* 43, no. 1 (2022): 5–23.

Said, Edward W. *The World, the Text, and the Critic*. Harvard University Press, 1983.

Salmón, Enrique. "Kincentric Ecology: Indigenous Perceptions of the Human-Nature Relationship." *Ecological Applications* 10, no. 5 (2000): 1327–32.

Sands, Kathleen. "Feminisms and Secularisms." In *Secularisms*, edited by Janet R. Jakobsen and Ann Pellegrini, 308–29. Duke University Press, 2008.

Sankrityayan, Rahul. *Bauddh Darshan*. Allahabad Law Journal Press, 1944.

Sankrityayan, Rahul. "Buddhist Dialectics." In Rahul Sankrityayan, *Buddhism: A Marxist Approach*, edited by Debiprasad Chattopadhyay, Y. Balaramamoorty, Ram Vilas Sharma, and Mulk Raj Anand, 1–8. People's Publishing House, 1970.

Sankrityayan, Rahul. *Ghumakkar Shastra*. Rajkamal Prakashan, 1949.

Savransky, Martin. *Around the Day in Eighty Worlds: Politics of the Pluriverse*. Duke University Press, 2021.

Savransky, Martin, and Isabelle Stengers. "Relearning the Art of Paying Attention: A Conversation." *SubStance* 47, no. 1 (2018): 130–45.

Schlegel, Friedrich. *Kritische Friedrich-Schlegel-Ausgabe*. Vol. 18. Edited by Ernst Behler. Schöningh, 1963.

Schlegel, Friedrich. *Kritische Friedrich-Schlegel-Ausgabe*. Vol. 20. Edited by Ernst Behler. Schöningh, 1995.

Schmidt, Leigh. *Restless Souls: The Making of American Spirituality*. University of California Press, 2012.

Schmitt, Carl. *The Concept of the Political*. Translated by George Schwab. University of Chicago Press, 1996.

Schmitt, Carl. *The Nomos of the Earth in the International Law of the Jus Publicum Europaeum*. Translated by G. L. Ulmen. Telos, 2006.

Schmitt, Carl. *Political Theology: Four Chapters on the Concept of Sovereignty*. Translated by George Schwab. University of Chicago Press, 2005.

Schmitt, Carl. *Political Theology II: The Myth of the Closure of Any Political Theology*. Translated by Michael Hoelzl and Graham Ward. Polity, 2008.

Schmitt, Carl. *Politische Theologie II: Die Legende von der Erledigung jeder Politischen Theologie. Dritte Auflage*. Duncker and Humblot, 1990.

Scholem, Gershom. *On Jews and Judaism in Crisis: Selected Essays*. Edited by Werner Dannhauser. Schocken, 1976.

Scholem, Gershom. *Tagebücher nebst Aufsätzen und Entwürfen bis 1923*. 2 vols. Edited by Karlfried Gründer. Jüdischer Verlag im Suhrkamp: 1995–2000.

Schuller, Florian. "Foreword." In Jürgen Habermas and Pope Benedict XVI, *Dialectics of Secularization: On Reason and Religion*, 7–18. Ignatius, 2006.

Schutte, Ofelia. *Cultural Identity and Social Liberation in Latin American Thought*. State University of New York Press, 1993.

Schwartz, Regina. *Sacramental Poetics at the Dawn of Secularism: When God Left the World*. Stanford University Press, 2008.

Scott, David. *Conscripts of Modernity: The Tragedy of Colonial Enlightenment*. Duke University Press, 2004.

Scott, Joan Wallach. *Sex and Secularism*. Princeton University Press, 2018.

Sedgwick, Eve. *Touching Feeling: Affect, Pedagogy, Performativity*. Duke University Press, 2003.

Seremetakis, C. Nadia. *The Last Word: Women, Death, and Divination in Inner Mani*. University of Chicago Press, 1991.

Sexton, Jared. "The Social Life of Social Death: On Afro-Pessimism and Black Optimism." *InTensions* 5 (2011). https://doi.org/10.25071/1913-5874/37359.

Sharma, Ram Vilas. "Some Aspects of the Teachings of the Buddha." In Rahul Sankrityayan, *Buddhism: A Marxist Approach*, edited by Debiprasad Chattopadhyay, Y. Balaramamoorty, Ram Vilas Sharma, and Mulk Raj Anand, 54–65. People's Publishing House, 1970.

Shenhav, Yehouda. "Imperialism, Exceptionalism, and the Contemporary World." In *Agamben and Colonialism*, edited by Marcelo Svirsky and Simone Bignall, 17–31. Edinburgh University Press, 2012.

Shortall, Sara, and Daniel Jenkins, eds. *Christianity and Human Rights Reconsidered*. Cambridge University Press, 2020.

Shorter, David Delgado. "Spirituality." In *Oxford Handbook of American Indian History*, edited by Frederick E. Hoxie, 433–52. Oxford University Press, 2016.

Shulman, George. *American Prophecy: Race and Redemption in American Political Culture*. University of Minnesota Press, 2008.

Shulman, George. "Fred Moten's Refusals and Consents: The Politics of Fugitivity," *Political Theory* 49, no. 2 (2021): 272–313. https://doi.org/10.1177/0090591720937375.

Shulman, George. *Radicalism and Reverence: The Political Theory of Gerrard Winstanley*. University of California Press, 1987.

Shulman, George. "Theorizing Life Against Death." *Contemporary Political Theory* 17, no. 1 (2017): 118–28.

Shuster, Martin. "Adorno and Negative Theology." *Graduate Faculty Philosophy Journal* 37, no. 1 (2015): 97–130.

Shuster, Martin. *Autonomy after Auschwitz: Adorno, German Idealism, and Modernity*. University of Chicago Press, 2014.

Shuster, Martin. "The Philosophy of History." In *The Routledge Companion to the Frankfurt School*, edited by Peter E. Gordon, Espen Hammer, and Axel Honneth, 48–64. Routledge, 2018.

Simpson, Audra. *Mohawk Interruptus: Political Life Across the Borders of Settler States*. Duke University Press, 2014.

Simpson, Leanne Betasamosake. "Land as Pedagogy: Nishnaabeg Intelligence and Rebellious Transformation." *Decolonization: Indigeneity, Education and Society* 3, no. 3 (2014): 1–25.

Simpson, Leanne Betasamosake. "The Place Where We All Live and Work Together: A Gendered Analysis of 'Sovereignty.'" In *Native Studies Keywords*,
edited by Stephanie Nohelani Teves, Andrea Smith, and Michelle H. Raheja, 18–24. University of Arizona Press, 2015.

Singer, Dorothea Waley. *Giordano Bruno, His Life and Thought, with an Annotated Translation of His Work* On the Infinite Universe and Worlds. Henry
Schuman, 1950.

Singer, Peter. *Marx: A Very Short Introduction*. Oxford University Press, 2018.

Singh, Nikhil Pal. *Black Is a Country: Race and the Unfinished Struggle for Democracy*. Harvard University Press, 2004.

Singh, Nikhil Pal. "Culture/Wars: Recoding Empire in an Age of Democracy."
American Quarterly 50, no. 3 (1998): 471–522.

Skaria, Ajay. "Ambedkar, Marx and the Buddhist Question." *South Asia: Journal
of South Asian Studies* 38, no. 3 (2015): 450–65.

Skaria, Ajay. *Unconditional Equality: Gandhi's Religion of Resistance*. University
of Minnesota Press, 2016.

Slabodsky, Santiago. *Decolonial Judaism: Triumphal Failures of Barbaric Thinking*. Palgrave Macmillan, 2014.

Sloterdijk, Peter. *After God*. Translated by Ian Alexander Moore. Polity, 2020.

Sloterdijk, Peter. *Spheres, Volume 2: Globes*. Translated by Wieland Hoban.
Semiotext(e), 2014.

Smith, Anthony Paul. "Against Tradition to Liberate Tradition." *Angelaki* 19,
no. 2 (2014): 145–59.

Smith, Graeme. *A Short History of Secularism*. Bloomsbury, 2007.

Smith, Jesse, and Gary J. Adler Jr. "What *Isn't* Christian Nationalism? A Call for
Conceptual and Empirical Splitting." *Socius*, no. 8 (2022): 1–14.

Smith, Selden. *The Atheist's Guide to Quaker Process: Spirit-Led Decisions for the
Secular*. Pendle Hill, 2021.

Sostaita, Barbara. "On Grief and Capitalist Humanitarianism." *Religious Studies
Review* 50, no. 3 (2024): 520–23.

Spillers, Hortense. "A Day in the Life of Civil Rights." *Black Scholar* 9, nos. 8–9
(1978): 20–27.

Spillers, Hortense. "A Lament." *Black Scholar* 8, no. 5 (1977): 12–16.

Spillers, Hortense. "Mama's Baby, Papa's Maybe: An American Grammar Book."
Diacritics 17, no. 2 (1987): 64–81.

Spillers, Hortense. "Moving on Down the Line: Variations on the African-
American Sermon." In *Black, White, and in Color: Essays on American Literature and Culture*, 251–76. University of Chicago Press, 2003.

Stark, Heidi Kiiwetinepinesiik. "Stories as Law: A Method to Live By." In *Sources
and Methods in Indigenous Studies*, edited by Chris Andersen and Jean M.
O'Brien, 249–56. Routledge, 2017.

Stengers, Isabelle. "*Aude Sapere*: Dare Betray the Testator's Demands." *Parallax*
24, no. 4 (2018): 406–15.

Stengers, Isabelle. "Beyond Conversation: The Risks of Peace." In *Process and Difference*, edited by Catherine Keller and Anne Danielle, 235–56. State University of New York Press, 2002.

Stengers, Isabelle. "The Challenge of Ontological Politics." In *A World of Many Worlds*, edited by Marisol de la Cadena and Mario Blaser, 83–111. Duke University Press, 2018.

Stengers, Isabelle. *Cosmopolitics II*. Translated by Robert Bononno. University of Minnesota Press, 2011.

Stengers, Isabelle. "The Doctor and the Charlatan." *Cultural Studies Review* 9, no. 2 (2003): 11–36.

Stengers, Isabelle. "Experimenting with *What Is Philosophy?*" In *Deleuzian Intersections: Science, Technology, Anthropology*, edited by Casper Bruun Jensen and Kjetil Rödje, 39–56. Berghahn, 2009.

Stengers, Isabelle. *The Invention of Modern Science*. Translated by Daniel W. Smith. University of Minnesota Press, 2000.

Stengers, Isabelle. *Power and Invention: Situating Science*. Translated by Paul Bains. University of Minnesota Press, 1997.

Stengers, Isabelle. "Whitehead's Account of the Sixth Day." *Configurations* 13, no. 1 (2005): 35–55.

Stengers, Isabelle, and Vinciane Despret. *Women Who Make a Fuss: The Unfaithful Daughters of Virginia Woolf*. Translated by April Knutson. Univocal, 2014.

Stevens, Wallace. *The Necessary Angel: Essays on Reality and the Imagination*. Knopf Doubleday, 1965.

Stimilli, Elettra. *The Debt of the Living: Ascesis and Capitalism*. Translated by Arianna Bove. State University of New York Press, 2018.

Stout, Jeffrey. *Democracy and Tradition*. Princeton University Press, 2004.

Stoyanov, Yuri. *The Other God: Dualist Religions from Antiquity to the Cathar Heresy*. Yale University Press, 2000.

Stroumsa, Guy G. "God's Rule in Late Antiquity." In *The Making of the Abrahamic Religions in Late Antiquity*, 123–35. Oxford University Press, 2015.

Sullivan, Winnifred. *Church, State, Corporation: Construing Religion in US Law*. University of Chicago Press, 2020.

Suzack, Cheryl. *Indigenous Women Writers and the Cultural Study of Law*. University of Toronto Press, 2017.

Svirsky, Marcelo, and Simone Bignall. "Introduction." In *Agamben and Colonialism*, edited by Marcelo Svirsky and Simone Bignall, 1–14. Edinburgh University Press, 2012.

Swain, Dan, Petr Urban, and Petr Kouba. *Unchaining Solidarity: On Mutual Aid and Anarchism with Catherine Malabou*. Rowman and Littlefield, 2021.

Taubes, Jacob. *From Cult to Culture: Fragments Towards a Critique of Historical Reason*. Edited by Charlotte Elisheva Fonrobert and Amir Engel. Stanford University Press, 2010.

Taubes, Jacob. *The Political Theology of Paul*. Translated by Dana Hollander. Stanford University Press, 2003.

Taubes, Jacob. "Walter Benjamin—Ein moderner Marcionit? Scholems Benjamin-Interpretation religionsgeschichtlich überprüft." In *Der Preis des Messianismus. Briefe von Jacob Taubes und Gershom Scholem und andere Materialien,* edited by Elettra Stimilli, 53–65. Königshausen and Neuman, 2006.

Taylor, Charles. *A Secular Age.* Harvard University Press, 2007.

Taylor, Mark L. *The Theological and the Political.* Fortress, 2011.

Teves, Stephanie Nohelani, Andrea Smith, and Michelle H. Raheja. "Sovereignty." In *Native Studies Keywords,* edited by Stephanie Nohelani Teves, Andrea Smith, and Michelle H. Raheja, 3–17. University of Arizona Press, 2015.

Thatamanil, John. "How Not to Be a Religion: Genealogy, Identity, Wonder." In *Common Goods: Economy, Ecology, and Political Theology,* edited by Melanie Johnson-Debaufre, Catherine Keller, and Elias Ortega-Aponte, 54–72. Fordham University Press, 2015.

Thiellement, Pacôme. *La victoire des Sans Roi: Révolution Gnostique.* PUF, 2017.

Thiem, Yannik. "Political Theology." In *The Encyclopedia of Political Thought,* edited by Michael T. Gibbons, 2807–22. John Wiley and Sons, 2015.

Tiqqun. *Introduction to Civil War.* Translated by Alexander R. Galloway and Jason E. Smith. MIT Press, 2010.

Tisby, Jemar. "The Patriotic Witness of Black Christians." In *Christian Nationalism and the January 6, 2021 Insurrection,* 7–9. Baptist Joint Committee for Religious Liberty and the Freedom from Religion Foundation, February 9, 2022. https://bjconline.org/wp-content/uploads/2022/02/Christian_Nationalism_and_the_Jan6_Insurrection-2-9-22.pdf.

Tomasky, Michael. "Jamie Raskin, Democracy's Defender." *New Republic,* January 3, 2022.

Tomba, Massimiliano. *Insurgent Universality: An Alternative Legacy of Modernity.* Oxford University Press, 2019.

Tranvik, Isak. "George Shulman's Letters on Political Theology." *Political Theology Network,* May 24, 2022. Accessed December 3, 2024. https://politicaltheology.com/symposium/george-shulmans-letters-on-political-theology.

Turner, Victor. *The Ritual Process: Structure and Anti-Structure.* Aldine Transaction, 1969.

US Army. *Field Manual 3-24 MCWP 3-33.5: Insurgencies and Countering Insurgencies.* US Army, 2014.

Vardoulakis, Dimitris. "The Ends of Stasis: Spinoza as a Reader of Agamben." *Culture, Theory, and Critique* 51, no. 2 (2010): 145–56. https://doi.org/10.1080/14735784.2010.496592.

Vardoulakis, Dimitris. *Stasis Before the State: Nine Theses on Agonistic Democracy.* Fordham University Press, 2018.

Vatter, Miguel. *Divine Democracy: Political Theology After Carl Schmitt.* Oxford University Press, 2020.

Vatter, Miguel. "The Political Theology of Carl Schmitt." In *The Oxford Handbook of Carl Schmitt,* edited by Jens Meierhenrich and Oliver Simons, 245–68. Oxford University Press, 2014.

Verma, Ajay. "Epistemological Foundations of Caste Identities: A Review of Buddhist Critique of Classical Orthodox Indian Realism." In *Classical Buddhism, Neo-Buddhism and the Question of Caste*, edited by Pradeep P. Gokhale, 65–76. Routledge, 2021.

Viveiros de Castro, Eduardo. *Cannibal Metaphysics*. Translated by Peter Skafish. Univocal, 2014.

Viveiros de Castro, Eduardo. "The Gift and the Given: Three Nano-Essays on Kinship and Magic." In *Kinship and Beyond: The Genealogical Model Reconsidered*, edited by Sandra Bamford and James Leach. Berghahn, 2009.

Viveiros de Castro, Eduardo. "Intensive Filiation and Demonic Alliance." In *Deleuzian Intersections: Science, Technology, Anthropology*, edited by Casper Bruun Jensen and Kjetil Rödje. Berghahn, 2009.

Vizcaíno, Rafael. "Liberation Philosophy, Anti-Fetishism, and Decolonization." *Journal of World Philosophies* 6, no. 2 (2021): 61–75.

Vizcaíno, Rafael. "Postsecular Philosophy as Metaphoric Theology: On Dussel's Reading of Marx." *Journal of the American Academy of Religion* (2025). https://doi.org/10.1093/jaarel/lfaf001.

Vizcaíno, Rafael. "Sylvia Wynter's New Science of the Word and the Autopoetics of the Flesh." *Comparative and Continental Philosophy* 14, no. 1 (2022): 72–88.

Vizcaíno, Rafael. "Which Secular Grounds? The Atheism of Liberation Philosophy." APA *Newsletter on Hispanic/Latino Issues in Philosophy* 20, no. 2 (2021): 2–5.

Warner, Michael. "Is Liberalism a Religion?" In *Religion: Beyond a Concept*, edited by Hent De Vries, 610–17. Fordham University Press, 2008.

Warrior, Robert. *Tribal Secrets: Recovering American Indian Intellectual Traditions*. University of Minnesota Press, 1994.

Watson, Matthew. "Derrida, Stengers, Latour, and Subalternist Cosmopolitics." *Theory, Culture and Society* 31, no. 1 (2014): 75–98.

Weber, Max. *Charisma and Disenchantment: The Vocation Lectures*. NYRB, 2020.

Weber, Max. *The Protestant Ethic and the Spirit of Capitalism: And Other Writings*. Translated by Peter Baehr and Gordon C. Wells. Penguin, 2002.

Westhelle, Vitor. *After Heresy: Colonial Practices and Post-Colonial Theologies*. Cascade, 2010.

Whitehead, Andrew, and Samuel Perry, "What Is Christian Nationalism?" In *Christian Nationalism and the January 6, 2021 Insurrection*, 1–3. Baptist Joint Committee for Religious Liberty and the Freedom from Religion Foundation, February 9, 2022. https://bjconline.org/wp-content/uploads/2022/02/Christian_Nationalism_and_the_Jan6_Insurrection-2-9-22.pdf.

Wilder, Craig. *Ebony and Ivory: Race, Slavery, and the Troubled History of America's Universities*. Bloomberg, 2013.

Wilderson, Frank, III. "Gramsci's Black Marx: Whither the Slave in Civil Society?" *Social Identities* 9, no. 2 (2003). https://doi.org/10.1080/1350463032000101579.

Wilson, Elizabeth. *Gut Feminism*. Duke University Press, 2015.

Winant, Gabriel. "On Mourning and Statehood: A Response to Joshua Leifer." *Dissent*, October 13, 2023. https://www.dissentmagazine.org/online_articles/a-response-to-joshua-leifer/.

Wittfogel, Karl. *Oriental Despotism: A Study of Total Power.* Yale University Press, 1957.

Wittgenstein, Ludwig. *Philosophical Investigations.* 4th ed. Edited by P. M. S. Hacker and Joachim Schulte. Translated by G. E. M. Anscombe, P. M. S. Hacker, and Joachim Schulte. Wiley-Blackwell, 2009.

Wolin, Sheldon. "Fugitive Democracy." In *Fugitive Democracy and Other Essays,* edited by Nicolas Xenos, 100–114. Princeton University Press, 2019.

Woodly, Deva. "Black Feminist Visions and the Politics of Healing in the Movement for Black Lives." In *Women Mobilizing Memory,* edited by Ayşe Gül Altınay, María José Contreras, Marianne Hirsch, Jean Howard Banu Karaca, and Alisa Solomon, 219–37. Columbia University Press, 2019.

Wynter, Sylvia. "The Ceremony Found: Towards the Autopoetic Turn/Overturn, Its Autonomy of Human Agency and Extraterritoriality of (Self-)Cognition." In *Black Knowledges/Black Struggles: Essays in Critical Epistemology,* edited by Jason R. Ambroise and Sabine Broeck, 184–253. Liverpool University Press, 2015.

Wynter, Sylvia. "The Ceremony Must Be Found: After Humanism." *boundary 2,* nos. 12–13 (1984): 19–70.

Wynter, Sylvia. "1492: A New World View." In *Race, Discourse, and the Origin of the Americas: A New World View,* edited by Vera Lawrence Hyatt and Rex Nettleford, 5–57. Smithsonian Institution Press, 1995.

Wynter, Sylvia. "Towards the Sociogenic Principle: Fanon, Identity, the Puzzle of Conscious Experience." In *National Identities and Socio-Political Changes in Latin America,* edited by Mercedes F. Durán-Cogan and Antonio Gómez-Moriana, 30–66. Routledge, 2001.

Wynter, Sylvia. "Unsettling the Coloniality of Being/Power/Truth/Freedom: Towards the Human, After Man, Its Overrepresentation—An Argument." *CR: New Centennial Review* 3, no. 3 (2003): 257–337.

Wynter, Sylvia. *We Must Learn to Sit Down Together and Talk About a Little Culture: Decolonizing Essays, 1967–1984.* Edited by Demetrius L. Eudell. Peepal Tree, 2022.

Wynter, Sylvia, and Katherine McKittrick. "Unparalleled Catastrophe for Our Species? Or, to Give Humanness a Different Future: Conversations." In *Sylvia Wynter: On Being Human as Praxis,* edited by Katherine McKittrick, 9–89. Duke University Press, 2015.

Wynter, Sylvia, and Greg Thomas. "Proud Flesh Inter/Views: Sylvia Wynter." *Proud Flesh: New Afrikan Journal of Culture, Politics and Consciousness* 4 (2006): 1–35.

Yelle, Robert. "Deprovincializing Political Theology: An Introduction." *Political Theology* 23, nos. 1–2 (2022): 8–12.

Yetman, Hailey E., Nevada Cox, Shelley R. Adler, Kathryn T. Hall, and Valerie E. Stone. "What Do Placebo and Nocebo Effects Have to Do with Health Equity? The Hidden Toll of Nocebo Effects on Racial and Ethnic Minority Patients in Clinical Care." *Frontiers in Psychology* 12 (2021). https://doi.org/10.3389/fpsyg.2021.788230.

Contributors

Prathama Banerjee, a historian and political theorist, is professor at the Centre for the Study of Developing Societies, New Delhi.

Agata Bielik-Robson is professor of Jewish studies at the University of Nottingham.

Kirill Chepurin is an incoming assistant professor of humanities at Bilkent University and a fellow at ICI Berlin.

Alex Dubilet is assistant professor of English at Vanderbilt University.

James Edward Ford III is associate professor of English and Black studies at Occidental College.

Lucia Hulsether is assistant professor of religious studies at Skidmore College.

Basit Kareem Iqbal is assistant professor of anthropology at McMaster University.

Ada S. Jaarsma is professor of philosophy at Mount Royal University.

Siobhan Kelly is a postdoctoral fellow at Boston University's Society of Fellows.

David Kline is teaching associate professor in religious studies at the University of Tennessee, Knoxville.

Adam Kotsko is associate professor in the Shimer Great Books School at North Central College.

Dana Lloyd is assistant professor of global interdisciplinary studies at Villanova University.

Vincent W. Lloyd is professor of theology and religious studies at Villanova University.

Beatrice Marovich is associate professor of theological studies at Hanover College.

Aseel Najib is assistant professor of history at Dartmouth College.

Milad Odabaei is assistant professor of anthropology at the University of Arkansas.

Inese Radzins is assistant professor of philosophy at California State University Stanislaus.

George Shulman, a political theorist, is professor emeritus in New York University's Gallatin School of Individualized Study.

Martin Shuster is professor of philosophy and Isaac Swift Distinguished Professor of Jewish Studies at the University of North Carolina, Charlotte.

Rafael Vizcaíno is assistant professor of philosophy at DePaul University.

Index

Raskin, Jamie (US Representative), 319–22, 329–31
Raskin, Tabitha, 319, 321, 330–31
Raskin, Tommy, 330
Ray, Avishek 163
Raymond, Janice, 307
religion: Ambedkar on 156–58, 160–61, 165; Asad on politics and, 118–19, 125n1; category of, 9, 72–74; etymology of, 104; Lefort on modernity and, 135; and liberalism, 99–101. *See also* autoreligion
religious criticism, 158–60, 165
religious, the, and the secular: as binary, 15, 156; as complex, 143; divide between, 98–101, 104, 147, 152; Federici on religious-secular dyad, 15, 294
reproductive: politics, 268–72; power, 296–97
Riedl, Anna Maria, 313–14
Rifkin, Mark, 285
Robinson, Cedric, 50
Roediger, David, 221–22

Said, Edward, 25n7
salvation, 2–4, 138; and Gnosticism, 51–53, 55, 59, 180
Sankrityayan, Rahul, 159, 162, 167–68
scale: cosmic, 174–75, 177, 181–85; political theology of, 175. *See also* upscaling
Schmitt, Carl: and Agamben, 211, 213; and Ambedkar, 156; and bad intentions, 275, 277, 282–83, 287n5; and Baldwin, 199; and Butler , 310; on colonialism, 154n37; *The Concept of the Political*, 59, 291; in Dussel, 148, 150; and Federici, 295, 298; and genealogical political theology, 291–93; on Gnosticism, 52–53, 56, 58, 63n61; and Moten's countertheology, 204–5; *Nomos of the Earth*, 213; *Political Theology*, 150; *Political Theology II*, 52, 58, 59, 126n12; on political theology, 1, 119, 126n12, 128–29; on sovereignty and civil war, 47–50; on secularization, 65; on stasis, 59

Scholem, Gershom, 33, 34, 38–40, 44n11, 45n20
Schwartz, Regina, 12–13
scientific method, 87
secular, the: in Adorno's messianism, 32–40; Asad on, 118–25; and the Christian, 49; and the religious, 65–67, 179, 293
Secular Age, A (Taylor), 65
secularism: Ambedkar on, 156; Dussel on Enlightened, 147–48; French, 119–20; as ideological project, 150; Karatani and the schema of, 65–66; in Taylor's work, 65; Wynter's critique of "biocentric," 235. *See also* laïcité
secularity: in Dussel's critique of liberation theology; in Habermas, 98; and religion, 100, 147; Wynter's "true," 235–36
secularization: academic debates concerning, 14; Asad on, 119; Marx and, 64–65; 150; modern, 150; Schmitt on, 52, 65–66; Taylor on, 65; theories of, 64–65
sex, 311
sexual difference, ethics of, 268–70
sexual monoculture, 268, 271
sexuate, 266–67
Sharma, Ram Vilas, 168
Shorter, David Delgado, 286
Simpson, Audra, 277
Simpson, Leanne Betasamosake, 2, 280, 284
slavery: 217–20, 222–23; African chattel, 214–15, 220–22; Agamben and, 212–14, 218; Aristotle on, 212, 217–18; de Vitoria on, 213; Grotius on, 213; Hobbes on, 213; Suárez on, 213
Smith, Andrea, 277–78
Socialisme ou Barbarie (revolutionary group), 132
sociogenesis, 228–30, 233–34
sociopoetics: of Black life, 203; of Black insurgency, 205, 207
Solon's law, 48
sovereign: decision, 204–5; in opposition to the non-sovereign, 211
sovereignty: Agamben on, 210–11; antagonism and, 60; Black feminist

www.ingramcontent.com/pod-product-compliance
Lightning Source LLC
Jackson TN
JSHW021006050825
88823JS00002B/15